Reasoning
from the
Scriptures

"According to Paul's custom he went
inside to them, and . . . he reasoned
with them from the Scriptures,
explaining and proving by references
that it was necessary for the Christ
to suffer and to rise from the dead."
—Acts 17:2, 3.

Publishers
WATCHTOWER BIBLE AND TRACT SOCIETY
OF NEW YORK, INC.
International Bible Students Association
Brooklyn, New York, U.S.A.

First Printing in English:
2,000,000 copies

Reasoning From the Scriptures
English (rs-E)

Made in the United States of America

Principal Subjects

128162

Bible Translations Referred to in This Book

Unless otherwise indicated, Scripture quotations are from the *New World Translation of the Holy Scriptures,* 1984 edition (*NW*). Explanations of the abbreviations used to designate other translations of the Bible are provided below:

AS - *American Standard Version* (1901; as printed in 1944), American Revision Committee.

AT - *The Bible—An American Translation* (1935), J. M. Powis Smith and Edgar J. Goodspeed.

By - *The Bible in Living English* (published in 1972), Steven T. Byington.

CBW - *The New Testament—A Translation in the Language of the People* (1937; as printed in 1950), Charles B. Williams.

CC - *The New Testament* (1941; as printed in 1947), Confraternity of Christian Doctrine Revision.

CKW - *The New Testament—A New Translation in Plain English* (1963), Charles K. Williams.

Da - *The 'Holy Scriptures'* (1882; as printed in 1949), J. N. Darby.

Dy - Catholic *Challoner-Douay Version* (1750; as printed in 1941).

ED - *The Emphatic Diaglott* (1864; as printed in 1942), Benjamin Wilson.

Int - *The Kingdom Interlinear Translation of the Greek Scriptures* (1969).

JB - *The Jerusalem Bible* (1966), Alexander Jones, general editor.

JP - *The Holy Scriptures According to the Masoretic Text* (1917), Jewish Publication Society of America.

KJ - *King James Version* (1611; as printed in 1942).

Kx - *The Holy Bible* (1954; as printed in 1956), Ronald A. Knox.

LEF - *The Christian's Bible—New Testament* (1928), George N. LeFevre.

LXX - Greek *Septuagint Version.*

Mo - *A New Translation of the Bible* (1934), James Moffatt.

NAB - *The New American Bible,* Saint Joseph Edition (1970).

NE - *The New English Bible* (1970).

NTIV - *The New Testament in an Improved Version* (1808), published in London.

Ro - *The Emphasised Bible* (1897), Joseph B. Rotherham.

RS - *Revised Standard Version,* Second Edition (1971).

Sd - *The Authentic New Testament* (1958), Hugh J. Schonfield.

SE - *The Simple English Bible—New Testament,* American Edition (1981).

TC - *The Twentieth Century New Testament,* Revised Edition (1904).

TEV - *Good News Bible—Today's English Version* (1976).

We - *The New Testament in Modern Speech* (1929; as printed in 1944), Richard F. Weymouth.

Yg - *The Holy Bible,* Revised Edition (1887), Robert Young.

How to Use
"Reasoning From the Scriptures"

The pattern to follow in helping others to understand the Bible is that provided by Jesus Christ and his apostles. In answer to questions, Jesus quoted scriptures and at times used appropriate illustrations that would help honest-hearted persons to be receptive to what the Bible says. (Matt. 12:1-12) The apostle Paul made it a practice to 'reason from the Scriptures, explaining and proving by references' what he taught. (Acts 17:2, 3) The material contained in this book can help you to do the same.

Instead of providing a broad, general coverage of each subject, *Reasoning From the Scriptures* focuses primary attention on questions that are currently being asked by many people.

This publication has not been prepared for the purpose of helping anyone to "win arguments" with people who show no respect for the truth. Rather, it provides valuable information that is meant to be used in reasoning with individuals who will allow you to do so. Some of them may ask questions to which they really want satisfying answers. Others, in the course of conversation, may simply state their own beliefs and they may do so with some conviction. But are they reasonable persons who are willing to listen to another viewpoint? If so, you can share with them what the Bible says, doing so with the conviction that it will find welcome response in the hearts of lovers of truth.

How can you locate in this handbook the specific material you need? Often you will find it most readily by turning directly to the main heading that represents the subject being discussed. Under all the main headings, the principal questions are easy to isolate; they are in boldface type that extends to the left-hand margin. If you do not quickly find what you need, consult the Index in the back of the book.

Advance preparation for a discussion is always beneficial. But if you are not yet familiar with certain sections of the book, you can still make good use of them. How? When you locate the question that most nearly corresponds to the point you want to discuss, look at any subheadings under it. These subheadings are set in bold italics and are indented under the questions to which they relate. If you already have some knowledge of the subject, a review of those subheadings and a quick glance at some of the thoughts under them may be all that you need, because they outline a helpful line of reasoning that might be used. Do not hesitate to express the ideas in your own words.

Do you feel that you need more—perhaps the actual scriptures, the reasoning to use in connection with those scriptures, some illustrations to help you to make clear the reasonableness of what the Bible says, and so forth? If so, you may want to show the person with whom you are talking what you have in this book and then read together the portion that deals with the question he has brought up. Even if you have not studied the material in advance, you can use it to give a satisfying answer. Everything is right here in the book, stated in a simple and concise manner.

Keep in mind that this book is only an aid. The Bible is the authority. That is God's Word. When quotations in the book are from the Bible, impress this fact on those with whom you are speaking. Wherever possible, ask them to get out their Bible and look up the scriptures so they will see that what you are saying is actually in their own copy of the Scriptures. If some popularly used Bible translations render key portions of certain texts in a different way, attention is often drawn to this, and the renderings from a variety of translations are provided for comparison.

In harmony with the example set by the apostle Paul in referring to the altar "To an Unknown God" and in quoting some generally accepted secular sources when preaching to the Athenians (Acts 17:22-28), this book makes limited use of quotations from secular history, encyclopedias, religious reference books, and Bible-language lexicons. Thus, instead of making assertions as to the origin of false religious practices, the development of certain doctrines, and the meanings of Hebrew and Greek terms, the book shows the reasons for statements made. However, it directs attention to the Bible as the basic source of truth.

As further aids in paving the way to share Bible truth with others, the opening sections of this book provide a listing of "Introductions for Use in the Field Ministry" and a compilation of suggestions as to "How You Might Respond to Potential Conversation Stoppers." Many other potential "conversation stoppers" relate to particular beliefs, and these are considered at the end of each of the main sections dealing with those beliefs. It is not intended that you memorize these replies, but no doubt you will find it helpful to analyze why others have found them to be effective; then express the ideas in your own words.

Use of this handbook should help you to cultivate the ability to reason from the Scriptures and to use them effectively in helping others to learn about "the magnificent things of God."
—Acts 2:11.

Introductions

For Use in the Field Ministry

Comments: In determining the kind of introduction to use when you share in the field ministry, three things deserve careful consideration: (1) The message that we are commissioned to deliver is "this good news of the kingdom." (Matt. 24:14) Even when we are not discussing it directly, we should have in mind helping people to see the need for it, or perhaps clearing out of the way obstacles to their being willing to consider it. (2) Genuine concern for the welfare of the people we meet will help us, as it did Jesus, to reach hearts. (Mark 6:34) Such genuine interest may be indicated by a warm smile and a friendly manner, willingness to listen when they speak and then adapting our remarks accordingly, also by our use of questions that encourage them to express themselves so we can better understand their viewpoint. First Corinthians 9:19-23 shows that the apostle Paul adapted his presentation of the good news to the circumstances of the people to whom he spoke. (3) In some parts of the world, visitors are expected to observe certain formalities before stating the reason they are calling. Elsewhere the householder may expect an uninvited visitor to get to the point quickly.—Compare Luke 10:5.

The following introductions show how some experienced Witnesses begin conversations. If the introductions you are now using seldom open the way for conversations, try some of these suggestions. When you do so, you will no doubt want to put them in your own words. Also, you will find it helpful to get suggestions from other Witnesses in your congregation who have good success in approaching people.

ARMAGEDDON

● 'Many people are concerned about Armageddon. They have heard world leaders use that term with reference to all-out nuclear war. What do you believe Armageddon will mean to mankind? ... Actually, the name Armageddon is taken from the Bible, and it means something quite different from what the word is commonly used to express. (Rev. 16:14, 16) The Bible also shows that there are things you personally can do with a view to survival. (Zeph. 2:2, 3)' (See also pages 44-49, under the main heading "Armageddon.")

9

BIBLE/GOD

● 'Hello. I'm making just a brief call to share an important message with you. Please note what it says here in the Bible. (Read scripture, such as Revelation 21:3, 4.) What do you think about that? Does it sound good to you?'

● 'We're talking to our neighbors about where to find practical help to cope with problems of life. In the past, many people consulted the Bible. But we live in a time when attitudes are changing. How do you feel about it? Do you believe that the Bible is God's Word or do you feel that it is just a good book written by men? . . . If it is from God, how do you think a person can be sure of that?' (See pages 58-68, under the main heading "Bible.")

● 'I'm glad to find you at home. I'm sharing with my neighbors an encouraging thought from the Bible (or, the Holy Scriptures). Have you ever wondered: . . . ? (Ask a question that leads into your topic for discussion.)'

● 'We're encouraging folks to read their Bible. The answers that it gives to important questions often surprise people. For example: . . . (Ps. 104:5; or Dan. 2:44; or some other).'

● 'We're making just a brief visit on our neighbors today. Some people to whom we talk have confidence in God. Others find it difficult to believe in him. How do you feel? . . . The Bible encourages us to consider the significance of the physical universe. (Ps. 19:1) The One whose laws govern these heavenly bodies has also provided valuable direction for us. (Ps. 19:7-9)' (See also pages 145-151, 84-88, under the main headings "God" and "Creation.")

CRIME/SAFETY

● 'Hello. We're talking with folks about the matter of personal safety. There is a lot of crime around us, and it affects our lives. Do you think the time will come when people like you and me will be able to walk the streets at night and feel safe? (Or, Do you feel that anyone has a real solution to the problem?) . . . (Prov. 15:3; Ps. 37:10, 11)'

● 'My name is ——. I live in the neighborhood. As I was coming along this morning, I observed that everyone is talking about (mention a recent neighborhood crime or other matter of local concern). What do you think about it? . . . Is there anything that you feel would help to make our lives more secure? . . . (Prov. 1:33; 3:5, 6)'

CURRENT EVENTS

● 'Good evening. My name is ——. I'm a neighbor from (name street or area). Did you see the TV news last night? . . . That report on (mention some current item of concern)—what do you think about it? . . . It is not unusual to hear people ask, What is this world coming to? We as Jehovah's Witnesses believe that we are living in what the Bible calls "the last days." Notice this detailed description at 2 Timothy 3:1-5.' (See also pages 234-243.)

● 'Did you read this in the newspaper this week? (Show appropriate clipping.) What do you think . . . ?'

● 'I'd like to ask you a question. If you could choose, which of the many problems now facing the world would you like to see corrected first? (After learning what is of greatest concern to the householder, use this as the basis for your discussion.)'

EMPLOYMENT/HOUSING

● 'We've been talking with your neighbors about what can be done to assure that there will be employment and housing for everyone. Do you believe that it is reasonable to expect that human governments will accomplish this? . . . But there is someone who knows how to solve these problems; that is mankind's Creator. (Isa. 65:21-23)'

● 'We are sharing with our neighbors a thought about good government. Most people would like to have the kind of government that is free from corruption, one that provides employment and good housing for everyone. What kind of government do you think can do all of that? . . . (Ps. 97:1, 2; Isa. 65:21-23)' (See also pages 152-156, under the main heading "Government.")

FAMILY/CHILDREN

● 'We're talking to folks who are interested in how we can better cope with the problems of family life. We all try to do the best we can, but if there is something that can help us to have greater success, we're interested, aren't we? . . . (Col. 3:12, 18-21) The Bible sets before us a hope that offers a real future for our families. (Rev. 21:3, 4)'

● 'We all want our children to have happy lives. But do you think there is sound reason to expect a happy outcome for the trouble the world is in today? . . . So, what kind of world do you think our children are going to face when they grow up? . . . The Bible shows that God is going to make this earth a wonderful place in which to live. (Ps. 37: 10, 11) But whether our children will share in it may depend to a large extent on the choice *we* make. (Deut. 30:19)'

FUTURE/SECURITY

● 'Good morning. How are you? . . . We're endeavoring to share with our neighbors a positive view of the future. Is that the way you try

to look at life? . . . Do you find that some situations make this hard
to do? . . . I have found that the Bible is very helpful in this respect.
It realistically describes the conditions that exist in our day, but it
also explains their meaning and tells us what the outcome will be.
(Luke 21:28, 31)'

● 'Hello. My name is ——. What's yours? . . . I'm encouraging young
folks like you to consider the grand future that the Bible holds out to
us. (Read scripture, such as Revelation 21:3, 4.) Does that sound good
to you?'

HOME BIBLE STUDY

● 'I'm calling to offer you a free home Bible course. If I may, I'd like
to take just a few minutes to demonstrate how people in some 200
lands discuss the Bible at home as family groups. We can use any of
these topics as a basis for discussion. (Show the table of contents from
study book.) Which one especially interests you?'

● 'We are showing this Bible study aid to our neighbors. (Show it.)
Have you seen it before? . . . If you have just a few minutes, I'd like
to demonstrate how it can be used with your own copy of the Bible.'

INJUSTICE/SUFFERING

● 'Have you ever wondered: Does God really care about the injustice
and suffering that humans experience? . . . (Eccl. 4:1; Ps. 72:12-14)'
(See also the main headings "Suffering" and "Encouragement.")

KINGDOM

● 'In speaking with my neighbors, I have observed that many long to
live under a government that can really solve the big problems that
face us today—crime and the high cost of living (or whatever is
currently on the minds of many). That would be desirable, don't you
agree? . . . Is there such a government today? . . . Many people have
actually prayed for a government that can do those things. No doubt
you have prayed for it, but not many people think of it as a government. (Dan. 2:44; Ps. 67:6, 7; Mic. 4:4)' (See also pages 225-234 and
152-156, under the main headings "Kingdom" and "Government.")

● 'We are asking our neighbors a question. We'd appreciate your
comment on it. You know, Jesus taught us to pray for God's Kingdom
to come and for His will to be done on earth as it is in heaven. Do you
think this prayer will ever be answered so that God's will really will
be done here on earth? . . . (Isa. 55:10, 11; Rev. 21:3-5)'

● 'I'm discussing with my neighbors an issue that we all must face:
Do we favor government by God, or do we prefer human rulership?

In view of conditions in the world today, do you feel that we need something other than what men have produced? ... (Matt. 6:9, 10; Ps. 146:3-5)'

LAST DAYS

● 'We're calling to discuss the meaning of what's happening around us in the world today. Among many people there has been a decline in interest in God and in his standards for living as set out in the Bible. This has greatly influenced the attitude of people toward one another. Please let me share with you this description recorded at 2 Timothy 3:1-5 and tell me whether you think it fits the world today. (Read) ... Is there sound reason to expect better conditions in the future? (2 Pet. 3:13)'

● 'Many people believe that time is fast running out for this world. They speak of our time as being "the last days." But did you realize that the Bible tells us how we can survive the end of the present world and live on an earth that will be made a paradise? (Zeph. 2:2, 3)' (See also pages 234-243, under the main heading "Last Days.")

See also "Current Events" in this list of suggested introductions.

LIFE/HAPPINESS

● 'We're visiting our neighbors to find people who are deeply concerned about the meaning of life. Most people experience some happiness. But they face a lot of problems too. As we get up in years, we realize that life is very short. Is this all that life is meant to be? How do you feel about it? ... (Comment on God's original purpose as reflected in Eden; then John 17:3 and Revelation 21:3, 4.)' (See also pages 243-248, under the main heading "Life.")

● 'Today we are asking our neighbors what they think when they read in their Bibles the expression "everlasting life." It is of special interest because that expression appears in the Bible some 40 times. What might such life mean for us? ... How can we get it? (John 17:3; Rev. 21:4)'

● 'We're speaking with people who are truly concerned about the quality of life today. Most of us are glad to be alive, but many wonder, Is a genuinely happy life possible? How do you feel about that? ... What would you say is one of the biggest obstacles to happiness today? ... (Ps. 1:1, 2; further texts to fit what concerns the householder)'

LOVE/KINDNESS

● 'We have found that many people are quite concerned about the lack of real love in the world. Do you feel that way too? ... Why do you think this is the trend? . . . Did you know that the Bible foretold this situation? (2 Tim. 3:1-4) It also explains the reason for it. (1 John 4:8)'

● 'My name is ——. I'm one of your neighbors. I'm making just a brief visit to talk with my neighbors about something that concerns me a great deal, and I'm sure you've noticed it too. Kindness does not cost much, but it seems to be so rare today. Did you ever wonder why that situation exists? . . . (Matt. 24:12; 1 John 4:8)'

OLD AGE/DEATH

● 'Have you ever wondered why we grow old and die? Some sea turtles live for hundreds of years. Certain trees have lived for thousands of years. But humans live just 70 or 80 years and then die. Have you wondered why? . . . (Rom. 5:12) Will that situation ever change? . . . (Rev. 21:3, 4)'

● 'Have you ever asked: Is death the end of it all? Or is there something else after death? . . . The Bible clears up any question we might have about death. (Eccl. 9:5, 10) It also shows that there is a real hope for persons who have faith. (John 11:25)' (See also pages 98-104 and 118, under the headings "Death" and "Encouragement.")

WAR/PEACE

● 'Just about everyone these days is concerned about the threat of nuclear war. Do you think we will ever see real peace on this earth? . . . (Ps. 46:8, 9; Isa. 9:6, 7)'

● 'I'm looking for people who would like to live in a world free from war. In this century alone there have been hundreds of wars, including two world wars. Now we are faced with the threat of a nuclear conflict. What do you feel is needed if such a war is to be avoided? . . . Who can bring about a peaceful world? . . . (Mic. 4:2-4)'

● 'We find that just about everyone says he wants world peace. Most of the world leaders also say that. Why, then, is it so hard to attain? . . . (Rev. 12:7-12)'

WHEN MANY PEOPLE SAY: 'I HAVE MY OWN RELIGION'

● 'Good morning. We are visiting all the families on your block (or, in this area), and we find that most of them have their own religion. No doubt you do too. . . . But, regardless of our religion, we are affected by many of the same problems—high cost of living, crime, illness—is that not so? . . . Do you feel that there is any real solution to these things? . . . (2 Pet. 3:13; etc.)'

WHEN MANY PEOPLE SAY: 'I'M BUSY'

● 'Hello. We're visiting everyone in this neighborhood with an important message. No doubt you are a busy person, so I'll be brief.'

● 'Greetings. My name is ——. The purpose of my coming is to discuss with you blessings of God's Kingdom and how we can share in them. But I can see that you are busy (or, about to go out). May I leave you with just a brief thought?'

IN TERRITORY OFTEN WORKED

● 'I'm glad to find you at home. We're making our weekly visit in the neighborhood, and we have something more to share with you about the wonderful things that God's Kingdom will do for mankind.'

● 'Hello. It's good to see you again. . . . Is everyone in the family in good health? . . . I stopped by to share with you a thought on . . . '

● 'Good morning. How are you? . . . I've been wanting another opportunity to talk with you. (Then name the specific subject you want to discuss.)'

How You Might Respond to Potential

Conversation Stoppers

Comments: The life prospects of people depend on their attitude toward Jehovah God and his Kingdom by Christ Jesus. The message of God's Kingdom is thrilling, and it points to the only dependable hope for humankind. It is a message that transforms lives. We want everyone to hear it. We realize that only a minority will receive it appreciatively, but we know that people at least need to hear it if they are to make an informed choice. Yet not everyone is willing to listen, and we do not try to force them. But with discernment it is often possible to turn potential conversation stoppers into opportunities for further discussion. Here are examples of what some experienced Witnesses have used in their efforts to search out deserving ones. (Matt. 10:11) Our recommendation is not that you memorize any of these replies but that you get the idea in mind, put it in your own words and express it in a manner that conveys your genuine interest in the person to whom you are speaking. As you do so, you can have confidence that those whose hearts are rightly disposed will listen and respond appreciatively to what Jehovah is doing to draw them to his loving provisions for life.—John 6:44; Acts 16:14.

'I'M NOT INTERESTED'

● 'May I ask, Do you mean that you are not interested in *the Bible,* or is it religion in general that does not interest you? I ask that because we have met many who at one time were religious but no longer go to church because they see much hypocrisy in the churches (or, they feel that religion is just another money-making business; or, they do not approve of religion's involvement in politics; etc.). The Bible does not approve of such practices either and it provides the only basis on which we can look to the future with confidence.'

● 'If you mean that you are not interested in another religion, I can understand that. But more than likely you are interested in what kind of future we can expect in view of the threat of nuclear war (or, how we can safeguard our children against drug abuse; or, what can be done about crime so that we won't have to be afraid to walk the streets; etc.). Can you see any prospect for a real solution?'

● 'Is that because you already have a religion? . . . Tell me, Do you think we will ever see a time when everyone belongs to the same religion? . . . What seems to stand in the way? . . . For it to be meaningful, what sort of foundation would be needed?'

● 'I can appreciate that. A few years ago I felt the same way. But I read something in the Bible that helped me to view matters in a different light. (Show the person what it was.)'

● 'Would you be interested if I could show you from the Bible how you could see your dead loved ones again (or, what the real purpose of life is; or, how it can help us to keep our families united; etc.)?'

● 'If you mean that you are not interested in buying something, let me put your mind at ease. I'm not engaged in a commercial work. But would you be interested in the opportunity to live on a paradise earth, free from sickness and crime, with neighbors who really love you?'

● 'Is that your usual reply when Jehovah's Witnesses call? . . . Have you ever really wondered why we keep calling or what we have to say? . . . Briefly, the reason I came to see you is that I know something that you should know too. Why not listen just this once?'

'I'M NOT INTERESTED IN RELIGION'

● 'I can understand how you feel. Frankly, the churches are not making this world a safer place to live, are they? . . . May I ask, Have you always felt the way you do now? . . . But do you believe in God?'

● 'There are a lot of people who share your view. Religion has not really helped them. That is one reason why we are calling—because the churches have not told people the truth about God and his wonderful purpose for mankind.'

● 'But I am sure that you are interested in your own future. Did you know that the Bible foretold the very conditions that exist in the world today? . . . And it shows what the outcome will be.'

● 'Have you always felt that way? . . . How do you feel about the future?'

'I'M NOT INTERESTED IN JEHOVAH'S WITNESSES'

● 'Many folks tell us that. Have you ever wondered why people like me volunteer to make these calls even though we know that the majority of householders may not welcome us? (Give the gist of Matthew 25:31-33, explaining that a separating of people of all nations is taking place and that their response to the Kingdom message is an important factor in this. Or state the gist of Ezekiel 9: 1-11, explaining that, on the basis of people's reaction to the Kingdom message, everyone is being "marked" either for preservation through the great tribulation or for destruction by God.)'

● 'I can appreciate that, because I used to feel the same way. But, just to be fair, I decided to listen to one of them. And I found out that I hadn't been told the truth about them. (Mention a common false accusation and then explain what we believe.)'

● 'Not long ago I said the same thing to a Witness who called at my door. But before he left I raised a question that I was sure he could not answer. Would you like to know what it was? . . . (As an example: Where did Cain get his wife?)' (For use by those who really had such an experience.)

● 'If you are a religious person, I can appreciate that. Your own religion no doubt means much to you. But I think you'll agree that we are both interested in (name an appropriate topic).'

● 'Then no doubt you have your own religion. Do you mind my asking which religion it is? . . . We enjoy talking with people of your faith. How do you feel about (mention your topic for discussion)?'

● 'Yes, I understand. But the reason we are calling is that we are a family that would like to see people live together in peace. We're sick and tired of the news every night with reports of fighting and suffering. I suppose you are the same. . . . But what can bring the needed change? . . . We've found encouragement in the Bible's promises.'

● 'I appreciate your letting me know how you feel. Would you mind telling me what there is about us that you don't like? Is it what we show you from the Bible, or is it our coming to visit you?'

'I HAVE MY OWN RELIGION'

● 'Would you mind telling me, Does your religion teach that the time will come when people who love what is right will live on earth forever? . . . That is an appealing thought, isn't it? . . . It is right here in the Bible. (Ps. 37:29; Matt. 5:5; Rev. 21:4)'

● 'I agree that in this matter each person must make his own decision. But did you know that God himself is looking for a certain kind of people to be his true worshipers? Notice here at John 4:23, 24. What would it mean to worship God "with truth"? . . . What has God given us to help us to know what is true and what is not? . . . (John 17:17) And notice how important it is to us personally. (John 17:3)'

● 'Have you been a religious person all your life? . . . Do you think mankind will ever be united in one religion? . . . I've thought a lot about that because of what is recorded here at Revelation 5:13. . . . What is needed in order for us to fit into this picture?'

● 'I was hoping to find someone like yourself who has an interest in spiritual things. So many today do not. May I ask how you feel about the Bible's promise that God will clear out all wickedness and make this earth a place where only people who love righteousness will live? Does that appeal to you?'

● 'Are you quite active in church affairs? . . . Is the church usually well filled for services these days? . . . Do you find that most members are really showing a sincere desire to apply God's Word in everyday life? (Or, Do you find that there is unity of thinking among the members as to the solution to the problems that face the world?) We find that personal home Bible instruction helps.'

● 'Evidently you are satisfied with your religion. But most people are not satisfied with world conditions. Perhaps that is true of you too; is it? . . . What is it all leading up to?'

● 'Are you a person who enjoys reading the Bible? . . . Do you find time to read it on a regular basis?'

● 'I appreciate your telling me that. I am sure that you will agree that, no matter what our religious background, we are all very much interested in world peace (or, ways to protect our children against bad influences; or, having a neighborhood in which people really love one another; or, enjoying good relationships with other people, and that can present a challenge when everyone feels under pressure).'

● 'I'm glad to know that you are religiously inclined. Many people today do not take religion seriously. Some even think there is no God. But, according to what you have been taught, what kind of person do you think of God as being? . . . Notice that the Bible gives us his personal name. (Ex. 6:3; Ps. 83:18)'

● 'When Jesus sent out his disciples to preach, he told them to go to every part of the earth, so they would meet many people whose religion was different from theirs. (Acts 1:8) But he knew that those hungering and thirsting for righteousness would listen. What is the particular message that he said would be delivered in our day? (Matt. 24:14) What does that Kingdom mean to us?'

'WE ARE ALREADY CHRISTIANS HERE'

● 'I'm glad to know that. Then you no doubt know that Jesus himself did a work like this, calling on people in their homes, and he commissioned his disciples to do it too. Are you familiar with the theme of the preaching they did? . . . That's what we came to talk about today. (Luke 8:1; Dan. 2:44)'

● 'Then I'm sure you will appreciate the seriousness of what Jesus said here in the Sermon on the Mount. He was being very straightforward but also loving when he said . . . (Matt. 7:21-23) The question that we need to ask ourselves, then, is, How well do I know the will of the heavenly Father? (John 17:3)'

'I'M BUSY'

● 'Then I'll be very brief. I called to share just one important thought with you. (State the gist of your topic for discussion in about two sentences.)'

● 'All right. I'll be glad to call at another time, when it is more convenient for you. But before I leave, I'd like to read just one scripture that really gives us something important to think about.'

● 'I understand. As a mother (or, workingman; or, student) I have a full schedule too. So I'll be brief. All of us are faced with a serious situation. The Bible shows that we are very near the time when God will destroy the present wicked system of things. But there will be survivors. The question is, What must you and I do to be among them? The Bible answers that question. (Zeph. 2:2, 3)'

● 'You know, that's exactly the reason why I'm calling. We're all busy —so busy that really important things in life sometimes get neglected, isn't that so? . . . I'll be very brief, but I'm sure you will be interested in just this one text. (Luke 17:26, 27) None of us want to find ourselves in that situation, so we need to make time in our busy lives to consider what the Bible says. (Make literature offer.)'

● 'Would it be more convenient if we called back in about half an hour, after we have visited some of your neighbors?'

● 'Then I won't keep you. Perhaps I can call another day. But before I leave, I would like to give you the opportunity to obtain this special offer. (Display the offer for the month.) This publication contains a study course that will acquaint you with the Bible's own answers to such questions as (mention just one or two).'

● 'I'm sorry that I caught you at an inconvenient moment. As you may know, I am one of Jehovah's Witnesses. I wanted to share with you an important thought from the Bible. But since you don't have time to listen right now, I would like to give you this tract, which discusses (name the subject). It won't take long to read, but you will find it very interesting.'

● 'That's not hard for me to understand. There just does not seem to be enough time to get everything done. But have you ever thought how different life might be if you could live forever? I know that may sound strange. But let me show you just one Bible text that explains how such a thing is possible. (John 17:3) So, what we need to do now is to take in this knowledge of God and his Son. That is why we leave this literature.'

'WHY DO YOU PEOPLE CALL SO OFTEN?'

● 'Because we believe that we are living in the last days referred to in the Bible. We feel that it is important for all of us to think about what the outcome of present conditions will be. (Mention one or two recent events or current situations.) The question is, What do we need to do if we are to survive the end of this system of things?'

● 'Because we love God and our neighbors. That is what we all should do, isn't it?'

'I AM ALREADY WELL ACQUAINTED WITH YOUR WORK'

● 'I am very glad to hear that. Do you have a close relative or a friend that is a Witness? . . . May I ask: Do you *believe* what we teach from the Bible, namely, that we are living in "the last days," that soon God is going to destroy the wicked, and that this earth will become a paradise in which people can live forever in perfect health among neighbors who really love one another?'

'WE HAVE NO MONEY'

● 'We are not soliciting funds. But we are offering a free home Bible study course. One of the subjects that it covers is (use a chapter title from a current publication). May I take a few minutes to show you how it works? It won't cost you a penny.'

● 'We're interested in people, not their money. (Continue with discussion. Show them one of the publications and explain how it can benefit them. If they manifest genuine interest and promise to read it, leave it with them. If appropriate, explain how our worldwide preaching activity is financed.)'

WHEN SOMEONE SAYS, 'I'M A BUDDHIST'

● Do not conclude that the person's beliefs are the same as those of all other Buddhists. Buddhist teachings are vague and the interpretation varies from one person to another. Japanese Buddhism is quite different from the Buddhism of Southeast Asia. Individuals, too, differ as to their viewpoint. In general, however, the following points may be helpful: (1) Buddhism does not recognize an external God, a personal Creator. But many Buddhists worship images and relics of Buddha. (2) Siddhartha Gautama, who was given the title Buddha, came to be viewed as the religious ideal of his followers, to be imitated by them. He encouraged gaining enlightenment by studying mankind from a human standpoint, also severing the roots of suffering by controlling the mind so as to eliminate all earthly desire. He taught that in this way one might attain to Nirvana, free from the rebirths of transmigration. (3) Buddhists worship their ancestors, because they view these as the source of their life.

Suggestions for conversation: (1) When speaking with Buddhists, emphasize that you are no part of Christendom. (2) Buddhists have respect for "holy books," and generally they respect the Bible for that reason. Instead of dwelling on Buddhist philosophy, present the positive message of the Bible. Let them know that the Bible is not mere human philosophy but the authoritative Word of mankind's Creator, Jehovah God. Ask politely if you may show them an interesting point in this holy book, the Bible. (3) Many Buddhists are keenly interested in peace and family life and want to live moral lives. Discussion on any of these matters is often welcomed. (4) Show that the Bible points to a righteous heavenly government over the earth as the real solution to the problems facing mankind. It explains the future of the earth and the wonderful prospect of living forever in an earthly paradise. (5) You might point out that the Bible explains the origin of life, the meaning of life, the condition of the dead and the resurrection hope, the reason for the existence of wickedness. A kindly presentation of the clear truths of God's Word will find appreciative response in the hearts of sheeplike ones.

The booklet *In Search of a Father* was prepared especially for the benefit of sincere Buddhists.

WHEN SOMEONE SAYS, 'I'M A HINDU'

● You ought to be aware that Hindu philosophy is very complex and does not conform to normal logic. You may find it helpful to have the following points in mind: (1) Hinduism teaches that the god Brahman includes three forms—Brahma the Creator, Vishnu the Preserver, and Siva the Destroyer. But Hindus do not think of a personal god with an individual existence. (2) Hindus believe that all natural objects possess a soul that never dies, that the soul experiences a virtually endless cycle of reincarnation, that the forms in which it is reborn are determined by deeds (Karma), that release from this "endless wheel" is possible only by extinguishing all physical desire, and that if this is achieved, the soul will merge with the universal spirit. (3) In general, Hindus respect other religions. Hindus believe that, in spite of the fact that they teach conflicting doctrines, all religions lead to the same truth.

Instead of trying to deal with the complexities of Hindu philosophy, present the satisfying truths found in the Holy Bible. Jehovah's loving provisions for life are open to people of all kinds, and the clear truths in his Word will reach the hearts of those who hunger and thirst for righteousness. Only the Bible provides a truly well-founded hope for the future; only the Bible gives really satisfying answers to the important questions that face all mankind. Give them opportunity to hear those answers. It is of interest that the Hindu *Rig-Veda* hymn, 10. 121, is entitled "To the Unknown God." In some cases you may find it appropriate to refer to this in a manner similar to the apostle Paul's reference to the altar "To an Unknown God" in Athens. (Acts 17:22, 23) Interestingly, the name of the Hindu god Vishnu, without the digamma, is Ish-nuh, which in Chaldee means "the man Noah." Point out what the Bible says about the significance of the global Flood in the days of Noah. Those who are distressed by the prospect of endless reincarnations may be helped by the material on pages 320, 321, under the main heading "Reincarnation."

The booklets *The Path of Divine Truth Leading to Liberation* and *From Kurukshetra to Armageddon—And Your Survival* contain information that will be very beneficial to sincere Hindus.

WHEN SOMEONE SAYS, 'I'M A JEW'

● First, ascertain how the person views himself as a Jew. Few are religious. For many, being Jewish is simply an ethnic designation.

Here are a few points that are beneficial to have in mind: (1) Religious Jews view the pronouncing of God's name as forbidden. (2) Many Jews think of "the Bible" as a Christian book, but if you refer to "the Hebrew Scriptures," "the Scriptures," or "the Torah," that problem does not arise. (3) Tradition is a central part of their faith and is viewed by many religious Jews as equal in authority with the Scriptures. (4) They may associate Jesus Christ with the brutal persecution experienced by the Jews at the hands of Christendom in the name of Jesus. (5) They frequently believe that God requires the Jews to keep the Sabbath, which belief includes refraining from handling money on that day.

To establish a common ground, you might say: (1) 'You would no doubt agree that, regardless of our background, we all face many of the same difficulties in today's world. Do you believe that there will really be a lasting solution to the great problems that face this generation? (Ps. 37:10, 11, 29; Ps. 146:3-5; Dan. 2:44)' (2) 'We are no part of Christendom and do not believe in a Trinity but worship the God of Abraham. We are especially interested in the matter of religious truth. Do you mind if I ask how you determine what is true, especially in view of the fact that there are great differences of beliefs among Jewish people? . . . (Deut. 4:2; Isa. 29:13, 14; Ps. 119:160)' (3) 'We are keenly interested in God's promise to Abraham that through his seed people of all nations will be blessed. (Gen. 22:18)'

If the person expresses lack of faith in God, ask whether he has always felt that way. Then perhaps discuss why God has permitted wickedness and suffering. Memories of the Nazi holocaust have caused many Jews to be concerned about this.

If you discuss the importance of using God's name, find out first how the other person feels about it. Point out that Exodus 20:7 forbids taking up God's name in a worthless way, but *it does not forbid using it with respect.* Then reason on texts such as Exodus 3:15 (or Psalm 135:13); 1 Kings 8:41-43; Isaiah 12:4; Jeremiah 10:25; Malachi 3:16.

When you discuss the Messiah: (1) Talk first about the future blessings under his rule, instead of his identity. (2) Then reason on texts that point to a *personal* Messiah. (Gen. 22:17, 18; Zech. 9:9, 10; Dan. 7:13, 14) (3) You may need to discuss the *two* comings of the Messiah. (Contrast Daniel 7:13, 14 with Daniel 9:24-26.) (4) When referring to Jesus, do so in a context that emphasizes the progressive nature of God's purpose. Mention that when Jesus taught, the time was near when God allowed the second temple to be destroyed, never to be rebuilt. But Jesus emphasized the *fulfillment* of the Law and of the Prophets and the glorious future to which these would direct persons with faith.

WHEN SOMEONE SAYS, 'I'M A MUSLIM'

● A few points to have in mind are these: (1) The Koran is their principal "holy book." Some will agree that the Bible is God's Word, but they believe that it is superseded by the Koran. (2) They believe that there is only one true God. (3) They say that Jesus was one of the prophets, as was Muhammad, and that Muhammad (570-632 C.E.) was the Comforter foretold by Jesus. They believe Muhammad was the last and most important prophet. (4) They strongly believe that God has no son.

A common ground can sometimes be established in the following ways: (1) You might say: 'I have come to discuss the Word of God with you. It tells about the problems of life that people like you and me experience and it shows us what the real solution is.' Then discuss the Kingdom. (2) You could say: 'I do not believe in Christendom's Trinity. I worship the one true God, the Creator of heaven and earth.' (3) 'Am I right that you believe that Jesus (or Moses) was a prophet? . . . Was he a true prophet? . . . Then what he said was from God and if other teachings do not agree with it, they must be from another source, is that not so?' Then use statements made by Jesus (or Moses) as a basis for further discussion.

If they make strong assertions concerning their beliefs, it can be beneficial to ask them, tactfully, to show you the point in the Koran, sura (chapter) and verse. (Wait while they search for it.) When they are unable to find it, some give evidence of greater willingness to listen to what you show them in the Bible.

Possible topics for discussion: (1) After laying a foundation, as above, you may be able to point out what God said to Moses about His personal name. (Ex. 3:15; Deut. 6:4, 5) (2) Material in this book under the main headings "Fate" and "Suffering" can be used to help some to see that God is not responsible for the injustice and suffering they experience and that lasting relief will come by means of God's Kingdom. (3) If you are asked about your view regarding the Comforter, you can point out how Jesus spoke of it, showing that it is not a person and that it would remind his disciples of all the things that Jesus had taught them, rather than introduce a new religion. (John 14:26, *KJ, NW;* Acts 1:8) (4) If the objection is raised that God cannot have a Son, you might endeavor to reason on the matter. God's having a Son does not mean that he had sexual relations with a wife. But God is the Creator. Since he gives life to those that he creates, can he not refer to himself as their Father? He speaks of his very first creation as his Son. He calls the angels sons of God, and he refers to Adam as his son. Why? Because he gave them life. How did Mary conceive Jesus? Not by sexual relations with God but, as the Bible says, it was by means of holy spirit, the same active force that God used in creation.—Matt. 3:17; 16:16, 17; Luke 1:35.

The booklet *The Time for True Submission to God* can be a real aid to sincere Muslims in understanding God's purpose.

Abortion

Definition: Abortion is the expulsion of an embryo or a fetus that is not normally able to live outside the womb. Spontaneous abortion or miscarriage may result from human imperfection or from an accident. Deliberately induced abortion simply to avoid the birth of an unwanted child is the willful taking of human life.

How should the Source of human life affect our view of this matter?

Acts 17:28: "By him [God] we have life and move and exist."

Ps. 36:9: "With you [Jehovah God] is the source of life."

Rom. 14:12: "Each of us will render an account for himself to God."

Does Jehovah view the life of a child as precious even during the very early stages of development after conception?

Ps. 139:13-16: "You [Jehovah] kept me screened off in the belly of my mother. . . . Your eyes saw even the embryo of me, and in your book all its parts were down in writing."

Has God ever stated that a person would be called to account for injury to an unborn child?

Ex. 21:22, 23: "In case men should struggle with each other and they really hurt a pregnant woman and her children do come out but no fatal accident occurs, he is to have damages imposed upon him without fail according to what the owner of the woman may lay upon him; and he must give it through the justices. But if a fatal accident should occur, then you must give soul for soul." (Some translations make it appear that in this law to Israel the crucial matter was what happened to the mother, not to the fetus. The original Hebrew text, however, refers to a fatal accident to either mother or child.)

How serious is the willful taking of a human life for a reason not authorized by God?

Gen. 9:6: "Anyone shedding man's blood, by man will his own blood be shed, for in God's image he made man."

1 John 3:15: "No manslayer has everlasting life remaining in him."

Ex. 20:13: "You must not murder."

Does a doctor's opinion that allowing a pregnancy to go full term would be harmful to the health of the mother justify an abortion?

Medical opinions are sometimes wrong. Would it be right to kill a fellow human because that one *might* harm his fellowman? If *at the time of childbirth* a choice must be made between the life of the mother and that of the child, it is up to the individuals concerned to make that choice. However, advances in medical procedures in many lands have made this situation very rare.

If Someone Says—

'But I have a right to decide on matters affecting my own body.'

You might reply: 'I can understand how you feel. So often today our rights are trampled on by others; many just don't care what happens to other people. But the Bible provides guidelines that can protect us. To receive the benefits, though, we must also accept the responsibilities.' **Then perhaps add:** (1) 'Many mothers have been abandoned by the men who fathered their children. But in a home where both husband and wife live by Bible standards, the husband will really love his wife and children and loyally stay with them and provide for them. (1 Tim. 5:8; Eph. 5:28-31)' (2) 'If we personally are to receive that kind of love and respect, we also have to apply Bible standards in our attitude toward the members of our family. How does the Bible say that we should view the children that we produce? (Ps. 127:3; contrast Isaiah 49:15.)'

Adam and Eve

Definition: Adam was the first human creature. The Hebrew term *'a·dham'* is also properly translated "man," "earthling man," and "mankind." Eve, the first woman, was Adam's wife.

Were Adam and Eve merely allegorical (fictional) persons?

Is it unreasonable to believe that all of us descended from the same original parents?

"Science now corroborates what most great religions have long been preaching: Human beings of all races are . . . descended from the same first man."—*Heredity in Humans* (Philadelphia and New York, 1972), Amram Scheinfeld, p. 238.

"The Bible story of Adam and Eve, father and mother of the whole human race, told centuries ago the same truth that science has shown today: that all the peoples of the earth are a single family and have a common origin."—*The Races of Mankind* (New York, 1978), Ruth Benedict and Gene Weltfish, p. 3.

Acts 17:26: "[God] made out of one man every nation of men, to dwell upon the entire surface of the earth."

Does the Bible present Adam simply as an allegorical character representing all early mankind?

Jude 14: "The seventh one in line from Adam, Enoch, prophesied." (Enoch was not the seventh in line from all early mankind.)

Luke 3:23-38: "Jesus himself, when he commenced his work, was about thirty years old, being the . . . son of David . . . son of Abraham . . . son of Adam." (David and Abraham are well-known historical persons. So is it not reasonable to conclude that Adam was a real person?)

Gen. 5:3: "Adam lived on for a hundred and thirty years. Then he became father to a son in his likeness, in his image, and called his name Seth." (Seth certainly was not fathered by all early men, nor did all early men father sons at 130 years of age.)

Does the statement that a serpent spoke to Eve require that the account be allegorical?

Gen. 3:1-4: "Now the serpent proved to be the most cautious of all the wild beasts of the field that Jehovah God had made. So it began to say to the woman: 'Is it really so that God said you must not eat from every tree of the garden?' At this the woman said to the serpent: ' . . . God has said, "You must not eat from it, no, you must not touch it that you do not die."' At this the serpent said to the woman: 'You positively will not die.'"

John 8:44: "[Jesus said:] The Devil . . . is a liar and the *father of the lie*." (So the Devil was the source of the first lie, spoken in Eden. He used the serpent as a visible mouthpiece. The Genesis account is not using fictional creatures to teach a lesson. See also Revelation 12:9.)

Illustration: It is not unusual for a ventriloquist to make it appear that his voice comes from another source. Compare Numbers 22:26-31, which tells that Jehovah caused Balaam's she-ass to speak.

If "the first man Adam" was simply allegorical, what about "the last Adam," Jesus Christ?

1 Cor. 15:45, 47: "It is even so written: 'The first man Adam became a living soul.' The last Adam became a life-giving spirit. The first man is out of the earth and made of dust; the second man is out of heaven." (Thus denial that Adam was a real person who sinned against God implies doubt as to the identity of Jesus Christ. Such denial leads to rejection of the reason it was necessary for Jesus to give his life for mankind. Rejection of that means repudiation of the Christian faith.)

How did Jesus himself view the Genesis account?

Matt. 19:4, 5: "[Jesus] said: 'Did you not read [at Genesis 1:27; 2:24] that he who created them [Adam and Eve] from the beginning made them male and female and said, "For this reason a man will leave his father and his mother and will stick to his wife, and the two will be one flesh"?'" (Since Jesus believed the Genesis account to be factual, should we not believe it too?)

If Someone Says—

'Adam's sin was God's will, God's plan.'

You might reply: 'Many people have said that. But if I were to do something that you wanted me to do, would you condemn me for it? . . . Then, if Adam's sin was God's will, why was Adam driven out of Eden as a sinner? (Gen. 3: 17-19, 23, 24)'

Or you could say: 'That's an interesting point, and the answer really involves the kind of person God is. Would it be just or loving to condemn a person for doing something that you yourself planned for him to do?' **Then perhaps add:** (1) 'Jehovah is a God of love. (1 John 4:8) All his ways are just. (Ps. 37:28; Deut. 32:4) It was not God's will for Adam to sin; he warned Adam against it. (Gen. 2:17)' (2) 'God did allow Adam, as he does us, the freedom to choose what he would do. Perfection did not rule out the exercise of free will to disobey. Adam chose to rebel against God, despite the warning that death would result.' (See also page 142.)

Ancestor Worship

Definition: The practice of honoring and venerating dead ancestors (ceremonially or otherwise) in the belief that they are conscious in an invisible realm and can help or bring harm to the living and are therefore to be appeased. *Not a Bible teaching*.

Are dead ancestors aware of what the living do and are these ancestors able to help living persons?

Eccl. 9:5: "The living are conscious that they will die; but as for the dead, they are conscious of nothing at all."

Job 14:10, 21: "An earthling man expires, and where is he? His sons get honored, but he does not know it."

Ps. 49:10, 17-19: "Even the wise ones die, together the stupid one and the unreasoning one perish, and they must leave to others their means of maintenance. . . . At his death he cannot take along anything at all; his glory will not go down along with him himself. . . . His soul finally comes only as far as the generation of his forefathers. Nevermore will they see the light."

Is it not true that food placed on an altar or a grave remains untouched? Does not this indicate that the dead are unable to benefit from it?

See also the main heading "Spiritism."

Is there reason to fear that our dead ancestors will harm us?

Eccl. 9:5, 6: "As for the dead, . . . their love and their hate and their jealousy have already perished, and they have no portion anymore to time indefinite in anything that has to be done under the sun."

Is there a spiritual part of a person that survives the death of the body?

Ezek. 18:4: "Look! All the souls—to me they belong. As the soul of the father so likewise the soul of the son—to me they belong. The soul that is sinning—it itself will die." (Also verse 20)

Ps. 146:3, 4: "Do not put your trust in nobles, nor in the son of earthling man . . . His spirit goes out, he goes back to his ground; in that day his thoughts do perish."

Scientists and surgeons have found no evidence of any conscious, living part of humans that survives when the body dies.

See also pages 100-102, under the heading "Death."

Would you prefer that your children and grandchildren show respect and love for you

while you are alive or that they perform rituals at your grave after you are dead?

Eph. 6:2, 3: "'Honor your father and your mother'; which is the first command with a promise: 'That it may go well with you and you may endure a long time on the earth.'" (Children trained in Bible principles show such honor that brings joy to the hearts of their parents while they are alive.)

Prov. 23:22: "Listen to your father who caused your birth, and do not despise your mother just because she has grown old."

1 Tim. 5:4: "If any widow has children or grandchildren, let these learn first to practice godly devotion in their own household and to keep paying a due compensation to their parents and grandparents, for this is acceptable in God's sight."

When spirit mediums claim to deliver messages from the dead, from where do these actually come?

Isa. 8:19: "In case they should say to you people: 'Apply to the spiritistic mediums or to those having a spirit of prediction who are chirping and making utterances in low tones,' is it not to its God that any people should apply? Should there be application to dead persons in behalf of living persons?" (Would God warn us against such a practice if it truly put us in touch with our loved ones?)

Acts 16:16: "As we were going to the place of prayer, a certain servant girl with a spirit, *a demon* of divination, met us. She used to furnish her masters with much gain by practicing the art of prediction."

See also pages 384-386, under "Spiritism."

To whom should our worship be directed?

Luke 4:8: "Jesus said to him: 'It is written, "It is Jehovah your God you must worship, and it is to him alone you must render sacred service."'"

John 4:23, 24: "The hour is coming, and it is now, when the true worshipers will worship the Father with spirit and truth, for, indeed, the Father is looking for suchlike ones to worship him. God is a Spirit, and those worshiping him must worship with spirit and truth."

What hope is there for a future uniting of family members, including those who have died?

John 5:28, 29: "Do not marvel at this, because the hour is coming in which all those in the memorial tombs will hear his voice and come out, those who did good things to a resurrection of life, those who practiced vile things to a resurrection of judgment."

Antichrist

Definition: Antichrist means *against* or *instead of* Christ. The term applies to all who deny what the Bible says about Jesus Christ, all who oppose his Kingdom, and all who mistreat his followers. It also includes individuals, organizations, and nations that falsely claim to represent Christ or that improperly ascribe to themselves the role of Messiah.

Does the Bible refer to only one antichrist?

1 John 2:18: "Young children, it is the last hour, and, just as you have heard that antichrist is coming, even now there have come to be *many* antichrists; from which fact we gain the knowledge that it is the last hour."

2 John 7: "Many deceivers have gone forth into the world, persons not confessing Jesus Christ as coming in the flesh. This is the deceiver and the antichrist." (Notice that the "many antichrists" of 1 John 2:18 are here referred to collectively as "the antichrist.")

Is the coming of the antichrist reserved for some future time?

1 John 4:3: "Every inspired expression that does not confess Jesus does not originate with God. Furthermore, this

is the antichrist's inspired expression which you have heard was coming, and *now it is already* in the world." (That was written near the end of the first century C.E.)

1 John 2:18: *"Even now* there have come to be many antichrists; from which fact we gain the knowledge that it is the last hour." (By "last hour" John evidently meant the end of the apostolic period. The other apostles had died, and John himself was very old.)

Some of those identified as antichrist—

Persons who deny that Jesus is truly the Messiah

1 John 2:22: "Who is the liar if it is not the one that denies that Jesus is the Christ [or, Messiah, anointed one]? This is the antichrist."

All who deny that Jesus is the unique Son of God

1 John 2:22: "This is the antichrist, the one that denies the Father and the Son."

Compare John 10:36; Luke 9:35.

Apostates

1 John 2:18, 19: "There have come to be many antichrists . . . *They went out from us,* but they were not of our sort."

Those who oppose Christ's true followers

John 15:20, 21: "If they have persecuted me, they will persecute you also . . . But they will do all these things against you on account of my name."

Individuals and nations that oppose Christ as King or that themselves falsely claim the Messianic role

Ps. 2:2: "The kings of earth take their stand and high officials themselves have massed together as one against Jehovah and against his anointed one [Christ, or Messiah]."

See also Revelation 17:3, 12-14; 19:11-21.

Matt. 24:24: "False Christs and false prophets will arise and will give great signs and wonders so as to mislead, if possible, even the chosen ones."

Apostasy

Definition: Apostasy is abandoning or deserting the worship and service of God, actually a rebellion against Jehovah God. Some apostates profess to know and serve God but reject teachings or requirements set out in his Word. Others claim to believe the Bible but reject Jehovah's organization.

Should we expect that apostates will arise within the Christian congregation?

1 Tim. 4:1: "The inspired utterance says definitely that in later periods of time some will fall away from the faith, paying attention to misleading inspired utterances and teachings of demons."

2 Thess. 2:3: "Let no one seduce you in any manner, because [the day of Jehovah] will not come unless the apostasy comes first and the man of lawlessness gets revealed, the son of destruction."

Some identifying marks of apostates—

They seek to make others their followers, thus causing sectarian divisions

Acts 20:30: "From among you yourselves men will rise and speak twisted things to draw away the disciples after themselves."

2 Pet. 2:1, 3: "There will also be false teachers among you. These very ones will quietly bring in destructive sects and will disown even the owner that bought them . . . Also, with covetousness they will exploit you with counterfeit words."

They may profess to believe in Christ but treat lightly the preaching and teaching work he assigned to his followers

Luke 6:46: "Why, then, do you call me 'Lord! Lord!' but do not do the things I say?"

Matt. 28:19, 20: "Go therefore and make disciples of

34

people of all the nations, baptizing them . . . teaching them to observe all the things I have commanded you."

Matt. 24:14: "This good news of the kingdom will be preached in all the inhabited earth for a witness to all the nations; and then the end will come."

They may claim to serve God but reject his representatives, his visible organization

Jude 8, 11: "These men, too, indulging in dreams, are defiling the flesh and disregarding lordship and speaking abusively of glorious ones. Too bad for them, because they . . . have perished in the rebellious talk of Korah!"

Num. 16:1-3, 11, 19-21: "Korah . . . proceeded to get up, together with . . . two hundred and fifty men of the sons of Israel, chieftains of the assembly . . . So they congregated themselves against Moses and Aaron and said to them: 'That is enough of you, because the whole assembly are all of them holy and Jehovah is in their midst. Why, then, should you lift yourselves up above the congregation of Jehovah?' . . . [Moses said:] 'You and all your assembly who are gathering together are against Jehovah. As for Aaron, what is he that you men should murmur against him?' When Korah got all the assembly together against them at the entrance of the tent of meeting, then Jehovah's glory appeared to all the assembly. Jehovah now spoke to Moses and Aaron, saying: 'Separate yourselves from the midst of this assembly, that I may exterminate them in an instant.'"

Not only do they abandon the true faith but they then "beat" their former associates, using public criticism and other methods to hinder their work; the efforts of such apostates are devoted to tearing down, not building up

Matt. 24:45-51: "Who really is the faithful and discreet slave whom his master appointed over his domestics, to give them their food at the proper time? . . . But if ever that evil slave should say in his heart, 'My master is delaying,' and should start to beat his fellow slaves and should eat and drink with the confirmed drunkards, the master of that slave will come on a day that he does not expect and in an hour that he does not know, and will punish him with the greatest severity and will assign him his part with the hypocrites."

2 Tim. 2:16-18: "Shun empty speeches that violate what is holy; for they will advance to more and more ungodliness, and their word will spread like gangrene. Hymenaeus and Philetus are of that number. These very men have deviated from the truth, saying that the resurrection has already occurred; and they are subverting the faith of some."

Would faithful Christians welcome apostates into their presence, either personally or by reading their literature?

2 John 9, 10: "Everyone that pushes ahead and does not remain in the teaching of the Christ does not have God. . . . If anyone comes to you and does not bring this teaching, never receive him into your homes or say a greeting to him."

Rom. 16:17, 18: "I exhort you, brothers, to keep your eye on those who cause divisions and occasions for stumbling contrary to the teaching that you have learned, and avoid them. . . . By smooth talk and complimentary speech they seduce the hearts of guileless ones."

Would any serious harm come from satisfying one's curiosity about the thinking of apostates?

Prov. 11:9: "By his mouth the one who is an apostate brings his fellowman to ruin."

Isa. 32:6: "The senseless one himself will speak mere senselessness, and his very heart will work at what is hurtful, to work at apostasy and to speak against Jehovah what is wayward, to cause the soul of the hungry one to go empty, and he causes even the thirsty one to go without drink itself." (Compare Isaiah 65:13, 14.)

How serious is apostasy?

2 Pet. 2:1: "These very ones will quietly bring in destructive sects and will disown even the owner that bought them, bringing speedy destruction upon themselves."

Job 13:16: "Before him [God] no apostate will come in."

Heb. 6:4-6: "It is impossible as regards those who have once for all been enlightened, and who have tasted the heavenly free gift, and who have become partakers of holy spirit, and who have tasted the fine word of God and powers of the coming system of things, but who have fallen away ["if they then commit apostasy," *RS*], to revive them again to repentance, because they impale the Son of God afresh for themselves and expose him to public shame."

Apostolic Succession

Definition: The doctrine that the 12 apostles have successors to whom authority has been passed by divine appointment. In the Roman Catholic Church, the bishops as a group are said to be successors of the apostles, and the pope is claimed to be the successor of Peter. It is maintained that the Roman pontiffs come immediately after, occupy the position and perform the functions of Peter, to whom Christ is said to have given primacy of authority over the whole Church. *Not a Bible teaching*.

Was Peter the "rock" on which the church was built?

Matt. 16:18, *JB:* "I now say to you: You are Peter and on this rock I will build my Church. And the gates of the underworld can never hold out against it." (Notice in the context [vss. 13, 20] that the discussion centers on the identity of *Jesus*.)

Whom did the apostles Peter and Paul understand to be the "rock," the "cornerstone"?

Acts 4:8-11, *JB:* "Peter, filled with the Holy Spirit, addressed them, 'Rulers of the people, and elders! . . . it was by the name of Jesus Christ the Nazarene, the one you crucified, whom God raised from the dead, by this name and by no other that this man is able to stand up perfectly healthy, here in your presence, today. This is the stone rejected by you the builders, but which has proved to be the keystone ["cornerstone," *NAB*].'"

1 Pet. 2:4-8, *JB:* "Set yourselves close to him [the Lord Jesus Christ] so that you too . . . may be living stones making a spiritual house. As scripture says: See how I lay in Zion a precious cornerstone that I have chosen and the man who rests his trust on it will not be disappointed. That means that for you who are believers, it is precious; but for unbelievers, the stone rejected by the builders has proved to be the keystone, a stone to stumble over, a rock to bring men down."

Eph. 2:20, *JB:* "You are part of a building that has the apostles and prophets for its foundations, and Christ Jesus himself for its main cornerstone."

What was the belief of Augustine (who was viewed as a saint by the Catholic Church)?

"In this same period of my priesthood, I also wrote a book against a letter of Donatus . . . In a passage in this book, I said about the Apostle Peter: 'On him as on a rock the Church was built.' . . . But I know that very frequently at a later time, I so explained what the Lord said: 'Thou art Peter, and upon this rock I will build my Church,' that it be understood as built upon Him whom Peter confessed saying: 'Thou art the Christ, the Son of the living God,' and so Peter, called after this rock, represented the person of the Church which is built upon this rock, and has received 'the keys of the kingdom of heaven.' For, 'Thou art Peter' and not 'Thou art the rock' was said to him. But 'the rock was Christ,' in confessing whom as also the whole Church confesses, Simon was called Peter."—*The Fathers of the Church—Saint Augustine, the Retractations* (Washington, D.C.; 1968), translated by Mary I. Bogan, Book I, p. 90.

Did the other apostles view Peter as having primacy among them?

Luke 22:24-26, *JB:* "A dispute arose also between them [the apostles] about which should be reckoned the greatest, but he said to them, 'Among pagans it is the kings who lord it over them, and those who have authority over them are

given the title Benefactor. This must not happen with you.'"
(If Peter were the "rock," would there have been any question as to which one of them "should be reckoned the greatest"?)

Since Jesus Christ, the head of the congregation, is alive, does he need successors?

Heb. 7:23-25, *JB:* "Then there used to be a great number of those other priests [in Israel], because death put an end to each one of them; but this one [Jesus Christ], because he remains for ever, can never lose his priesthood. It follows, then, that his power to save is utterly certain, since he is living for ever to intercede for all who come to God through him."

Rom. 6:9, *JB:* "Christ, as we know, having been raised from the dead will never die again."

Eph. 5:23, *JB:* "Christ is head of the Church."

What were "the keys" entrusted to Peter?

Matt. 16:19, *JB:* "I will give you the keys of the kingdom of heaven: whatever you bind on earth shall be considered bound in heaven; whatever you loose on earth shall be considered loosed in heaven."

In Revelation, Jesus referred to a symbolic key used by himself to open up privileges and opportunities to humans

Rev. 3:7, 8, *JB:* "Here is the message of the holy and faithful one who has the key of David, so that when he opens, nobody can close, and when he closes, nobody can open: . . . I have opened in front of you a door that nobody will be able to close."

Peter used "keys" entrusted to him to open up (to Jews, Samaritans, Gentiles) the opportunity to receive God's spirit with a view to their entering the heavenly Kingdom

Acts 2:14-39, *JB:* "Peter stood up with the Eleven and addressed them in a loud voice: 'Men of Judaea, and all you who live in Jerusalem . . . God has made this Jesus whom you crucified both Lord and Christ.' Hearing this, they were cut to the heart and said to Peter and the apostles, 'What must we do, brothers?' 'You must repent,' Peter answered 'and every one of you must be baptised in the name of Jesus Christ for the forgiveness of your sins, and you will receive the gift of the Holy Spirit. The promise that was made is for you and your children, and for all those who are far away, for all those whom the Lord our God will call to himself.'"

Acts 8:14-17, *JB:* "When the apostles in Jerusalem heard that Samaria had accepted the word of God, they sent Peter and John to them, and they went down there, and prayed for the Samaritans to receive the Holy Spirit, for as yet he had not come down on any of them: they had only been baptised in the name of the Lord Jesus. Then they laid hands on them, and they received the Holy Spirit." (Verse 20 indicates that Peter was the one taking the lead on this occasion.)

Acts 10:24-48, *JB:* "They reached Caesarea the following day, and Cornelius [an uncircumcised Gentile] was waiting for them. . . . Peter addressed them . . . While Peter was still speaking the Holy Spirit came down on all the listeners."

Did heaven wait on Peter to make decisions and then follow his lead?

Acts 2:4, 14, *JB:* "They were all filled with the Holy Spirit, and began to speak foreign languages as the Spirit gave them the gift of speech. . . . Then [after Christ, the head of the congregation, had stirred them up by means of the holy spirit] Peter stood up with the Eleven and addressed them." (See verse 33.)

Acts 10:19, 20, *JB:* "The Spirit had to tell him [Peter], 'Some men have come to see you. Hurry down, and do not hesitate about going back with them [to the home of the Gentile Cornelius]; it was I who told them to come.'"

Compare Matthew 18:18, 19.

Is Peter the judge as to who is worthy to enter the Kingdom?

2 Tim. 4:1, *JB:* "Christ Jesus . . . is to be judge of the living and the dead."

2 Tim. 4:8, *JB:* "All there is to come now is the crown of

righteousness reserved for me, which the Lord [Jesus Christ], the righteous judge, will give to me on that Day; and not only to me but to all those who have longed for his Appearing."

Was Peter in Rome?

Rome is referred to in nine verses of the Holy Scriptures; none of these say that Peter was there. First Peter 5:13 shows that he was in Babylon. Was this a cryptic reference to Rome? His being in Babylon was consistent with his assignment to preach to the Jews (as indicated at Galatians 2:9), since there was a large Jewish population in Babylon. The *Encyclopaedia Judaica* (Jerusalem, 1971, Vol. 15, col. 755), when discussing production of the Babylonian Talmud, refers to Judaism's "great academies of Babylon" during the Common Era.

Has an unbroken line of successors been traced from Peter to modern-day popes?

Jesuit John McKenzie, when professor of theology at Notre Dame, wrote: "Historical evidence does not exist for the entire chain of succession of church authority."—*The Roman Catholic Church* (New York, 1969), p. 4.

The *New Catholic Encyclopedia* admits: "... the scarcity of documents leaves much that is obscure about the early development of the episcopate ... "—(1967), Vol. I, p. 696.

Claims of divine appointment mean nothing if those who make them are not obedient to God and Christ

Matt. 7:21-23, *JB:* "It is not those who say to me, 'Lord, Lord', who will enter the kingdom of heaven, but the person who does the will of my Father in heaven. When the day comes many will say to me, 'Lord, Lord, did we not prophesy in your name, cast out demons in your name, work many miracles in your name?' Then I shall tell them to their faces: I have never known you; away from me, you evil men!"

See also Jeremiah 7:9-15.

Have the claimed successors to the apostles adhered to the teachings and practices of Jesus Christ and his apostles?

A Catholic Dictionary states: "The Roman Church is Apostolic, because her doctrine is the faith once revealed to the Apostles, which faith she guards and explains, without adding to it or taking from it." (London, 1957, W. E. Addis and T. Arnold, p. 176) Do the facts agree?

Identity of God

"The Trinity is the term employed to signify the central doctrine of the Christian religion."—*The Catholic Encyclopedia* (1912), Vol. XV, p. 47.

"Neither the word Trinity, nor the explicit doctrine as such, appears in the New Testament . . . The doctrine developed gradually over several centuries and through many controversies."—*The New Encyclopædia Britannica* (1976), Micropædia, Vol. X, p. 126.

"There is the recognition on the part of exegetes and Biblical theologians, including a constantly growing number of Roman Catholics, that one should not speak of Trinitarianism in the New Testament without serious qualification. There is also the closely parallel recognition on the part of historians of dogma and systematic theologians that when one does speak of an unqualified Trinitarianism, one has moved from the period of Christian origins to, say, the last quadrant of the 4th century."—*New Catholic Encyclopedia* (1967), Vol. XIV, p. 295.

Celibacy of the clergy

Pope Paul VI, in his encyclical *Sacerdotalis Caelibatus* (Priestly Celibacy, 1967), endorsed celibacy as a requirement for the clergy, but he admitted that "the New Testament which preserves the teaching of Christ and the Apostles . . . does not openly demand celibacy of sacred ministers . . . Jesus Himself did not make it a prerequisite in His choice of the Twelve, nor did the Apostles for those who presided over the first Christian communities."—*The Papal Encyclicals 1958-1981* (Falls Church, Va.; 1981), p. 204.

1 Cor. 9:5, *NAB:* "Do we not have the right to marry a believing woman like the rest of the apostles and the brothers of the Lord and Cephas?" ("Cephas" is an Aramaic name given to Peter; see John 1:42. See also Mark 1:29-31, where reference is made to the mother-in-law of Simon, or Peter.)

1 Tim. 3:2, *Dy:* "It behoveth, therefore, a bishop to be . . . the husband of one wife ["married only once," *NAB*]."

Before the Christian era, Buddhism required its priests and monks to be celibate. (*History of Sacerdotal Celibacy in the Christian Church,* London, 1932, fourth ed., revised, Henry C. Lea, p. 6) Even earlier, the higher orders of the Babylonian priesthood were required to practice celibacy, according to *The Two Babylons* by A. Hislop.—(New York, 1943), p. 219.

1 Tim. 4:1-3, *JB:* "The Spirit has explicitly said that during the last times there will be some who will desert the faith and choose to listen to deceitful spirits and doctrines that come from the devils; . . . they will say marriage is forbidden."

Separateness from the world

Pope Paul VI, when addressing the United Nations in 1965, said: "The peoples of the earth turn to the United Nations as the last hope of concord and peace; We presume to present here, together with Our own, their tribute of honor and of hope."—*The Pope's Visit* (New York, 1965), Time-Life Special Report, p. 26.

John 15:19, *JB:* "[Jesus Christ said:] If you belonged to the world, the world would love you as its own; but because you do not belong to the world, because my choice withdrew you from the world, therefore the world hates you."

Jas. 4:4, *JB:* "Don't you realise that making the world your friend is making God your enemy?"

Resorting to weapons of war

Catholic historian E. I. Watkin writes: "Painful as the admission must be, we cannot in the interest of a false edification or dishonest loyalty deny or ignore the historical fact that Bishops have consistently supported all wars waged by the government of their country. I do not know in fact of a single instance in which a national hierarchy has condemned as unjust any war . . . Whatever the official theory, in practice 'my country always right' has been the maxim followed in wartime by Catholic Bishops."—*Morals and Missiles* (London, 1959), edited by Charles S. Thompson, pp. 57, 58.

Matt. 26:52, *JB:* "Jesus then said, 'Put your sword back, for all who draw the sword will die by the sword.'"

1 John 3:10-12, *JB:* "In this way we distinguish the children of God from the children of the devil: anybody . . . not loving his brother is no child of God's. . . . We are to love one another; not to be like Cain, who belonged to the Evil One and cut his brother's throat."

In the light of the foregoing, have those who claim to be successors to the apostles really taught and practiced what Christ and his apostles did?

Armageddon

Definition: The Greek *Har Ma·ge·don'*, taken from Hebrew and rendered "Armageddon" by many translators, means "Mountain of Megiddo," or "Mountain of Assembly of Troops." The Bible associates the name, not with a nuclear holocaust, but with the coming universal "war of the great day of God the Almighty." (Rev. 16:14, 16) This name is applied specifically to "the place [Greek, *to'pon;* that is, condition or situation]" to which earth's political rulers are being gathered in opposition to Jehovah and his Kingdom by Jesus Christ. Such opposition will be shown by global action against Jehovah's servants on earth, the visible representatives of God's Kingdom.

Will humans be permitted by God to ruin the earth by what some call a "thermonuclear Armageddon"?

Ps. 96:10: "Jehovah himself has become king. The productive land [Hebrew, *te·vel';* the earth, as fertile and inhabited, the habitable globe] also becomes firmly established so that it cannot be made to totter."

Ps. 37:29: "The righteous themselves will possess the earth, and they will reside forever upon it."

Rev. 11:18: "The nations became wrathful, and your own [Jehovah's] wrath came, and the appointed time . . . to bring to ruin those ruining the earth."

What is Armageddon, as referred to in the Bible?

Rev. 16:14, 16: "They are, in fact, expressions inspired by demons and perform signs, and they go forth to the kings of the entire inhabited earth, to gather them together to the *war of the great day of God the Almighty*. And they gathered them together to the place that is called in Hebrew Har–Magedon [Armageddon]."

Will Armageddon be fought only in the Middle East?

Rulers and armies of all nations will be assembled in opposition to God

Rev. 16:14: "They go forth to the kings of *the entire inhabited earth,* to gather them together to the war of the great day of God the Almighty."

Rev. 19:19: "I saw the wild beast [human political rulership as a whole] and the kings of the earth and their armies gathered together to wage the war with the one seated on the horse and with his army."

Jer. 25:33: "Those slain by Jehovah will certainly come to be in that day from one end of the earth clear to the other end of the earth."

Use of the name Armageddon (Har–Magedon) cannot mean that the war will be fought at a literal Mountain of Megiddo

There is no literal Mountain of Megiddo; only a mound about 70 feet (21 m) high where ruins of ancient Megiddo are found.

The kings and military forces of "the entire inhabited earth" could not fit into the literal Plain of Esdraelon, below Megiddo. The plain is triangular, only 20 miles (32 km) long and 18 miles (29 km) wide at the eastern end.—*The Geography of the Bible* (New York, 1957), Denis Baly, p. 148.

The name is fitting because of Megiddo's role in history; the plain below Megiddo was the site of decisive wars

There Jehovah caused the defeat of Sisera, the chief of the Canaanite army, before Judge Barak.—Judg. 5:19, 20; 4:12-24.

Thutmose III, pharaoh of Egypt, said: "The capturing of Megiddo is the capturing of a thousand towns!"—*Ancient Near Eastern Texts Relating to the Old Testament* (Princeton, N.J.; 1969), edited by James Pritchard, p. 237.

The reference to Megiddo (meaning "Assembly of Troops") is appropriate because Armageddon is a world situation in which the troops and other supporters of the rulers of all nations will be involved.

Who or what will be destroyed at Armageddon?

Dan. 2:44: "The God of heaven will set up a kingdom . . . It will crush and put an end to all these kingdoms, and it itself will stand to times indefinite."

Rev. 19:17, 18: "I saw also an angel standing in the sun, and he cried out with a loud voice and said to all the birds that fly in midheaven: 'Come here, be gathered together to the great evening meal of God, that you may eat the fleshy parts of kings and the fleshy parts of military commanders and the fleshy parts of strong men and the fleshy parts of horses and of those seated upon them, and the fleshy parts of all, of freemen as well as of slaves and of small ones and great.'"

1 John 2:16, 17: "Everything in the world—the desire of the flesh and the desire of the eyes and the showy display of one's means of life—does not originate with the Father, but originates with the world. Furthermore, the world is passing away and so is its desire, but he that does the will of God remains forever."

Rev. 21:8: "As for the cowards and those without faith and those who are disgusting in their filth and murderers and fornicators and those practicing spiritism and idolaters and all the liars, their portion will be in the lake that burns with fire and sulphur. This means the second death."

Will the destruction be forever?

Matt. 25:46: "These [who refused to do good to Christ's "brothers"] will depart into everlasting cutting-off."

2 Thess. 1:8, 9: "Those who do not know God and those who do not obey the good news about our Lord Jesus . . . will undergo the judicial punishment of everlasting destruction."

Will there be survivors?

Zeph. 2:3: "Seek Jehovah, all you meek ones of the earth, who have practiced His own judicial decision. Seek righteousness, seek meekness. Probably you may be concealed in the day of Jehovah's anger."

Rom. 10:13: "Everyone who calls on the name of Jehovah will be saved."

Ps. 37:34: "Hope in Jehovah and keep his way, and he will exalt you to take possession of the earth. When the wicked ones are cut off, you will see it."

John 3:16: "God . . . gave his only-begotten Son, in order that everyone exercising faith in him might not be destroyed but have everlasting life."

Rev. 7:9, 10, 14: "I saw, and, look! a great crowd, which no man was able to number, out of all nations and tribes and peoples and tongues, standing before the throne and before the Lamb, dressed in white robes; and there were palm branches in their hands. And they keep on crying with a loud voice, saying: 'Salvation we owe to our God, who is seated on the throne, and to the Lamb.' . . . 'These are the ones that come out of the great tribulation.'"

What will happen to young children at Armageddon?

The Bible does not directly answer that question, and we are not the judges. However, the Bible does show that God views the young children of true Christians as "holy." (1 Cor.

7:14) It also reveals that in times past when God destroyed the wicked he likewise destroyed their little ones. (Num. 16: 27, 32; Ezek. 9:6) God does not want anyone to be destroyed, so he is having a warning sounded now to benefit both parents and children. Would it not be wise for parents to pursue a course that would result in their children being looked on with favor by God both now and at Armageddon?

Is the love of God violated by destruction of the wicked?

2 Pet. 3:9: "Jehovah . . . is patient with you because he does not desire any to be destroyed but desires all to attain to repentance."

Luke 18:7, 8: "Shall not God cause justice to be done for his chosen ones who cry out to him day and night, even though he is long-suffering toward them? I tell you, He will cause justice to be done to them speedily."

2 Thess. 1:6: "It is righteous on God's part to repay tribulation to those who make tribulation for you [his servants]."

Is it possible to take a neutral position?

2 Thess. 1:8: "He brings vengeance upon those who [by choice] do not know God and those who do not obey the good news about our Lord Jesus."

Matt. 24:37-39: "Just as the days of Noah were . . . they took no note until the flood came and swept them all away, so the presence of the Son of man will be."

Matt. 12:30: "He that is not on my side is against me, and he that does not gather with me scatters."

Compare Deuteronomy 30:19, 20.

Whose influence is pushing the nations to the world situation that will result in war against God?

Rev. 16:13, 14: "I saw three unclean inspired expressions that looked like frogs come out of the mouth of the dragon

[Satan the Devil; Rev. 12:9] and out of the mouth of the wild beast and out of the mouth of the false prophet. They are, in fact, expressions inspired by demons and perform signs, and they go forth to the kings of the entire inhabited earth, to gather them together to the war of the great day of God the Almighty."

Compare Luke 4:5, 6; 1 John 5:19; also Acts 5:38, 39; 2 Chronicles 32:1, 16, 17.

Babylon the Great

Definition: The world empire of false religion, embracing all religions whose teachings and practices do not conform to the true worship of Jehovah, the only true God. Following the Flood of Noah's day, false religion had its beginning at Babel (later known as Babylon). (Gen. 10:8-10; 11:4-9) In time, Babylonish religious beliefs and practices spread to many lands. So Babylon the Great became a fitting name for false religion as a whole.

What evidence points to the identity of Babylon the Great, referred to in Revelation?

It could not be the ancient city of Babylon. Revelation was written at the end of the first century C.E. and describes events that would reach down to our day. *The Encyclopedia Americana* says: "The city [Babylon] was taken by the Persians under Cyrus the Great in 539 B.C. Later Alexander the Great planned to make Babylon the capital of his eastern empire, but after his death Babylon gradually lost importance." (1956, Vol. III, p. 7) Today the city is an uninhabited ruin.

In the symbolism of Revelation, Babylon the Great is referred to as a "great city," a "kingdom" that rules other kings. (Rev. 17:18) Like a city, it would have many organizations within it; and like a kingdom that includes other kings in its domain, it would be international in scope. It is described as having relations with political rulers and contributing much to the wealth of men in commerce, while itself being a third element that "has become a dwelling place of demons" and a persecutor of "prophets and of holy ones."—Rev. 18:2, 9-17, 24.

Ancient Babylon was outstandingly noted for its religion and its defiance of Jehovah

Gen. 10:8-10: "Nimrod . . . displayed himself a mighty hunter in opposition to Jehovah. . . . And the beginning of his kingdom came to be Babel [later known as Babylon]."

Dan. 5:22, 23: "As for you [Belshazzar king of Babylon] . . . against the Lord of the heavens you exalted yourself, . . . and you have praised mere gods of silver and of gold, copper, iron, wood and stone, that are beholding nothing or hearing nothing or knowing nothing; but the God in whose hand your breath is and to whom all your ways belong you have not glorified."

An ancient cuneiform inscription reads: "Altogether there are in Babylon 53 temples of the chief gods, 55 chapels of Marduk, 300 chapels for the earthly deities, 600 for the heavenly deities, 180 altars for the goddess Ishtar, 180 for the gods Nergal and Adad and 12 other altars for different gods."—Quoted in *The Bible as History* (New York, 1964), W. Keller, p. 301.

The Encyclopedia Americana comments: "Sumerian civilization [which was part of Babylonia] was dominated by priests; at the head of the state was the *lugal* (literally 'great man'), the representative of the gods."—(1977), Vol. 3, p. 9.

Reasonably, therefore, Babylon the Great as referred to in Revelation is *religious*. Being like a city and an empire, it is not limited to one religious group but includes all religions that are in opposition to Jehovah, the true God.

Ancient Babylonian religious concepts and practices are found in religions worldwide

"Egypt, Persia, and Greece felt the influence of the Babylonian religion . . . The strong admixture of Semitic elements both in early Greek mythology and in Grecian cults is now so generally admitted by scholars as to require no further comment. These Semitic elements are to a large extent more specifically Babylonian."—*The Religion of*

Babylonia and Assyria (Boston, 1898), M. Jastrow, Jr., pp. 699, 700.

Their gods: There were triads of gods, and among their divinities were those representing various forces of nature and ones that exercised special influence in certain activities of mankind. (*Babylonian and Assyrian Religion,* Norman, Okla.; 1963, S. H. Hooke, pp. 14-40) "The Platonic trinity, itself merely a rearrangement of older trinities dating back to earlier peoples, appears to be the rational philosophic trinity of attributes that gave birth to the three hypostases or divine persons taught by the Christian churches. . . . This Greek philosopher's [Plato's] conception of the divine trinity . . . can be found in all the ancient [pagan] religions." —*Nouveau Dictionnaire Universel* (Paris, 1865-1870), edited by M. Lachâtre, Vol. 2, p. 1467.

Use of images: "[In Mesopotamian religion] the role of the image was central in the cult as well as in private worship, as the wide distribution of cheap replicas of such images shows. Fundamentally, the deity was considered present in its image if it showed certain specific features and paraphernalia and was cared for in the appropriate manner." —*Ancient Mesopotamia—Portrait of a Dead Civilization* (Chicago, 1964), A. L. Oppenheim, p. 184.

Belief regarding death: "Neither the people nor the leaders of religious thought [in Babylon] ever faced the possibility of the total annihilation of what once was called into existence. Death was a passage to another kind of life." —*The Religion of Babylonia and Assyria,* p. 556.

Position of the priesthood: "The distinction between priest and layman is characteristic of this [Babylonian] religion."—*Encyclopædia Britannica* (1948), Vol. 2, p. 861.

Practice of astrology, divination, magic, and sorcery: Historian A. H. Sayce writes: "[In] the religion of ancient Babylonia . . . every object and force of nature was supposed to have its *zi* or spirit, who could be controlled by the magical exorcisms of the Shaman, or sorcerer-priest." (*The History of Nations,* New York, 1928, Vol. I, p. 96) "The Chaldeans [Babylonians] made great progress in the study of astronomy through an effort to discover the future in the

stars. This art we call 'astrology.'"—*The Dawn of Civilization and Life in the Ancient East* (Chicago, 1938), R. M.
Engberg, p. 230.

Babylon the Great is like an immoral harlot, one living in shameless luxury

Revelation 17:1-5 says: "'Come, I will show you the
judgment upon the great harlot who sits on many waters
[peoples], with whom the kings [political rulers] of the earth
committed fornication, whereas those who inhabit the earth
were made drunk with the wine of her fornication.' . . . And
upon her forehead was written a name, a mystery: 'Babylon
the Great, the mother of the harlots and of the disgusting
things of the earth.'" Revelation 18:7 adds that "she glorified herself and lived in shameless luxury."

Is it not true that the dominant religious organizations
have made it a practice to consort with political rulers for
power and material gain, though this has resulted in suffering for the common people? Is it not also true that their
higher clergy live in luxury, even though many of the people
to whom they should minister may be impoverished?

Why can religions that profess to be Christian properly be viewed as a part of Babylon the Great, along with those who know nothing of the God of the Bible?

Jas. 4:4: "Adulteresses, do you not know that the friendship with the world is enmity with God? Whoever, therefore,
wants to be a friend of the world is constituting himself an
enemy of God." (So, though they know what the Bible says
about God, they make themselves his enemies if they choose
friendship with the world by imitating its ways.)

2 Cor. 4:4; 11:14, 15: "The god of this system of things
has blinded the minds of the unbelievers, that the illumination of the glorious good news about the Christ, who is the
image of God, might not shine through." "Satan himself
keeps transforming himself into an angel of light. It is
therefore nothing great if his ministers also keep transforming themselves into ministers of righteousness. But their
end shall be according to their works." (Thus Jehovah's chief

adversary, Satan the Devil himself, is really being honored by all who do not worship the true God in the manner that He has appointed, even though they may claim to be Christians. See also 1 Corinthians 10:20.)

Matt. 7:21-23: "Not everyone saying to me [Jesus Christ], 'Lord, Lord,' will enter into the kingdom of the heavens, but the one doing the will of my Father who is in the heavens will. Many will say to me in that day, 'Lord, Lord, did we not prophesy in your name, and expel demons in your name, and perform many powerful works in your name?' And yet then I will confess to them: I never knew you! Get away from me, you workers of lawlessness."

Why is it urgent to get out of Babylon the Great without delay?

Rev. 18:4: "Get out of her, my people, if you do not want to share with her in her sins, and if you do not want to receive part of her plagues."

Rev. 18:21: "A strong angel lifted up a stone like a great millstone and hurled it into the sea, saying: 'Thus with a swift pitch will Babylon the great city be hurled down, and she will never be found again.'"

Luke 21:36: "Keep awake, then, all the time making supplication that you may succeed in escaping all these things that are destined to occur, and in standing before the Son of man."

What will happen to people who did not know Bible truth but lived and died in the past as part of Babylon the Great?

Acts 17:30: "God has overlooked the times of such ignorance, yet now he is telling mankind that they should all everywhere repent."

Acts 24:15: "There is going to be a resurrection of both the righteous and the unrighteous." (As to which ones of "the unrighteous" will be raised, God will decide.)

Job 34:12: "For a fact, God himself does not act wickedly, and the Almighty himself does not pervert judgment."

Baptism

Definition: The word "baptize" comes from the Greek *ba·pti'-zein*, meaning "to dip, to plunge." (*A Greek-English Lexicon*, by Liddell and Scott) Christian water baptism is an outward symbol that the one being baptized has made a complete, unreserved, and unconditional dedication through Jesus Christ to do the will of Jehovah God. The Scriptures also refer to John's baptism, baptism with holy spirit, and baptism with fire, among others.

Do persons who really believe God's Word hold back from being baptized?

Matt. 28:19, 20: "Go therefore and make disciples of people of all the nations, baptizing them in the name of the Father and of the Son and of the holy spirit, teaching them to observe all the things I have commanded you."

Acts 2:41: "Those who embraced his word heartily were baptized."

Acts 8:12: "When they believed Philip, who was declaring the good news of the kingdom of God and of the name of Jesus Christ, they proceeded to be baptized, both men and women."

Acts 8:36-38: "Now as they were going over the road, they came to a certain body of water, and the [Ethiopian] eunuch said: 'Look! A body of water; what prevents me from getting baptized?' With that he commanded the chariot to halt, and . . . [Philip] baptized him."

Christian water baptism—is it by sprinkling or by complete immersion?

Mark 1:9, 10: "Jesus . . . was baptized ["immersed," *ED, Ro*] in the Jordan [River] by John. And immediately on *coming up out of the water* he saw the heavens being parted."

Acts 8:38: "They both *went down into the water,* both Philip and the eunuch; and he baptized ["immersed," *ED, Ro*] him."

Was infant baptism practiced by first-century Christians?

Matt. 28:19: "Go therefore and make *disciples . . . baptizing them.*"

Acts 8:12: "When they believed Philip . . . they proceeded to be baptized, both *men and women.*"

However, later on, Origen (185-254 C.E.) wrote: "It is the custom of the church that baptism be administered even to infants." (*Selections From the Commentaries and Homilies of Origen,* Madras, India; 1929, p. 211) The practice was confirmed by the Third Council of Carthage (253 C.E.).

Religious historian Augustus Neander wrote: "Faith and baptism were always connected with one another; and thus it is in the highest degree probable . . . that the practice of infant baptism was unknown at this period [in the first century]. . . . That it first became recognised as an apostolic tradition in the course of the third century, is evidence rather *against* than *for* the admission of its apostolic origin." —*History of the Planting and Training of the Christian Church by the Apostles* (New York, 1864), p. 162.

Does Christian water baptism result in forgiveness of sins?

1 John 1:7: "If we are walking in the light as he himself is in the light, . . . the blood of Jesus his Son cleanses us from all sin." (Thus, not baptismal water but the blood of Jesus cleanses us from sin.)

Matt. 3:11: "I [John the Baptist] . . . baptize you with water because of your repentance; but the one coming after me [Jesus Christ] is stronger than I am, whose sandals I am not fit to take off." (Verses 5, 6, also Acts 13:24, show that what John did was directed, not to all people, but to the Jews. Why? Because of the sins of the Jews against the Law covenant and to prepare them for Christ.)

Acts 2:38: "Repent, and let each one of you be baptized in the name of Jesus Christ for forgiveness of your sins." (Did the baptism itself bring forgiveness to them? Consider: This was stated to Jews who shared responsibility for the death of Christ. [See verses 22, 23.] Their baptism would give evidence of something. Of what? That they now put faith in Jesus as the Messiah, the Christ. Only by their doing this could their sins be forgiven. [Acts 4:12; 5:30, 31])

Acts 22:16: "Rise, get baptized and wash your sins away *by your calling upon his name.*" (Also Acts 10:43)

Who is baptized with holy spirit?

1 Cor. 1:2; 12:13, 27: "To you who have been sanctified in union with Christ Jesus, called to be *holy ones* . . . For truly by one spirit we were all baptized into one body, whether Jews or Greeks, whether slaves or free, and we were all made to drink one spirit. Now you are Christ's body." (As Daniel 7:13, 14, 27 shows, such "holy ones" share in the Kingdom with the Son of man, Jesus Christ.)

John 3:5: "Unless anyone is born from water and spirit, he cannot enter into the kingdom of God." (A person is 'born from spirit' at the time of his baptism with that spirit. Luke 12:32 shows that only a "little flock" have that privilege. See also Revelation 14:1-3.)

Do all who are baptized with holy spirit speak in tongues or have the gift of healing?

1 Cor. 12:13, 29, 30: "For truly by one spirit we were all baptized into one body . . . Not all are apostles, are they? . . . Not all perform powerful works, do they? Not all have gifts of healings, do they? Not all speak in tongues, do they?"

See also "Healing" and "Tongues, Speaking in."

'Baptism for the dead'—what does it mean?

1 Cor. 15:29, *KJ:* "Else what shall they do which are baptized for the dead, if the dead rise not at all? why are they then baptized for the dead?"

The Greek preposition *hy·per'*, here translated "for," also means "over," "on behalf of," "instead of," "for the purpose of," etc. (*A Greek-English Lexicon,* by Liddell and Scott) What does it mean in this text? Was Paul suggesting baptizing living persons in behalf of those who had died unbaptized?

The only other scriptures that directly mention death in connection with baptism refer to a baptism that the individual himself undergoes, not a baptism on behalf of another person, one who is dead

Rom. 6:3: "Do you not know that all of us who were baptized into Christ Jesus were baptized into his death?" (Also Mark 10:38, 39)

Col. 2:12: "For you [living members of the congregation in Colossae] were buried with him in his baptism, and by relationship with him you were also raised up together through your faith in the operation of God, who raised him up from the dead."

Rendering in "New World Translation" is grammatically correct and in agreement with these other Bible texts

1 Cor. 15:29: "Otherwise, what will they do who are being baptized for the purpose of being dead ones? If the dead are not to be raised up at all, why are they also being baptized for the purpose of being such?" (So they are baptized, or immersed, into a course of life that will lead to a death of integrity like that of Christ and then to being raised to spirit life as he was.)

What results from baptism with fire?

Luke 3:16, 17: "He [Jesus Christ] will baptize you people with . . . fire. His winnowing shovel is in his hand to clean up his threshing floor completely . . . The chaff he will burn up with fire that cannot be put out." (Its destruction would be forever.)

Matt. 13:49, 50: "That is how it will be in the conclusion of the system of things: the angels will go out and separate the wicked from among the righteous and will cast them into the fiery furnace."

Luke 17:29, 30: "On the day that Lot came out of Sodom it rained fire and sulphur from heaven and destroyed them all. The same way it will be on that day when the Son of man is to be revealed."

Not the same as baptism with holy spirit, which was for disciples

Acts 1:5: "John, indeed, baptized with water, but you [Jesus' faithful apostles] will be baptized in holy spirit not many days after this."

Acts 2:2-4: "Suddenly there occurred from heaven a noise just like that of a rushing stiff breeze, and it filled the whole house in which they were sitting. And tongues as if of fire became visible to them and were distributed about, and one sat upon [but did not envelop or immerse] each one of them, and they all became filled with holy spirit and started to speak with different tongues, just as the spirit was granting them to make utterance."

Bible

Definition: Jehovah God's written Word to humankind. He used some 40 human secretaries over a period of 16 centuries to record it, but God himself actively directed the writing by his spirit. Thus it is inspired by God. A large portion of the record is made up of actual pronouncements made by Jehovah and details as to the teachings and activities of Jesus Christ, the Son of God. In these we find statements of God's requirements for his servants and what he will do to bring his grand purpose for the earth to completion. To deepen our appreciation for these things, Jehovah also preserved in the Bible a record demonstrating what happens when individuals and nations listen to God and work in harmony with his purpose, as well as the outcome when they go their own way. By means of this reliable historical record Jehovah acquaints us with his dealings with humankind and thus with his own marvelous personality.

Reasons for considering the Bible

The Bible itself says it is from God, mankind's Creator

2 Tim. 3:16, 17: "All Scripture is inspired of God and beneficial for teaching, for reproving, for setting things straight, for disciplining in righteousness, that the man of

God may be fully competent, completely equipped for every good work."

Rev. 1:1: "A revelation by Jesus Christ, which God gave him, to show his slaves the things that must shortly take place."

2 Sam. 23:1, 2: "The utterance of David the son of Jesse . . . The spirit of Jehovah it was that spoke by me, and his word was upon my tongue."

Isa. 22:15: "This is what the Sovereign Lord, Jehovah of armies, has said."

We would expect God's message to all mankind to be available around the globe. The Bible, the whole or in part, has been translated into some 1,800 languages. Its circulation totals in the billions. Says *The World Book Encyclopedia:* "The Bible is the most widely read book in history. It is probably also the most influential. More copies have been distributed of the Bible than of any other book. It has also been translated more times into more languages than any other book."—(1984), Vol. 2, p. 219.

Bible prophecy explains the meaning of world conditions

Many world leaders acknowledge that mankind is on the brink of disaster. The Bible foretold these conditions long ago; it explains their meaning and what the outcome will be. (2 Tim. 3:1-5; Luke 21:25-31) It tells what we must do in order to survive the impending world destruction, with the opportunity to gain eternal life under righteous conditions here on earth.—Zeph. 2:3; John 17:3; Ps. 37:10, 11, 29.

The Bible enables us to understand the purpose of life

It answers such questions as: Where did life come from? (Acts 17:24-26) Why are we here? Is it just to live a few years, get what we can out of life, and then die?—Gen. 1: 27, 28; Rom. 5:12; John 17:3; Ps. 37:11; Ps. 40:8.

The Bible shows how we can have the very things that lovers of righteousness desire most

It tells us where to find wholesome associates who truly

love one another (John 13:35), what can give assurance that
we will have sufficient food for ourselves and our families
(Matt. 6:31-33; Prov. 19:15; Eph. 4:28), how we can be
happy in spite of difficult conditions that surround us.—Ps.
1:1, 2; 34:8; Luke 11:28; Acts 20:35.

It explains that God's Kingdom, his government, will
remove the present wicked system (Dan. 2:44), and under
its rule mankind will be able to enjoy perfect health and
eternal life.—Rev. 21:3, 4; compare Isaiah 33:24.

*Surely a book that claims to be from God, that explains
both the meaning of world conditions and the purpose of
life, and that shows how our problems will be solved is
worthy of consideration.*

Evidences of inspiration

It is filled with prophecies reflecting detailed knowledge of the future—something impossible for humans

2 Pet. 1:20, 21: "No prophecy of Scripture springs from
any private interpretation. For prophecy was at no time
brought by man's will, but men spoke from God as they were
borne along by holy spirit."

■ Prophecy: Isa. 44:24, 27, 28; 45:1-4: "Jehovah . . . the
One saying to the watery deep, 'Be evaporated; and all your
rivers I shall dry up'; the One saying of Cyrus, 'He is my
shepherd, and all that I delight in he will completely carry
out'; even in my saying of Jerusalem, 'She will be rebuilt,'
and of the temple, 'You will have your foundation laid.' This
is what Jehovah has said to his anointed one, to Cyrus, whose
right hand I have taken hold of, to subdue before him
nations, so that I may ungird even the hips of kings; to open
before him the two-leaved doors, so that even the gates will
not be shut: 'Before you I myself shall go, and the swells of
land I shall straighten out. The copper doors I shall break
in pieces, and the iron bars I shall cut down. . . . For the sake
of my servant Jacob and of Israel my chosen one, I even
proceeded to call you by your name.'" (Writing by Isaiah was
completed by about 732 B.C.E.)

□ Fulfillment: Cyrus had not been born when the prophecy was written. The Jews were not taken into exile to in the city royed until 617-607 B.C.E., and Jerusalem and its temple Cyrus. Thereafter, until 607 B.C.E. In detail the prophecy sent them back to Jerusalem in 539 B.C.E. Cyrus diverted the waters of the River into an artificial lake, the river Jehovah's temple there.—*The Entire* Jewish exiles and (1956), Vol. III, p. 9; *Light From the Ancient Americana* ton, 1959), Jack Finegan, pp. 227-229; *"All Scripture is Inspired of God and Beneficial"* (New York, 1963), pp. 282, 284, 295.

■ Prophecy: Jer. 49:17, 18: "'Edom must become an object of astonishment. Everyone passing along by her will stare in astonishment and whistle on account of all her plagues. Just as in the overthrow of Sodom and Gomorrah and her neighbor towns,' Jehovah has said, 'no man will dwell there.'" (Jeremiah's recording of prophecies was completed by 580 B.C.E.)

□ Fulfillment: "They [the Edomites] were driven from Palestine in the 2nd century B.C. by Judas Maccabæus, and in 109 B.C. John Hyrcanus, Maccabæan leader, extended the kingdom of Judah to include the w. part of Edomitic lands. In the 1st century B.C. Roman expansion swept away the last vestige of Edomitic independence . . . After the destruction of Jerusalem by the Romans in 70 A.D. . . . the name Idumæa [Edom] disappeared from history." (*The New Funk & Wagnalls Encyclopedia,* 1952, Vol. 11, p. 4114) Notice that the fulfillment extends down to our day. In no way can it be argued that this prophecy was written *after* the events had taken place.

■ Prophecy: Luke 19:41-44; 21:20, 21: "He [Jesus Christ] viewed the city [Jerusalem] and wept over it, saying: . . . 'The days will come upon you when your enemies will build around you a fortification with pointed stakes and will encircle you and distress you from every side, and they will dash you and your children within you to the ground, and

they will not leave a stone upon a stone in ~~Judea~~ ~~eso~~ begin
did not discern the time of your being in~~to~~ the midst of her
later, he counseled his disciples: "W~~~~ the midst of her
surrounded by encamped armies~~~~ Christ in 33 C.E.)
lating of her has drawn near ~~~~ revolted against Rome, and in
fleeing to the mountains ~~~~ revolted against Rome, and in
withdraw." (Prophecy under Cestius Gallus attacked the

□ Fulfillment~~~~ historian Josephus reports, the Roman
66 C.E. the R~~~~ historian Josephus reports, the Roman
city. But ~~r~~ "suddenly called off his men, abandoned hope
comm~~~~ had suffered no reverse, and flying in the face of
though ~~~~ had suffered no reverse, and flying in the face of
all reason retired from the City." (*Josephus, the Jewish War*,
Penguin Classics, 1969, p. 167) This provided opportunity
for Christians to flee from the city, which they did, moving
to Pella, beyond the Jordan, according to Eusebius Pamphi-
lus in his *Ecclesiastical History*. (Translated by C. F. Crusé,
London, 1894, p. 75) Then around Passover time of the year
70 C.E. General Titus besieged the city, an encircling fence
4.5 miles (7.2 km) long was erected in just three days, and
after five months Jerusalem fell. "Jerusalem itself was sys-
tematically destroyed and the Temple left in ruins. Archae-
ological work shows us today just how effective was the
destruction of Jewish buildings all over the land."—*The
Bible and Archaeology* (Grand Rapids, Mich.; 1962), J. A.
Thompson, p. 299.

Its contents are scientifically sound on matters that human researchers discovered only at a later date

Origin of the Universe: Gen. 1:1: "In the beginning
God created the heavens and the earth." In 1978, astronomer
Robert Jastrow wrote: "Now we see how the astronomical
evidence leads to a biblical view of the origin of the world.
The details differ, but the essential elements in the astronomical and biblical accounts of Genesis are the same: the
chain of events leading to man commenced suddenly and
sharply at a definite moment in time, in a flash of light and
energy."—*God and the Astronomers* (New York, 1978),
p. 14.

Shape of Planet Earth: Isa. 40:22: "There is One who is dwelling above the circle of the earth." In ancient times the general opinion was that the earth was flat. It was not until over 200 years after this Bible text had been written that a school of Greek philosophers reasoned that the earth likely was spherical, and in about another 300 years a Greek astronomer calculated the approximate radius of the earth. But the idea of a spherical earth was not the general view even then. Only in the 20th century has it been possible for humans to travel by airplane, and later into outer space and even to the moon, thus giving them a clear view of "the circle" of earth's horizon.

Animal Life: Lev. 11:6: "The hare . . . is a chewer of the cud." Though this was long attacked by some critics, the rabbit's cud chewing was finally observed by Englishman William Cowper in the 18th century. The unusual way in which it is done was described in 1940 in *Proceedings of the Zoological Society of London,* Vol. 110, Series A, pp. 159-163.

Its internal harmony is significant

This is especially so in view of the fact that the books of the Bible were recorded by some 40 men as diverse as king, prophet, herdsman, tax collector, and physician. They did the writing over a period of 1,610 years; so there was no opportunity for collusion. Yet their writings agree, even in the smallest detail. To appreciate the extent to which the various portions of the Bible are harmoniously intertwined, you must read and study it personally.

How can we be sure the Bible has not been changed?

"In the number of ancient MSS. [manuscripts] attesting a writing, and in the number of years that had elapsed between the original and the attesting MSS., the Bible enjoys a decided advantage over classical writings [those of Homer, Plato, and others]. . . . Altogether classical MSS. are but a handful compared with Biblical. No ancient book is so well attested as the Bible."—*The Bible From the Beginning* (New York, 1929), P. Marion Simms, pp. 74, 76.

A report published in 1971 shows that there are possibly 6,000 handwritten copies containing all or part of the Hebrew Scriptures; the oldest dates back to the third century B.C.E. Of the Christian Greek Scriptures, there are some 5,000 in Greek, the oldest dating back to the beginning of the second century C.E. There are also many copies of early translations into other languages.

In the introduction to his seven volumes on *The Chester Beatty Biblical Papyri,* Sir Frederic Kenyon wrote: "The first and most important conclusion derived from the examination of them [the papyri] is the satisfactory one that they confirm the essential soundness of the existing texts. No striking or fundamental variation is shown either in the Old or the New Testament. There are no important omissions or additions of passages, and no variations which affect vital facts or doctrines. The variations of text affect minor matters, such as the order of words or the precise words used . . . But their essential importance is their confirmation, by evidence of an earlier date than was hitherto available, of the integrity of our existing texts."—(London, 1933), p. 15.

It is true that some translations of the Bible adhere more closely to what is in the original languages than others do. Modern paraphrase Bibles have taken liberties that at times alter the original meaning. Some translators have allowed personal beliefs to color their renderings. But these weaknesses can be identified by comparison of a variety of translations.

If Someone Says—

'I don't believe in the Bible'

You might reply: 'But you do believe there is a God, don't you? . . . May I ask what there is in the Bible that you find hard to accept?'

Or you could say: 'May I ask, Have you always felt that way? . . . I've heard others say that, even though they have not made a thorough study of the Bible. But since the Bible clearly says that it is a message from God himself and that he offers us eternal life if we believe and live by what it says, don't you agree that it would be worthwhile at least to examine it to find out whether its claims are true or not? (Use material on pages 60-63.)'

'The Bible contradicts itself'

You might reply: 'I've had other people tell me that, but no one has ever been able to show me what is actually a contradiction. And in my own personal reading of the Bible I've never seen one. Could you give me an example?' **Then perhaps add:** 'What I *have* found is that many persons simply never found answers to questions that the Bible made them think about. For example, Where did Cain get his wife? (Use material on pages 301, 302.)'

'Men wrote the Bible'

You might reply: 'That's true. About 40 of them had a part in it. But it was *inspired* by God.' **Then perhaps add:** (1) 'What does that mean? That God directed the writing, much as a businessman uses a secretary to write letters for him.' (2) 'The idea of receiving messages from someone out in space should not surprise us. Even humans have sent messages and pictures from the moon. How did they do it? By using laws that originated long ago with God himself.' (3) 'But how can we be sure that what the Bible contains is really from God? It contains information that could not possibly have come from a human source. What kind? Details about the future; and these have always proved to be completely accurate. (For examples, see pages 60-62, also pages 234-239, under the heading "Last Days.")'

'Everyone has his own interpretation of the Bible'

You might reply: 'And obviously not all of them are right.' **Then perhaps add:** (1) 'Twisting the Scriptures to fit our own ideas can result in lasting harm. (2 Pet. 3:15, 16)' (2) 'Two things can help us to understand the Bible correctly. First, consider the context (surrounding verses) of any statement. Next, compare texts with other statements in the Bible that deal with the same subject. In that way we are letting God's own Word guide our thinking, and the interpretation is not ours but his. That is the approach taken in the Watch Tower publications.' (See pages 204, 205, under the heading "Jehovah's Witnesses.")

'It is not practical for our day'

You might reply: 'And we are interested in things that are practical for us today, aren't we?' **Then perhaps add:** (1) 'Would you agree that putting an end to war would be practical? . . . Don't you agree that if people learned to live together in peace with those of other nations, this would be a good start? . . . The Bible foretold exactly that. (Isa. 2:2, 3) As a result of Bible education, this is taking place today among Jehovah's Witnesses.' (2) 'Something more is needed —the removal of all men and nations that cause wars. Will such a thing ever happen? Yes, and the Bible explains how. (Dan. 2:44; Ps. 37:10, 11)'

Or you could say: 'I appreciate your concern. If a guidebook was not practical, we would be foolish to use it, wouldn't we?' **Then perhaps add:** 'Would you agree that a book that provides sound counsel that can enable us to have a happy family life is practical? . . . Theories and practices involving family life have changed many times, and the results we see today are not good. But those who know and apply what the Bible says have stable, happy families. (Col. 3:12-14, 18-21)'

'The Bible is a good book, but there is no such thing as absolute truth'

You might reply: 'It's true that everyone seems to have a different opinion. And even if someone thinks he has a thing figured out, he often finds that there is at least one other factor that he didn't consider. But there is someone who does not have such a limitation. Who might that be? . . . Yes, the Creator of the universe.' **Then perhaps add:** (1) 'That is why Jesus Christ said to him: "Your word is truth." (John 17:17) That truth is in the Bible. (2 Tim. 3:16, 17)' (2) 'God does not want us to grope in ignorance; he has said that his will is for us to come to an accurate knowledge of truth. (1 Tim. 2:3, 4) In a thoroughly satisfying manner the Bible answers such questions as . . . ' (To help some people, you may first need to discuss evidence for belief in the existence of God. See pages 145-151, under the heading "God.")

'The Bible is a white man's book'

You might reply: 'It certainly is true that they have printed many copies of the Bible. But the Bible does not say that one race is better than another.' **Then perhaps add:** (1) 'The Bible is from our Creator, and he is impartial. (Acts 10:34, 35)' (2) 'God's Word holds out to people of all nations and tribes the opportunity to live forever here on earth under his Kingdom. (Rev. 7:9, 10, 17)'

Or you could say: 'Not at all! Mankind's Creator was the one to choose the men whom he would inspire to write the 66 books of the Bible. And if he chose to use people with light-colored skin, that was his responsibility. But the Bible's message was not to be confined to white people.' **Then perhaps add:** (1) 'Notice what Jesus said . . . (John 3:16) "Everyone" includes persons of whatever skin color. Also, before ascending to heaven, Jesus said these parting words to his disciples . . . (Matt. 28:19)' (2) 'Interestingly, Acts 13:1 speaks of a certain man named Niger, which name means "black." He was one of the prophets and teachers of the congregation of Antioch, Syria.'

'I believe only the *King James Version*'

You might reply: 'If you have yours handy, I would like to share with you something that I have found to be very encouraging.'

Or you could say: 'Many people use that Bible version, and I personally have one in my library.' **Then perhaps add:** (1) 'Did you know that the Bible was originally written in the Hebrew, Aramaic, and Greek languages? . . . Do you read those languages? . . . So we are grateful that the Bible has been translated into English.' (2) 'This chart ("Table of the Books of the Bible," in *NW*) shows that Genesis, the first book of the Bible, was completed in 1513 B.C.E. Did you know that, after Genesis was written, some 2,900 years passed before the complete Bible was translated into English? And over 200 more years elapsed before translation of the *King James Version* was completed (1611 C.E.).' (3) 'Since the 17th century, English has undergone many changes. We have seen that in our own lifetime, haven't we? . . . So we appreciate modern translations that carefully express the same original truths in the language that we speak today.'

'You have your own Bible'

See the main heading "New World Translation."

Birthday

Definition: The day of one's birth or the anniversary of that day. In some places the anniversary of one's birth, especially that of a child, is celebrated with a party and the giving of gifts. *Not a Biblical practice.*

Do Bible references to birthday celebrations put them in a favorable light? The Bible makes only two references to such celebrations:

Gen. 40:20-22: "Now on the third day it turned out to be Pharaoh's birthday, and he proceeded to make a feast . . . Accordingly he returned the chief of the cupbearers to his post of cupbearer . . . But the chief of the bakers he hung up."

Matt. 14:6-10: "When Herod's birthday was being celebrated the daughter of Herodias danced at it and pleased Herod so much that he promised with an oath to give her whatever she asked. Then she, under her mother's coaching, said: 'Give me here upon a platter the head of John the Baptist.' . . . He sent and had John beheaded in the prison."

Everything that is in the Bible is there for a reason.

(2 Tim. 3:16, 17) Jehovah's Witnesses take note that God's Word reports unfavorably about birthday celebrations and so shun these.

How did early Christians and Jews of Bible times view birthday celebrations?

"The notion of a *birthday festival* was far from the ideas of the Christians of this period in general."—*The History of the Christian Religion and Church, During the Three First Centuries* (New York, 1848), Augustus Neander (translated by Henry John Rose), p. 190.

"The later Hebrews looked on the celebration of birthdays as a part of idolatrous worship, a view which would be abundantly confirmed by what they saw of the common observances associated with these days."—*The Imperial Bible-Dictionary* (London, 1874), edited by Patrick Fairbairn, Vol. I, p. 225.

What is the origin of popular customs associated with birthday celebrations?

"The various customs with which people today celebrate their birthdays have a long history. Their origins lie in the realm of magic and religion. The customs of offering congratulations, presenting gifts and celebrating—complete with lighted candles—in ancient times were meant to protect the birthday celebrant from the demons and to ensure his security for the coming year. . . . Down to the fourth century Christianity rejected the birthday celebration as a pagan custom."—*Schwäbische Zeitung* (magazine supplement *Zeit und Welt*), April 3/4, 1981, p. 4.

"The Greeks believed that everyone had a protective spirit or *daemon* who attended his birth and watched over him in life. This spirit had a mystic relation with the god on whose birthday the individual was born. The Romans also subscribed to this idea. . . . This notion was carried down in human belief and is reflected in the guardian angel, the fairy godmother and the patron saint. . . . The custom of lighted candles on the cakes started with the Greeks. . . . Honey cakes round as the moon and lit with tapers were placed on the temple altars of [Artemis]. . . . Birthday candles, in folk belief, are endowed with special magic for granting wishes. . . . Lighted tapers and sacrificial fires have had a special mystic significance ever since man first set up altars to his gods. The birthday candles are thus an honor and tribute to the birthday child and bring good fortune. . . . Birthday greetings and wishes for happiness are an intrinsic part of this holiday. . . . Originally the idea was rooted in magic. . . . Birthday greetings have power for good or ill because one is closer to the spirit world on this day."—*The Lore of Birthdays* (New York, 1952), Ralph and Adelin Linton, pp. 8, 18-20.

Wholesome gatherings of family and friends at other times to eat, drink, and rejoice are not objectionable

Eccl. 3:12, 13: "There is nothing better for them than to rejoice and to do good during one's life; and also that every man should eat and indeed drink and see good for all his hard work. It is the gift of God."

See also 1 Corinthians 10:31.

Blood

Definition: A truly marvelous fluid that circulates in the vascular system of humans and most multicelled animals, supplying nourishment and oxygen, carrying away waste products, and playing a major role in safeguarding the body against infection. So intimately is blood involved in the life processes that the Bible says "the soul of the flesh is in the blood." (Lev. 17:11) As the Source of life, Jehovah has provided definite instructions regarding the use to which blood may be put.

Christians are commanded to 'abstain from blood'

Acts 15:28, 29: "The holy spirit and we ourselves [the governing body of the Christian congregation] have favored adding no further burden to you, except these necessary things, to keep abstaining from things sacrificed to idols and from blood and from things strangled [or, killed without draining their blood] and from fornication. If you carefully keep yourselves from these things, you will prosper. Good health to you!" (There the eating of blood is equated with idolatry and fornication, things that we should not want to engage in.)

Animal flesh may be eaten, but not the blood

Gen. 9:3, 4: "Every moving animal that is alive may serve as food for you. As in the case of green vegetation, I do give it all to you. Only flesh with its soul—its blood—you must not eat."

Any animal used for food should be properly bled. One that is strangled or that dies in a trap or that is found after it has died is not suitable for food. (Acts 15:19, 20; compare Leviticus 17:13-16.) Similarly, any food to which whole blood or even some blood fraction has been added should not be eaten.

Only sacrificial use of blood has ever been approved by God

Lev. 17:11, 12: "The soul of the flesh is in the blood, and I myself have put it upon the altar for you to make atonement for your souls, because it is the blood that makes atonement by the soul in it. That is why I have said to the sons of Israel: 'No soul of you must eat blood and no alien resident who is residing as an alien in your midst should eat blood.'" (All those animal sacrifices under the Mosaic Law foreshadowed the one sacrifice of Jesus Christ.)

Heb. 9:11-14, 22: "When Christ came as a high priest . . . he entered, no, not with the blood of goats and of young bulls, but with his own blood, once for all time into the holy place and obtained an everlasting deliverance for us. For if the blood of goats and of bulls and the ashes of a heifer sprinkled on those who have been defiled sanctifies to the extent of cleanness of the flesh, how much more will the blood of the Christ, who through an everlasting spirit offered himself without blemish to God, cleanse our consciences from dead works that we may render sacred service to the living God? . . . Unless blood is poured out no forgiveness takes place."

Eph. 1:7: "By means of him [Jesus Christ] we have the release by ransom through the blood of that one, yes, the forgiveness of our trespasses, according to the riches of his undeserved kindness."

How did those who claimed to be Christians in early centuries C.E. understand the Bible's commands regarding blood?

Tertullian (c. 160-230 C.E.): "Let your unnatural ways blush before the Christians. We do not even have the blood of animals at our meals, for these consist of ordinary food. . . . At the trials of Christians you [pagan Romans] offer them sausages filled with blood. You are convinced, of course, that the very thing with which you try to make them deviate from the right way is unlawful for them. How is it that, when you are confident that they will shudder at the blood of an animal, you believe they will pant eagerly after human blood?"—*Tertullian, Apologetical Works, and Minucius Felix, Octavius* (New York, 1950), translated by Emily Daly, p. 33.

Minucius Felix (third century C.E.): "So much do we shrink from human blood, that we do not use the blood even of eatable animals in our food."—*The Ante-Nicene Fathers* (Grand Rapids, Mich.; 1956), edited by A. Roberts and J. Donaldson, Vol. IV, p. 192.

Blood Transfusions

Does the Bible's prohibition include human blood?

Yes, and early Christians understood it that way. Acts 15:29 says to "keep abstaining from . . . blood." It does not say merely to abstain from *animal* blood. (Compare Leviticus 17:10, which prohibited eating "any sort of blood.") Tertullian (who wrote in defense of the beliefs of early

Christians) stated: "The interdict upon 'blood' we shall understand to be (an interdict) much more upon *human* blood."
—*The Ante-Nicene Fathers,* Vol. IV, p. 86.

Is a transfusion really the same as eating blood?

In a hospital, when a patient cannot eat through his mouth, he is fed intravenously. Now, would a person who never put blood into his mouth but who accepted blood by transfusion really be obeying the command to "keep abstaining from . . . blood"? (Acts 15:29) To use a comparison, consider a man who is told by the doctor that he must abstain from alcohol. Would he be obedient if he quit drinking alcohol but had it put directly into his veins?

In the case of a patient that refuses blood, are there any alternative treatments?

Often simple *saline solution, Ringer's solution,* and *dextran* can be used as plasma volume expanders, and these are available in nearly all modern hospitals. Actually, the risks that go with use of blood transfusions are avoided by using these substances. The *Canadian Anaesthetists' Society Journal* (January 1975, p. 12) says: "The risks of blood transfusion are the advantages of plasma substitutes: avoidance of bacterial or viral infection, transfusion reactions and Rh sensitization." Jehovah's Witnesses have no religious objection to the use of nonblood plasma expanders.

Jehovah's Witnesses actually benefit from better medical treatment because they do not accept blood. A doctor writing in the *American Journal of Obstetrics and Gynecology* (June 1, 1968, p. 395) acknowledged: "There is no doubt that the situation where you [the surgeon] are operating without the possibility of transfusion tends to improve your surgery. You are a little bit more aggressive in clamping every bleeding vessel."

All types of surgery can be performed successfully without blood transfusions. This includes open-heart operations, brain surgery, amputation of limbs, and total removal of cancerous organs. Writing in the *New York State Journal of Medicine* (October 15, 1972, p. 2527), Dr. Philip Roen said: "We have not hesitated to perform any and all indicated surgical procedures in the face of proscribed blood replacement." Dr. Denton Cooley, at the Texas Heart Institute, said: "We became so impressed with the results [from using nonblood plasma expanders] on the Jehovah's Witnesses that we started using the procedure on all our heart patients." (The San Diego *Union,* December 27, 1970, p. A-10) "'Bloodless' open-heart surgery, originally developed for adult members of the Jehovah's Witnesses sect because their religion forbids blood transfusions, now has been safely adapted for use in delicate cardiac procedures in infants and children."—*Cardiovascular News,* February 1984, p. 5.

If Someone Says—

'You let your children die because you refuse blood transfusions. I think that's terrible'

You might reply: 'But we do allow them to have *transfusions*—the safer kind. We accept the kind of transfusions that don't carry the risk of such things as AIDS, hepatitis, and malaria. We want the *best* treatment for our children, as I am sure that any loving parent would.' **Then perhaps add:** (1) 'When there is severe blood loss, the greatest need is to restore the fluid volume. No doubt you realize that our blood is actually over 50 percent water; then there are the red and white cells, and so forth. When much blood is lost, the body itself pours large reserves of blood cells into the system and speeds up production of new ones. But fluid volume is needed. Plasma volume expanders that contain no blood can be used to fill that need, and we accept these.' (2) 'Plasma volume expanders have been used on thousands of persons, with excellent results.' (3) 'Even more important to us is what the Bible itself says at Acts 15:28, 29.'

Or you could say: 'I can understand your point of view. I suppose you are imagining your own child in that situation. As parents we would do everything possible to safeguard our child's welfare, wouldn't we? So if folks like you and me were going to refuse some sort of medical treatment for our child, there would certainly have to be some compelling reason for it.' **Then perhaps add:** (1) 'Do you think that some parents might be influenced by what God's Word says here at Acts 15:28, 29?' (2) 'So the question is, Do we have enough faith to do what God commands?'

'You people don't believe in blood transfusions'

You might reply: 'The newspapers have published stories about some situations in which they felt that Witnesses might die if they did not accept blood. Is that what you have in mind? . . . Why do we take the position we do?' **Then perhaps add:** (1) 'Do you love your wife (husband) enough that you would be willing to risk your life for her (him)? . . . There are also men who risk their lives for their country, and they are viewed as heroes, aren't they? But there is someone who is greater than any person or thing here on earth, and that is God. Would you risk your life because of love for him and loyalty to his rulership?' (2) 'The issue here really is loyalty to God. It is God's Word that tells us to abstain from blood. (Acts 15:28, 29)'

Or you could say: 'There are many things that are rather common today and that Jehovah's Witnesses shun—for example, lying, adultery, stealing, smoking, and as you mentioned, the use of blood. Why? Because we govern our lives by God's Word.' **Then perhaps add:** (1) 'Did you know that the *Bible* says we should "abstain from blood"? I would like to show it to you. (Acts 15:28, 29)' (2) 'Perhaps you recall that God told our first parents, Adam and Eve, that they could eat from every tree in Eden except one. But they disobeyed, ate that forbidden fruit, and lost everything. How unwise! Now, of course, there is no tree with forbidden fruit. But after the Flood of Noah's day God again set out one prohibition for mankind. This time it involved blood. (Gen. 9:3, 4)' (3) 'So the real question is, Do we have faith in God? If we obey him, we have before us the prospect of eternal life in perfection under his Kingdom. Even if we die, he assures us of a resurrection.'

'What if a doctor says, "You will die without a blood transfusion"?'

You might reply: 'If the situation is really that serious, can the doctor guarantee that the patient will not die if he is given blood?' **Then perhaps add:** 'But there is someone who can give a person life again, and that is God. Don't you agree that, when face to face with death, turning one's back on God by violating his law would be a poor decision? I truly have faith in God. Do you? His Word promises a resurrection for those who put faith in his Son. Do you believe that? (John 11:25)'

Or you could say: 'It may mean that he personally does not know how to handle the case without the use of blood. If possible, we try to put him in touch with a doctor who has had the needed experience, or we engage the services of another doctor.'

Born Again

Definition: Being born again involves being baptized in water ("born from water") and begotten by God's spirit ("born from . . . spirit"), thus becoming a son of God with the prospect of sharing in the Kingdom of God. (John 3:3-5) Jesus had this experience, as do the 144,000 who are heirs with him of the heavenly Kingdom.

Why is it necessary for any Christians to be "born again"?

God has purposed to associate a limited number of faithful humans with Jesus Christ in the heavenly Kingdom

Luke 12:32: "Have no fear, little flock, because your Father has approved of giving you the kingdom."

Rev. 14:1-3: "I saw, and, look! the Lamb [Jesus Christ] standing upon the Mount Zion, and with him a hundred and forty-four thousand . . . who have been bought from the earth." (See pages 166, 167, under the heading "Heaven.")

Humans cannot go to heaven with bodies of flesh and blood

1 Cor. 15:50: "This I say, brothers, that flesh and blood cannot inherit God's kingdom, neither does corruption inherit incorruption."

John 3:6: "What has been born from the flesh is flesh, and what has been born from the spirit is spirit."

Only persons who have been "born again," thus becoming God's sons, can share in the heavenly Kingdom

John 1:12, 13: "As many as did receive him [Jesus Christ], to them he gave authority to become God's children, because they were exercising faith in his name; and they were born, not from blood or from a fleshly will or from man's will, but from God." ("As many as did receive him" does not mean all humans who have put faith in Christ. Notice who is being referred to, as indicated by verse 11 ["his own people," the Jews]. The same privilege has been extended to others of mankind, but only to a "little flock.")

Rom. 8:16, 17: "The spirit itself bears witness with our spirit that we are God's children. If, then, we are children, we are also heirs: heirs indeed of God, but joint heirs with Christ, provided we suffer together that we may also be glorified together."

1 Pet. 1:3, 4: "Blessed be the God and Father of our Lord Jesus Christ, for according to his great mercy he gave us a new birth to a living hope through the resurrection of Jesus Christ from the dead, to an incorruptible and undefiled and unfading inheritance. It is reserved in the heavens for you."

What will they do in heaven?

Rev. 20:6: "They will be priests of God and of the Christ, and will rule as kings with him for the thousand years."

1 Cor. 6:2: "Do you not know that the holy ones will judge the world?"

Can a person who is not "born again" be saved?

Rev. 7:9, 10, 17: "After these things [after the apostle John heard the number of those who would be "born again," those who would make up spiritual Israel and would be with Christ in heaven; compare Romans 2:28, 29 and Galatians 3:26-29] I saw, and, look! a great crowd, which no man was able to number, out of all nations and tribes and peoples and tongues, standing before the throne and before the Lamb, dressed in white robes; and there were palm branches in their hands. And they keep on crying with a loud voice, saying: 'Salvation we owe to our God, who is seated on the throne, and to the Lamb.' . . . 'The Lamb [Jesus Christ], who is in the midst of the throne, will shepherd them, and will guide them to fountains of waters of life.'"

After listing many pre-Christian persons of faith, Hebrews 11:39, 40 says: "All these, although they had witness borne to them through their faith, did not get the fulfillment of the promise, as God foresaw something better for us, in order that they might not be made perfect apart from us." (Who are here meant by "us"? Hebrews 3:1 shows that they are "partakers of the heavenly calling." The pre-Christian persons who had faith, then, must have a hope for perfect life somewhere other than in heaven.)

Ps. 37:29: "The righteous themselves will possess the earth, and they will reside forever upon it."

Rev. 21:3, 4: "Look! The tent of God is with mankind, and he will reside with them, and they will be his peoples. And God himself will be with them. And he will wipe out every tear from their eyes, and death will be no more, neither will mourning nor outcry nor pain be anymore. The former things have passed away."

Is it possible for a person to have God's spirit and yet not be "born again"?

Regarding John the baptizer, Jehovah's angel said: "He will be filled with holy spirit right from his mother's womb." (Luke 1:15) And Jesus later said: "Among those born of women there has not been raised up a greater than John the Baptist; but a person that is a lesser one in the kingdom of the heavens is greater than he is [Why? Because John will not be in the heavens and so there was no need for him to be "born again"]. But from the days of John the Baptist until now [when Jesus stated this] the kingdom of the heavens is the goal toward which men press."—Matt. 11:11, 12.

The spirit of Jehovah was "operative" upon David and "spoke" by him (1 Sam. 16:13; 2 Sam. 23:2), but nowhere does the Bible say that he was "born again." There was no need for him to be "born again," because, as Acts 2:34 says: "David did not ascend to the heavens."

What identifies persons today who have God's spirit?

See pages 381, 382, under the main heading "Spirit."

If Someone Says—

'I've been born again'

You might reply: 'That means that you expect someday to be with Christ in heaven, doesn't it? . . . Have you ever wondered what those who go to heaven will do there?' **Then perhaps add:** (1) 'They will be kings and priests, ruling with Christ. (Rev. 20:6; 5:9, 10) Jesus said that these would be just a "little flock." (Luke 12:32)' (2) 'If they are kings, there must also be subjects over whom they will rule. Who will these be? . . . Here are some points that I found to be very interesting when they were drawn to my attention. (Ps. 37: 11, 29; Prov. 2:21, 22)'

'Have you been born again?'

You might reply: 'I find that what people mean by "born again" is not always the same. Would you tell me what it means to you?'

Or you could say: 'You want to know whether I have accepted Jesus as my Savior and have received holy spirit, is that right? May I assure you that the answer is Yes; otherwise I would not be talking to you about Jesus.' **Then perhaps add:** (1) 'But when I think of having the holy spirit, I find that evidence of that spirit is sadly missing in many who claim to be Christians. (Gal. 5:22, 23)' (2) 'Would you enjoy living on this earth if everyone reflected those godly qualities? (Ps. 37:10, 11)'

Another possibility: 'If you mean by that, "Have I accepted Christ as my Savior?" the answer is Yes. All of Jehovah's Witnesses have done that. But, to us, being born again involves much more than that.' **Then perhaps add:** (1) 'When Jesus spoke about being born again he said that it was necessary in order to enter the Kingdom of God, that is, to be part of God's Kingdom, his heavenly government. (John 3:5)' (2) 'The Bible also shows that many people who do the will of God will live here on earth, as happy subjects of that Kingdom. (Matt. 6:10; Ps. 37:29)'

An additional suggestion: Those who are of the heavenly class could reply: 'Yes, I am. But the Bible cautions all of us not to be overconfident of our position. We need to keep examining ourselves to be sure that we are really doing what God and Christ require of us. (1 Cor. 10:12)' **Then perhaps add:** 'What responsibility did Jesus lay upon his true disciples? (Matt. 28:19, 20; 1 Cor. 9:16)'

Confession

Definition: A declaration or an acknowledgment, either publicly or in private, (1) of what a person believes or (2) of his sins.

Is the rite of reconciliation, including auricular confession (personal confession into the ear of a priest), as taught by the Catholic Church Scriptural?

The manner in which the priest is addressed

The traditional formula, still often used, is: "Bless me, Father, for I have sinned. It has been [length of time] since my last Confession."—*U.S. Catholic* magazine, October 1982, p. 6.

Matt. 23:1, 9, *JB:* "Jesus said, . . . 'You must call no one on earth your father, since you have only one Father, and he is in heaven.'"

Sins that can be forgiven

"The Church has always taught that every sin, no matter how serious, can be forgiven."—*The Catholic Encyclopedia* (bearing the nihil obstat and the imprimatur), R. C. Broderick (Nashville, Tenn.; 1976), p. 554.

Heb. 10:26, *JB:* "If, after we have been given knowledge of the truth, we should deliberately commit any sins, then there is no longer any sacrifice for them."

Mark 3:29, *JB:* "Let anyone blaspheme against the Holy Spirit and he will never have forgiveness: he is guilty of an eternal sin."

How penance is to be shown

Frequently the confessor directs that the penitent say a specified number of "Our Fathers" and "Hail Marys."

Matt. 6:7, *JB:* "In your prayers do not babble [that is, utter in a meaninglessly repetitious manner] as the pagans do, for they think that by using many words they will make themselves heard."

Matt. 6:9-12, *JB:* "You should pray like this: '*Our Father* in heaven, . . . forgive us our debts.'" (Nowhere in the Bible are we commanded to pray to or through Mary. See Philippians 4:6, also pages 258, 259, under "Mary.")

Rom. 12:9, *JB:* "Do not let your love be a pretence, but sincerely prefer good to evil."

Did not Jesus authorize his apostles to forgive sins?

John 20:21-23, *JB:* "'As the Father sent me, so am I sending you.' After saying this he breathed on them and said: 'Receive the Holy Spirit. For those whose sins you forgive, they are forgiven; for those whose sins you retain, they are retained.'"

How did the apostles understand and apply this? There is no record in the Bible of a single instance in which an apostle listened to a private confession and then pronounced absolution. However, the requirements for being forgiven by God are set out in the Bible. The apostles, under the direction of holy spirit, could discern whether individuals were meeting such requirements and could on this basis declare that *God* had either forgiven them or not forgiven them. For examples, see Acts 5:1-11, also 1 Corinthians 5:1-5 and 2 Corinthians 2:6-8.

See also the main heading "Apostolic Succession."

Viewpoints of scholars as to the origin of auricular confession differ

The Catholic Encyclopedia, by R. C. Broderick, states: "Since the fourth century auricular confession has been the accepted method."—P. 58.

The *New Catholic Encyclopedia* says: "Many contemporary historians, both Catholic and Protestant, trace the origins of private penance as a normal discipline to the churches of Ireland, Wales, and Britain, where the Sacraments, including Penance, were administered usually by the abbot of a monastery and his priest-monks. With the monastic practice of confession and public and private spiritual direction as the model, repeated confession and confession of devotion seem to have been introduced for the laity. . . . However, it was not until the 11th century that secret sins were absolved at the time of confession and before the fulfillment of penance."—(1967), Vol. XI, p. 75.

Historian A. H. Sayce reports: "The ritual texts show that both public and private confession was practised in Babylonia. Indeed, private confession seems to have been the older and more usual method."—*The Religions of Ancient Egypt and Babylonia* (Edinburgh, 1902), p. 497.

What are the beliefs of Jehovah's Witnesses as to confession?

Confessing one's faith by public declaration

Rom. 10:9, 10: "If you publicly declare that 'word in your own mouth,' that Jesus is Lord, and exercise faith in your heart that God raised him up from the dead, you will be saved. For with the heart one exercises faith for righteousness, but with the mouth one makes public declaration for salvation."

Matt. 10:32, 33: "Everyone, then, that confesses union with me [Jesus Christ] before men, I will also confess union with him before my Father who is in the heavens; but whoever disowns me before men, I will also disown him before my Father who is in the heavens."

When a person sins against God

Matt. 6:6-12: "When you pray, go into your private room and, after shutting your door, pray *to your Father* who is in secret . . . 'Our Father in the heavens, let your name be sanctified . . . and forgive us our debts, as we also have forgiven our debtors.'"

Ps. 32:5: "My sin I finally confessed to you [God], and my error I did not cover. I said: 'I shall make confession over my transgressions *to Jehovah.*' And you yourself pardoned the error of my sins."

1 John 2:1: "If anyone does commit a sin, we have a helper with the Father, Jesus Christ, a righteous one."

When an individual wrongs his fellowman or when he has been wronged

Matt. 5:23, 24: "If, then, you are bringing your gift to the altar and you there remember that your brother has something against you, leave your gift there in front of the altar, and go away; first make your peace with your brother, and then, when you have come back, offer up your gift."

Matt. 18:15: "If your brother commits a sin, go lay bare his fault between you and him alone."

Luke 17:3: "If your brother commits a sin give him a rebuke, and if he repents forgive him."

Eph. 4:32: "Become kind to one another, tenderly compassionate, freely forgiving one another just as God also by Christ freely forgave you."

When someone becomes involved in serious wrongdoing and wants spiritual help

Jas. 5:14-16: "Is there anyone [spiritually] sick among you? Let him call the older men of the congregation to him, and let them pray over him, greasing him with oil in the name of Jehovah. And the prayer of faith will make the indisposed one well, and Jehovah will raise him up. Also, if he has committed sins, it will be forgiven him [by God]. Therefore openly confess your sins to one another and pray for one another, that you may get healed."

Prov. 28:13: "He that is covering over his transgressions will not succeed, but he that is confessing and leaving them will be shown mercy."

What if persons who commit sins do not seek help?

Gal. 6:1: "Brothers, even though a man takes some false step before he is aware of it, you who have spiritual qualifications try to readjust such a man in a spirit of mildness, as you each keep an eye on yourself, for fear you also may be tempted."

1 Tim. 5:20: "Reprove before all onlookers [that is, those who personally know about the matter] persons who *practice* sin, that the rest also may have fear."

1 Cor. 5:11-13: "Quit mixing in company with anyone called a brother that is a fornicator or a greedy person or an idolater or a reviler or a drunkard or an extortioner, not even eating with such a man. . . . 'Remove the wicked man from among yourselves.'"

Creation

Definition: Creation, as explained in the Bible, means that Almighty God designed and brought into existence the universe, including other spirit persons and all the basic kinds of life upon the earth.

In this modern, scientific world, is it reasonable to believe in creation?

"The natural laws of the universe are so precise that we have no difficulty building a spaceship to fly to the moon and can time the flight with the precision of a fraction of a second. These laws must have been set by somebody."

—Quoted from Wernher von Braun, who had much to do with sending American astronauts to the moon.

Physical universe: If you found a precision timepiece, would you conclude that it was formed by a chance blowing together of some dust particles? Obviously, someone with intelligence made it. There is an even more magnificent "clock." The planets in our solar system, also the stars in the entire universe, move at a rate that is more precise than most clocks designed and manufactured by man. The galaxy in which our solar system is located includes over 100 billion stars, and astronomers estimate that there are 100 billion of such galaxies in the universe. If a clock is evidence of intelligent design, how much more so is the far more vast and complicated universe! The Bible describes the Designer of it as "the true God, Jehovah, . . . the Creator of the heavens and the Grand One stretching them out."—Isa. 42:5; 40:26; Ps. 19:1.

Planet Earth: When crossing a barren desert, if you came to a beautiful house, well equipped in every way and stocked with food, would you believe that it got there by some chance explosion? No; you would realize that someone with considerable wisdom built it. Well, scientists have not yet found life on any of the planets of our solar system except the earth; available evidence indicates that the others are barren. This planet is, as the book *The Earth* says, "the wonder of the universe, a unique sphere." (New York, 1963, Arthur Beiser, p. 10) It is at just the right distance from the sun for human life, and it moves at just the right speed to be held in orbit. The atmosphere, of a kind found only around the earth, is made up of just the right proportion of gases to sustain life. Marvelously, light from the sun, carbon dioxide from the air, and water and minerals from fertile soil combine to produce food for earth's inhabitants. Did it all come about as a result of some uncontrolled explosion in space? *Science News* admits: "It seems as if such particular and precise conditions could hardly have arisen at random." (August 24 and 31, 1974, p. 124) The Bible's conclusion is reasonable when it states: "Of course, every house is constructed by someone, but he that constructed all things is God."—Heb. 3:4.

Human brain: Modern computers are a product of intensive research and careful engineering. They did not "just happen." What about the human brain? Unlike the brain of any animal, the brain of a human infant triples in size during its first year. How it functions is still largely a mystery to scientists. In humans, there is the built-in capacity to learn complex languages, to appreciate beauty, to compose music, to contemplate the origin and meaning of life. Said brain surgeon Robert White: "I am left with no choice but to acknowledge the existence of a Superior Intellect, responsible for the design and development of the incredible brain-mind relationship—something far beyond man's capacity to understand." (*The Reader's Digest,* September 1978, p. 99) The development of this marvel begins from a tiny fertilized cell in the womb. With remarkable insight, the Bible writer David said to Jehovah: "I shall laud you because in a fear-inspiring way I am wonderfully made. Your works are wonderful, as my soul is very well aware."—Ps. 139:14.

Living cell: A single living cell is sometimes referred to as being a "simple" form of life. But a one-celled animal can catch food, digest it, get rid of wastes, build a house for itself and engage in sexual activity. Each cell of the human body has been likened to a walled city, with a central government to maintain order, a power plant to generate energy, factories to produce proteins, a complex transportation system, and guards to regulate what is permitted to enter. And a single human body is made up of as many as 100 trillion cells. How appropriate the words of Psalm 104:24: "How many your works are, O Jehovah! All of them in wisdom you have made"!

Does the Bible allow for the idea that God used evolution to produce the various kinds of living things?

Genesis 1:11, 12 says that grass and trees were made to produce each "according to its kind." Verses 21, 24, 25 add that God created sea creatures, flying creatures and land animals, each "according to its kind." There is no allowance here for one basic kind to evolve or change into another.

Regarding man, Genesis 1:26 reports that God said: "Let us make man in our image, according to our likeness." So he was to have godlike qualities, not traits that were simply a development of those of a beast. Genesis 2:7 adds: "Jehovah God proceeded to form the man [not out of some preexisting life form but] out of dust from the ground and to blow into his nostrils the breath of life." There is no hint of evolution here, but, rather, description of a new creation.

Did God create all the millions of varieties of organisms that exist on earth today?

Genesis chapter 1 says simply that God created each "according to its kind." (Gen. 1:12, 21, 24, 25) In preparation for the global Flood in Noah's day, God directed that representative members of each "kind" of land animal and flying creature be taken into the ark. (Gen. 7:2, 3, 14) Each "kind" has the genetic potential for great variety. Thus there are reportedly more than 400 different breeds of dogs and upwards of 250 breeds and types of horses. All interfertile varieties of any animal are just one Genesis "kind." Similarly, all varieties of humans—Oriental, African, Caucasian, those as tall as the seven-foot Dinka in the Sudan and as short as the four-foot-four-inch Pygmies—stem from the one original pair, Adam and Eve.—Gen. 1:27, 28; 3:20.

What accounts for the basic similarities in the structure of living things?

"God . . . created all things." (Eph. 3:9) Thus everything has the same Great Designer.

"All things came into existence through him [God's only-begotten Son, who became Jesus Christ when on earth], and apart from him not even one thing came into existence." (John 1:3) Thus there was one Master Worker through whom Jehovah performed his works of creation.—Prov. 8: 22, 30, 31.

What is the origin of the raw material of which the universe is made?

Scientists have learned that matter is a concentrated form of energy. This is demonstrated with the explosion of nuclear weapons. Astrophysicist Josip Kleczek states: "Most and possibly all elementary particles may be created by materialization of energy."—*The Universe* (Boston, 1976), Vol. 11, p. 17.

From where could such energy come? After asking, "Who has created these things [the stars and planets]?", the Bible states regarding Jehovah God, "Due to the abundance of dynamic energy, he also being vigorous in power, not one of them is missing." (Isa. 40:26) So God himself is the Source of all the "dynamic energy" that was needed to create the universe.

Was all physical creation accomplished in just six days sometime within the past 6,000 to 10,000 years?

The facts disagree with such a conclusion: (1) Light from the Andromeda nebula can be seen on a clear night in the northern hemisphere. It takes about 2,000,000 years for that light to reach the earth, indicating that the universe must be at least millions of years old. (2) End products of radioactive decay in rocks in the earth testify that some rock formations have been undisturbed for billions of years.

Genesis 1:3-31 is not discussing the original creation of matter or of the heavenly bodies. It describes the preparation of the already existing earth for human habitation. This included creation of the basic kinds of vegetation, marine life, flying creatures, land animals, and the first human pair. All of this is said to have been done within a period of six "days." However, the Hebrew word translated "day" has a variety of meanings, including 'a long time; the time covering an extraordinary event.' (*Old Testament Word Studies*, Grand Rapids, Mich.; 1978, W. Wilson, p. 109) The term used allows for the thought that each "day" could have been thousands of years in length.

Cross

Definition: The device on which Jesus Christ was executed is referred to by most of Christendom as a cross. The expression is drawn from the Latin *crux*.

Why do Watch Tower publications show Jesus on a stake with hands over his head instead of on the traditional cross?

The Greek word rendered "cross" in many modern Bible versions ("torture stake" in *NW*) is *stau·ros'*. In classical Greek, this word meant merely an upright stake, or pale. Later it also came to be used for an execution stake having a crosspiece. *The Imperial Bible-Dictionary* acknowledges this, saying: "The Greek word for cross, [*stau·ros'*], properly signified a *stake,* an upright pole, or piece of paling, on which anything might be hung, or which might be used in impaling [fencing in] a piece of ground. . . . Even amongst the Romans the *crux* (from which our *cross* is derived) appears to have been originally an upright pole."—Edited by P. Fairbairn (London, 1874), Vol. I, p. 376.

Was that the case in connection with the execution of God's Son? It is noteworthy that the Bible also uses the word *xy'lon* to identify the device used. *A Greek-English Lexicon,* by Liddell and Scott, defines this as meaning: "*Wood* cut and ready for use, *firewood, timber,* etc. . . . *piece of wood, log, beam, post . . . cudgel, club . . . stake* on which criminals were impaled . . . of live wood, *tree.*" It also says "in *NT,* of the *cross,*" and cites Acts 5:30 and 10:39 as examples. (Oxford, 1968, pp. 1191, 1192) However, in those verses *KJ, RS, JB,* and *Dy* translate *xy'lon* as "tree." (Compare this rendering with Galatians 3:13; Deuteronomy 21:22, 23.)

The book *The Non-Christian Cross,* by J. D. Parsons (London, 1896), says: "There is not a single sentence in any of the numerous writings forming the New Testament, which, in the original Greek, bears even indirect evidence to the effect that the stauros used in the case of Jesus was other than an ordinary stauros; much less to the effect that it consisted, not of one piece of timber, but of two pieces nailed together in the form of a cross. . . . It is not a little misleading upon the part of our teachers to translate the word stauros as 'cross' when rendering the Greek documents of the Church into our native tongue, and to support that action by putting 'cross' in our lexicons as the meaning of stauros without carefully explaining that that was at any rate not the primary meaning of the word in the days of the Apostles, did not become its primary signification till long afterwards, and became so then, if at all, only because, despite the absence of corroborative evidence, it was for some reason or other assumed that the particular stauros upon which Jesus was executed had that particular shape." —Pp. 23, 24; see also *The Companion Bible* (London, 1885), Appendix No. 162.

Thus the weight of the evidence indicates that Jesus died on an upright stake and not on the traditional cross.

What were the historical origins of Christendom's cross?

"Various objects, dating from periods long anterior to the Christian era, have been found, marked with crosses of different designs, in almost every part of the old world. India, Syria, Persia and Egypt have all yielded numberless examples . . . The use of the cross as a religious symbol in pre-Christian times and among non-Christian peoples may probably be regarded as almost universal, and in very many cases it was connected with some form of nature worship." —*Encyclopædia Britannica* (1946), Vol. 6, p. 753.

"The shape of the [two-beamed cross] had its origin in ancient Chaldea, and was used as the symbol of the god Tammuz (being in the shape of the mystic Tau, the initial of his name) in that country and in adjacent lands, including Egypt. By the middle of the 3rd cent. A.D. the churches had either departed from, or had travestied, certain doctrines of the Christian faith. In order to increase the prestige of the apostate ecclesiastical system pagans were received into the churches apart from regeneration by faith, and were permitted largely to retain their pagan signs and symbols. Hence the Tau or T, in its most frequent form, with the cross-piece lowered, was adopted to stand for the cross of Christ."—*An Expository Dictionary of New Testament Words* (London, 1962), W. E. Vine, p. 256.

"It is strange, yet unquestionably a fact, that in ages long before the birth of Christ, and since then in lands untouched by the teaching of the Church, the Cross has been used as a sacred symbol. . . . The Greek Bacchus, the Tyrian Tammuz, the Chaldean Bel, and the Norse Odin, were all symbolised to their votaries by a cruciform device."—*The Cross in Ritual, Architecture, and Art* (London, 1900), G. S. Tyack, p. 1.

"The cross in the form of the 'Crux Ansata' . . . was carried in the hands of the Egyptian priests and Pontiff kings as the symbol of their authority as priests of the Sun god and was called 'the Sign of Life.' "—*The Worship of the Dead* (London, 1904), Colonel J. Garnier, p. 226.

"Various figures of crosses are found everywhere on Egyptian monuments and tombs, and are considered by many authorities as symbolical either of the phallus [a representation of the male sex organ] or of coition. . . . In Egyptian tombs the crux ansata [cross with a circle or handle on top] is found side by side with the phallus."—*A Short History of Sex-Worship* (London, 1940), H. Cutner, pp. 16, 17; see also *The Non-Christian Cross,* p. 183.

"These crosses were used as symbols of the Babylonian sun-god, $\oplus$, and are first seen on a coin of Julius Cæsar, 100-44 B.C., and then on a coin struck by Cæsar's heir (Augustus), 20 B.C. On the coins of Constantine the most frequent symbol is ⚥; but the same symbol is used without the surrounding circle, and with the four equal arms vertical and horizontal; and this was the symbol specially venerated as the 'Solar Wheel'. It should be stated that Constantine was a sun-god worshipper, and would not enter the 'Church' till some quarter of a century after the legend of his having seen such a cross in the heavens."—*The Companion Bible,* Appendix No. 162; see also *The Non-Christian Cross,* pp. 133-141.

Is veneration of the cross a Scriptural practice?

1 Cor. 10:14: "My beloved ones, flee from idolatry." (An idol is an image or symbol that is an object of intense devotion, veneration, or worship.)

Ex. 20:4, 5, *JB*: "You shall not make yourself a carved image or any likeness of anything in heaven or on earth beneath or in the waters under the earth; you shall not bow down to them or serve them." (Notice that God commanded that his people not even *make an image* before which people would bow down.)

Of interest is this comment in the *New Catholic Encyclopedia:* "The representation of Christ's redemptive death on Golgotha does not occur in the symbolic art of the first Christian centuries. The early Christians, influenced by the Old Testament prohibition of graven images, were reluctant to depict even the instrument of the Lord's Passion." —(1967), Vol. IV, p. 486.

Concerning first-century Christians, *History of the Christian Church* says: "There was no use of the crucifix and no material representation of the cross."—(New York, 1897), J. F. Hurst, Vol. I, p. 366.

Does it really make any difference if a person cherishes a cross, as long as he does not worship it?

How would you feel if one of your dearest friends was executed on the basis of false charges? Would you make a replica of the instrument of execution? Would you cherish it, or would you rather shun it?

In ancient Israel, unfaithful Jews wept over the death of the false god Tammuz. Jehovah spoke of what they were doing as being a 'detestable thing.' (Ezek. 8:13, 14) According to history, Tammuz was a Babylonian god, and the cross was used as his symbol. From its beginning in the days of Nimrod, Babylon was against Jehovah and an enemy of true worship. (Gen. 10:8-10; Jer. 50:29) So by cherishing the cross, a person is honoring a symbol of worship that is opposed to the true God.

As stated at Ezekiel 8:17, apostate Jews also 'thrust out the shoot to Jehovah's nose.' He viewed this as "detestable" and 'offensive.' Why? This "shoot," some commentators explain, was a representation of the male sex organ, used in phallic worship. How, then, must Jehovah view the use of the cross, which, as we have seen, was anciently used as a symbol in phallic worship?

Dates

Definition: Dates mark the time at which events occur. The Bible expresses dates in relation to the lifetime of individuals, the period during which certain rulers were in office, or other notable events. It contains the only complete chronology reaching back to the time of Adam's creation. Bible chronology also pinpointed in advance the time when certain important events in the fulfillment of God's purpose would take place. The Gregorian calendar, which is now popular in much of the world, did not come into use until 1582. In secular sources there is disagreement on dates given for events in ancient history. However, certain key dates, such as 539 B.C.E. for the fall of Babylon, and hence 537 B.C.E. for the Jews' return from captivity, are well established. (Ezra 1:1-3) Using such dates as starting points, it is possible to express in terms of current calendars the dates for ancient Biblical events.

Have scientists proved that humans have been on earth for millions of years, not merely some thousands of years as the Bible indicates?

The dating methods used by scientists are built on assumptions that can be useful but that often lead to very contradictory results. So, dates given by them are constantly being revised.

A report in *New Scientist* of March 18, 1982, reads: "'I am staggered to believe that as little as a year ago I made the statements that I made.' So said Richard Leakey, before the elegant audience of a Royal Institution evening discourse last Friday. He had come to reveal that the conventional wisdom, which he had so recently espoused in his BBC television series *The Making of Mankind,* was 'probably wrong in a number of crucial areas.' In particular, he now sees man's oldest ancestor as being considerably younger than the 15-20 million years he plumped for on television." —P. 695.

From time to time, new methods of dating are developed. How reliable are these? Regarding one known as thermoluminescence, *The New Encyclopædia Britannica* (1976, Macropædia, Vol. 5, p. 509) says: "Hope rather than accomplishment mainly characterizes the status of thermoluminescence dating at the present time." Also, *Science* (August 28, 1981, p. 1003) reports that a skeleton showing an age of 70,000 years by amino acid racemization gave only 8,300 or 9,000 years by radioactive dating.

Popular Science (November 1979, p. 81) reports that physicist Robert Gentry "believes that all of the dates determined by radioactive decay may be off—not only by a few years, but by orders of magnitude." The article points out that his findings would lead to the conclusion that "man, instead of having walked the earth for 3.6 million years, may have been around for only a few thousand."

It should be noted, however, that scientists believe that the age of the earth itself is much greater than the age of man. The Bible does not disagree with that.

Were the ages of people before the Flood, as stated in the Bible, measured according to the same kind of years that we use?

If it was reasoned that the "years" must be equivalent to our months, then Enosh became a father when he was seven years of age, and Kenan was only five years old when he fathered a son. (Gen. 5:9, 12) That is, clearly, impossible.

Detailed chronology provided in connection with the Flood indicates the length of months and years used at that time. Comparison of Genesis 7:11, 24 and 8:3, 4 shows that five months (from the 17th of the 2nd month to the 17th of the 7th month) was equal to 150 days, or five 30-day months. Specific reference is made to a "tenth month" and to further periods beyond that before coming to the next year. (Gen. 8: 5, 6, 8, 10, 12-14) Evidently, their years were made up of twelve 30-day months. At a very early time, the strictly lunar calendar was adjusted periodically to the length of the solar year, as indicated by Israel's holding *seasonal* festivals of ingathering on *specified dates*. In that way the festivals continued to fall in the appropriate seasons.—Lev. 23:39.

Keep in mind that God made humans to live forever. It was Adam's sin that led to death. (Gen. 2:17; 3:17-19; Rom. 5:12) Those who lived before the Flood were closer to perfection than we are today, so they lived much longer. But each one died within a thousand years.

Why do Jehovah's Witnesses say that God's Kingdom was established in 1914?

Two lines of evidence point to that year: (1) Bible chronology and (2) the events since 1914 in fulfillment of prophecy. Here we will consider the chronology. For fulfillment of prophecy, see the main heading "Last Days."

Read Daniel 4:1-17. Verses 20-37 show that this prophecy had a fulfillment upon Nebuchadnezzar. But it also has a larger fulfillment. How do we know that? Verses 3 and 17 show that the dream that God gave to King Nebuchadnezzar deals with the Kingdom of God and God's promise to give it "to the one whom he wants to . . . even the lowliest one of mankind." The entire Bible shows that Jehovah's purpose is for his own Son, Jesus Christ, to rule as His representative over mankind. (Ps. 2:1-8; Dan. 7:13, 14; 1 Cor. 15:23-25; Rev. 11:15; 12:10) The Bible's description of Jesus shows that he was indeed "the lowliest one of mankind." (Phil. 2: 7, 8; Matt. 11:28-30) The prophetic dream, then, points to the time when Jehovah would give rulership over mankind to his own Son.

What was to happen in the meantime? Rulership over mankind, as represented by the tree and its rootstock, would have "the heart of a beast." (Dan. 4:16) The history of mankind would be dominated by governments that displayed the characteristics of wild beasts. In modern times, the bear is commonly used to represent Russia; the eagle, the United

States; the lion, Britain; the dragon, China. The Bible also uses wild beasts as symbols of world governments and of the entire global system of human rulership under the influence of Satan. (Dan. 7:2-8, 17, 23; 8:20-22; Rev. 13:1, 2) As Jesus showed in his prophecy pointing to the conclusion of the system of things, Jerusalem would be "trampled on by the nations, until the appointed times of the nations" were fulfilled. (Luke 21:24) "Jerusalem" represented the Kingdom of God because its kings were said to sit on "the throne of the kingship of Jehovah." (1 Chron. 28:4, 5; Matt. 5: 34, 35) So, the Gentile governments, represented by wild beasts, would 'trample' on the right of God's Kingdom to direct human affairs and would themselves hold sway under Satan's control.—Compare Luke 4:5, 6.

For how long would such governments be permitted to exercise this control before Jehovah gave the Kingdom to Jesus Christ? Daniel 4:16 says "seven times" ("seven years," *AT* and *Mo,* also *JB* footnote on verse 13). The Bible shows that in calculating prophetic time, a day is counted as a year. (Ezek. 4:6; Num. 14:34) How many "days," then, are involved? Revelation 11:2, 3 clearly states that 42 months (3 1/2 years) in that prophecy are counted as 1,260 days. Seven years would be twice that, or 2,520 days. Applying the "day for a year" rule would result in 2,520 years.

When did the counting of the "seven times" begin? After Zedekiah, the last king in the typical Kingdom of God, was removed from the throne in Jerusalem by the Babylonians. (Ezek. 21:25-27) Finally, by early October of 607 B.C.E. the last vestige of Jewish sovereignty was gone. By that time the Jewish governor, Gedaliah, who had been left in charge by the Babylonians, had been assassinated, and the remaining Jews had fled to Egypt. (Jeremiah, chapters 40-43) Reliable Bible chronology indicates that this took place 70 years before 537 B.C.E., the year in which the Jews returned from captivity; that is, it took place by early October of 607 B.C.E. (Jer. 29:10; Dan. 9:2; for further details, see the book *"Let Your Kingdom Come,"* pages 186-189.)

How, then, is the time calculated down to 1914? Counting 2,520 years from early October of 607 B.C.E. brings us to early October of 1914 C.E., as shown on the chart.

CALCULATING THE "SEVEN TIMES"

"Seven times" = 7 X 360 = 2,520 years

A Biblical "time," or year = 12 X 30 days = 360. (Rev. 11:2, 3; 12:6, 14)
In the fulfillment of the "seven times" each day equals one year. (Ezek. 4:6; Num. 14:34)

Early October, 607 B.C.E., to December 31, 607 B.C.E.	= 1/4 year
January 1, 606 B.C.E., to December 31, 1 B.C.E.	= 606 years
January 1, 1 C.E., to December 31, 1913	= 1,913 years
January 1, 1914, to early October, 1914	= 3/4 year
	Total: 2,520 years

What happened at that time? Jehovah entrusted ruler-ship over mankind to his own Son, Jesus Christ, glorified in the heavens.—Dan. 7:13, 14.

Then why is there still so much wickedness on earth? After Christ was enthroned, Satan and his demons were hurled out of heaven and down to the earth. (Rev. 12:12) Christ as King did not immediately proceed to destroy all who refused to acknowledge Jehovah's sovereignty and him-self as the Messiah. Instead, as he had foretold, a global preaching work was to be done. (Matt. 24:14) As King he would direct a dividing of peoples of all nations, those prov-ing to be righteous being granted the prospect of everlasting life, and the wicked being consigned to everlasting cutting-off in death. (Matt. 25:31-46) In the meantime, the very difficult conditions foretold for "the last days" would prevail. As shown under the heading "Last Days," those events have been clearly in evidence since 1914. Before the last members of the generation that was alive in 1914 will have passed off the scene, all the things foretold will occur, including the "great tribulation" in which the present wicked world will end.—Matt. 24:21, 22, 34.

When will the end of this wicked world come?

Jesus answered: "Concerning that day and hour nobody knows, neither the angels of the heavens nor the Son, but only the Father." However, he also stated: "Truly I say to you that this generation [that was alive when "the sign" of "the last days" began its fulfillment] will by no means pass away until all these things occur."—Matt. 24:36, 34.

Also, after telling of events that would follow the establishment of the Kingdom in the hands of Jesus Christ in 1914, Revelation 12:12 adds: "Be glad, you heavens and you who reside in them! Woe for the earth and for the sea, because the Devil has come down to you, having great anger, knowing he has *a short period of time*."

Death

Definition: The ceasing of all functions of life. After breathing, heartbeat, and brain activity stop, the life-force gradually ceases to function in body cells. Death is the opposite of life.

Was man created by God to die?

On the contrary, Jehovah warned Adam against disobedience, which would lead to death. (Gen. 2:17) Later, God warned Israel against conduct that would lead even to premature death for them. (Ezek. 18:31) In time he sent his Son to die on behalf of mankind so that those who would put faith in this provision might enjoy everlasting life.—John 3: 16, 36.

Psalm 90:10 says that the usual human life span is 70 or 80 years. That was true when Moses wrote it, but that was not so from the beginning. (Compare Genesis 5:3-32.) Hebrews 9:27 says, "It is reserved for men to die once for all time." This, too, was true when it was written. But it was not the case before God passed judgment on sinful Adam.

Why do we grow old and die?

Jehovah created the first human couple perfect, with the prospect of living forever. They were endowed with free will. Would they obey their Creator out of love and appreciation for all that he had done for them? They were fully capable of doing so. God told Adam: "As for the tree of the knowledge of good and bad you must not eat from it, for in the day you eat from it you will positively die." Using a serpent as a mouthpiece, Satan enticed Eve to violate Jehovah's command. Adam did not reprove his wife but joined her in eating that forbidden fruit. True to his word, Jehovah passed sentence of death upon Adam, but before executing the sinful pair, Jehovah mercifully permitted them to bring forth children.—Gen. 2:17; 3:1-19; 5:3-5; compare Deuteronomy 32:4 and Revelation 12:9.

Rom. 5:12, 17, 19: "Through one man [Adam] sin entered into the world and death through sin, and thus death spread to all men because they had all sinned—. . . . By the trespass of the one man death ruled as king . . . Through the disobedience of the one man many were constituted sinners."

1 Cor. 15:22: "In Adam all are dying."

See also the main heading "Fate."

Why do babies die?

Ps. 51:5, *JB:* "You know I was born guilty, a sinner from the moment of conception." (See also Job 14:4; Genesis 8:21.)

Rom. 3:23; 6:23: *"All* have sinned and fall short of the glory of God . . . The wages sin pays is death."

God does not "take" children from their parents, as some have been told. Although the earth produces ample food, selfish political and commercial elements often hinder its distribution to those most in need, resulting in death due to malnutrition. Some children die in accidents, as adults do. But all of us have inherited sin; we are all imperfect. We were born in a system in which everyone—both the good and the bad—eventually dies. (Eccl. 9:5) But Jehovah 'yearns' to reunite children with their parents by means of the resurrection, and lovingly has made provision to do so. —John 5:28, 29; Job 14:14, 15; compare Jeremiah 31:15, 16; Mark 5:40-42.

Where are the dead?

Gen. 3:19: "In the sweat of your face you will eat bread until you return to the ground, for out of it you were taken. For dust you are and to dust you will return."

Eccl. 9:10: "All that your hand finds to do, do with your very power, for there is no work nor devising nor knowledge nor wisdom in Sheol ["the grave," *KJ, Kx;* "the world of the dead," *TEV*], the place to which you are going."

What is the condition of the dead?

Eccl. 9:5: "The living are conscious that they will die; but as for the dead, they are conscious of nothing at all."

Ps. 146:4: "His spirit goes out, he goes back to his ground; in that day his thoughts ["thoughts," *KJ,* 145:4 in *Dy;* "all his thinking," *NE;* "plans," *RS, NAB*] do perish."

John 11:11-14: "'Lazarus our friend has gone to rest, but I am journeying there to awaken him from sleep.' . . . Jesus said to them outspokenly: 'Lazarus has died.'" (Also Psalm 13:3)

Is there some part of man that lives on when the body dies?

Ezek. 18:4: "The soul ["soul," *RS, NE, KJ, Dy, Kx;* "man," *JB;* "person," *TEV*] that is sinning—it itself will die."

Isa. 53:12: "He poured out his soul ["soul," *RS, KJ, Dy;* "life," *TEV;* "himself," *JB, Kx, NAB*] to the very death." (Compare Matthew 26:38.)

See also the main headings "Soul" and "Spirit."

Are the dead in any way able to help or to harm the living?

Eccl. 9:6: "Their love and their hate and their jealousy have already perished, and they have no portion anymore to time indefinite in anything that has to be done under the sun."

Isa. 26:14: "They are dead; they will not live. Impotent in death, they will not rise up."

What about reports made by persons who were revived after being reported to be dead and who spoke of another life?

Normally, after a person stops breathing and the heart-beat ceases, it is several minutes before gradual cessation of the life-force in the body cells begins. If the body is subjected to severe cold, that process can be delayed for hours. For this reason, it is sometimes possible to revive persons by means of cardiopulmonary resuscitation. They were what is termed "clinically dead," but their body cells were still alive.

Many persons revived from "clinical death" remember nothing. Others report experiencing a floating sensation. Some say they saw beautiful things; others were terrified by their experience.

Is there a medical explanation for any of these experiences?

The medical editor of *The Arizona Republic* wrote: "When physical prowess is at its lowest ebb, as under anesthesia, or the result of disease or injury, automatic control of bodily functions diminishes accordingly. Thus, the neurohormones and catecholamines of the nervous system are released and pour out in uncontrolled quantity. The result, among other manifestations, is the hallucination, rationalized after returning to consciousness, of having died and returned to life."—May 28, 1977, p. C-1; also the German medical journal *Fortschritte der Medizin,* No. 41, 1979; *Psychology Today,* January 1981.

But is not the testimony of those who were revived confirmed by persons to whom deceased loved ones have appeared and spoken?

Read again, please, the scriptures quoted earlier regarding the condition of the dead. What is God's Word of truth telling us about the condition of the dead?

Who wants humans to believe otherwise? After Jehovah warned our first parents that disobedience would bring death, who contradicted that? "The serpent [used by Satan; see Revelation 12:9] said to the woman: 'You positively will not die.'" (Gen. 3:4) Later, of course, Adam and Eve did die. Reasonably, then, who invented the idea that a spirit part of man survives the death of the body? As we have already seen, this is not what God's Word says. God's law to ancient Israel condemned as "unclean" and "detestable" the practice of consulting the dead. (Lev. 19:31; Deut. 18:10-12; Isa.

8:19) Would a God of love condemn this practice if the living were simply communicating with loved ones who had departed? On the other hand, if demonic spirits were impersonating the dead and misleading mankind by conveying to their minds impressions that would perpetuate a lie, would it not be loving on God's part to safeguard his servants against such deception?—Eph. 6:11, 12.

Why do Jehovah's Witnesses not share in the traditional customs of mourning for the dead?

Grief over the death of a loved one is normal and may properly be expressed

After the death of his close friend Lazarus, "Jesus gave way to tears." (John 11:35) Sometimes the grief experienced by God's servants in connection with death has been intense. —2 Sam. 1:11, 12.

But because of the resurrection hope, Christians are told: "We do not want you to be ignorant concerning those who are sleeping in death; that you may not sorrow just as the rest also do who have no hope."—1 Thess. 4:13.

Jehovah's servants do not reject all customs that are associated with death

Gen. 50:2, 3: "Joseph commanded his servants, the physicians, to embalm his father . . . and they took fully forty days for him, for this many days they *customarily* take for the embalming."

John 19:40: "They took the body of Jesus and bound it up with bandages with the spices, just the way the Jews have the *custom* of preparing for burial."

Customs that conflict with God's Word are avoided by those who seek to please him

Some customs publicly advertise one's grief. But Jesus said: "When you are fasting [because of sorrow], stop becoming sad-faced like the hypocrites, for they disfigure their faces that they may appear to men to be fasting. Truly I say to you, They are having their reward in full. But you, when fasting, grease your head and wash your face, that you may appear to be fasting, not to men, but to your Father who is in secrecy; then your Father who is looking on in secrecy will repay you."—Matt. 6:16-18.

Certain customs reflect belief that man has an immortal soul that survives death of the body and, so, is aware of what the survivors are doing. But the Bible says: "The dead . . . are conscious of nothing at all." (Eccl. 9:5) Also, "The soul that is sinning—it itself will die."—Ezek. 18:4.

Many customs arise from belief that the dead need the help of the living or from fear that they may harm the living if not appeased. But God's Word shows that the dead are experiencing neither pain nor pleasure. "His spirit goes out, he goes back to his ground; in that day his thoughts do perish." (Ps. 146:4; see also 2 Samuel 12:22, 23.) "Their love and their hate and their jealousy have already perished, and they have no portion anymore to time indefinite in anything that has to be done under the sun."—Eccl. 9:6.

If Someone Says—

'It is the will of God'

You might reply: 'That's a very common belief. But I have found it helpful to search out what God himself says about this.' **Then perhaps add:** (1) '(Read Genesis 2:17.) If a father warns his son that doing a certain thing will cost him his life, would you say that the father wants the son to do it?' (2) 'Then what really is God's will regarding mankind? Jesus said: "This is the will of my Father, that everyone that beholds the Son [that is, perceives and acknowledges that Jesus truly is God's Son] and exercises faith in him should have everlasting life, and I will resurrect him at the last day." (John 6:40)'

'People will always die'

You might reply: 'That certainly is what has happened to humans right down to our day, isn't it?' **Then perhaps add:** 'But notice this wonderful promise made by God at Revelation 21:3, 4 (or Isaiah 25:8).'

'It comes when your time is up'

You might reply: 'Many people feel the way you do. Did you know that many of the ancient Greeks held that same view? They believed that there were three goddesses that determined the length of life that each human would have. But the Bible presents a very different view of life.' **Then perhaps add:** (1) '(Read Ecclesiastes 9:11.) Illustration: A piece of concrete may break off from a building and fall on a pedestrian. Did God cause it? If so, is it fair to charge the building owner with negligence? . . . As the Bible says, for the pedestrian, it was an unplanned and unforeseen occurrence that he was right there when the concrete fell.' (2) 'The Bible tells us that if we avoid bad conduct we safeguard our life. (Prov. 16:17) If you are a parent, I am sure that you apply that principle with your children. You warn them against things that could result in loss of life. Jehovah is doing the same thing for all mankind today.' (3) 'Jehovah knows what the future holds. By means of the Bible he tells us how we can enjoy a life much longer than that of people who ignore what he says. (John 17:3; Prov. 12:28)' (See also the main heading "Fate.")

Dreams

Definition: The thoughts or mental images of a person during sleep. The Bible refers to natural dreams, dreams from God, and dreams that involve divination.—Job 20:8; Num. 12:6; Zech. 10:2.

Do dreams in our time have special meaning?

What have researchers learned about dreams?

"Everyone dreams," says *The World Book Encyclopedia* (1984, Vol. 5, p. 279). "Most adults dream for about 100 minutes during eight hours of sleep." So dreams are a normal human experience.

Said Dr. Allan Hobson, of Harvard Medical School: "They are ambiguous stimuli which can be interpreted in any way a therapist is predisposed to. But their meaning is in the eye of the beholder—not in the dream itself." When reporting this, the "Science Times" section of *The New York Times* added: "Within the school that places great value on dreams, there are many approaches to finding the psychological message of a dream, each reflecting different theoretical outlooks. A Freudian will find one kind of meaning in a dream, while a Jungian will find another, and a Gestalt therapist will find still another meaning. . . . But the view that dreams have psychological meaning at all has come under strong attack from neuroscientists."—July 10, 1984, p. C12.

Can dreams that seem to impart special knowledge come from a source other than God?

Jer. 29:8, 9: "This is what Jehovah of armies . . . has said: 'Let not your prophets who are in among you and your *practicers of divination* deceive you, and do not you listen to their dreams that they are dreaming. For "it is in falsehood that they are prophesying to you in my name. I have not sent them," is the utterance of Jehovah.'"

Harper's Bible Dictionary informs us: "Babylonians had such trust in dreams that on the eve of important decisions they slept in temples, hoping for counsel. Greeks desiring health instruction slept in shrines of Aesculapius [whose emblem was a serpent], and Romans in temples of Serapis [at times associated with a coiled serpent]. Egyptians prepared elaborate books for dream interpretation."—(New York, 1961), Madeleine Miller and J. Lane Miller, p. 141.

In the past, God used dreams to give warnings, instruction, and prophecy, but is he leading his people in that way now?

References to such dreams originating with God are found at Matthew 2:13, 19, 20; 1 Kings 3:5; Genesis 40:1-8.

Heb. 1:1, 2: "God, who long ago spoke on many occasions and in many ways [including dreams] to our forefathers by means of the prophets, has at the end of these days spoken to us by means of a Son [Jesus Christ, whose teachings are recorded in the Bible]."

1 Cor. 13:8: "Whether there are gifts of prophesying [and at times God conveyed prophecies to his servants by means of dreams], they will be done away with."

2 Tim. 3:16, 17: "All Scripture is inspired of God and beneficial for teaching . . . that the man of God may be fully competent, *completely equipped* for every good work."

1 Tim. 4:1: "However, the inspired utterance says definitely that in later periods of time some will fall away from the faith, paying attention to misleading inspired utterances [sometimes conveyed in dreams] and teachings of demons."

Drugs

Definition: There are various definitions of the word "drugs." In the sense being discussed here, drugs are nonfood, mood-altering substances that are not deemed medically necessary but that are used in an effort to escape from the problems of life, to get a dreamy feeling, or a sense of well-being or of elation.

Does the Bible actually forbid the use of drugs for pleasure?

It does not name such substances as heroin, cocaine, LSD, PCP (angel dust), marijuana, and tobacco. But it does provide needed guidelines so that we can know what to do and what to avoid in order to please God. Similarly, the Bible does not say that it is wrong to use a gun to kill someone, but it does forbid murder.

Luke 10:25-27: "'By doing what shall I inherit everlasting life?' . . . '"You must love Jehovah your God with your whole heart and with your whole soul and with your whole strength and with your whole mind," and, "your neighbor as yourself."'" (Is a person really loving God with his whole soul and his whole mind if he makes a practice of things that needlessly shorten his life and cause his mind to be blurred? Is he showing love for his neighbor if he steals from others to support his drug habit?)

2 Cor. 7:1: "Since we have these promises [of having Jehovah as our God and our Father], beloved ones, let us cleanse ourselves of every defilement of flesh and spirit, perfecting holiness in God's fear." (But can we expect to have God's approval if we deliberately do things that defile our bodies?)

Titus 2:11, 12: "The undeserved kindness of God which brings salvation to all sorts of men has been manifested, instructing us to repudiate ungodliness and worldly desires and to live with soundness of mind ["be self-restrained," *JB;* 'to live self-controlled lives,' *TEV*] and righteousness and godly devotion amid this present system of things." (Is the use of drugs that impair one's judgment or that cause a person to lose self-control in harmony with that counsel?)

Gal. 5:19-21: "Now the works of the flesh are manifest, and they are . . . practice of spiritism, . . . revelries, and things like these. . . . Those who practice such things will not inherit God's kingdom." (The literal meaning of the Greek word *phar·ma·ki'a,* here rendered "practice of spiritism," is "druggery." *An Expository Dictionary of New Testament Words,* by W. E. Vine, in commenting on this Greek word, says: "In sorcery, the use of drugs, whether simple or potent, was generally accompanied by incantations and appeals to occult powers, with the provision of various charms, amulets, etc., professedly designed to keep the applicant or patient from the attention and power of demons, but actually to impress the applicant with the mysterious resources and powers of the sorcerer." [London, 1940, Vol. IV, pp. 51, 52] Similarly today, many who use drugs are involved in spiritistic practices or associate with those who are, because a blank mind or one that experiences hallucinations is easy prey to the demons. Compare Luke 11:24-26.)

Titus 3:1: "Be in subjection and be obedient to governments and authorities as rulers." (In many locations, possession or use of certain drugs is a violation of the law.)

Since some of the drugs may help a person to feel good, are they really so harmful?

2 Tim. 3:1-5: "In the last days critical times hard to deal with will be here. For men will be . . . lovers of pleasures

rather than lovers of God . . . From these turn away."
(Clearly the Bible warns against craving pleasure to such an
extent that we put it ahead of applying the righteous principles of God's Word and having his approval.)

Some NARCOTICS bring relief from pain and can produce a feeling of contentment, but they are also addictive
and can result in death from overdose. Sniffing some SOL-
VENTS can produce a feeling of excitement, but it can also
result in slurred speech, distortion of vision, loss of muscu-
lar control, in addition to irreversible damage to the brain,
liver, and kidneys. HALLUCINOGENS cause a "high" feeling and seem to dispel fatigue, but they also cause distor-
tions in perception of distance, impair logical thinking, can
cause irreversible personality changes, and produce suicidal
or homicidal inclinations.

What about marijuana—is it harmless?
Some doctors have said that it is

David Powelson, M.D., formerly chief of psychiatry, Cow-
ell Hospital, University of California, Berkeley, at one time
advocated legalizing the use of marijuana. Later, after more
evidence was available, he wrote: "I now believe that marijuana is the most dangerous drug we must contend with:
1. Its early use is beguiling. The user is given an illusion of
feeling good; he cannot sense the deterioration of his mental
and physiological processes. 2. Its continued use leads to
delusional thinking. After one to three years of continuous
use, the pathological forms of thinking begin to take over
the thought process."—*Executive Health Report,* October
1977, p. 8.

Dr. Robert L. DuPont, former director of the National
Institute on Drug Abuse in the United States, who in the
past was quoted as minimizing danger from marijuana, more
recently stated: "The real issue is the health danger posed
by this epidemic [of marijuana use by the younger genera-
tion], danger of at least two kinds. One is the effects of the
intoxication, ranging from the hazardous impact on driving
to caring less about everything. The other area is purely
physical. Here the concerns range from the regular occurrence of chronic bronchitis among marijuana users to the

very real possibilities of harmful hormonal effects, effects on the immune system and possibly even cancer."—Montreal *Gazette,* March 22, 1979, p. 9.

Science Digest provided these details: "Regular marijuana puffing may, in the long run, widen the gaps between nerve endings in the brain that are necessary for such vital functions as memory, emotion and behavior. In order for nerves to perform their functions, they must communicate between themselves." Then, commenting on the results of tests involving animals, the article continues: "The most marked effects occurred in the septal region, associated with emotions; the hippocampus, concerned with memory formation; and the amygdala, responsible for certain behavioral functions."—March 1981, p. 104.

Is use of marijuana any worse than the drinking of alcoholic beverages?

Alcohol is a food and is metabolized by the body to provide energy; the end products are disposed of by the body. However, a psychopharmacologist said: "Marijuana is a very potent drug, and the biggest mistake we make is comparing it to alcohol." "Molecule for molecule, THC [in marijuana] is *10,000 times stronger* than alcohol in its ability to produce mild intoxication . . . THC is removed slowly from the body, and many months are required to recover from its effects." (*Executive Health Report,* October 1977, p. 3) The Creator knows how we are made, and his Word permits moderate use of alcoholic beverages. (Ps. 104:15; 1 Tim. 5:23) But he also strongly condemns immoderate consumption of alcohol, just as he condemns gluttony.—Prov. 23:20, 21; 1 Cor. 6:9, 10.

Why do Jehovah's Witnesses view tobacco smoking as such a serious offense?

It shows disrespect for the gift of life

Acts 17:24, 25: "The God that made the world and all the things in it . . . gives to all persons life and breath and all things."

"The evidence that cigarettes shorten life is overwhelming; the causal connection is as firmly established as any in medicine."—*Science 80,* September/October, p. 42.

Reports show that in the United States the annual death toll from smoking has been tabulated as being 300,000; in Britain, 50,000; in Canada, 50,000. "More than one million people die annually because of smoking-related disease and the Third World, which accounts for 52% of world tobacco consumption, is making up a rapidly increasing proportion of those deaths."—*The Journal* (Toronto), September 1, 1983, p. 16.

Former U.S. Secretary of Health, Education, and Welfare, Joseph Califano, said: "Today there can be no doubt that smoking is truly slow-motion suicide."—*Scholastic Science World,* March 20, 1980, p. 13.

It is not consistent with what God requires Christians to render to him

Rom. 12:1: "I entreat you by the compassions of God, brothers, to present your bodies a sacrifice living, holy, acceptable to God, a sacred service with your power of reason."

The surgeon general of the United States, C. Everett Koop, said: "Cigarette smoking is clearly identified as the chief preventable cause of death in our society." (*The New York Times,* February 23, 1982, p. A1) "Medical studies show that . . . the average life expectancy of a smoker is three to four years less than that of a nonsmoker. The life expectancy of a heavy smoker—a person who smokes two or more packages of cigarettes a day—may be as much as eight years shorter than that of a nonsmoker." (*The World Book Encyclopedia,* 1984, Vol. 17, p. 430) Is it proper for a person to present his life for service to God and then slowly to destroy that life?

"Smoking is so devastating, especially to the heart and lungs, that the other aspects of preventive medicine become comparatively insignificant if the person smokes." (University of Southern California News Service, February 18, 1982) "Smoking is probably the largest single preventable cause of ill health in the world." (Dr. H. Mahler, director-general of the World Health Organization, in *World Health,* February/March 1980, p. 3) Is it consistent for a person to present himself to God for sacred service and then deliberately to ruin his health?

Smoking is a violation of the divine requirement that we love our neighbor

Jas. 2:8: "You must love your neighbor as yourself." —Compare Matthew 7:12.

"A recent study . . . revealed that the nonsmoking wives of men who smoke die on the average four years younger than women whose husbands are also nonsmokers." (*The New York Times,* November 22, 1978, p. C5) "Smoking during pregnancy can cause congenital malformations so severe that either the fetus dies, or the infant does shortly after birth." (*Family Health,* May 1979, p. 8) Such unloving treatment of family members is clear evidence that a person is not acting as a Christian.—Compare 1 Timothy 5:8.

"Studies have shown that since the average smoker actively smokes his cigarette for only a small portion of the time it is lit, a nonsmoker may actually be forced against his will to breathe almost as much carbon monoxide, tar and nicotine as the active smoker sitting next to him." (*Today's Health,* April 1972, p. 39) A person who is thus unloving toward his fellowman does not give evidence of loving God either.—See 1 John 4:20.

Why did God make plants from which drugs are derived if it is wrong to use them?

Things that are abused usually also have proper uses. That is true of man's reproductive abilities. It is true of wine. Marijuana is made from the dried leaves and flowering tops of the hemp plant, which provides useful fibers for making rope and cloth. Tobacco leaves, abused by smokers, can also be used in making disinfectants and insecticides. Regarding many of earth's resources, much is yet to be learned as to how they can be beneficially employed. Even weeds are beneficial in preventing erosion and providing mulch when soil is not under cultivation.

What can a person do if he has tried to break free from smoking or other use of drugs and has not succeeded?

First, by Bible study and meditation you need to cultivate a strong desire to please God and to live in his righteous new system of things. If you draw close to him, he will draw close to you, giving you the needed help.—Jas. 4:8.

It is important to be convinced of the badness of these practices and to develop genuine hatred for them. (Ps. 97:10) This can be done by reviewing the facts set out in this section of the book and meditating, not on temporary present pleasure that may come from the practices, but on what pleases God and how disgusting the results of the bad practices are.

If you feel a strong craving to smoke or to use one of the other drugs, pray earnestly to God for help. (Luke 11:9, 13; compare Philippians 4:13.) Do it right away. Also, get your Bible and read *aloud* from it, or get in touch with a mature Christian. Tell him what is happening and ask for his help.

Earth

Definition: The term "earth" is used in more than one sense in the Scriptures. Usually we think of it as referring to the planet itself, which Jehovah generously endowed so that it could sustain human life with a view to making our lives richly satisfying. It should be realized, however, that "earth" also may be used in a figurative sense, referring, for example, to people living on this planet or to a human society that has certain characteristics.

Will planet Earth be destroyed in a nuclear war?

What does the Bible show to be God's purpose regarding the earth?

Matt. 6:10: "Let your kingdom come. Let your will take place, as in heaven, *also upon earth.*"

Ps. 37:29: "The righteous themselves will possess the earth, and they will reside forever upon it."

See also Ecclesiastes 1:4; Psalm 104:5.

Is there a possibility that, since the nations show little regard for God's purpose, they might completely ruin the earth for habitation anyway?

Isa. 55:8-11: "[The utterance of Jehovah is:] As the heavens are higher than the earth, so my ways are higher than your ways, and my thoughts than your thoughts. . . . My word . . . will not return to me without results, but it will certainly do that in which I have delighted, and it will have certain success in that for which I have sent it."

Isa. 40:15, 26: "Look! [From the standpoint of Jehovah God] The nations are as a drop from a bucket; and as the film of dust on the scales they have been accounted. . . . 'Raise your eyes high up and see [the sun, the moon, and the billions of stars]. Who has created these things? It is the One who is bringing forth the army of them even by number, all of whom he calls even by name. Due to the abundance of dynamic energy, he also being vigorous in power, not one of them is missing.'" (The nuclear power developed by the nations is fear inspiring to men. But billions of stars employ nuclear power on a scale that is beyond our ability to comprehend. Who created and controls all these heavenly bodies? Can He not prevent the nations from using their nuclear weapons in a way that would hinder his purpose? That God would do this is illustrated by his destroying the military power of Egypt when Pharaoh sought to stop the deliverance of Israel.—Ex. 14:5-31.)

Rev. 11:17, 18: "We thank you, Jehovah God, the Almighty, the One who is and who was, because you have taken your great power and begun ruling as king. But the nations became wrathful, and your own wrath came, and the appointed time . . . to bring to ruin those ruining the earth."

Will God himself destroy the earth by fire?

Does 2 Peter 3:7, 10 (KJ) support that view? "The heavens and the earth, which are now, by the same word are kept in store, reserved unto fire against the day of judgment and perdition ["destruction," *RS*] of ungodly men. . . . The day of the Lord will come as a thief in the night; in the which the heavens shall pass away with a great noise, and the elements shall melt with fervent heat, the earth also and the works that are therein shall be burned up ["burned (burnt) up," *RS, JB;* "will vanish," *TEV;* "will be made manifest," *NAB;* "will be laid bare," *NE;* "will be discovered," *NW*]." (Note: The Codex Sinaiticus and Vatican MS 1209, both of the 4th century C.E., read "be discovered." Later manuscripts, the 5th-century Codex Alexandrinus and the 16th-century Clementine recension of the Vulgate, read "be burned up.")

Does Revelation 21:1 (KJ) indicate that our planet will be destroyed? "And I saw a new heaven and a new earth: for the first heaven and the first earth were passed away; and there was no more sea."

To be correct, the explanation of these verses must agree with the context and with the rest of the Bible

If these texts (2 Peter 3:7, 10 and Revelation 21:1) mean that the literal planet Earth is to be consumed by fire, then the literal heavens (the stars and other heavenly bodies) are also to be destroyed by fire. Such a literal view, however, conflicts with the assurance contained in such texts as Matthew 6:10, Psalm 37:29 and 104:5, also Proverbs 2:21, 22. Furthermore, what effect would fire have on the already intensely hot sun and stars? So the term "earth" in the above-quoted texts must be understood in a different sense.

At Genesis 11:1, First Kings 2:1, 2, First Chronicles 16:31, Psalm 96:1, etc., the term "earth" is used in a *figurative* sense, referring to mankind, to human society. Might that be the case at 2 Peter 3:7, 10 and Revelation 21:1?

Note that, in the context, at 2 Peter 3:5, 6 (also 2:5, 9), a parallel is drawn with the Flood of Noah's day, in which wicked human society was destroyed, but Noah and his household, as well as the globe itself, were preserved. Likewise, at 2 Peter 3:7 it says that the ones to be destroyed are "ungodly men." The view that "the earth" here refers to wicked human society fully agrees with the rest of the Bible, as is illustrated by the texts cited above. It is that symbolic "earth," or *wicked human society,* that is "discovered"; that is, Jehovah will sear away as by fire all disguise, *exposing* the wickedness of ungodly human society and showing it to be worthy of complete destruction. That wicked society of humans is also "the first earth," referred to at Revelation 21:1 (*KJ*).

Consistently, Jesus' expression at Luke 21:33 ("heaven and earth will pass away, but . . . ") must be understood in the light of the parallel statement at Luke 16:17 (*"it is easier* for heaven and earth to pass away *than . . .* "), both of which simply emphasize the impossibility of the situations presented.—See also Matthew 5:18.

Will the righteous be taken to heaven and then returned to earth after the wicked are destroyed?

Does Revelation 21:2, 3 support that view? It says: "I saw also the holy city, New Jerusalem, coming down out of heaven from God and prepared as a bride adorned for her husband. With that I heard a loud voice from the throne say: 'Look! The tent of God is with mankind, and he will reside with them, and they will be his peoples. And God himself will be with them.'" (Does the fact that God will "reside" with mankind and "be with them" mean that he will become a fleshly Being? That cannot be, because Jehovah told Moses: "No man may see me and yet live." [Ex. 33:20] Consistently, then, the members of the New Jerusalem will not return to earth as physical beings. In what sense, then, could God "be with" mankind and how would the New Jerusalem 'come down out of heaven'? No doubt an indication is found in Genesis 21:1, which says that God "visited" Sarah, blessing her with a son in her old age. Exodus 4:31 tells us that God "visited" Israel by sending Moses as a deliverer. Luke 7:16 says that by means of Jesus' ministry God "visited" his people. [All from *KJ* and *RS*] Other translations use the expression God "turned his attention" to his people [*NW*] or 'showed concern' for them [*NE*]. So Revelation 21:2, 3 must mean that God will 'visit,' or be with, mankind by means of the heavenly New Jerusalem, through which blessings will come to obedient humans.)

Prov. 2:21, 22, *KJ:* "The upright shall dwell in the land ["on earth," *NE*], and the perfect ["blameless men," *NE*] shall *remain* in it. But the wicked shall be cut off from the earth, and the transgressors shall be rooted out of it." (Notice that it does not say the blameless will *return* to the earth but that they "shall remain in it.")

Has God's original purpose for the earth changed?

Gen. 1:27, 28: "God proceeded to create the man in his image, in God's image he created him; male and female he created them. Further, God blessed them and God said to them: 'Be fruitful and become many and fill the earth and subdue it, and have in subjection the fish of the sea and the flying creatures of the heavens and every living creature that is moving upon the earth.'" (Thus God indicated his purpose to have the earth filled with the offspring of Adam and Eve as caretakers of a global paradise. After God had magnificently designed this earth for human habitation, making it unique among all the planets that man has examined with his telescopes and spaceships, did the Creator simply abandon his purpose, leaving it forever unfulfilled because of Adam's sin?)

Isa. 45:18: "This is what Jehovah has said, the Creator of the heavens, He the true God, the Former of the earth and the Maker of it, He the One who firmly established it, who did not create it simply for nothing, who formed it even to be inhabited: 'I am Jehovah, and there is no one else.'" (See also Isaiah 55:10, 11.)

If no one is ever going to die in God's New Order, how will all the people fit on earth?

Keep in mind that when God expressed his purpose for the earth he said: "Be fruitful and become many and *fill* the earth." (Gen. 1:28) God gave man the ability to procreate, and when His purpose in that regard is fulfilled He can cause procreation to cease on earth.

What kind of people will God favor with endless life on earth?

Zeph. 2:3: "Seek Jehovah, all you meek ones of the earth, who have practiced His own judicial decision. Seek righteousness, seek meekness. Probably you may be concealed in the day of Jehovah's anger."

Ps. 37:9, 11: "Those hoping in Jehovah are the ones that will possess the earth. . . . The meek ones themselves will possess the earth, and they will indeed find their exquisite delight in the abundance of peace."

Encouragement

Definition: Something that gives courage or imparts hope. Everyone needs encouragement. Giving it may require rendering personal help or expressing appreciation. Often it involves assisting someone to see how to cope with a difficult situation or discussing reasons for confidence in a better future. The Bible provides the finest basis for such encouragement, and the texts quoted below can be helpful in giving it to persons faced with various situations. At times much good is done by simply displaying a sympathetic attitude.—Rom. 12:15.

For those experiencing trials because of ILLNESS—

Rev. 21:4, 5: "'[God] will wipe out every tear from their eyes, and death will be no more, neither will mourning nor outcry nor pain be anymore. The former things have passed away.' And the One seated on the throne said: 'Look! I am making all things new.' Also, he says: 'Write, because these words are faithful and true.'"

Matt. 9:35: "Jesus set out on a tour of all the cities and villages, teaching . . . and preaching the good news of the kingdom and curing every sort of disease and every sort of infirmity." (By associating such healing with his preaching about the Kingdom, Jesus provided a marvelous foreview of what he will do for mankind during his Millennial Reign.)

2 Cor. 4:13, 16: "We too exercise faith . . . Therefore we

do not give up, but even if the man we are outside [our physical body] is wasting away, certainly the man we are inside is being renewed [or given fresh strength] from day to day." (We may be wasting away in a physical sense. But spiritually we are being renewed as we continue to feed on God's precious promises.)

See also Luke 7:20-23.

For persons who have lost loved ones in DEATH—

Isa. 25:8, 9: "He will actually swallow up death forever, and the Sovereign Lord Jehovah will certainly wipe the tears from all faces. . . . And in that day one will certainly say: 'Look! This is our God. We have hoped in him, and he will save us. This is Jehovah. We have hoped in him. Let us be joyful and rejoice in the salvation by him.'"

John 5:28, 29: "Do not marvel at this, because the hour is coming in which all those in the memorial tombs will hear his voice and come out, those who did good things to a resurrection of life, those who practiced vile things to a resurrection of judgment."

John 11:25, 26: "Jesus said to her: 'I am the resurrection and the life. He that exercises faith in me, even though he dies, will come to life; and everyone that is living and exercises faith in me will never die at all. Do you believe this?'"

Ps. 146:5, 9: "Happy is the one . . . whose hope is in Jehovah his God. . . . The fatherless boy and the widow he relieves." (Right now God has such loving concern for bereaved ones.)

See also Luke 7:11-16; 8:49-56.

For persons facing PERSECUTION because of doing God's will—

Ps. 27:10: "In case my own father and my own mother did leave me, even Jehovah himself would take me up."

1 Pet. 4:16: "If he suffers as a Christian, let him not feel shame, but let him keep on glorifying God in this name."

Prov. 27:11: "Be wise, my son, and make my heart rejoice, that I may make a reply to him that is taunting me." (By faithfulness we provide an answer to Satan's false charge that no one suffering great hardship will continue to serve God.)

Matt. 5:10-12: "Happy are those who have been persecuted for righteousness' sake, since the kingdom of the heavens belongs to them. Happy are you when people reproach you and persecute you and lyingly say every sort of wicked thing against you for my sake. Rejoice and leap for joy, since your reward is great in the heavens; for in that way they persecuted the prophets prior to you."

Acts 5:41, 42: "[The apostles], therefore, went their way from before the Sanhedrin, rejoicing because they had been counted worthy to be dishonored in behalf of his name. And every day in the temple and from house to house they continued without letup teaching and declaring the good news about the Christ, Jesus."

Phil. 1:27-29: "Only behave in a manner worthy of the good news about the Christ . . . and in no respect being frightened by your opponents. This very thing is a proof of destruction for them, but of salvation for you; and this indication is from God, because to you the privilege was given in behalf of Christ, not only to put your faith in him, but also to suffer in his behalf."

For those disheartened because of INJUSTICE—

Ps. 37:10, 11: "Just a little while longer, and the wicked one will be no more; and you will certainly give attention to his place, and he will not be. But the meek ones themselves will possess the earth, and they will indeed find their exquisite delight in the abundance of peace."

Isa. 9:6, 7: "There has been a child born to us, there has been a son given to us; and the princely rule will come to be upon his shoulder. And his name will be called Wonderful Counselor, Mighty God, Eternal Father, Prince of Peace. To the abundance of the princely rule and to peace there will be no end, upon the throne of David and upon his kingdom in order to establish it firmly and to sustain it *by means of justice and by means of righteousness,* from now on and to time indefinite. The very zeal of Jehovah of armies will do this."

Dan. 2:44: "In the days of those kings the God of heaven will set up a kingdom that will never be brought to ruin. And the kingdom itself will not be passed on to any other people. It will crush and put an end to all these kingdoms, and it itself will stand to times indefinite."

See also Isaiah 32:1, 2; 2 Peter 3:13.

For those hard pressed by ECONOMIC PROBLEMS—

Isa. 65:21, 22: "They will certainly build houses and have occupancy; and they will certainly plant vineyards and eat their fruitage. They will not build and someone else have occupancy; they will not plant and someone else do the eating. . . . The work of their own hands my chosen ones will use to the full."

Ps. 72:8, 16: "He [the Messianic King] will have subjects from sea to sea and from the River to the ends of the earth. There will come to be plenty of grain on the earth; on the top of the mountains there will be an overflow."

Matt. 6:33: "Keep on, then, seeking first the kingdom and his righteousness, and all these other things [material necessities of life] will be added to you."

Rom. 8:35, 38, 39: "Who will separate us from the love of the Christ? Will tribulation or distress or persecution or hunger or nakedness or danger or sword? For I am convinced that neither death nor life nor angels nor governments nor things now here nor things to come nor powers nor height nor depth nor any other creation will be able to separate us from God's love that is in Christ Jesus our Lord."

See also Hebrews 13:5, 6.

For individuals who are discouraged because of their own SHORTCOMINGS—

Ps. 34:18: "Jehovah is near to those that are broken at heart; and those who are crushed in spirit he saves."

Ps. 103:13, 14: "As a father shows mercy to his sons, Jehovah has shown mercy to those fearing him. For he himself well knows the formation of us, remembering that we are dust."

Neh. 9:17: "You are a God of acts of forgiveness, gracious and merciful, slow to anger and abundant in loving-kindness."

2 Pet. 3:9, 15: "Jehovah is not slow respecting his promise, as some people consider slowness, but he is patient with you because he does not desire any to be destroyed but desires all to attain to repentance. Furthermore, consider the patience of our Lord as salvation."

Evolution

Definition: Organic evolution is the theory that the first living organism developed from lifeless matter. Then, as it reproduced, it is said, it changed into different kinds of living things, ultimately producing all forms of plant and animal life that have ever existed on this earth. All of this is said to have been accomplished without the supernatural intervention of a Creator. Some persons endeavor to blend belief in God with evolution, saying that God created by means of evolution, that he brought into existence the first primitive life forms and that then higher life forms, including man, were produced by means of evolution. *Not a Bible teaching.*

Is evolution really scientific?

The "scientific method" is as follows: Observe what happens; based on those observations, form a theory as to what may be true; test the theory by further observations and by experiments; and watch to see if the predictions based on the theory are fulfilled. Is this the method followed by those who believe in and teach evolution?

Astronomer Robert Jastrow says: "To their chagrin [scientists] have no clear-cut answer, because chemists have never succeeded in reproducing nature's experiments on the creation of life out of nonliving matter. Scientists do not know how that happened."—*The Enchanted Loom: Mind in the Universe* (New York, 1981), p. 19.

Evolutionist Loren Eiseley acknowledged: "After having chided the theologian for his reliance on myth and miracle, science found itself in the unenviable position of having to create a mythology of its own: namely, the assumption that what, after long effort, could not be proved to take place today had, in truth, taken place in the primeval past."—*The Immense Journey* (New York, 1957), p. 199.

According to *New Scientist:* "An increasing number of scientists, most particularly a growing number of evolutionists . . . argue that Darwinian evolutionary theory is no genuine scientific theory at all. . . . Many of the critics have the highest intellectual credentials."—June 25, 1981, p. 828.

Physicist H. S. Lipson said: "The only acceptable explanation is *creation.* I know that this is anathema to physicists, as indeed it is to me, but we must not reject a theory that we do not like *if the experimental evidence supports it.*" (Italics added.)—*Physics Bulletin,* 1980, Vol. 31, p. 138.

Are those who advocate evolution in agreement? How do these facts make you feel about what they teach?

The introduction to the centennial edition of Darwin's *Origin of Species* (London, 1956) says: "As we know, there is a great divergence of opinion among biologists, not only about the causes of evolution but even about the actual process. This divergence exists because the evidence is unsatisfactory and does not permit any certain conclusion. It is therefore right and proper to draw the attention of the non-scientific public to the disagreements about evolution." —By W. R. Thompson, then director of the Commonwealth Institute of Biological Control, Ottawa, Canada.

"A century after Darwin's death, we still have not the slightest demonstrable or even plausible idea of how evolution really took place—and in recent years this has led to an extraordinary series of battles over the whole question. . . . A state of almost open war exists among the evolutionists themselves, with every kind of [evolutionary] sect urging some new modification."—C. Booker (London *Times* writer), *The Star,* (Johannesburg), April 20, 1982, p. 19.

The scientific magazine *Discover* said: "Evolution . . . is not only under attack by fundamentalist Christians, but is also being questioned by reputable scientists. Among paleontologists, scientists who study the fossil record, there is growing dissent."—October 1980, p. 88.

What view does the fossil record support?

Darwin acknowledged: "If numerous species . . . have really started into life at once, the fact would be fatal to the theory of evolution." (*The Origin of Species,* New York, 1902, Part Two, p. 83) Does the evidence indicate that "numerous species" came into existence at the same time, or does it point to gradual development, as evolution holds?

Have sufficient fossils been found to draw a sound conclusion?

Smithsonian Institution scientist Porter Kier says: "There are a hundred million fossils, all catalogued and identified, in museums around the world." (*New Scientist,* January 15, 1981, p. 129) *A Guide to Earth History* adds: "By the aid of fossils palaeontologists can now give us an excellent picture of the life of past ages."—(New York, 1956), Richard Carrington, Mentor edition, p. 48.

What does the fossil record actually show?

The *Bulletin* of Chicago's Field Museum of Natural History pointed out: "Darwin's theory of [evolution] has always been closely linked to evidence from fossils, and probably most people assume that fossils provide a very important part of the general argument that is made in favor of darwinian interpretations of the history of life. Unfortunately, this is not strictly true. . . . the geologic record did not then and still does not yield a finely graduated chain of slow and progressive evolution."—January 1979, Vol. 50, No. 1, pp. 22, 23.

A View of Life states: "Beginning at the base of the Cambrian period and extending for about 10 million years, all the major groups of skeletonized invertebrates made their first appearance in the most spectacular rise in diversity ever recorded on our planet."—(California, 1981), Salvador E. Luria, Stephen Jay Gould, Sam Singer, p. 649.

Paleontologist Alfred Romer wrote: "Below this [Cambrian period], there are vast thicknesses of sediments in which the progenitors of the Cambrian forms would be expected. But we do not find them; these older beds are almost barren of evidence of life, and the general picture could reasonably be said to be consistent with the idea of a special creation at the beginning of Cambrian times."—*Natural History,* October 1959, p. 467.

Zoologist Harold Coffin states: "If progressive evolution from simple to complex is correct, the ancestors of these full-blown living creatures in the Cambrian should be found; but they have not been found and scientists admit there is little prospect of their ever being found. On the basis of the facts alone, on the basis of what is actually found in the earth, the theory of a sudden creative act in which the major forms of life were established fits best."—*Liberty,* September/October 1975, p. 12.

Carl Sagan, in his book *Cosmos,* candidly acknowledged: "The fossil evidence could be consistent with the idea of a Great Designer."—(New York, 1980), p. 29.

Might it be that the evolutionary process took place as a result of mutations, that is, sudden drastic changes in genes?

Science Digest states: "Evolutionary revisionists believe mutations in key regulatory genes may be just the genetic jackhammers their quantum-leap theory requires." However, the magazine also quotes British zoologist Colin Patterson as stating: "Speculation is free. We know nothing about these regulatory master genes." (February 1982, p. 92) In other words, there is no evidence to support the theory.

The Encyclopedia Americana acknowledges: "The fact that most mutations are damaging to the organism seems hard to reconcile with the view that mutation is the source of raw materials for evolution. Indeed, mutants illustrated in biology textbooks are a collection of freaks and monstrosities and mutation seems to be a destructive rather than a constructive process."—(1977), Vol. 10, p. 742.

What about those "ape-men" depicted in schoolbooks, encyclopedias and museums?

"The flesh and hair on such reconstructions have to be filled in by resorting to the imagination. . . . Skin color; the color, form, and distribution of the hair; the form of the features; and the aspect of the face—of these characters we know absolutely nothing for any prehistoric men." —*The Biology of Race* (New York, 1971), James C. King, pp. 135, 151.

"The vast majority of artists' conceptions are based more on imagination than on evidence. . . . Artists must create something between an ape and a human being; the older the specimen is said to be, the more apelike they make it." —*Science Digest,* April 1981, p. 41.

"Just as we are slowly learning that primitive men are not necessarily savages, so we must learn to realize that the early men of the Ice Age were neither brute beasts nor semi-apes nor cretins. Hence the ineffable stupidity of all attempts to reconstruct Neanderthal or even Peking man." —*Man, God and Magic* (New York, 1961), Ivar Lissner, p. 304.

Do not textbooks present evolution as fact?

"Many scientists succumb to the temptation to be dogmatic, . . . over and over again the question of the origin of the species has been presented as if it were finally settled. Nothing could be further from the truth. . . . But the tendency to be dogmatic persists, and it does no service to the cause of science."—*The Guardian,* London, England, December 4, 1980, p. 15.

But is it reasonable to believe that everything on this earth was created in six days?

There are some religious groups that teach that God created everything in six 24-hour days. But that is not what the Bible says.

Genesis 1:3-31 tells how God prepared the already existing earth for human habitation. It says that this was done during a period of six days, but it does not say that these were 24-hour days. It is not unusual for a person to refer to his "grandfather's day," meaning that one's entire lifetime. So, too, the Bible often uses the term "day" to describe an extended period of time. (Compare 2 Peter 3:8.) Thus the 'days' of Genesis chapter 1 could reasonably be thousands of years long.

For further details, see page 88.

If Someone Says—

'I believe in evolution'

You might reply: 'Do you believe that God had any hand in matters, or is it your belief that from the very start the development of life was strictly a matter of chance? (Then proceed on the basis of what the person says.)'

Or you could say: 'It wouldn't be realistic to reject something that has been fully proved to be a scientific fact, would it? . . . I have here some comments of scientists that are very interesting regarding this point. (Use material on pages 121, 122, under the subheading "Is evolution really scientific?" or on pages 122, 123, under "Are those who advocate evolution in agreement? . . . ")'

Another possibility: 'When there is solid evidence proving something, that is what we should all believe, isn't it? . . . I recall in my school textbooks that pictures of fossils were provided to support evolution. But since then I have read some very interesting comments by scientists concerning the fossil record. I have some of them here. (Use material on pages 123, 124, under the subheading "What view does the fossil record support?")'

An additional suggestion: 'Am I right in concluding that you are a person who likes to face life the way it really is? . . . I do too.' **Then perhaps add:** 'If I walk in the countryside and find that some wood and stones have been shaped into a house, it should be obvious to me that someone was there before me and built it; right? . . . But, now, would it be logical for me to conclude that flowers growing along-side the house resulted just from chance? If I feel that way I need to look closely and notice the intricate design, because I know that it is a basic truth that where there is design there must be a designer. This is what the Bible tells us at Hebrews 3:4.'

Or you might answer (an older person): 'One of the basic ideas in evolution is that it accounts for man's progress, his development to what he is today, isn't that right?' **Then perhaps add:** (1) 'You are an individual who has lived quite some time. Do you remember how things were when you were a child? Was there as much crime as there is now? . . . Did you always have to keep the door locked? . . . Would you say that people back then showed greater concern for their neighbors, and for older folks, than they do today? . . . So, while there has been great progress in technical fields, humans themselves seem to be losing some of the qualities that count most. Why is this?' (2) 'I find that these realities of life that we have both observed agree with what is written here in the Bible at Romans 5:12. . . . So, really there has been a downhill trend.' (3) 'But the Bible shows how that will change. (Dan. 2:44; Rev. 21:3, 4)'

'I believe that God created man by means of evolution'

You might reply: 'I've talked with others who share your view. Am I right in concluding that you are a person who has strong faith in God? . . . So your faith really holds first place in your life; with it as a guide, you endeavor to evaluate other things, is that right? . . . That's the way I view matters too.' **Then perhaps add:** (1) 'I know that if what I believe is really truth, it is not going to conflict with proved scientific facts. At the same time I know that it would be foolish for me to ignore what God's Word says, because God knows much more about his works than any of us do. I'm impressed with what the Bible, God's inspired Word, says here at Genesis 1:21 (emphasize "according to their kinds").' (2) 'Then in Genesis 2:7 we learn that God formed man, not from earlier animals, but from the dust.' (3) 'And in verses

21, 22 we find that Eve was formed, not from an animal, but with one of Adam's ribs as starting material.'

Or you could say: '(After establishing a common ground, as above . . .) Some say that the Bible's reference to Adam was just an allegory. But if that is true, to what conclusion does it lead?' (1) 'Well, notice what is stated here at Romans 5:19: "Just as through the disobedience of the one man [Adam] many were constituted sinners, likewise also through the obedience of the one person [Jesus Christ] many will be constituted righteous." Similarly, 1 Corinthians 15:22 says: "Just as in Adam all are dying, so also in the Christ all will be made alive." But if there really was no "one man" named Adam, then such a man never sinned. If he did not sin and pass an inheritance of sin on to his offspring, then there was no need for Christ to give his life on behalf of mankind. If Christ really did not give his life on our behalf, then there is no prospect for life beyond our present few years. That would mean that there actually is nothing left to Christianity.' (2) 'Yet, embodied in Christianity are the highest moral principles that can be found anywhere. Is it possible that the finest teachings as to truth and honesty could originate with something that is basically false?' (See also pages 27-29, under the main heading "Adam and Eve.")

'But highly educated people believe it'

You might reply: 'True, yet I have come to realize that even those who say they believe it may strongly disagree with others who believe in evolution. (Cite examples from material on pages 122, 123.) So, we must personally examine the evidence to see which we should believe—evolution or creation.'

Or you could say: 'That's true. And yet I have come to realize that there are other highly educated people who do not believe it.' **Then perhaps add:** (1) 'Why the difference? They are all acquainted with the same evidence. Might motive enter the picture? Possibly.' (2) 'How can you decide which ones to believe? Well, viewing the group as a whole (and not criticizing individuals), which group do you believe would be the more honest—those who believe that man wa created by God and so feel accountable to him, or those who say they are a product of chance and so are accountable only to themselves?' (3) 'So, then, we personally need to examine the evidence to see whether creation or evolution provides the most satisfying answers to life.'

Faith

Definition: "Faith is the assured expectation of things hoped for, the evident demonstration of realities though not beheld." (Heb. 11:1) True faith is not credulity, that is, a readiness to believe something without sound evidence or just because a person wants it to be so. Genuine faith requires basic or fundamental knowledge, acquaintance with evidence, as well as heartfelt appreciation of what that evidence indicates. Thus, although it is impossible to have real faith without accurate knowledge, the Bible says that it is "with the heart" that one exercises faith.—Rom. 10:10.

Why do many people not have faith?

Faith is a fruit of God's spirit, and God gladly gives his spirit to those who seek it. (Gal. 5:22; Luke 11:13) So persons without faith are not seeking that spirit, or they are doing so for a wrong purpose or are resisting its operation in their lives. Many things influence this:

Lack of accurate Bible knowledge: The Bible is a product of God's spirit, being inspired by God. (2 Tim. 3:16, 17; 2 Sam. 23:2) Failure to study it hinders any development of true faith. Although church members may have Bibles, if they have been taught the ideas of men instead of the Word of God, they will lack real faith in God and his purpose. To solve life's problems, they will be inclined to rely on their own ideas and those of other humans.—Compare Matthew 15:3-9.

Disillusionment with religion: Many have been disillusioned by the hypocrisy of the churches of Christendom, which claim to teach God's Word but fail to live in harmony with what it says. Others were adherents to a non-Christian religion, but they saw bad fruitage from its practices or found that their beliefs did not really help them to cope with the problems of life. Lacking accurate knowledge of the true God, such persons draw away from everything related to religion.—Compare Romans 3:3, 4; Matthew 7:21-23.

Do not understand God's permission of wickedness: Most people do not understand why God permits wickedness and so blame him for all the bad things that take place. They do not realize that man's inclination toward badness is not because of God's will but because of the sin of Adam. (Rom. 5:12) They may be unaware of the existence of Satan the Devil and of his influence on world affairs, so they ascribe to God the vile things perpetrated by Satan. (1 John 5:19; Rev. 12:12) If they are to some extent aware of these things, they may feel that God is slow about taking action, because they do not see clearly the issue of universal sovereignty and do not grasp the fact that God's patience down till this time affords them an undeserved opportunity for salvation. (Rom. 2:4; 2 Pet. 3:9) Also, they do not fully realize that God has a set time when he will destroy forever all who practice wickedness.—Rev. 22:10-12; 11:18; Hab. 2:3.

Lives dominated by fleshly desires and viewpoints: Generally, persons who lack faith that has real substance have devoted themselves to the pursuit of other interests. Some may say that they believe the Bible but they may never have thoroughly studied it or may have failed to meditate appreciatively on what they read, on the reasons for it, and how it applies to everyday life. (Compare 1 Chronicles 28:9.) In some cases, they failed to nourish the faith they had but, instead, allowed a desire for unrighteous things to dominate the inclination of their heart so that they drew away from God and his ways.—Heb. 3:12.

How can a person acquire faith?

Rom. 10:17: "Faith follows the thing heard." (Compare Acts 17:11, 12; John 4:39-42; 2 Chronicles 9:5-8. A person must first find out what the Bible says, and he will strengthen his conviction if he examines it carefully so as to be convinced of its reliability.)

Rom. 10:10: "With the heart one exercises faith." (By meditating on godly things to build up appreciation for them, a person impresses them on his figurative heart.)

Faith is strengthened when a person acts on God's promises and then sees the evidence of God's blessing on what he has done.—See Psalm 106:9-12.

Illustration: Perhaps you have a friend of whom you would say: 'I trust that man. I can count on him to keep his word; and I know that if I have a problem, he will come to my help.' It is not likely that you would be saying that about anyone you met for the first time yesterday, is it? He would have to be someone with whom you had long association, someone who had proved his dependability time and again. It is similar with religious faith. To have faith, you need to take time to get to know Jehovah and his way of doing things.

Faith that there is a God

See pages 145-151, under the main heading "God."

Faith in the prospect of a righteous new system of things

When a person becomes well acquainted with the record of Jehovah's dealings with his servants, he comes to share the viewpoint of Joshua, who said: "You well know with all your hearts and with all your souls that not one word out of all the good words that Jehovah your God has spoken to you has failed. They have all come true for you. Not one word of them has failed."—Josh. 23:14.

The Bible's promises of renewed health, resurrection from the dead, and so forth, are fortified by the record of miracles performed by Jesus Christ. These are not fables. Read the Gospel accounts and see the evidence that they bear all the marks of historical authenticity. Geographical locations are named; the names of contemporary secular rulers are given; more than one eyewitness account has been preserved. Meditating on this evidence can strengthen your faith in the Bible's promises.

Go to the Kingdom Halls of Jehovah's Witnesses and to their general conventions, and you can then see for yourself evidence that application of Bible counsel transforms lives, that it can make people honest and morally upright, that it can enable people of all races and nationalities to live and work together in a spirit of genuine brotherhood.

Are works really necessary if a person has faith?

Jas. 2:17, 18, 21, 22, 26: "Faith, if it does not have works, is dead in itself. Nevertheless, a certain one will say: 'You have faith, and I have works. Show me your faith apart from the works, and I shall show you my faith by my works.' Was not Abraham our father declared righteous by works after he had offered up Isaac his son upon the altar? You behold that his faith worked along with his works and by his works his faith was perfected. Indeed, as the body without spirit is dead, so also faith without works is dead."

Illustration: A young man may court a young lady, telling her that he loves her. But if he never asks her to marry him, is he really demonstrating that his love is thorough? Likewise, works are a means of demonstrating the genuineness of our faith and our love. If we do not obey God we do not really love him or have faith in the rightness of his ways. (1 John 5:3, 4) But we cannot *earn* salvation no matter what works we do. Eternal life is a *gift* from God through Jesus Christ, not payment for our works.—Eph. 2:8, 9.

False Prophets

Definition: Individuals and organizations proclaiming messages that they attribute to a superhuman source but that do not originate with the true God and are not in harmony with his revealed will.

How can true prophets and false ones be identified?

True prophets make known their faith in Jesus, but more is required than claiming to preach in his name

1 John 4:1-3: "Test the inspired expressions to see wheth-

er they originate with God, because many false prophets have gone forth into the world. You gain the knowledge of the inspired expression from God by this: Every inspired expression that confesses Jesus Christ as having come in the flesh originates with God, but every inspired expression that does not confess Jesus does not originate with God."

Matt. 7:21-23: "Not everyone saying to me, 'Lord, Lord,' will enter into the kingdom of the heavens, but the one doing the will of my Father who is in the heavens will. Many will say to me in that day, 'Lord, Lord, did we not prophesy in your name . . . ?' And yet then I will confess to them: I never knew you! Get away from me, you workers of lawlessness."

True prophets speak in the name of God, but merely claiming to represent him is not enough

Deut. 18:18-20: "A prophet I shall raise up for them from the midst of their brothers, like you [like Moses]; and I shall indeed put my words in his mouth, and he will certainly speak to them all that I shall command him. And it must occur that the man who will not listen to my words that he will speak in my name, I shall myself require an account from him. However, the prophet who presumes to speak in my name a word that I have not commanded him to speak or who speaks in the name of other gods, that prophet must die." (Compare Jeremiah 14:14; 28:11, 15.)

Jesus said: "I do nothing of my own initiative; but just as the Father taught me I speak these things." (John 8:28) He said: "I have come in the name of my Father." (John 5:43) Jesus also said: "He that speaks of his own originality is seeking his own glory."—John 7:18.

If any individuals or organizations claim to represent God but decline to use God's personal name, and make it a practice to express their own opinions on matters, are they measuring up to this important qualification of a true prophet?

Ability to perform "great signs," or "miracles," is not necessarily proof of a true prophet

Matt. 24:24: "False Christs and false prophets will arise

and will give great signs ["miracles," *TEV*] and wonders so as to mislead, if possible, even the chosen ones."

2 Thess. 2:9, 10: "The lawless one's presence is according to the operation of Satan with every powerful work and lying signs and portents and with every unrighteous deception for those who are perishing, as a retribution because they did not accept the love of the truth that they might be saved."

On the other hand, Moses performed miracles at Jehovah's direction. (Ex. 4:1-9) Jehovah also empowered Jesus to perform miracles. (Acts 2:22) But more than the miracles gave evidence that God had truly sent them.

What true prophets foretell comes to pass, but they may not understand just when or how it will be

Dan. 12:9: "Go, Daniel, because the words are made secret and sealed up until the time of the end."

1 Pet. 1:10, 11: "The prophets . . . kept on investigating what particular season or what sort of season the spirit in them was indicating concerning Christ when it was bearing witness beforehand about the sufferings for Christ and about the glories to follow these."

1 Cor. 13:9, 10: "We have partial knowledge and we prophesy partially; but when that which is complete arrives, that which is partial will be done away with."

Prov. 4:18: "The path of the righteous ones is like the bright light that is getting lighter and lighter until the day is firmly established."

The apostles and other early Christian disciples had certain wrong expectations, but the Bible does not classify them with the "false prophets."—See Luke 19:11; John 21:22, 23; Acts 1:6, 7.

Nathan the prophet encouraged King David to go ahead with what was in his heart regarding the building of a house for Jehovah's worship. But later Jehovah told Nathan to inform David that he was not the one who would build it. Jehovah did not reject Nathan for what he had said earlier but continued to use him because he humbly corrected the matter when Jehovah made it plain to him.—1 Chron. 17: 1-4, 15.

The pronouncements of a true prophet promote true worship and are in harmony with God's revealed will

Deut. 13:1-4: "In case a prophet or a dreamer of a dream arises in your midst and does give you a sign or a portent, and the sign or the portent does come true of which he spoke to you, saying, 'Let us walk after other gods, whom you have not known, and let us serve them,' you must not listen to the words of that prophet or to the dreamer of that dream, because Jehovah your God is testing you to know whether you are loving Jehovah your God with all your heart and all your soul. After Jehovah your God you should walk, and him you should fear, and his commandments you should keep, and to his voice you should listen, and him you should serve, and to him you should cling."

Since the Bible says that "a friend of the world" is an enemy of God, are clergymen who urge their parishioners to get involved in the affairs of the world promoting true worship? (Jas. 4:4; 1 John 2:15-17) The true God said that the nations "will have to know that I am Jehovah," and the Bible states that God would take out of the nations "a people for his name," but are religious organizations that minimize the importance of using God's personal name acting in harmony with this revealed will of God? (Ezek. 38:23; Acts 15:14) Jesus taught his followers to pray for God's Kingdom, and the Bible cautions against putting one's trust in earthling men, so are clergymen or political organizations that urge people to place their confidence in human rulership true prophets?—Matt. 6:9, 10; Ps. 146:3-6; compare Revelation 16:13, 14.

True prophets and the false can be recognized by the fruitage manifest in their lives and the lives of those who follow them

Matt. 7:15-20: "Be on the watch for the false prophets that come to you in sheep's covering, but inside they are ravenous wolves. By their fruits you will recognize them. . . . Every good tree produces fine fruit, but every rotten tree produces worthless fruit . . . Really, then, by their fruits you will recognize those men."

What characterizes their way of life? "The works of the flesh are . . . fornication, uncleanness, loose conduct, idolatry, practice of spiritism, enmities, strife, jealousy, fits of anger, contentions, divisions, sects, envies, drunken bouts, revelries, and things like these. . . . Those who practice such things will not inherit God's kingdom. On the other hand, the fruitage of [God's] spirit is love, joy, peace, long-suffering, kindness, goodness, faith, mildness, self-control."—Gal. 5: 19-23; see also 2 Peter 2:1-3.

Have not Jehovah's Witnesses made errors in their teachings?

Jehovah's Witnesses do not claim to be inspired prophets. They have made mistakes. Like the apostles of Jesus Christ, they have at times had some wrong expectations.—Luke 19:11; Acts 1:6.

The Scriptures provide time elements related to Christ's presence, and Jehovah's Witnesses have studied these with keen interest. (Luke 21:24; Dan. 4:10-17) Jesus also described a many-featured sign that would tie in with the fulfillment of time prophecies to identify the generation that would live to see the end of Satan's wicked system of things. (Luke 21:7-36) Jehovah's Witnesses have pointed to evidence in fulfillment of this sign. It is true that the Witnesses have made mistakes in their understanding of what would occur at the end of certain time periods, but they have not made the mistake of losing faith or ceasing to be watchful as to fulfillment of Jehovah's purposes. They have continued to keep to the fore in their thinking the counsel given by Jesus: "Keep on the watch, therefore, because you do not know on what day your Lord is coming."—Matt. 24:42.

Matters on which corrections of viewpoint have been needed have been relatively minor when compared with the vital Bible truths that they have discerned and publicized. Among these are the following: Jehovah is the only true God. Jesus Christ is not part of a Trinitarian godhead but is the only-begotten Son of God. Redemption from sin is possible only through faith in Christ's ransom sacrifice. The holy spirit is not a person but is Jehovah's active force, and its fruitage must be evident in the lives of true worshipers. The human soul is not immortal, as the ancient pagans claimed; it dies, and the hope for future life is in the resurrection. God's permission of wickedness has been because of the issue of universal sovereignty. God's Kingdom is the only hope for mankind. Since 1914 we have been living in the last days of the global wicked system of things. Only 144,000 faithful Christians will be kings and priests with Christ in heaven, whereas the rest of obedient mankind will receive eternal life on a paradise earth.

Another factor to consider regarding the teachings of Jehovah's Witnesses is this: Have these truly uplifted people morally? Are those who adhere to these teachings outstanding in their communities because of their honesty? Is their family life beneficially influenced by applying these teachings? Jesus said that his disciples would be readily identified because of having love among themselves. (John 13:35) Is this quality outstanding among Jehovah's Witnesses? We let the facts speak for themselves.

If Someone Says—

'My minister said that Jehovah's Witnesses are the false prophets'

You might reply: 'May I ask, Did he show you anything in the Bible that describes what we believe or do and that says people of that sort would be false prophets? . . . May I show you how the Bible describes false prophets? (Then use one or more of the points outlined on pages 132-136.)'

Or you could say: 'I'm sure you'll agree that specific evidence should back up such a serious charge. Did your minister mention any specific examples? (If householder refers to some claimed "predictions" that did not come to pass, use material on page 134, and from the bottom of page 135 to the top of 137.)'

Another possibility: 'I'm sure that if someone accused you of something similar, you would welcome the opportunity at least to explain your position or point of view, wouldn't you? . . . So may I show you from the Bible . . . ?'

Fate

Definition: An inevitable and often adverse outcome. Fatalism is the belief that all events are determined by the divine will or by some force greater than man, that every event must take place as it does because it has been predetermined. *Not a Bible word or teaching*.

Does everyone have a predetermined "time to die"?

This belief was popular among the Greeks and Romans. According to pagan Greek mythology, the Fates were three goddesses that spun the thread of life, determined its length, and cut it.

Ecclesiastes 3:1, 2 speaks of "a time to die." But, showing that this is not a predetermined fixed moment for the individual, Ecclesiastes 7:17 counsels: "Do not be wicked overmuch, nor become foolish. Why should *you die when it is not your time?*" Proverbs 10:27 says: "The years themselves of the wicked ones will be cut short." And Psalm 55:23 adds: "As for bloodguilty and deceitful men, they will not live out half their days." What, then, does Ecclesiastes 3:1, 2 mean? It is simply discussing the continuous cycle of life and death in this imperfect system of things. There is a time when people are born and a time when they die—usually at not more than 70 or 80 years of age, but sometimes sooner and sometimes later.—Ps. 90:10; see also Ecclesiastes 9:11.

If each one's moment and manner of death were already fixed at the time of birth or earlier, there would be no need to avoid dangerous situations or to care for one's health, and safety precautions would not alter mortality rates. But do you believe that a battlefield during war is as safe as one's home far away from the war zone? Do you care for your health or take your children to the doctor? Why do smokers die three to four years younger, on an average, than nonsmokers? Why are there fewer fatal accidents when automobile passengers wear seat belts and when drivers obey traffic laws? Obviously, taking precautions is beneficial.

Is everything that happens "the will of God"?

2 Pet. 3:9: "Jehovah . . . is patient with you because he does not desire any to be destroyed but desires all to attain to repentance." (But not all respond to his patience. Clearly, it is not "the will of God" when some fail to repent. Compare Revelation 9:20, 21.)

Jer. 7:23-26: "This word I did express in command upon them [Israel], saying: 'Obey my voice, and I will become your God, and you yourselves will become my people; and you must walk in all the way that I shall command you, in order that it may go well with you.' But they did not listen . . . I kept sending to you all my servants the prophets, daily getting up early and sending them. But they did not listen to me, and they did not incline their ear, but they kept hardening their neck." (Obviously, the badness taking place in Israel was not "the will of God.")

Mark 3:35: "Whoever does the will of God, this one is my brother and sister and mother." (If whatever anyone did was "the will of God," then everyone would have enjoyed the kind of relationship with Jesus that he there described. But he said to some: "You are from your father the Devil."—John 8:44.)

What accounts for many seemingly unexplainable things that occur?

Eccl. 9:11: "Time and unforeseen occurrence ["chance," *NE, RS*] befall them all." (Thus, not due to any foreseeing of a person's life, but due to chance he may become a victim of unfortunate circumstances.)

Do humans bear responsibility for much of the hardship suffered by themselves and others of humankind?

Rom. 5:12: "Through one man [Adam] sin entered into the world and death through sin, and thus death spread to all men because they had all sinned." (Imperfections, including inclinations toward wrongdoing, are inherited from Adam by all of us.)

Eccl. 8:9: "Man has dominated man to his injury."

Prov. 13:1: "A son is wise where there is a father's

discipline." (What parents do has a great influence on the lives of their offspring.)

Gal. 6:7: "Do not be misled: God is not one to be mocked. For whatever a man is sowing, this he will also reap." (Also Proverbs 11:17; 23:29, 30; 29:15; 1 Corinthians 6:18)

Are there superhuman forces that also cause woe to mankind?

Rev. 12:12: "Woe for the earth and for the sea, because the Devil has come down to you, having great anger, knowing he has a short period of time." (Also Acts 10:38)

Does God foreknow and foreordain everything?

Isa. 46:9, 10: "I am the Divine One and there is no other God, nor anyone like me; the One telling from the beginning the finale, and from long ago the things that have not been done; the One saying, 'My own counsel will stand, and everything that is my delight I shall do.'" (He makes known his purpose, foreordains certain matters in connection with its accomplishment, and has the almighty power to assure that these will be fulfilled.)

Isa. 11:1-3: "There must go forth a twig out of the stump of Jesse; and out of his roots a sprout will be fruitful. [Jesus was born in the line of Jesse.] And upon him the spirit of Jehovah must settle down, . . . and there will be enjoyment by him in the fear of Jehovah." (Jehovah could confidently foretell this regarding his Son because He had observed his attitude and conduct in the heavens since the beginning of creation.) (Regarding Jesus' prehuman existence, see pages 216, 217, under the heading "Jesus Christ.")

Deut. 31:20, 21: "I shall bring them [the nation of Israel] to the ground that I have sworn about to their forefathers, which flows with milk and honey, and they will certainly eat and be satisfied and grow fat and turn to other gods, and they will indeed serve them and treat me with disrespect and break my covenant. And it must occur that when many calamities and distresses will come upon them, this song [recounting how they acted because of failing to appreciate

God's favor] must also answer before them as a witness, . . . for I well know their inclination that they are developing today before I bring them into the land about which I have sworn." (Note that God's ability to discern the outcome of their course did not mean that he was responsible for it or that it was what he wanted for them, but on the basis of what they were doing he could foresee the outcome. Similarly, on the basis of what is observed, a weather forecaster may predict the weather with a great degree of accuracy, but he does not cause it or necessarily like it.)

Does God's ability to foreknow and foreordain events prove that he does this regarding all the actions of all his creatures?

Rev. 22:17: "Let anyone hearing say: 'Come!' And let anyone thirsting come; *let anyone that wishes* take life's water free." (The choice is not foreordained; it is left to the individual.)

Rom. 2:4, 5: "Do you despise the riches of his kindness and forbearance and long-suffering, because you do not know that the kindly quality of God is trying to lead you to repentance? But according to your hardness and unrepentant heart you are storing up wrath for yourself on the day of wrath and of the revealing of God's righteous judgment." (There is no forcing of individuals to pursue a prescribed course. But there is accountability for what one does.)

Zeph. 2:3: "Seek Jehovah, all you meek ones of the earth . . . Seek righteousness, seek meekness. Probably you may be concealed in the day of Jehovah's anger." (Would a just and loving God encourage people to do what is right, in hope of a reward, if he knew that they were foreordained not to succeed?)

Illustration: The owner of a radio can listen to the world news. But the fact that he *can* listen to a certain station does not mean that he *does*. He must first turn on the radio and then select the station. Likewise, Jehovah has the ability to foreknow events, but the Bible shows that he makes *selective* and *discretionary* use of that ability, with due regard for the free will with which he has endowed his human creation.—Compare Genesis 22:12; 18:20, 21.

When God created Adam, did he know that Adam would sin?

Here is what God set before Adam and Eve: "Be fruitful and become many and fill the earth and subdue it, and have in subjection the fish of the sea and the flying creatures of the heavens and every living creature that is moving upon the earth." "And Jehovah God also laid this command upon the man: 'From every tree of the garden you may eat to satisfaction. But as for the tree of the knowledge of good and bad you must not eat from it, for in the day you eat from it you will positively die.'" (Gen. 1:28; 2:16, 17) Would you encourage your children to undertake a project with a marvelous future, knowing from the start that it was doomed to failure? Would you warn them of harm, while knowing that you had planned everything so that they were sure to come to grief? Is it reasonable, then, to attribute such to God?

Matt. 7:11: "If you, although being wicked [or, "bad as you are," *NE*], know how to give good gifts to your children, how much more so will your Father who is in the heavens give good things to those asking him?"

If God foreordained and foreknew Adam's sin and all that would result from this, it would mean that by creating Adam, God deliberately set in motion all the wickedness committed in human history. He would be the Source of all the wars, the crime, the immorality, the oppression, the lying, the hypocrisy, the disease. But the Bible clearly says: "You are not a God taking delight in wickedness." (Ps. 5:4) "Anyone loving violence His soul certainly hates." (Ps. 11:5) "God . . . cannot lie." (Titus 1:2) "From oppression and from violence he [the One designated by God as Messianic King] will redeem their soul, and their blood will be precious in his eyes." (Ps. 72:14) "God is love." (1 John 4:8) "He is a lover of righteousness and justice."—Ps. 33:5.

Did God predestinate Jacob and Esau?

Gen. 25:23: "Jehovah proceeded to say to her [Rebekah]: 'Two nations are in your belly, and two national groups will be separated from your inward parts; and the one national group will be stronger than the other national group, and the older [Esau] will serve the younger [Jacob].'" (Jehovah was able to read the genetic pattern of the unborn twins. He may have considered this when foreseeing the qualities that each of the boys would develop and foretelling the outcome. [Ps. 139:16] But there is no indication here that he fixed their *eternal destinies* or that he predetermined how *each event* in their lives would turn out.)

Was Judas Iscariot predestined to betray Jesus?

Ps. 41:9: "The man at peace with me, in whom I trusted, who was eating my bread, has magnified his heel against me." (Notice that the prophecy does not specify *which* close associate of Jesus it would be. Jehovah knew that the Devil had used David's counselor Ahithophel to betray him, and He had that recorded because it demonstrated how the Devil operated and what he would do in the future. It was not God but "the Devil . . . [who] put it into the heart of Judas Iscariot, the son of Simon, to betray him [Jesus]." [John 13:2] Instead of resisting, Judas yielded to that satanic influence.)

John 6:64: "From the beginning Jesus knew . . . who was the one that would betray him." (Not from the beginning of creation, nor from the time of Judas' birth, but "from the beginning" of his acting treacherously. Compare Genesis 1: 1, Luke 1:2, and 1 John 2:7, 13, in each of which texts "beginning" is used in a relative sense. Take note also of John 12:4-6.)

Does not the apostle Paul speak of Christians as being "predestinated"?

Rom. 8:28, 29: "We know that God makes all his works cooperate together for the good of those who love God, those who are the ones called according to his purpose; because those whom he gave his first recognition he also fore-ordained ["predestinated," *KJ*] to be patterned after the image of his Son, that he might be the firstborn among many brothers." (Also Eph. 1:5, 11) Yet, to these same ones, 2 Peter 1:10 says: "Do your utmost to make the calling and choosing of you sure for yourselves; for *if you keep on doing these things* you will by no means ever fail." (If the individuals were predestinated to salvation, they could not possibly fail, regardless of what they did. Since effort is required on the part of the individuals, it must be the *class* that is foreordained. God purposed that the entire class would conform to the pattern set by Jesus Christ. Those selected by God to be part of that class, however, must prove faithful if they are actually to attain the reward set before them.)

Eph. 1:4, 5: "He chose us in union with him [Jesus Christ] *before the founding of the world,* that we should be holy and without blemish before him in love. For he foreordained us to the adoption through Jesus Christ as sons to himself, according to the good pleasure of his will." (It is noteworthy that, at Luke 11:50, 51, Jesus parallels "the founding of the world" with the time of Abel. Abel is the first human who continued to have God's favor throughout his life. Thus, it was after the rebellion in Eden but before the conception of Abel that God formed his purpose to produce a "seed" through which deliverance would be provided. [Gen. 3:15] God purposed that associated with the principal Seed, Jesus Christ, would be a group of his faithful followers who would share with him in a new government over the earth, the Messianic Kingdom.)

Do the stars and the planets influence events in our lives or provide omens that we should weigh when making decisions?

What is the origin of astrology?

"Western astrology can be traced directly to the theories and practices of the Chaldeans and Babylonians of the 2000's B.C."—*The Encyclopedia Americana* (1977), Vol. 2, p. 557.

"Astrology was based upon two Babylonic ideas: the zodiac, and the divinity of the heavenly bodies. . . . The Babylonians credited the planets with the influences that one would expect of their respective deities."—*Great Cities of the Ancient World* (New York, 1972), L. Sprague de Camp, p. 150.

"In Babylonia as well as in Assyria as a direct offshoot of Babylonian culture . . . astrology takes its place in the official cult as one of the two chief means at the disposal of the priests . . . for ascertaining the will and intention of the gods, the other being through the inspection of the liver of the sacrificial animal. . . . The movements of the sun, moon and five planets were regarded as representing the activity of the five gods in question, together with the moon-god Sin and the sun-god Shamash, in preparing the occurrences on earth."—*Encyclopœdia Britannica* (1911), Vol. II, p. 796.

What is the viewpoint of mankind's Creator toward this practice?

Deut. 18:10-12: "There should not be found in you anyone who . . . employs divination, a practicer of magic or anyone who looks for omens . . . For everybody doing these things is something detestable to Jehovah."

To the Babylonians he said: "Let your astrologers, your star-gazers who foretell your future month by month, persist, and save you! But look, they are gone like chaff . . . So much for your magicians with whom you have trafficked all your life: they have stumbled off, each his own way, and there is no one to save you."—Isa. 47:13-15, *NE*.

God

Definition: The Supreme Being, whose distinctive name is Jehovah. The Hebrew language uses terms for "God" that convey the idea of strength, also of majesty, dignity, and excellence. In contrast to the true God, there are false gods. Some of these have set themselves up as gods; others have been made objects of worship by those who serve them.

Are there sound reasons for believing in God?

Ps. 19:1: "The heavens are declaring the glory of God; and of the work of his hands the expanse is telling."

Ps. 104:24: "How many your works are, O Jehovah! All of them in wisdom you have made. The earth is full of your productions."

Rom. 1:20: "His invisible qualities are clearly seen from

the world's creation onward, because they are perceived by the things made."

New Scientist magazine said: "The lay view persists—of scientists having 'disproved' religion. It is a view that commonly expects scientists to be nonbelievers; that Darwin put the last nails in God's coffin; and that a succession of scientific and technological innovations since have ruled out the possibility of any resurrection. It is a view that is wildly wrong."—May 26, 1977, p. 478.

A member of the French Academy of Sciences stated: "Natural order was not invented by the human mind or set up by certain perceptive powers. . . . The existence of order presupposes the existence of organizing intelligence. Such intelligence can be none other than God's."—*Dieu existe? Oui* (Paris, 1979), Christian Chabanis, quoting Pierre-Paul Grassé, p. 94.

Scientists have identified over 100 chemical elements. Their atomic structure displays an intricate mathematical interrelationship of the elements. The periodic table points to obvious design. Such amazing design could not possibly be accidental, a product of chance.

Illustration: When we see a camera, a radio, or a computer, we readily acknowledge that it must have been produced by an intelligent designer. Would it be reasonable, then, to say that far more complex things—the eye, the ear, and the human brain—did not originate with an intelligent Designer?

See also pages 84-86, under the heading "Creation."

Does the existence of wickedness and of suffering prove that there is no God?

Consider examples: Does the fact that knives have been used to murder prove that no one designed them? Is the use of jet aircraft to drop bombs in time of war evidence that they had no designer? Or is it rather the use to which these are being put that is causing grief to mankind?

Is it not true that much disease is a result of man's own poor living habits and his spoiling of the environment for himself and others? Are not the wars fought by humans a major cause of human suffering? Is it not also true that, while millions suffer from lack of food, there is more than enough in other lands, so that one of the underlying problems is human greed? All these things give evidence, not that there is no God, but that humans are sadly misusing their God-given abilities and the earth itself.

Does God really care what happens to us humans?

Yes, indeed! Consider the evidence: The Bible tells us that God gave man a perfect start. (Gen. 1:27, 31; Deut. 32:4) Man's continued enjoyment of God's favor, however, depended on obedience to his Maker. (Gen. 2:16, 17) If man was obedient, he would continue to enjoy perfect human life—no sickness, no suffering, no death. The Creator would provide man with needed guidance and would use His power to safeguard mankind against any calamity. But man rejected God's guidance; he chose the course of self-rule. In trying to do something for which he was never designed, he has brought calamity upon himself. (Jer. 10:23; Eccl. 8:9; Rom. 5:12) Yet, over the centuries God has been patiently seeking out those who, because of love for him and his ways, are willing to serve him. He sets before them the opportunity to enjoy all the blessings of which they have been deprived because of man's imperfections and misrule. (Rev. 21:3-5) The provision God made by means of his Son to redeem humans from sin and death is a marvelous evidence of God's great love for mankind. (John 3:16) God has also set an appointed time when he will destroy those who ruin the earth and will cause lovers of righteousness to enjoy life in harmony with his own original purpose.—Rev. 11:18; Ps. 37:10, 11; see also the main headings "Suffering" and "Wickedness."

Is God a real person?

Heb. 9:24: "Christ entered . . . into heaven itself, now to appear before *the person* of God for us."

John 4:24: "God is a Spirit."

John 7:28: "He that sent me is real," said Jesus.

1 Cor. 15:44: "If there is a physical body, there is also a spiritual one."

Does God have feelings of the sort that we associate with living people?

John 16:27: "The Father himself has affection for you, because you have had affection for me and have believed that I came out as the Father's representative."

Isa. 63:9: "During all their distress it was distressing to him. . . . In his love and in his compassion he himself repurchased them."

1 Tim. 1:11: "The happy God."

Did God have a beginning?

Ps. 90:2: "Before the mountains themselves were born, or you proceeded to bring forth as with labor pains the earth and the productive land, even from time indefinite to time indefinite you are God."

Is that reasonable? Our minds cannot fully comprehend it. But that is not a sound reason for rejecting it. *Consider examples:* (1) *Time.* No one can point to a certain moment as the beginning of time. And it is a fact that, even though our lives end, time does not. We do not reject the idea of time because there are aspects of it that we do not fully comprehend. Rather, we regulate our lives by it. (2) *Space.* Astronomers find no beginning or end to space. The farther they probe into the universe, the more there is. They do not reject what the evidence shows; many refer to space as being infinite. The same principle applies to the existence of God.

Other examples: (1) Astronomers tell us that the *heat of the sun* at its core is 27,000,000 degrees Fahrenheit (15,000,-000° C.). Do we reject that idea because we cannot fully comprehend such intense heat? (2) They tell us that the *size of our Milky Way* is so great that a beam of light traveling at over 186,000 miles per second (300,000 km/sec) would require 100,000 years to cross it. Do our minds really comprehend such a distance? Yet we accept it because scientific evidence supports it.

Which is more reasonable—that the universe is the product of a living, intelligent Creator? or that it must have arisen simply by chance from a nonliving source without intelligent direction? Some persons adopt the latter viewpoint because to believe otherwise would mean that they would have to acknowledge the existence of a Creator whose qualities they cannot fully comprehend. But it is well known that scientists do not fully comprehend the functioning of the genes that are within living cells and that determine how these cells will grow. Nor do they fully understand the functioning of the human brain. Yet, who would deny that these exist? Should we really expect to understand everything about a Person who is so great that he could bring into existence the universe, with all its intricate design and stupendous size?

Is it important to use God's name?

Rom. 10:13: "Everyone who calls on the name of Jehovah will be saved."

Ezek. 39:6: "People will have to know that I am Jehovah."

Jesus said to his Father: "I have made your name known to them [his true followers] and will make it known."—John 17:26.

See also pages 196, 197, under "Jehovah."

Is it important which God we serve, as long as we have some religion?

1 Cor. 10:20: "The things which the nations sacrifice they sacrifice to demons, and not to God."

2 Cor. 4:4: "The god of this system of things has blinded the minds of the unbelievers, that the illumination of the glorious good news about the Christ, who is the image of God, might not shine through." (Here the Devil is referred to as a "god." See 1 John 5:19; Revelation 12:9.)

Matt. 7:22, 23: "Many will say to me [Jesus Christ] in that day, 'Lord, Lord, did we not prophesy in your name, and expel demons in your name, and perform many powerful works in your name?' And yet then I will confess to them: I never knew you! Get away from me, you workers of lawlessness." (Even professing to be a Christian is not a guarantee that we are acceptably serving the true God.)

See also pages 322, 323, under the heading "Religion."

If Jehovah is "the only true God," what kind of "God" is Jesus?

Jesus himself referred to his Father as "the only true God." (John 17:3) Jehovah himself said: "Besides me there is no God." (Isa. 44:6) The apostle Paul wrote that, to true Christians, "there is . . . one God the Father." (1 Cor. 8:5, 6) So Jehovah is unique; no one else shares his position. Jehovah stands in utter contrast to all such objects of worship as idols, deified humans, and Satan. All these are false gods.

Jesus is spoken of in the Scriptures as "a god," even as "Mighty God." (John 1:1; Isa. 9:6) But nowhere is he spoken of as being Almighty, as Jehovah is. (Gen. 17:1) Jesus is said to be "the reflection of [God's] glory," but the Father is the Source of that glory. (Heb. 1:3) Jesus in no way seeks the position of his Father. He said: "It is Jehovah your God you must worship, and it is to him alone you must render sacred service." (Luke 4:8) He exists "in God's form," and the Father has commanded that "in the name of Jesus every knee should bend," but this is all done "to the glory of God the Father."—Phil. 2:5-11; see also pages 212-216.

If Someone Says—

'I don't believe in God'

You might reply: 'Have you always felt that way? . . . Before you came to that conclusion, did you examine some body of evidence that you found to be persuasive?' **Then perhaps add:** 'This is a subject that greatly interests me and I have given it considerable thought. Some points that I found to be very helpful were these: . . . (On page 145, see the subheading "Are there sound reasons for believing in God?" also see pages 84-86, under "Creation.")'

Or you could say: 'Do you mean that you do not believe that there is a Creator, or is it that you have seen so much hypocrisy in the churches that you have no faith in what they teach?' If it is the latter, **you might add:** 'There is a great difference between the churches of Christendom and true Christianity. It is true that Christendom has oppressed people, but Christianity has not. Christendom has waged war, but Christianity has not. Christendom has failed to provide proper moral direction, but Christianity has not. God's Word, the Bible, does not support Christendom. On the contrary, it condemns Christendom.'

Another possibility: 'I have had interesting conversations with others who felt as you do. Some of them said that they just could not reconcile belief in God with all the suffering and wickedness in the world. Is that how you feel? (If so, use some of the material on pages 146, 147, under the subheading "Does the existence of wickedness and of suffering prove that there is no God?")'

'I believe only what I can see, and I have never seen God'

You might reply: 'That view is quite common nowadays. And there is a reason for it. We live in a society that emphasizes material possessions. But you are a person who likes to be realistic, aren't you?' **Then perhaps add:** (1) 'Are there some things that we cannot see with our eyes but that we believe exist because there are sound reasons to do so? What about the *air* we breathe? We may feel it when there is a breeze. We can tell that it fills our lungs, even though we do not see it. Because we see the effects, there is good reason to believe in it, isn't that so?' (2) 'And we cannot see *gravity*. But when we drop something we see evidence that gravity is at work. Nor do we see *odors,* but our nose picks them up. We cannot see *sound waves,* but our ears detect them. So we believe in things we cannot see—provided there is good reason to do so, isn't that right?' (3) 'Well, is there evidence that an invisible God really exists? (Use material on pages 145, 146, under the subheading "Are there sound reasons for believing in God?")'

'I have my own concept of God'

You might reply: 'I'm glad to hear that you are a person who has given this matter some thought and that you believe in God. May I ask, What is your concept of God?' **Then perhaps add:** 'I am sure you appreciate that it is important to make certain that whatever we believe is in harmony with what God himself says. May I share with you just one thought from the Bible on this matter? (Ps. 83:18)'

Government

Definition: The arrangement for making and administering laws. Governments are frequently classified according to the source and scope of their authority. Jehovah God is the Universal Sovereign, who confers authority on others in accord with his will and purpose. However, Satan the Devil, the foremost rebel against Jehovah's sovereignty, is "the ruler of the world" —this by God's permission for a limited period of time. The Bible depicts the global system of political rulership as a wild beast and says that "the dragon [Satan the Devil] gave to the beast its power and its throne and great authority."—John 14:30; Rev. 13:2; 1 John 5:19.

Is it possible for humans to establish a government that will really bring lasting happiness?

What does the record of human history show?

Eccl. 8:9: "Man has dominated man to his injury." (This is true even though some governments and rulers have started off with high ideals.)

"Every civilization that has ever existed has ultimately collapsed. History is a tale of efforts that failed, or aspirations that weren't realized. . . . So, as a historian, one has to live with a sense of the inevitability of tragedy."—Henry Kissinger, political scientist and professor of government, as quoted in *The New York Times,* October 13, 1974, p. 30B.

What hinders human efforts in the field of government?

Jer. 10:23: "I well know, O Jehovah, that to earthling man his way does not belong. It does not belong to man who is walking even to direct his step." (God did not authorize his human creation to chart its own path independent from God.)

Gen. 8:21: "The inclination of the heart of man is bad from his youth up." (Not only the rulers but also those ruled are all born in sin, with selfish inclinations.)

2 Tim. 3:1-4: "In the last days critical times hard to deal

with will be here. For men will be lovers of themselves, lovers of money, . . . not open to any agreement, . . . puffed up with pride." (The problems facing mankind today cannot be lastingly solved by just one nation; they require complete international cooperation. But selfish interests prevent that and also seriously hinder any real cooperation among the various organizations within nations.)

The Bible also reveals that superhuman forces are manipulating the affairs of men. "The whole world is lying in the power of the wicked one." (1 John 5:19) "We have a wrestling, not against blood and flesh, but against . . . the world rulers of this darkness, against the wicked spirit forces in the heavenly places." (Eph. 6:12) "Expressions inspired by demons . . . go forth to the kings of the entire inhabited earth, to gather them together to the war of the great day of God the Almighty."—Rev. 16:14.

How can people get lasting relief from governmental corruption and oppression?

Will putting other men in office solve the problem?

Is it not true that where there are free elections the men in power are usually voted out of office in a relatively few years? Why? A majority are not satisfied with their performance.

Ps. 146:3, 4: "Do not put your trust in nobles, nor in the son of earthling man, to whom no salvation belongs. His spirit goes out, he goes back to his ground; in that day his thoughts do perish." (So, any programs for betterment that rulers institute soon pass into the hands of others and are frequently abandoned.)

No matter who the ruler is, he will still be part of this world that lies in Satan's power.—1 John 5:19.

Is violent revolution the answer?

Even if corrupt rulers are ousted and unjust laws are discarded, the new government will be made up of imperfect humans and will still be part of the political system that the Bible clearly says is under the control of Satan.

Matt. 26:52: "Return your sword to its place, for all those who take the sword will perish by the sword." (Jesus said this to one of his apostles at a time when governmental authority was being used unjustly against the Son of God himself. For what more worthy cause could a person have fought, if that were the right thing to do?)

Prov. 24:21, 22: "My son, fear Jehovah and the king. With those who are for a change, do not intermeddle. For their disaster will arise so suddenly, that who is aware of the extinction of those who are for a change?"

What, then, is the answer to the problems of corruption and oppression?

Dan. 2:44: "The God of heaven will set up a kingdom [a government] that will never be brought to ruin. And the kingdom itself will not be passed on to any other people. It will crush and put an end to all these kingdoms, and it itself will stand to times indefinite."

Ps. 72:12-14: "He [Jehovah's appointed king, Jesus Christ] will deliver the poor one crying for help, also the afflicted one and whoever has no helper. He will feel sorry for the lowly one and the poor one, and the souls of the poor ones he will save. From oppression and from violence he will redeem their soul, and their blood will be precious in his eyes." (His concern for such people when he was on earth —his healing them, feeding multitudes, even laying down his life for them—shows that he will truly be the kind of ruler foretold in the prophecy.)

See also pages 227-232, under the heading "Kingdom."

Why should we seriously consider what the Bible says about the future of government?

Human rulers are not providing what mankind urgently needs

Consider these things that people everywhere need, that human governments are not providing but that God has promised: (1) Life in a world free from the threat of war. —Isa. 2:4; Ps. 46:9, 10. (2) Ample food for everyone.—Ps. 72:16. (3) Comfortable housing for everyone.—Isa. 65:21.

(4) Satisfying employment for all who need it, so they can provide for themselves and their families.—Isa. 65:22. (5) Life that is not marred by sickness and disease.—Rev. 21:3, 4. (6) Justice; freedom from religious, racial, economic, and national prejudice.—Isa. 9:7; 11:3-5. (7) Enjoyment of security, without danger to one's person or property from criminals.—Mic. 4:4; Prov. 2:22. (8) A world in which qualities most highly prized include love, kindness, concern for one's fellowman, and truthfulness. —Ps. 85:10, 11; Gal. 5:22, 23.

For thousands of years, political rulers have been promising their people better conditions. With what results? Although the people in many nations have more material possessions, they are not happier, and the problems confronting them are more complex than ever.

Bible prophecies have proved completely reliable

A century in advance God's Word foretold Babylon's position of world dominance, also how its power would finally be broken, and the fact that, once desolated, its capital would never again be inhabited. (Isa. 13:17-22) Nearly two centuries in advance, even before Cyrus was born, the Bible foretold him by name as well as his role in international affairs. (Isa. 44:28; 45:1, 2) Before Medo-Persia became a world power, its ascendancy, its dual nature, and how it would end were all foretold. Over two centuries in advance the course of the Grecian world empire under its first king was foretold, also the subsequent division of the empire into four parts.—Dan. 8:1-8, 20-22.

The Bible foretold in detail the world conditions of our day, and it puts us on notice that all human governments will come to their end at the hands of God and that God's Kingdom in the hands of his Son, Jesus Christ, will rule over all mankind.—Dan. 2:44; 7:13, 14.

Is it not the course of wisdom to heed a source of information that has proved to be so consistently reliable?

Government by God is the only real solution to the problems of mankind

The problems that need to be resolved require power,

abilities, and qualities that no humans possess. God can free mankind from the influence of the Devil and his demons, and He has promised to do so, but no human can. God has made provision to do what medical science could never accomplish —remove sin, thus ending sickness and death and making it possible for people to be the kind of persons that they really want to be. The Creator has the needed knowledge (of the earth and of all life processes) to solve the problems of food production and to prevent dangerous pollution, but human efforts often create more problems. God's Word is already transforming lives so that those who respond to its leading become kind, loving persons with high morals, a society of persons who refuse to take up arms against their fellowman and who live in genuine peace and brotherhood although they are from all nations, races, and language groups.

When will God's Kingdom clear out the present world system? See the main headings "Dates" and "Last Days."

Healing

Definition: Causing a person who has been physically, mentally, or spiritually sick to gain good health. Some of the pre-Christian Hebrew prophets as well as Jesus Christ and certain members of the early Christian congregation were enabled by God's spirit to perform miraculous healing.

Is miraculous healing in our day done by means of the spirit of God?

Can the ability to perform miracles come from a source other than the true God?

Moses and Aaron appeared before Pharaoh of Egypt to request that Israel be allowed to go into the wilderness to offer sacrifices to Jehovah. As evidence of divine backing, Moses directed Aaron to throw down his rod and it became a big snake. That miracle was done by God's power. But then the magic-practicing priests of Egypt threw down their rods and these, too, became big snakes. (Ex. 7:8-12) By whose power did they perform their miracle?—Compare Deuteronomy 18:10-12.

In the 20th century some faith healing is performed in services conducted by the clergy of Christendom. Among non-Christian religions there are voodoo priests, witch doctors, medicine men, and others who also do healing; they often employ magic and divination. Some "psychic healers" say that their cures have nothing to do with religion. In all these instances, does the healing power come from the true God?

Matt. 24:24: "False Christs and false prophets will arise and will give great signs ["miracles," *TEV*] and wonders so as to mislead, if possible, even the chosen ones."

Matt. 7:15-23: "Be on the watch for the false prophets ... Many will say to me in that day, 'Lord, Lord, did we not prophesy in your name, and expel demons in your name, and perform many powerful works ["miracles," *JB, NE, TEV*] in your name?' And yet then I will confess to them: I never knew you! Get away from me, you workers of lawlessness."

Are the sensational cures of our day performed in the same way as the miraculous cures of Jesus and his early disciples?

Cost of services: "Cure sick people, raise up dead persons, make lepers clean, expel demons. *You received free, give free.*" (Matt. 10:8) (Are healers today doing that—giving free, as Jesus commanded?)

Rate of success: "All the crowd were seeking to touch him [Jesus], because power was going out of him and *healing them all.*" (Luke 6:19) "They brought the sick out even into the broad ways and laid them there upon little beds and cots, in order that, as Peter would go by, at least his shadow might fall upon some one of them. Also, the multitude from the cities around Jerusalem kept coming together, bearing sick people and those troubled with unclean spirits, and *they would one and all be cured.*" (Acts 5:15, 16) (In our day, do *all* who go to religious practitioners or to religious shrines seeking a cure get healed?)

Does the way of life of members of the organiza-
tions of which "healers" are a part give evidence
that they have God's spirit?

As a group do they outstandingly manifest such fruits of
the spirit as love, long-suffering, mildness, and self-control?
—Gal. 5:22, 23.

Are they truly "no part of the world," shunning all involvement in the world's political affairs? Have they remained clean of bloodguilt during wartime? Do they have a
fine reputation because of avoiding the world's immoral
conduct?—John 17:16; Isa. 2:4; 1 Thess. 4:3-8.

Are true Christians today identified by the ability to do miraculous healing?

John 13:35: "By this all will know that you are my
disciples, if you have love among yourselves." (This is what
Jesus said. If we really believe him, we look for love, not
miraculous healing, as evidence of true Christianity.)

Acts 1:8: "You will receive power when the holy spirit
arrives upon you, and you will be witnesses of me . . . to the
most distant part of the earth." (Just before leaving his
apostles to return to heaven, Jesus told them that this, not
healing, was the vital work they were to do. See also Matthew 24:14; 28:19, 20.)

1 Cor. 12:28-30: "God has set the respective ones in the
congregation, first, apostles; second, prophets; third, teachers; then powerful works; then gifts of healings; helpful
services, abilities to direct, different tongues. Not all are
apostles, are they? Not all are prophets, are they? Not all
are teachers, are they? Not all perform powerful works, do
they? Not all have gifts of healings, do they?" (So, the Bible
clearly shows that not all true Christians would have the gift
of healing.)

Does not Mark 16:17, 18 show that ability to heal
the sick would be a sign identifying believers?

Mark 16:17, 18, *KJ:* "These signs shall follow them that
believe; In my name shall they cast out devils; they shall
speak with new tongues; they shall take up serpents; and if

they drink any deadly thing, it shall not hurt them; they shall lay hands on the sick, and they shall recover."

These verses appear in certain Bible manuscripts and versions of the fifth and sixth centuries C.E. But they do not appear in the older Greek manuscripts, the Sinaiticus and Vatican MS. 1209 of the fourth century. Dr. B. F. Westcott, an authority on Bible manuscripts, said that "the verses . . . are no part of the original narrative but an appendage." (*An Introduction to the Study of the Gospels,* London, 1881, p. 338) Bible translator Jerome, in the fifth century, said that "almost all the Greek codices [are] without this passage." (*The Last Twelve Verses of the Gospel According to S. Mark,* London, 1871, J. W. Burgon, p. 53) The *New Catholic Encyclopedia* (1967) says: "Its vocabulary and style differ so radically from the rest of the Gospel that it hardly seems possible Mark himself composed it [that is, verses 9-20]." (Vol. IX, p. 240) There is no record that early Christians either drank poison or handled serpents to prove they were believers.

Why were such gifts as the ability to do miraculous healing given to first-century Christians?

Heb. 2:3, 4: "How shall we escape if we have neglected a salvation of such greatness in that it began to be spoken through our Lord and was verified for us by those who heard him, while God joined in bearing witness with signs as well as portents and various powerful works and with distributions of holy spirit according to his will?" (Here was convincing evidence, indeed, that the Christian congregation, which was then new, was truly of God. But once that was fully established, would it be necessary to prove it again and again?)

1 Cor. 12:29, 30; 13:8, 13: "Not all are prophets, are they? . . . Not all have gifts of healings, do they? Not all speak in tongues, do they? . . . Love never fails. But whether there are gifts of prophesying, they will be done away with; whether there are tongues, they will cease . . . Now, however, there remain faith, hope, love, these three; but the greatest of these is love." (When they had accomplished their purpose, those miraculous gifts would cease. But price-

less qualities that are the fruitage of God's spirit would still be manifest in the lives of true Christians.)

As long as a person is healed, is it really important how it is done?

2 Thess. 2:9, 10: "The lawless one's presence is according to the operation of Satan with every powerful work ["all kinds of miracles," *JB*] and lying signs and portents and with every unrighteous deception for those who are perishing, as a retribution because they did not accept the love of the truth that they might be saved."

Luke 9:24, 25: "Whoever wants to save his soul ["life," *RS, JB, TEV*] will lose it; but whoever loses his soul for my sake is the one that will save it. Really, what does a man benefit himself if he gains the whole world but loses his own self or suffers damage?"

What hope is there for real healing from all sickness?

Rev. 21:1-4: "I saw a new heaven and a new earth; for the former heaven and the former earth had passed away . . . 'And he [God] will wipe out every tear from their eyes, and death will be no more, neither will mourning nor outcry nor pain be anymore. The former things have passed away.'"

Isa. 25:8: "He will actually swallow up death forever, and the Sovereign Lord Jehovah will certainly wipe the tears from all faces." (Also Revelation 22:1, 2)

Isa. 33:24: "No resident will say: 'I am sick.'"

If Someone Says—

'Do you believe in healing?'

You might reply: 'Anyone who doesn't believe that God has the power to heal doesn't believe the Bible. But I can't help but wonder whether people are going about it in the right way today.' **Then perhaps add:** (1) 'Let me read you a scripture, and see if you notice a practice that is very different in our day. (Matt. 10:7, 8) . . . Do you also notice something here that Jesus said his disciples could do but that healers today have not been able to do? (They cannot raise the dead.)' (2) 'We are not the judges of other people, but it is noteworthy that Matthew 24:24 mentions something that we need to be on guard against.'

Or you could say: 'I certainly do believe that what the Bible says about healing is true. But any healing done in this system of things brings only temporary benefits, doesn't it? Eventually we all die. Will there ever be a time when everyone living will enjoy good health and never have to die? (Rev. 21:3, 4)'

Heaven

Definition: The dwelling place of Jehovah God and of faithful spirit creatures; a realm invisible to human eyes. The Bible also uses the term "heaven(s)" in a variety of other senses; for example: to represent God himself, his organization of faithful spirit creatures, a position of divine favor, the physical universe apart from the earth, the expanse surrounding planet Earth, human governments under Satan's domination, and the righteous new heavenly government in which Jesus Christ with his joint heirs are empowered by Jehovah to rule.

Did we all exist in the spirit realm before our birth as humans?

John 8:23: "[Jesus Christ said:] 'You are from the realms below; I am from the realms above. You are from this world; I am not from this world.'" (Jesus did come from the spirit realm. But, as Jesus said, other men did not.)

Rom. 9:10-12: "Rebekah conceived twins . . . When they had not yet been born nor had practiced anything good or vile, in order that the purpose of God respecting the choosing might continue dependent, not upon works, but upon the One who calls, it was said to her: 'The older will be the slave of the younger.'" (Of course, if the twins Jacob and Esau had lived previously in a spirit realm they certainly would have built up a record based on their conduct there, would they not? But they had no such record until after their birth as humans.)

Do all good people go to heaven?

Acts 2:34: "David [whom the Bible refers to as being 'a man agreeable to Jehovah's heart'] did not ascend to the heavens."

Matt. 11:11: "Truly I say to you people, Among those born of women there has not been raised up a greater than John the Baptist; but a person that is a lesser one in the kingdom of the heavens is greater than he is." (So John did not go to heaven when he died.)

Ps. 37:9, 11, 29: "Evildoers themselves will be cut off, but those hoping in Jehovah are the ones that will possess the earth . . . The meek ones themselves will possess the earth, and they will indeed find their exquisite delight in the abundance of peace. The righteous themselves will possess the earth, and they will reside forever upon it."

If Adam had not sinned, would he eventually have gone to heaven?

Gen. 1:26: "God went on to say: 'Let us make man in our image, according to our likeness, and let them have in subjection the fish of the sea and the flying creatures of the heavens and the domestic animals and all the earth and every moving animal that is moving upon the earth.'" (So, God's purpose for Adam was that he be caretaker of the earth and of the animal life there. Nothing is said about his going to heaven.)

Gen. 2:16, 17: "Jehovah God also laid this command upon the man: 'From every tree of the garden you may eat to satisfaction. But as for the tree of the knowledge of good and bad you must not eat from it, for in the day you eat from it you will positively die.'" (It was not Jehovah's original purpose for man someday to die. God's command here quoted shows that he warned against the course that would lead to death. Death was to be punishment for disobedience, not the doorway to a better life in heaven. Obedience would have been rewarded by continued life, eternal life, in the Paradise that God had given to man. See also Isaiah 45:18.)

Must a person go to heaven to have a truly happy future?

Ps. 37:11: "The meek ones themselves will possess the earth, and they will indeed find their exquisite delight in the abundance of peace."

Rev. 21:1-4: "I saw a new heaven *and a new earth* . . . I heard a loud voice from the throne say: 'Look! The tent of God is with mankind, and he will reside with them, and they will be his peoples. And God himself will be with them. And he will wipe out every tear from their eyes, and death will be no more, neither will mourning nor outcry nor pain be anymore. The former things have passed away.'"

Mic. 4:3, 4: "They will not lift up sword, nation against nation, neither will they learn war anymore. And they will actually sit, each one under his vine and under his fig tree, and there will be no one making them tremble; for the very mouth of Jehovah of armies has spoken it."

Did Jesus open the way to heaven for those who had died before his own death?

What does 1 Peter 3:19, 20 mean? "In this state [in the spirit, following his resurrection] also he [Jesus] went his way and preached to the spirits in prison, who had once been disobedient when the patience of God was waiting in Noah's days, while the ark was being constructed, in which a few people, that is, eight souls ["souls," *KJ, Dy;* "people," *TEV, JB;* "persons," *RS*], were carried safely through the water." (Were those "spirits in prison" the souls of the humans who had refused to take heed to Noah's preaching before the Flood, and was the way now open for them to go to heaven? Comparison of 2 Peter 2:4 and Jude 6 with Genesis 6:2-4 shows that these spirits were angelic sons of God that had materialized and married in Noah's day. At 1 Peter 3:19, 20 the Greek word for "spirits" is *pneu'ma·sin,* while the word rendered "souls" is *psy·khai'.* The "spirits" were not disembodied souls but disobedient angels; the "souls" here referred to were living people, humans, Noah and his household. What was preached to "spirits in prison" must therefore have been a message of judgment.)

What is the meaning of 1 Peter 4:6? "In fact, for this

purpose the good news was declared also to the dead, that they might be judged as to the flesh from the standpoint of men but might live as to the spirit from the standpoint of God." (Were these "dead" the people who had died prior to the death of Christ? As already shown, the dead are not "the spirits in prison." Those spirits were disobedient angels. And preaching would not have benefited physically dead humans because, as Ecclesiastes 9:5 says, they "are conscious of nothing at all," and Psalm 146:4 adds that at death a person's "thoughts do perish." But Ephesians 2:1-7, 17 does refer to persons who were spiritually dead and who came to life spiritually as a result of accepting the good news.)

Is heavenly life set out in the "New Testament" as the hope for all Christians?

John 14:2, 3: "In the house of my Father there are many abodes. Otherwise, I would have told you, because I am going my way to prepare a place for you. Also, if I go my way and prepare a place for you, I am coming again and will receive you home to myself, that where I am you also may be." (Jesus here shows that his faithful apostles, to whom he was speaking, would, in time, be in his Father's "house," in heaven, with Jesus. But he does not here say how many others would also go to heaven.)

John 1:12, 13: "As many as did receive him [Jesus], to them he gave authority to become God's children, because they were exercising faith in his name; and they were born, not from blood or from a fleshly will or from man's will, but from God." (Notice that the context, in verse 11, refers to Jesus' "own people," the Jews. As many of them as did receive him when he came to them in the first century became God's children, with heavenly life in view. The verbs in the text are in the past tense, so this passage is not referring to all people who have become Christians since then.)

Rom. 8:14, 16, 17: "All who are led by God's spirit, these are God's sons. The spirit itself bears witness with our spirit that we are God's children. If, then, we are children, we are also heirs: heirs indeed of God, but joint heirs with Christ, provided we suffer together that we may also be glorified together." (At the time this was written it was true that all who were led by God's spirit were God's sons whose hope was that they would be glorified with Christ. But this had not always been true. Luke 1:15 says that John the Baptizer would be filled with holy spirit, but Matthew 11:11 makes clear that he will not share in the glory of the heavenly Kingdom. So, too, after the gathering of the heirs of the heavenly Kingdom, there would be others who would serve God as followers of his Son and yet not share in heavenly glory.)

What specific references are there in the "New Testament" to a provision for Christians to be rewarded with eternal life on earth?

Matt. 5:5: "Happy are the mild-tempered ones, since they will inherit the earth."

Matt. 6:9, 10: "Our Father in the heavens, let your name be sanctified. Let your kingdom come. Let your will take place, as in heaven, *also upon earth."* (What is God's will regarding the earth? What do Genesis 1:28 and Isaiah 45:18 indicate?)

Matt. 25:31-33, 40, 46: "When the Son of man arrives in his glory, and all the angels with him, then he will sit down on his glorious throne. And all the nations will be gathered before him, and he will separate people one from another, just as a shepherd separates the sheep from the goats. And he will put the sheep on his right hand, but the goats on his left. . . . The king will say to them [the sheep], 'Truly I say to you, To the extent that you did it to one of the least of these my brothers, you did it to me.' And [the goats] will depart into everlasting cutting-off, but the righteous ones [the sheep] into everlasting life." (Notice that these "sheep" are not the same as the King's brothers, who are "partakers of the heavenly calling." [Heb. 2:10–3:1] But these sheep-like ones would be alive during the time that Christ was on his throne and during the time when some of his "brothers" would still be experiencing hardship on earth.)

John 10:16: "I have other sheep, which are not of this fold; those also I must bring, and they will listen to my voice, and they will become one flock, one shepherd." (Who are these "other sheep"? They are followers of the Fine Shepherd, Jesus Christ, but are not in the "new covenant" sheepfold, with hope of heavenly life. Yet they do come to be closely associated with those who are in that sheepfold.)

2 Pet. 3:13: "There are new heavens *and a new earth* that we are awaiting according to his promise, and in these righteousness is to dwell." (Also Revelation 21:1-4)

Rev. 7:9, 10: "After these things [after the apostle John saw the full number of "sealed" ones who had been "bought from the earth" to be with Christ on heavenly Mount Zion; see Revelation 7:3, 4; 14:1-3] I saw, and, look! a great crowd, which no man was able to number, out of all nations and tribes and peoples and tongues, standing before the throne and before the Lamb, dressed in white robes; and there were palm branches in their hands. And they keep on crying with a loud voice, saying: 'Salvation we owe to our God, who is seated on the throne, and to the Lamb.'"

To how many does the Bible hold out hope of heavenly life?

Luke 12:32: "Have no fear, *little flock,* because your Father has approved of giving you the kingdom."

Rev. 14:1-3: "I saw, and, look! the Lamb [Jesus Christ] standing upon the Mount Zion [in heaven; see Hebrews 12: 22-24], and with him a hundred and forty-four thousand having his name and the name of his Father written on their foreheads. . . . And they are singing as if a new song . . . and no one was able to master that song but the hundred and forty-four thousand, who have been *bought from the earth."*

Are the 144,000 only natural Jews?

Rev. 7:4-8: "I heard the number of those who were sealed, a hundred and forty-four thousand, sealed out of every tribe of the sons of Israel: . . . Judah . . . Reuben . . . Gad . . . Asher . . . Naphtali . . . Manasseh . . . Simeon . . . Levi . . . Issachar . . . Zebulun . . . Joseph . . . Benjamin." (These cannot be the tribes of natural Israel because there never was a tribe of Joseph, the tribes of Ephraim and Dan are not included in the list here, and the Levites were set aside for service in connection with the temple but were not reckoned as one of the 12 tribes. See Numbers 1:4-16.)

Rom. 2:28, 29: "He is not a Jew who is one on the outside, nor is circumcision that which is on the outside upon the flesh. But he is a Jew who is one on the inside, and his circumcision is that of the heart by spirit, and not by a written code."

Gal. 3:26-29: "You are all, in fact, sons of God through your faith in Christ Jesus. . . . There is neither Jew nor Greek, there is neither slave nor freeman, there is neither male nor female; for you are all one person in union with Christ Jesus. Moreover, if you belong to Christ, you are really Abraham's seed, heirs with reference to a promise."

Is the number 144,000 merely symbolic?

The answer is indicated by the fact that, after mention of the definite number 144,000, Revelation 7:9 refers to "a great crowd, which no man was able to number." If the number 144,000 were not literal it would lack meaning as a contrast to the "great crowd." Viewing the number as literal agrees with Jesus' statement at Matthew 22:14 regarding the Kingdom of the heavens: "There are many invited, but *few* chosen."

Do those of the "great crowd" referred to at Revelation 7:9, 10 also go to heaven?

Revelation does not say of them, as it does of the 144,000, that they are "bought from the earth" to be with Christ on heavenly Mount Zion.—Rev. 14:1-3.

The description of them as "standing before the throne and before the Lamb" indicates, not necessarily a location, but an approved condition. (Compare Revelation 6:17; Luke 21:36.) The expression "before the throne" (Greek, e·no'pi·on tou thro'nou; literally, "in sight of the throne") does not require that they be in heaven. Their position is simply "in sight" of God, who tells us that from heaven he beholds the sons of men.—Ps. 11:4; compare Matthew 25:31-33; Luke 1:74, 75; Acts 10:33.

The "great crowd in heaven" referred to at Revelation 19:1, 6 is not the same as the "great crowd" of Revelation 7:9. The ones in heaven are not described as being "out of all nations" or as ascribing their salvation to the Lamb; they are angels. The expression "great crowd" is used in a variety of contexts in the Bible.—Mark 5:24; 6:34; 12:37.

What will those who go to heaven do there?

Rev. 20:6: "They will be priests of God and of the Christ, and will rule as kings with him for the thousand years." (Also Daniel 7:27)

1 Cor. 6:2: "Do you not know that the holy ones will judge the world?"

Rev. 5:10: "You made them to be a kingdom and priests to our God, and they are to rule as kings over ["on," *RS, KJ, Dy;* "over," *AT, Da, Kx, CC*] the earth." (The same Greek word and grammatical structure is found at Revelation 11:6. There *RS, KJ, Dy,* etc., all render it "over.")

Who selects the ones who will go to heaven?

2 Thess. 2:13, 14: "We are obligated to thank God always for you, brothers loved by Jehovah, because *God selected* you from the beginning for salvation by sanctifying you with spirit and by your faith in the truth. To this very destiny he called you through the good news we declare, for the purpose of acquiring the glory of our Lord Jesus Christ."

Rom. 9:6, 16: "Not all who spring from Israel are really 'Israel.' . . . It depends, not upon the one wishing nor upon the one running, but upon God, who has mercy."

Hell

Definition: The word "hell" is found in many Bible translations. In the same verses other translations read "the grave," "the world of the dead," and so forth. Other Bibles simply transliterate the original-language words that are sometimes rendered "hell"; that is, they express them with the letters of our alphabet but leave the words untranslated. What are those words? The Hebrew *she'ohl'* and its Greek equivalent *hai'des,* which refer, not to an individual burial place, but to the common grave of dead mankind; also the Greek *ge'en·na,* which is used as a symbol of eternal destruction. However, both in Christendom and in many non-Christian religions it is taught that hell is a place inhabited by demons and where the wicked, after death, are punished (and some believe that this is with torment).

Does the Bible indicate whether the dead experience pain?

Eccl. 9:5, 10: "The living are conscious that they will die; but as for the dead, they are conscious of nothing at all . . . All that your hand finds to do, do with your very power, for there is no work nor devising nor knowledge nor wisdom in Sheol,* the place to which you are going." (If they are conscious of nothing, they obviously feel no pain.) (*"Sheol," *AS, RS, NE, JB;* "the grave," *KJ, Kx;* "hell," *Dy;* "the world of the dead," *TEV.*)

Ps. 146:4: "His spirit goes out, he goes back to his ground; in that day his thoughts* do perish." (*"Thoughts," *KJ,* 145:4 in *Dy;* "schemes," *JB;* "plans," *RS, TEV.*)

Does the Bible indicate that the soul survives the death of the body?

Ezek. 18:4: "The soul* that is sinning—it itself will die." (*"Soul," *KJ, Dy, RS, NE, Kx;* "the man," *JB;* "the person," *TEV.*)

"The concept of 'soul,' meaning a purely spiritual, immaterial reality, separate from the 'body,' . . . does not exist in the Bible."—*La Parole de Dieu* (Paris, 1960), Georges Auzou, professor of Sacred Scripture, Rouen Seminary, France, p. 128.

"Although the Hebrew word *nefesh* [in the Hebrew Scriptures] is frequently translated as 'soul,' it would be inaccurate to read into it a Greek meaning. *Nefesh* . . . is never conceived of as operating separately from the body. In the New Testament the Greek word *psyche* is often translated as 'soul' but again should not be readily understood to have the meaning the word had for the Greek philosophers. It

usually means 'life,' or 'vitality,' or, at times, 'the self.'"
—*The Encyclopedia Americana* (1977), Vol. 25, p. 236.

What sort of people go to the Bible hell?

Does the Bible say that the wicked go to hell?

Ps. 9:17, *KJ:* "The wicked shall be turned into hell,* and all the nations that forget God." (*"Hell," 9:18 in *Dy;* "death," *TEV;* "the place of death," *Kx;* "Sheol," *AS, RS, NE, JB, NW.*)

Does the Bible also say that upright people go to hell?

Job 14:13, *Dy:* "[Job prayed:] Who will grant me this, that thou mayst protect me in hell,* and hide me till thy wrath pass, and appoint me a time when thou wilt remember me?" (God himself said that Job was "a man blameless and upright, fearing God and turning aside from bad."—Job 1:8.) (*"The grave," *KJ;* "the world of the dead," *TEV;* "Sheol," *AS, RS, NE, JB, NW.*)

Acts 2:25-27, *KJ:* "David speaketh concerning him [Jesus Christ], . . . Because thou wilt not leave my soul in hell,* neither wilt thou suffer thine Holy One to see corruption." (The fact that God did not "leave" Jesus in hell implies that Jesus was in hell, or Hades, at least for a time, does it not?) (*"Hell," *Dy;* "death," *NE;* "the place of death," *Kx;* "the world of the dead," *TEV;* "Hades," *AS, RS, JB, NW.*)

Does anyone ever get out of the Bible hell?

Rev. 20:13, 14, *KJ:* "The sea gave up the dead which were in it; and death and hell* delivered up the dead which were in them: and they were judged every man according to their works. And death and hell were cast into the lake of fire." (So the dead will be delivered from hell. Notice also that hell is not the same as the lake of fire but will be cast into the lake of fire.) (*"Hell," *Dy, Kx;* "the world of the dead," *TEV;* "Hades," *NE, AS, RS, JB, NW.*)

Why is there confusion as to what the Bible says about hell?

"Much confusion and misunderstanding has been caused

through the early translators of the Bible persistently rendering the Hebrew Sheol and the Greek Hades and Gehenna by the word hell. The simple transliteration of these words by the translators of the revised editions of the Bible has not sufficed to appreciably clear up this confusion and misconception."—*The Encyclopedia Americana* (1942), Vol. XIV, p. 81.

Translators have allowed their personal beliefs to color their work instead of being consistent in their rendering of the original-language words. For example: (1) The *King James Version* rendered *she'ohl'* as "hell," "the grave," and "the pit"; *hai'des* is therein rendered both "hell" and "grave"; *ge'en·na* is also translated "hell." (2) *Today's English Version* transliterates *hai'des* as "Hades" and also renders it as "hell" and "the world of the dead." But besides rendering "hell" from *hai'des* it uses that same translation for *ge'en·na*. (3) *The Jerusalem Bible* transliterates *hai'des* six times, but in other passages it translates it as "hell" and as "the underworld." It also translates *ge'en·na* as "hell," as it does *hai'des* in two instances. Thus the exact meanings of the original-language words have been obscured.

Is there eternal punishment for the wicked?

Matt. 25:46, *KJ:* "These shall go away into everlasting punishment ["lopping off," *Int;* Greek, *ko'la·sin*]: but the righteous into life eternal." (*The Emphatic Diaglott* reads "cutting-off" instead of "punishment." A footnote states: *"Kolasin* . . . is derived from *kolazoo,* which signifies, 1. *To cut off;* as lopping off branches of trees, to prune. 2. *To restrain, to repress.* . . . 3. *To chastise, to punish.* To cut off an individual from life, or society, or even to restrain, is esteemed as *punishment;*—hence has arisen this *third* metaphorical use of the word. The primary signification has been adopted, because it agrees better with the second member of the sentence, thus preserving the force and beauty of the antithesis. The righteous go to *life,* the wicked to the *cutting off* from life, or *death.* See 2 Thess. 1.9.")

2 Thess. 1:9, *RS:* "They shall suffer the punishment of *eternal destruction** and exclusion from the presence of the Lord and from the glory of his might." (*"Eternal ruin,"

NAB, NE; "lost eternally," *JB;* "condemn them to eternal punishment," *Kx;* "eternal punishment in destruction," *Dy*.)

Jude 7, *KJ:* "Even as Sodom and Gomorrha, and the cities about them in like manner, giving themselves over to fornication, and going after strange flesh, are set forth for an example, suffering the vengeance of eternal fire." (The fire that destroyed Sodom and Gomorrah ceased burning thousands of years ago. But the effect of that fire has been lasting; the cities have not been rebuilt. God's judgment, however, was against not merely those cities but also their wicked inhabitants. What happened to them is a warning example. At Luke 17:29, Jesus says that they were "destroyed"; Jude 7 shows that the destruction was eternal.)

What is the meaning of the 'eternal torment' referred to in Revelation?

Rev. 14:9-11; 20:10, *KJ:* "If any man worship the beast and his image, and receive his mark in his forehead, or in his hand, the same shall drink of the wine of the wrath of God, which is poured out without mixture into the cup of his indignation; and he shall be tormented with fire and brimstone in the presence of the holy angels, and in the presence of the Lamb: and the smoke of their torment [Greek, *basa·ni·smou'*] ascendeth up for ever and ever: and they have no rest day nor night, who worship the beast and his image, and whosoever receiveth the mark of his name." "And the devil that deceived them was cast into the lake of fire and brimstone, where the beast and the false prophet are, and shall be tormented day and night for ever and ever."

What is the 'torment' to which these texts refer? It is noteworthy that at Revelation 11:10 (*KJ*) reference is made to 'prophets that torment those dwelling on the earth.' Such torment results from humiliating exposure by the messages that these prophets proclaim. At Revelation 14:9-11 (*KJ*) worshipers of the symbolic "beast and his image" are said to be "tormented with fire and brimstone." This cannot refer to conscious torment after death because "the dead know not any thing." (Eccl. 9:5, *KJ*) Then, what causes them to experience such torment while they are still alive? It is the proclamation by God's servants that worshipers of the "beast and his image" will experience second death, which is represented by "the lake which burneth with fire and brimstone." The smoke, associated with their fiery destruction, ascends forever because the destruction will be eternal and will never be forgotten. When Revelation 20:10 says that the Devil is to experience 'torment forever and ever' in "the lake of fire and brimstone," what does that mean? Revelation 21:8 (*KJ*) says clearly that "the lake which burneth with fire and brimstone" means "the second death." So the Devil's being "tormented" there forever means that there will be no relief for him; he will be held under restraint forever, actually in eternal death. This use of the word "torment" (from the Greek *ba'sa·nos*) reminds one of its use at Matthew 18:34, where the same basic Greek word is applied to a 'jailer.'—*RS, AT, ED, NW*.

What is the 'fiery Gehenna' to which Jesus referred?

Reference to Gehenna appears 12 times in the Christian Greek Scriptures. Five times it is directly associated with fire. Translators have rendered the Greek expression *ge'en·nan tou py·ros'* as "hell fire" (*KJ, Dy*), "fires of hell" (*NE*), "fiery pit" (*AT*), and "fires of Gehenna" (*NAB*).

Historical background: The Valley of Hinnom (Gehenna) was outside the walls of Jerusalem. For a time it was the site of idolatrous worship, including child sacrifice. In the first century Gehenna was being used as the incinerator for the filth of Jerusalem. Bodies of dead animals were thrown into the valley to be consumed in the fires, to which sulfur, or brimstone, was added to assist the burning. Also bodies of executed criminals, who were considered undeserving of burial in a memorial tomb, were thrown into Gehenna. Thus, at Matthew 5:29, 30, Jesus spoke of the casting of one's "whole body" into Gehenna. If the body fell into the constantly burning fire it was consumed, but if it landed on a ledge of the deep ravine its putrefying flesh became infested with the ever-present worms, or maggots. (Mark 9:47, 48) Living humans were not pitched into Gehenna; so it was not a place of conscious torment.

At Matthew 10:28, Jesus warned his hearers to "be in fear

of him that can destroy both soul and body in Gehenna." What does it mean? Notice that there is no mention here of *torment* in the fires of Gehenna; rather, he says to 'fear him that can *destroy* in Gehenna.' By referring to the "soul" separately, Jesus here emphasizes that God can destroy all of a person's life prospects; thus there is no hope of resurrection for him. So, the references to the 'fiery Gehenna' have the same meaning as 'the lake of fire' of Revelation 21: 8, namely, destruction, "second death."

What does the Bible say the penalty for sin is?

Rom. 6:23: "The wages sin pays is death."

After one's death, is he still subject to further punishment for his sins?

Rom. 6:7: "He who has died has been acquitted from his sin."

Is eternal torment of the wicked compatible with God's personality?

Jer. 7:31: "They [apostate Judeans] have built the high places of Topheth, which is in the valley of the son of Hinnom, in order to burn their sons and their daughters in the fire, a thing that I had not commanded and that had not come up into my heart." (If it never came into God's heart, surely he does not have and use such a thing on a larger scale.)

Illustration: What would you think of a parent who held his child's hand over a fire to punish the child for wrongdoing? "God is love." (1 John 4:8) Would he do what no right-minded human parent would do? Certainly not!

By what Jesus said about the rich man and Lazarus, did Jesus teach torment of the wicked after death?

Is the account, at Luke 16:19-31, literal or merely an illustration of something else? The Jerusalem Bible, in a footnote, acknowledges that it is a "parable in story form without reference to any historical personage." If taken literally, it would mean that those enjoying divine favor could all fit at the bosom of one man, Abraham; that the

water on one's fingertip would not be evaporated by the fire
of Hades; that a mere drop of water would bring relief to one
suffering there. Does that sound reasonable to you? If it
were literal, it would conflict with other parts of the Bible.
If the Bible were thus contradictory, would a lover of truth
use it as a basis for his faith? But the Bible does not
contradict itself.

What does the parable mean? The "rich man" represented
the Pharisees. (See verse 14.) The beggar Lazarus represented the common Jewish people who were despised by the
Pharisees but who repented and became followers of Jesus.
(See Luke 18:11; John 7:49; Matthew 21:31, 32.) Their
deaths were also symbolic, representing a change in circumstances. Thus, the formerly despised ones came into a position of divine favor, and the formerly seemingly favored
ones were rejected by God, while being tormented by the
judgment messages delivered by the ones whom they had
despised.—Acts 5:33; 7:54.

What is the origin of the teaching of hellfire?

In ancient Babylonian and Assyrian beliefs the "nether
world . . . is pictured as a place full of horrors, and is presided over by gods and demons of great strength and fierce-
ness." (*The Religion of Babylonia and Assyria,* Boston,
1898, Morris Jastrow, Jr., p. 581) Early evidence of the
fiery aspect of Christendom's hell is found in the religion
of ancient Egypt. (*The Book of the Dead,* New Hyde
Park, N.Y., 1960, with introduction by E. A. Wallis Budge,
pp. 144, 149, 151, 153, 161) Buddhism, which dates back to
the 6th century B.C.E., in time came to feature both hot and
cold hells. (*The Encyclopedia Americana,* 1977, Vol. 14,
p. 68) Depictions of hell portrayed in Catholic churches
in Italy have been traced to Etruscan roots.—*La civiltà
etrusca* (Milan, 1979), Werner Keller, p. 389.

But the real roots of this God-dishonoring doctrine go
much deeper. The fiendish concepts associated with a hell of
torment slander God and originate with the chief slanderer
of God (the Devil, which name means "Slanderer"), the one
whom Jesus Christ called "the father of the lie."—John 8:44.

Holidays

Definition: Days usually marked by time off from secular work and school for commemoration of an event. Such days may also be occasions for family or community festivities. Participants may view them as being religious or as being largely social or secular affairs.

Is Christmas a celebration based on the Bible?

Date of the celebration

M'Clintock and Strong's *Cyclopædia* says: "The observance of Christmas is not of divine appointment, nor is it of N[ew] T[estament] origin. The day of Christ's birth cannot be ascertained from the N[ew] T[estament], or, indeed, from any other source."—(New York, 1871), Vol. II, p. 276.

Luke 2:8-11 shows that shepherds were in the fields *at night* at the time of Jesus' birth. The book *Daily Life in the Time of Jesus* states: "The flocks . . . passed the winter under cover; and from this alone it may be seen that the traditional date for Christmas, in the winter, is unlikely to be right, since the Gospel says that the shepherds were in the fields." —(New York, 1962), Henri Daniel-Rops, p. 228.

The Encyclopedia Americana informs us: "The reason for establishing December 25 as Christmas is somewhat obscure, but it is usually held that the day was chosen to correspond to pagan festivals that took place around the time of the winter solstice, when the days begin to lengthen, to celebrate the 'rebirth of the sun.' . . . The Roman Saturnalia (a festival dedicated to Saturn, the god of agriculture, and to the renewed power of the sun), also took place at this time, and some Christmas customs are thought to be rooted in this ancient pagan celebration."—(1977), Vol. 6, p. 666.

The *New Catholic Encyclopedia* acknowledges: "The date of Christ's birth is not known. The Gospels indicate neither the day nor the month . . . According to the hypothesis suggested by H. Usener . . . and accepted by most scholars today, the birth of Christ was assigned the date of the winter solstice (December 25 in the Julian calendar, January 6 in the Egyptian), because on this day, as the sun began its return to northern skies, the pagan devotees of Mithra celebrated the *dies natalis Solis Invicti* (birthday of the invincible sun). On Dec. 25, 274, Aurelian had proclaimed the sun-god principal patron of the empire and dedicated a temple to him in the Campus Martius. Christmas originated at a time when the cult of the sun was particularly strong at Rome."—(1967), Vol. III, p. 656.

Wise men, or Magi, led by a star

Those Magi were actually astrologers from the east. (Matt. 2:1, 2, *NW; NE*) Although astrology is popular among many people today, the practice is strongly disapproved in the Bible. (See pages 144, 145, under the main heading "Fate.") Would God have led to the newborn Jesus persons whose practices He condemned?

Matthew 2:1-16 shows that the star led the astrologers first to King Herod and then to Jesus and that Herod then sought to have Jesus killed. No mention is made that anyone other than the astrologers saw the "star." After they left, Jehovah's angel warned Joseph to flee to Egypt to safeguard the child. Was that "star" a sign from God or was it from someone who was seeking to have God's Son destroyed?

Note that the Bible account does not say that they found the babe Jesus in a manger, as customarily depicted in Christmas art. When the astrologers arrived, Jesus and his parents were living in a house. As to Jesus' age at that time, remember that, based on what Herod had learned from the astrologers, he decreed that all the boys in the district of Bethlehem two years of age and under were to be destroyed. —Matt. 2:1, 11, 16.

Gift giving as part of the celebration; stories about Santa Claus, Father Christmas, etc.

The practice of Christmas gift giving is not based on what was done by the Magi. As shown above, they did not arrive at the time of Jesus' birth. Furthermore, they gave gifts, not to one another, but to the child Jesus, in accord with what was then customary when visiting notable persons.

The Encyclopedia Americana states: "During the Saturnalia . . . feasting prevailed, and gifts were exchanged." (1977, Vol. 24, p. 299) In many instances that represents the spirit of Christmas giving—an *exchanging* of gifts. The spirit reflected in such gift giving does not bring real happiness, because it violates Christian principles such as those found at Matthew 6:3, 4 and 2 Corinthians 9:7. Surely a Christian can give gifts to others as an expression of love at other times during the year, doing so as often as he wants to.

Depending on where they live, children are told that gifts are brought by Santa Claus, St. Nicholas, Father Christmas, Père Noël, Knecht Ruprecht, the Magi, the elf Jultomten (or Julenissen), or a witch known as La Befana. (*The World Book Encyclopedia,* 1984, Vol. 3, p. 414) Of course, none of these stories are actually true. Does the telling of such stories build in children a respect for truth, and does such a practice honor Jesus Christ, who taught that God must be worshiped with truth?—John 4:23, 24.

Is there any objection to sharing in celebrations that may have unchristian roots as long as it is not done for religious reasons?

Eph. 5:10, 11: "Keep on making sure of what is acceptable to the Lord; and quit sharing with them in the unfruitful works that belong to the darkness, but, rather, even be reproving them."

2 Cor. 6:14-18: "What fellowship do righteousness and lawlessness have? Or what sharing does light have with darkness? Further, what harmony is there between Christ and Be'lial? Or what portion does a faithful person have with an unbeliever? And what agreement does God's temple have with idols? . . . '"Therefore get out from among them, and separate yourselves," says Jehovah, "and quit touching the unclean thing"'; '"and I will take you in, . . . and you will be sons and daughters to me," says Jehovah the Almighty.'" (Genuine love for Jehovah and a strong desire to be pleasing to him will help a person to break free from unchristian practices that may have had emotional appeal. A person who

really knows and loves Jehovah does not feel that by shunning practices that honor false gods or that promote falsehood he is in any way deprived of happiness. Genuine love causes him to rejoice, not over unrighteousness, but with the truth. See 1 Corinthians 13:6.)

Compare Exodus 32:4-10. Notice that the Israelites adopted an Egyptian religious practice but gave it a new name, "a festival to Jehovah." But Jehovah severely punished them for this. Today we see only 20th-century practices associated with holidays. Some may appear harmless. But Jehovah observed firsthand the pagan religious practices from which these originated. Should not his view be what matters to us?

Illustration: Suppose a crowd come to a gentleman's home saying they are there to celebrate his birthday. He does not favor the celebration of birthdays. He does not like to see people overeat or get drunk or engage in loose conduct. But some of them do all those things, and they bring presents for everyone there except him! On top of all that, they pick the birthday of one of the man's enemies as the date for the celebration. How would the man feel? Would you want to be a party to it? This is exactly what is being done by Christmas celebrations.

What is the origin of Easter and the customs associated with it?

The Encyclopædia Britannica comments: "There is no indication of the observance of the Easter festival in the New Testament, or in the writings of the apostolic Fathers. The sanctity of special times was an idea absent from the minds of the first Christians."—(1910), Vol. VIII, p. 828.

The Catholic Encyclopedia tells us: "A great many pagan customs, celebrating the return of spring, gravitated to Easter. The egg is the emblem of the germinating life of early spring. . . . The rabbit is a pagan symbol and has always been an emblem of fertility."—(1913), Vol. V, p. 227.

In the book *The Two Babylons,* by Alexander Hislop, we read: "What means the term Easter itself? It is not a

Christian name. It bears its Chaldean origin on its very forehead. Easter is nothing else than Astarte, one of the titles of Beltis, the queen of heaven, whose name, . . . as found by Layard on the Assyrian monuments, is Ishtar. . . . Such is the history of Easter. The popular observances that still attend the period of its celebration amply confirm the testimony of history as to its Babylonian character. The hot cross buns of Good Friday, and the dyed eggs of Pasch or Easter Sunday, figured in the Chaldean rites just as they do now."—(New York, 1943), pp. 103, 107, 108; compare Jeremiah 7:18.

Are New Year's celebrations objectionable for Christians?

According to *The World Book Encyclopedia,* "The Roman ruler Julius Caesar established January 1 as New Year's Day in 46 B.C. The Romans dedicated this day to Janus, the god of gates, doors, and beginnings. The month of January was named after Janus, who had two faces—one looking forward and the other looking backward."—(1984), Vol. 14, p. 237.

Both the date and the customs associated with New Year's celebrations vary from one country to another. In many places revelry and drinking are part of the festivities. However, Romans 13:13 counsels: "As in the daytime let us walk decently, not in revelries and drunken bouts, not in illicit intercourse and loose conduct, not in strife and jealousy." (See also 1 Peter 4:3, 4; Galatians 5:19-21.)

What underlies holidays in memory of the "spirits of the dead"?

The 1910 edition of *The Encyclopædia Britannica* states: "All Souls' Day . . . the day set apart in the Roman Catholic Church for the commemoration of the faithful departed. The celebration is based on the doctrine that the souls of the faithful which at death have not been cleansed from venial sins, or have not atoned for past transgressions, cannot attain the Beatific Vision, and that they may be helped to do so by prayer and by the sacrifice of the mass. . . . Certain popular beliefs connected with All Souls' Day are of pagan origin and immemorial antiquity. Thus the dead are believed by the peasantry of many Catholic countries to return to their former homes on All Souls' night and partake of the food of the living."—Vol. I, p. 709.

The Encyclopedia Americana says: "Elements of the customs connected with Halloween can be traced to a Druid ceremony in pre-Christian times. The Celts had festivals for two major gods—a sun god and a god of the dead (called Samhain), whose festival was held on November 1, the beginning of the Celtic New Year. The festival of the dead was gradually incorporated into Christian ritual."—(1977), Vol. 13, p. 725.

The book *The Worship of the Dead* points to this origin: "The mythologies of all the ancient nations are interwoven with the events of the Deluge . . . The force of this argument is illustrated by the fact of the observance of a great festival of the dead in commemoration of the event, not only by nations more or less in communication with each other, but by others widely separated, both by the ocean and by centuries of time. This festival is, moreover, held by all on or about the very day on which, according to the Mosaic account, the Deluge took place, viz., *the seventeenth day of the second month*—the month nearly corresponding with our November." (London, 1904, Colonel J. Garnier, p. 4) Thus these celebrations actually began with an honoring of people whom God had destroyed because of their badness in Noah's day.—Gen. 6:5-7; 7:11.

Such holidays honoring "spirits of the dead" as if they were alive in another realm are contrary to the Bible's description of death as a state of complete unconsciousness. —Eccl. 9:5, 10; Ps. 146:4.

Regarding the origin of belief in immortality of the human soul, see pages 101, 102, under the main heading "Death," and pages 379, 380, under "Soul."

What is the origin of Valentine's Day?

The World Book Encyclopedia informs us: "Valentine's Day comes on the feast day of two different Christian martyrs named Valentine. But the customs connected with the day . . . probably come from an ancient Roman festival called *Lupercalia* which took place every February 15. The festival honored Juno, the Roman goddess of women and marriage, and Pan, the god of nature."—(1973), Vol. 20, p. 204.

What is the origin of the practice of setting aside a day to honor mothers?

The *Encyclopædia Britannica* says: "A festival derived from the custom of mother worship in ancient Greece. Formal mother worship, with ceremonies to Cybele, or Rhea, the Great Mother of the Gods, were performed on the Ides of March throughout Asia Minor."—(1959), Vol. 15, p. 849.

What Bible principles explain the viewpoint of Christians toward ceremonies commemorating events in a nation's political history?

John 18:36: "Jesus answered [the Roman governor]: 'My kingdom is no part of this world.'"

John 15:19: "If you [Jesus' followers] were part of the world, the world would be fond of what is its own. Now because you are no part of the world, but I have chosen you out of the world, on this account the world hates you."

1 John 5:19: "The whole world is lying in the power of the wicked one." (Compare John 14:30; Revelation 13:1, 2; Daniel 2:44.)

Other local and national holidays

There are many. Not all can be discussed here. But the historical information provided above gives indications as to what to look for in connection with any holiday, and the Bible principles already discussed supply ample guidance for those whose foremost desire is to do what is pleasing to Jehovah God.

Images

Definition: Usually, visible representations of persons or things. An image that is an object of worship is an idol. Those who perform acts of worship before images often say that their worship actually is directed to the spirit being represented by the image. Such use of images is customary in many non-Christian religions. Regarding Roman Catholic practice, the *New Catholic Encyclopedia* (1967, Vol. VII, p. 372) says: "Since the worship given to an image reaches and terminates in the person represented, the same type of worship due the person can be rendered to the image as representing the person." *Not a Bible teaching*.

What does God's Word say about the making of images used as objects of worship?

Ex. 20:4, 5, *JB:* "*You shall not make* yourself *a carved image or any likeness* of anything in heaven or on earth beneath or in the waters under the earth; *you shall not bow down to them* or serve them ["bow down before them or worship them," *NAB*]. For I, Yahweh your God, am a jealous God." (Italics added.) (Notice that the prohibition was against *making* images and *bowing down* before them.)

Lev. 26:1, *JB:* "You must make no idols; you must set up neither carved image nor standing-stone ["sacred pillar," *NW*], set up no sculptured stone in your land, to prostrate yourselves in front of it; for it is I, Yahweh, who am your God." (No image before which people might bow in worship was ever to be set up.)

2 Cor. 6:16, *JB:* "The temple of God has no common ground with idols, and that is what we are—the temple of the living God."

1 John 5:21, *NAB:* "My little children, be on your guard against idols ["idols," *Dy, CC;* "false gods," *JB*]."

May images be used simply as aids in worship of the true God?

John 4:23, 24, *JB:* "True worshippers will worship the

Father in spirit and truth: that is the kind of worshipper the Father wants. God is spirit, and those who worship must worship in spirit and truth." (Those who rely on images as aids to devotion are not worshiping God "in spirit" but they depend on what they can see with their physical eyes.)

2 Cor. 5:7, *NAB:* "We walk by faith, not by sight."

Isa. 40:18, *JB:* "To whom could you liken God? What image could you contrive of him?"

Acts 17:29, *JB:* "Since we are the children of God, we have no excuse for thinking that the deity looks like anything in gold, silver or stone that has been carved and designed by a man."

Isa. 42:8, *JB:* "My name is Yahweh, I will not yield my glory to another, nor my honour to idols ["graven things," *Dy*]."

Should we venerate "saints" as intercessors with God, perhaps using images of them as aids in our worship?

Acts 10:25, 26, *JB:* "As Peter reached the house Cornelius went out to meet him, knelt at his feet and prostrated himself. But Peter helped him up. 'Stand up,' he said 'I am only a man after all!'" (Since Peter did not approve of such adoration when he was personally present, would he encourage us to kneel before an image of him? See also Revelation 19:10.)

John 14:6, 14, *JB:* "Jesus said: 'I am the Way, the Truth and the Life. No one can come to the Father except through me. If you ask for anything in my name, I will do it.'" (Jesus here clearly states that our approach to the Father can be only through him and that our requests are to be made in Jesus' name.)

1 Tim. 2:5, *JB:* "There is only one God, and there is only one mediator between God and mankind, himself a man, Christ Jesus." (There is no allowance here for others to serve in the role of mediator for the members of Christ's congregation.)

See also pages 353, 354, under the heading "Saints."

Do worshipers have in mind primarily the person represented by an image, or are some images viewed as being superior to others?

The attitude of worshipers is an important factor to consider. Why? Because a key difference between an "image" and an "idol" is the use to which an image is put.

In the mind of the worshiper, does one image of a person have greater value or importance than another image of the same person? If so, it is the image, not the person, that the worshiper has primarily in mind. Why do people make long pilgrimages to worship at certain shrines? Is it not the image itself that is viewed as having "miraculous" powers? For example, in the book *Les Trois Notre-Dame de la Cathédrale de Chartres,* by the canon Yves Delaporte, we are told regarding images of Mary in the cathedral in Chartres, France: "These images, sculptured, painted or appearing on the stained glass windows, are not equally famous. . . . Only three are the object of a real worship: Our Lady of the Crypt, Our Lady of the Pillar, and Our Lady of the 'Belle Verriere.'" But if worshipers had primarily in mind the person, not the image, one image would be considered to be just as good as another, would it not?

How does God view images that are objects of worship?

Jer. 10:14, 15, *JB:* "Every goldsmith blushes for the idol he has made, since his images are nothing but delusion, with no breath in them. They are a Nothing, a laughable production."

Isa. 44:13-19, *JB:* "The wood carver takes his measurements, outlines the image with chalk, carves it with chisels, following the outline with dividers. He shapes it to human proportions, and gives it a human face, for it to live in a temple. He cut down a cedar, or else took a cypress or an oak which he selected from the trees in the forest, or maybe he planted a cedar and the rain made it grow. For the common man it is so much fuel; he uses it to warm himself, he also burns it to bake his bread. But this fellow makes a god of it and worships it; he makes an idol of it and bows down before it. Half of it he burns in the fire, on the live embers he roasts meat, eats it and is replete. He warms himself too. 'Ah!' says he 'I am warm; I have a fire here!' With the rest he makes his god, his idol; he bows down before it and worships it and prays to it. 'Save me,' he says 'because you are my god.' They know nothing, understand nothing. Their eyes are shut to all seeing, their heart to all reason. They never think, they lack the knowledge and wit to say, 'I burned half of it on the fire, I baked bread on the live embers, I roasted meat and ate it, and am I to make some abomination of what remains? Am I to bow down before a block of wood?'"

Ezek. 14:6, *JB:* "The Lord Yahweh says this: Come back, renounce your idols ["dungy idols," *NW*] and give up all your filthy practices."

Ezek. 7:20, *JB:* "They used to pride themselves on the beauty of their jewellery, out of which they made their loathsome images and idols. That is why I mean to make it an object of horror ["uncleanness," *Dy;* "refuse," *NAB*] to them."

How should we feel about any images that we may formerly have venerated?

Deut. 7:25, 26, *JB:* "You must set fire to all the carved images of their gods, not coveting the gold and silver that covers them; take it and you will be caught in a snare: it is detestable to Yahweh your God. You must not bring any detestable thing into your house or you, like it, will come under the ban too. You must regard them as unclean and loathsome ["thoroughly loathe it and absolutely detest it," *NW*]." (While Jehovah's people today are not authorized to destroy images that belong to other people, this command to Israel provides a pattern as to how they should view any images in their possession that they may have venerated. Compare Acts 19:19.)

1 John 5:21, *Dy:* "Little children, keep yourselves from idols ["false gods," *JB*]."

Ezek. 37:23, *JB:* "They will no longer defile themselves with their idols ... They shall be my people and I will be their God."

What effect could use of images in worship have on our own future?

Deut. 4:25, 26, *JB:* "If you act perversely, making a carved image in one shape or another ["some idol," *Kx;* "any similitude," *Dy*], doing what displeases Yahweh and angers him, on that day I will call heaven and earth to witness against you; . . . you shall be utterly destroyed." (God's viewpoint has not changed. See Malachi 3:5, 6.)

1 Cor. 10:14, 20, *JB:* "This is the reason, my dear brothers, why you must keep clear of idolatry. . . . The sacrifices that they offer they sacrifice to demons who are not God. I have no desire to see you in communion with demons."

Rev. 21:8, *JB:* "The legacy for cowards, for those who break their word, or worship obscenities, for murderers and fornicators, and for fortune-tellers, idolaters or any other sort of liars, is the second death [ftn., "eternal death"] in the burning lake of sulphur."

Ps. 115:4-8, *JB* (113:4-8, second set of numbers, *Dy*): "Their idols, in silver and gold, products of human skill, have mouths, but never speak, eyes, but never see, ears, but never hear, noses, but never smell, hands, but never touch, feet, but never walk, and not a sound from their throats. Their makers will end up like them, and so will anyone who relies on them."

Independence

Definition: A condition in which a person is not, or claims not to be, dependent on others, not subject to their direction or influence. Being endowed with free will, humans have a natural desire for a measure of independence. Carried too far, however, this desire gives rise to disobedience, even rebellion.

When people cast aside Bible standards, do they really gain freedom?

Rom. 6:16, 23: "Do you not know that if you keep presenting yourselves to anyone as slaves to obey him, you are slaves of him because you obey him, either of sin with death in view or of obedience with righteousness in view? . . . The wages sin pays is death, but the gift God gives is everlasting life by Christ Jesus our Lord."

Gal. 6:7-9: "Do not be misled: God is not one to be mocked. For whatever a man is sowing, this he will also reap; because he who is sowing with a view to his flesh will reap corruption from his flesh, but he who is sowing with a view to the spirit will reap everlasting life from the spirit. So let us not give up in doing what is fine."

Sexual morality: "He that practices fornication is sinning against his own body." (1 Cor. 6:18) "Anyone committing adultery with a woman . . . is bringing his own soul to ruin." (Prov. 6:32) (Regarding homosexuality, see Romans 1:24-27.) (Illicit sexual relations may, at the moment, seem pleasurable. But they lead to loathsome diseases, unwanted pregnancy, abortion, jealousy, a disturbed conscience, emotional turmoil, and certainly the disapproval of God, upon whom our prospects for future life depend.)

Materialistic pursuits: "Those who are determined to be rich fall into temptation and a snare and many senseless and hurtful desires, which plunge men into destruction and ruin. For the love of money is a root of all sorts of injurious things, and by reaching out for this love some have been led astray from the faith and have stabbed themselves all over with many pains." (1 Tim. 6:9, 10) "I will say to my soul: 'Soul, you have many good things laid up for many years; take your ease, eat, drink, enjoy yourself.' But God said to him, 'Unreasonable one, this night they are demanding your soul from you. Who, then, is to have the things you stored up?' So it goes with the man that lays up treasure for himself but is not rich toward God." (Luke 12:19-21) (Material possessions do not bring lasting happiness. Efforts to gain riches often lead to unhappy families, broken health, spiritual ruin.)

Overindulging in alcohol: "Who has woe? Who has uneasiness? Who has contentions? Who has concern? Who has wounds for no reason? Who has dullness of eyes? Those staying a long time with the wine, those coming in to search out mixed wine. At its end it bites just like a serpent, and it secretes poison just like a viper." (Prov. 23:29, 30, 32) (Drinking may at first seem to help a person to forget his problems, but it does not solve them. When he sobers up, the problems are still there, often with others added. When overused, alcohol ruins a person's self-respect, his health, his family life, his relationship with God.)

Drug abuse: See pages 106-112, under "Drugs."

Bad associations: If a gang were to tell you that they knew how to get plenty of money without a lot of work, would you go with them? "Do not go in the way with them. Hold back your foot from their roadway. For their feet are those that run to sheer badness, and they keep hastening to shed blood." (Prov. 1:10-19) If a person is not a worshiper of Jehovah, but he does seem to be really nice, would you view him as a suitable friend? Shechem was the son of a Caananite chieftain, and the Bible says he was the "most honorable of the whole house of his father," but he "took [Dinah] and lay down with her and violated her." (Gen. 34:1, 2, 19) Should the fact that other people may not believe the truths you have learned from God's Word make a difference to you? "Do not be misled. Bad associations spoil useful habits." (1 Cor. 15:33) How would Jehovah feel if you chose as your friends those who do not love him? To a king of Judah who did that, Jehovah's spokesman said: "For this there is indignation against you from the person of Jehovah."—2 Chron. 19:1, 2.

Who urged humans to feel free to make their own decisions without regard for God's commands?

Gen. 3:1-5: "Now the serpent [being used as a mouthpiece by Satan; see Revelation 12:9] . . . began to say to the woman: 'Is it really so that God said you must not eat from every tree of the garden?' At this the woman said to the serpent: 'Of the fruit of the trees of the garden we may eat. But as for eating of the fruit of the tree that is in the middle of the garden, God has said, "You must not eat from it, no, you must not touch it that you do not die."' At this the serpent said to the woman: 'You positively will not die. For God knows that in the very day of your eating from it your eyes are bound to be opened and you are bound to be like God, knowing good and bad.'"

What spirit is moving an individual when he ignores God's will in order to satisfy personal desires?

Eph. 2:1-3: "It is you God made alive though you were dead in your trespasses and sins, in which you at one time walked according to the system of things of this world [of which Satan is ruler], according to the ruler of the authority of the air, the spirit that now operates in the sons of disobedience. Yes, among them we all at one time conducted ourselves in harmony with the desires of our flesh, doing the things willed by the flesh and the thoughts, and we were naturally children of wrath even as the rest."

What independent attitudes is it vital for those who profess to be serving God to avoid?

Prov. 16:18: "Pride is before a crash, and a haughty spirit before stumbling."

Prov. 5:12: "You will have to say: 'How I have hated discipline and my heart has disrespected even reproof!'" (Such an attitude can lead a person into serious problems, as the context shows.)

Num. 16:3: "So they congregated themselves against Moses and Aaron [whom Jehovah was using as overseers of his people] and said to them: 'That is enough of you, because the whole assembly are all of them holy and Jehovah is in their midst. Why, then, should you lift yourselves up above the congregation of Jehovah?'"

Jude 16: "These men are murmurers, complainers about their lot in life, proceeding according to their own desires, and their mouths speak swelling things, while they are admiring personalities for the sake of their own benefit."

3 John 9: "Diotrephes, who likes to have the first place among them, does not receive anything from us with respect."

Prov. 18:1: "One isolating himself will seek his own

selfish longing; against all practical wisdom he will break forth."

Jas. 4:13-15: "Come, now, you who say: 'Today or tomorrow we will journey to this city and will spend a year there, and we will engage in business and make profits,' whereas you do not know what your life will be tomorrow. For you are a mist appearing for a little while and then disappearing. Instead, you ought to say: 'If Jehovah wills, we shall live and also do this or that.'"

When a person's desire for independence leads him to imitate the world outside the Christian congregation, under whose control does he come? And how does God view this?

1 John 2:15; 5:19: "Do not be loving either the world or the things in the world. If anyone loves the world, the love of the Father is not in him." "The whole world is lying in the power of the wicked one."

Jas. 4:4: "Whoever, therefore, wants to be a friend of the world is constituting himself an enemy of God."

Jehovah

Definition: The personal name of the only true God. His own self-designation. Jehovah is the Creator and, rightfully, the Sovereign Ruler of the universe. "Jehovah" is translated from the Hebrew Tetragrammaton, יהוה, which means "He Causes to Become." These four Hebrew letters are represented in many languages by the letters *JHVH* or *YHWH*.

Where is God's name found in Bible translations that are commonly used today?

The New English Bible: The name Jehovah appears at Exodus 3:15; 6:3. See also Genesis 22:14; Exodus 17:15; Judges 6:24; Ezekiel 48:35. (But if this and other translations use "Jehovah" in several places, why not be consistent in using it at every place where the Tetragrammaton appears in the Hebrew text?)

Revised Standard Version: A footnote on Exodus 3:15 says: "The word LORD when spelled with capital letters, stands for the divine name, *YHWH.*"

Today's English Version: A footnote on Exodus 6:3 states: "THE LORD: . . . Where the Hebrew text has Yahweh, traditionally transliterated as Jehovah, this translation employs LORD with capital letters, following a usage which is widespread in English versions."

King James Version: The name Jehovah is found at Exodus 6:3; Psalm 83:18; Isaiah 12:2; 26:4. See also Genesis 22:14; Exodus 17:15; Judges 6:24.

American Standard Version: The name Jehovah is used consistently in the Hebrew Scriptures in this translation, beginning with Genesis 2:4.

Douay Version: A footnote on Exodus 6:3 says: *"My name Adonai.* The name, which is in the Hebrew text, is that most proper name of God, which signifieth his *eternal, self-existing being,* (Exod. 3, 14,) which the Jews out of reverence never pronounce; but, instead of it, whenever it occurs in the Bible, they read *Adonai,* which signifies *the Lord;* and, therefore, they put the points or vowels, which belong to the name *Adonai,* to the four letters of that other ineffable name, Jod, He, Vau, He. Hence some moderns have framed the name of *Jehovah,* unknown to all the ancients, whether Jews or Christians; for the true pronunciation of the name, which is in the Hebrew text, by long disuse is now quite lost." (It is interesting that *The Catholic Encyclopedia* [1913, Vol. VIII, p. 329] states: *"Jehovah,* the proper name of God in the Old Testament; hence the Jews called it *the name* by excellence, the great name, the only name.")

The Holy Bible translated by Ronald A. Knox: The name Yahweh is found in footnotes at Exodus 3:14 and 6:3.

The New American Bible: A footnote on Exodus 3:14 favors the form "Yahweh," but the name does not appear in the main text of the translation. In the Saint Joseph Edition, see also the appendix Bible Dictionary under "Lord" and "Yahweh."

The Jerusalem Bible: The Tetragrammaton is translated Yahweh, starting with its first occurrence, at Genesis 2:4.

New World Translation: The name Jehovah is used in both the Hebrew and the Christian Greek Scriptures in this translation, appearing 7,210 times.

An American Translation: At Exodus 3:15 and 6:3 the name Yahweh is used, followed by "the LORD" in brackets.

The Bible in Living English, S. T. Byington: The name Jehovah is used throughout the Hebrew Scriptures.

The 'Holy Scriptures' translated by J. N. Darby: The name Jehovah appears throughout the Hebrew Scriptures, also in many footnotes on Christian Greek Scripture texts, beginning with Matthew 1:20.

The Emphatic Diaglott, Benjamin Wilson: The name Jehovah is found at Matthew 21:9 and in 17 other places in this translation of the Christian Greek Scriptures.

The Holy Scriptures According to the Masoretic Text—A New Translation, Jewish Publication Society of America, Max Margolis editor-in-chief: At Exodus 6:3 the Hebrew Tetragrammaton appears in the English text.

The Holy Bible translated by Robert Young: The name Jehovah is found throughout the Hebrew Scriptures in this literal translation.

Why do many Bible translations not use the personal name of God or use it only a few times?

The preface of the *Revised Standard Version* explains: "For two reasons the Committee has returned to the more familiar usage of the King James Version: (1) the word 'Jehovah' does not accurately represent any form of the Name ever used in Hebrew; and (2) the use of any proper name for the one and only God, as though there were other gods from whom he had to be distinguished, was discontinued in Judaism before the Christian era and is entirely inappropriate for the universal faith of the Christian Church." (Thus their own view of what is appropriate has been relied on as the basis for removing from the Holy Bible the personal name of its Divine Author, whose name appears in the original Hebrew more often than any other name or any title. They admittedly follow the example of the adherents of Judaism, of whom Jesus said: "You have made the word of God invalid because of your tradition."—Matt. 15:6.)

Translators who have felt obligated to include the personal name of God at least once or perhaps a few times in the main text, though not doing so every time it appears in Hebrew, have evidently followed the example of William Tyndale, who included the divine name in his translation of the Pentateuch published in 1530, thus breaking with the practice of leaving the name out altogether.

Was the name Jehovah used by the inspired writers of the Christian Greek Scriptures?

Jerome, in the fourth century, wrote: "Matthew, who is also Levi, and who from a publican came to be an apostle, first of all composed a Gospel of Christ in Judaea in the Hebrew language and characters for the benefit of those of the circumcision who had believed." (*De viris inlustribus,* chap. III) This Gospel includes 11 direct quotations of portions of the Hebrew Scriptures where the Tetragrammaton is found. There is no reason to believe that Matthew did not quote the passages as they were written in the Hebrew text from which he quoted.

Other inspired writers who contributed to the contents of the Christian Greek Scriptures quoted hundreds of passages from the *Septuagint,* a translation of the Hebrew Scriptures into Greek. Many of these passages included the Hebrew Tetragrammaton right in the Greek text of early copies of the *Septuagint.* In harmony with Jesus' own attitude regarding his Father's name, Jesus' disciples would have retained that name in those quotations.—Compare John 17:6, 26.

In *Journal of Biblical Literature,* George Howard of the University of Georgia wrote: "We know for a fact that Greek-speaking Jews continued to write יהוה within their Greek Scriptures. Moreover, it is most unlikely that early conservative Greek-speaking Jewish Christians varied from this practice. Although in secondary references to God they probably used the words [God] and [Lord], it would have been extremely unusual for them to have dismissed the Tetragram from the biblical text itself. . . . Since the Tetragram was still written in the copies of the Greek Bible which made up the Scriptures of the early church, it is reasonable to believe that the N[ew] T[estament] writers, when quoting from Scripture, preserved the Tetragram within the biblical text. . . . But when it was removed from the Greek O[ld] T[estament], it was also removed from the quotations of the O[ld] T[estament] in the N[ew] T[estament]. Thus somewhere around the beginning of the second century the use of surrogates [substitutes] must have crowded out the Tetragram in both Testaments."—Vol. 96, No. 1, March 1977, pp. 76, 77.

Which form of the divine name is correct —Jehovah or Yahweh?

No human today can be certain how it was originally pronounced in Hebrew. Why not? Biblical Hebrew was originally written with only consonants, no vowels. When the language was in everyday use, readers easily provided the proper vowels. In time, however, the Jews came to have the superstitious idea that it was wrong to say God's personal name out loud, so they used substitute expressions. Centuries later, Jewish scholars developed a system of points by which to indicate which vowels to use when reading ancient Hebrew, but they put the vowels for the *substitute expressions* around the four consonants representing the divine name. Thus the original pronunciation of the divine name was lost.

Many scholars favor the spelling "Yahweh," but it is uncertain and there is not agreement among them. On the other hand, "Jehovah" is the form of the name that is most readily recognized, because it has been used in English for centuries and preserves, equally with other forms, the four consonants of the Hebrew Tetragrammaton.

J. B. Rotherham, in *The Emphasised Bible,* used the form Yahweh throughout the Hebrew Scriptures. However, later in his *Studies in the Psalms* he used the form "Jehovah." He explained: "JEHOVAH—The employment of this English form of the Memorial name . . . in the present version of the Psalter does not arise from any misgiving as to the more correct pronunciation, as being Yahwéh; but solely from practical evidence personally selected of the desirability of keeping in touch with the public ear and eye in a matter of this kind, in which the principal thing is the easy recognition of the Divine name intended."—(London, 1911), p. 29.

After discussing various pronunciations, German professor Gustav Friedrich Oehler concluded: "From this point onward I use the word Jehovah, because, as a matter of fact, this name has now become more naturalized in our vocabulary, and cannot be supplanted."—*Theologie des Alten Testaments,* second edition (Stuttgart, 1882), p. 143.

Jesuit scholar Paul Joüon states: "In our translations, instead of the (hypothetical) form *Yahweh,* we have used the form *Jéhovah* . . . which is the conventional literary form used in French."—*Grammaire de l'hébreu biblique* (Rome, 1923), footnote on p. 49.

Most names change to some extent when transferred from one language to another. Jesus was born a Jew, and his name in Hebrew was perhaps pronounced Ye·shu′a′, but the inspired writers of the Christian Scriptures did not hesitate to use the Greek form of the name, I·e·sous′. In most other languages the pronunciation is slightly different, but we freely use the form that is common in our tongue. The same is true of other Bible names. How, then, can we show proper respect for the One to whom the most important name of all belongs? Would it be by never speaking or writing his name because we do not know exactly how it was originally pronounced? Or, rather, would it be by using the pronunciation and spelling that are common in our language, while speaking well of its Owner and conducting ourselves as his worshipers in a manner that honors him?

Why is it important to know and use God's personal name?

Do you have a close relationship with anyone whose personal name you do not know? For people to whom God is nameless he is often merely an impersonal force, not a real person, not someone that they know and love and to whom they can speak from the heart in prayer. If they do pray, their prayers are merely a ritual, a formalistic repetition of memorized expressions.

True Christians have a commission from Jesus Christ to make disciples of people of all nations. When teaching these people, how would it be possible to identify the true God as different from the false gods of the nations? Only by using His personal name, as the Bible itself does.—Matt. 28: 19, 20; 1 Cor. 8:5, 6.

Ex. 3:15: "God said . . . to Moses: 'This is what you are to say to the sons of Israel, "Jehovah the God of your fore-fathers . . . has sent me to you." This is my name to time indefinite, and this is the memorial of me to generation after generation.'"

Isa. 12:4: "Give thanks to Jehovah, you people! Call upon his name. Make known among the peoples his dealings. Make mention that his name is put on high."

Ezek. 38:17, 23: "This is what the Sovereign Lord Jeho-vah has said, ' . . . And I shall certainly magnify myself and sanctify myself and make myself known before the eyes of many nations; and they will have to know that I am Jeho-vah.'"

Mal. 3:16: "Those in fear of Jehovah spoke with one another, each one with his companion, and Jehovah kept paying attention and listening. And a book of remembrance began to be written up before him for those in fear of Jehovah and for those *thinking upon his name.*"

John 17:26: "[Jesus prayed to his Father:] I have made your name known to them [his followers] and will make it known, in order that the love with which you loved me may be in them and I in union with them."

Acts 15:14: "Symeon has related thoroughly how God for the first time turned his attention to the nations to take out of them *a people for his name.*"

Is Jehovah in the "Old Testament" Jesus Christ in the "New Testament"?

Matt. 4:10: "Jesus said to him: 'Go away, Satan! For it is written, "It is Jehovah ["the Lord," *KJ* and others] your God you must worship, and it is to him alone you must render sacred service.'"" (Jesus was obviously not saying that he himself was to be worshiped.)

John 8:54: "Jesus answered [the Jews]: 'If I glorify myself, my glory is nothing. It is my Father that glorifies me, he who you say is your God.'" (The Hebrew Scriptures clearly identify Jehovah as the God that the Jews professed to worship. Jesus said, not that he himself was Jehovah, but that Jehovah was his Father. Jesus here made it very clear that he and his Father were distinct individuals.)

Ps. 110:1: "The utterance of Jehovah to my [David's] Lord is: 'Sit at my right hand until I place your enemies as a stool for your feet.'" (At Matthew 22:41-45, Jesus explained that he himself was David's "Lord," referred to in this psalm. So Jesus is not Jehovah but is the one to whom Jehovah's words were here directed.)

Phil. 2:9-11: "For this very reason also God exalted him [Jesus Christ] to a superior position and kindly gave him the name that is above every other name, so that in the name of Jesus every knee should bend of those in heaven and those on earth and those under the ground, and every tongue should openly acknowledge that Jesus Christ is Lord to the glory of God the Father. [Dy reads: "... every tongue should confess that the Lord Jesus Christ is in the glory of God the Father." Kx and CC read similarly, but a footnote in Kx acknowledges: " ... the Greek is perhaps more naturally rendered 'to the glory,'" and NAB and JB render it that way.]" (Notice that Jesus Christ is here shown to be different from God the Father and subject to Him.)

How can a person love Jehovah if he is also to fear Him?

The Bible tells us that we should both love Jehovah (Luke 10:27) and fear him. (1 Pet. 2:17; Prov. 1:7; 2:1-5; 16:6) Wholesome fear of God will make us very careful to avoid incurring his displeasure. Our love for Jehovah will move us to want to do the things that are pleasing to him, to express our appreciation for the countless expressions of his love and undeserved kindness.

Illustrations: A son properly fears to displease his father, but appreciation for all that his father does for him should also move the son to express genuine love for his father. A scuba diver may say that he loves the sea, but a wholesome fear of it causes him to realize that there are certain things that he should avoid doing. Similarly, our love for God should be coupled with a wholesome fear of doing anything that will incur his displeasure.

Jehovah's Witnesses

Definition: The worldwide Christian society of people who actively bear witness regarding Jehovah God and his purposes affecting mankind. They base their beliefs solely on the Bible.

What beliefs of Jehovah's Witnesses set them apart as different from other religions?

(1) Bible: Jehovah's Witnesses believe that the *entire* Bible is the inspired Word of God, and instead of adhering to a creed based on human tradition, they hold to the Bible as the standard for *all* their beliefs.

(2) God: They worship Jehovah as the only true God and freely speak to others about him and his loving purposes toward mankind. Anyone who publicly witnesses about Jehovah is usually identified as belonging to the one group —"Jehovah's Witnesses."

(3) Jesus Christ: They believe, not that Jesus Christ is part of a Trinity, but that, as the Bible says, he is the Son of God, the first of God's creations; that he had a prehuman existence and that his life was transferred from heaven to the womb of a virgin, Mary; that his perfect human life laid down in sacrifice makes possible salvation to eternal life for those who exercise faith; that Christ is actively ruling as King, with God-given authority over all the earth since 1914.

(4) God's Kingdom: They believe that God's Kingdom is the only hope for mankind; that it is a real government; that it will soon destroy the present wicked system of things, including all human governments, and that it will produce a new system in which righteousness will prevail.

(5) Heavenly life: They believe that 144,000 spirit-anointed Christians will share with Christ in his heavenly Kingdom, ruling as kings with him. They do not believe that heaven is the reward for everyone who is "good."

(6) The earth: They believe that God's original purpose for the earth will be fulfilled; that the earth will be completely populated by worshipers of Jehovah and that these will be able to enjoy eternal life in human perfection; that even the dead will be raised to an opportunity to share in these blessings.

(7) Death: They believe that the dead are conscious of absolutely nothing; that they are experiencing neither pain nor pleasure in some spirit realm; that they do not exist except in God's memory, so hope for their future life lies in a resurrection from the dead.

(8) Last days: They believe that we are living now, since 1914, in the last days of this wicked system of things; that some who saw the events of 1914 will also see the complete destruction of the present wicked world; that lovers of righteousness will survive into a cleansed earth.

(9) Separate from the world: They earnestly endeavor to be no part of the world, as Jesus said would be true of his followers. They show genuine Christian love for their neighbors, but they do not share in the politics or the wars of any nation. They provide for the material needs of their families but shun the world's avid pursuit of material things and personal fame and its excessive indulgence in pleasure.

(10) Apply Bible counsel: They believe that it is important to apply the counsel of God's Word in everyday life now —at home, in school, in business, in their congregation. Regardless of a person's past way of life, he may become one of Jehovah's Witnesses if he abandons practices condemned by God's Word and applies its godly counsel. But if anyone thereafter makes a practice of adultery, fornication, homosexuality, drug abuse, drunkenness, lying, or stealing, he will be disfellowshipped from the organization.

(The above list briefly states some outstanding beliefs of

Jehovah's Witnesses but by no means all the points on which their beliefs are different from those of other groups. Scriptural basis for the above beliefs can be found through the Index of this book.)

Are Jehovah's Witnesses an American religion?

They are advocates of God's Kingdom, not of the political, economic, or social system of any nation of this old world.

It is true that Jehovah's Witnesses had their modern-day start in the United States. The location of their world headquarters there has helped to make it possible to print and ship Bible literature to most parts of the world. But the Witnesses do not favor one nation over another; they are found in almost every nation, and they have offices in many parts of the earth to supervise their activity in those areas.

Consider: Jesus as a Jew was born in Palestine, but Christianity is not a Palestinian religion, is it? The place of Jesus' human birth is not the most important factor to consider. What Jesus taught originated with his Father, Jehovah God, who deals impartially with people of all nations.—John 14:10; Acts 10:34, 35.

How is the work of Jehovah's Witnesses financed?

By voluntary contributions, as was true with the early Christians. (2 Cor. 8:12; 9:7) No collections are ever taken at their meetings; they do not beg for money from the public. Any donations from interested persons are used to further the worldwide work of Bible education conducted by the Witnesses.

Witnesses are not paid to go from house to house or to offer Bible literature on the streets. Love for God and for neighbor motivates them to talk about God's loving provisions for mankind.

The Watch Tower Bible and Tract Society of Pennsylvania, a legal religious corporation that is used by Jehovah's Witnesses, was incorporated in 1884 in accordance with the Nonprofit Corporation Law of the Commonwealth of Pennsylvania, U.S.A. Thus, by law it cannot be, and it is not, a profit-making enterprise, nor do individuals make a profit through this Society. The Society's charter states: "It [the Society] does not contemplate pecuniary gain or profit, incidentally or otherwise, to its members, directors or officers."

Are Jehovah's Witnesses a sect or a cult?

Some define *sect* to mean a group that has broken away from an established religion. Others apply the term to a group that follows a particular human leader or teacher. The term is usually used in a derogatory way. Jehovah's Witnesses are not an offshoot of some church but include persons from all walks of life and from many religious backgrounds. They do not look to any human, but rather to Jesus Christ, as their leader.

A *cult* is a religion that is said to be unorthodox or that emphasizes devotion according to prescribed ritual. Many cults follow a living human leader, and often their adherents live in groups apart from the rest of society. The standard for what is orthodox, however, should be God's Word, and Jehovah's Witnesses strictly adhere to the Bible. Their worship is a way of life, not a ritual devotion. They neither follow a human nor isolate themselves from the rest of society. They live and work in the midst of other people.

How old is the religion of Jehovah's Witnesses?

According to the Bible, the line of witnesses of Jehovah reaches back to faithful Abel. Hebrews 11:4–12:1 says: "By faith Abel offered God a sacrifice of greater worth than Cain . . . By faith Noah, after being given divine warning of things not yet beheld, showed godly fear . . . By faith Abraham, when he was called, obeyed in going out into a place he was destined to receive as an inheritance . . . By faith Moses, when grown up, refused to be called the son of the daughter of Pharaoh, choosing to be ill-treated with the people of God rather than to have the temporary enjoyment of sin . . . So, then, because we have so great a cloud of *witnesses* surrounding us, let us also put off every weight and the sin that easily entangles us, and let us run with endurance the race that is set before us."

With reference to Jesus Christ, the Bible states: "These are the things that the Amen says, *the faithful and true witness,* the beginning of the creation by God." Of whom was he a witness? He himself said that he made his Father's name manifest. He was the foremost witness of Jehovah. —Rev. 3:14; John 17:6.

Interestingly, some of the Jews asked whether the activity of Jesus Christ represented "a new teaching." (Mark 1:27) Later, some Greeks thought the apostle Paul was introducing a "new teaching." (Acts 17:19, 20) It was new to the ears of those who were hearing it, but the important thing was that it was the truth, in full harmony with God's Word.

The modern-day history of Jehovah's Witnesses began with the forming of a group for Bible study in Allegheny, Pennsylvania, U.S.A., in the early 1870's. At first they were known only as Bible Students, but in 1931 they adopted the Scriptural name Jehovah's Witnesses. (Isa. 43:10-12) Their beliefs and practices are not new but are a restoration of first-century Christianity.

Do Jehovah's Witnesses believe that their religion is the only right one?

The Bible does not agree with the modern view that there are many acceptable ways to worship God. Ephesians 4:5 says there is "one Lord, one faith." Jesus stated: "Narrow is the gate and cramped the road leading off into life, and few are the ones finding it. . . . Not everyone saying to me, 'Lord, Lord,' will enter into the kingdom of the heavens, but the one doing the will of my Father who is in the heavens will." —Matt. 7:13, 14, 21; see also 1 Corinthians 1:10.

Repeatedly the Scriptures refer to the body of true Christian teachings as "the truth," and Christianity is spoken of as "the way of the truth." (1 Tim. 3:15; 2 John 1; 2 Pet. 2:2) Because Jehovah's Witnesses base all of their beliefs, their standards for conduct, and organizational procedures on the

Bible, their faith in the Bible itself as God's Word gives them the conviction that what they have is indeed the truth. So their position is not egotistical but demonstrates their confidence that the Bible is the right standard against which to measure one's religion. They are not self-centered but are eager to share their beliefs with others.

Do not other religions also follow the Bible?

Many use it to some extent. But do they really teach and practice what it contains? Consider: (1) From most of their Bible translations they have removed the name of the true God thousands of times. (2) The Trinity doctrine, their concept of God himself, is borrowed from pagan sources and was developed in its present form centuries after Bible writing was completed. (3) Their belief in immortality of the human soul as the basis for continued life is not taken from the Bible; it has roots in ancient Babylon. (4) The theme of Jesus' preaching was the Kingdom of God, and he sent his disciples out to talk personally to others about it; but the churches today seldom mention that Kingdom and their members are not doing the work of preaching "this good news of the kingdom." (Matt. 24:14) (5) Jesus said that his true followers could be readily identified by their self-sacrificing love for one another. Is that true of the religions of Christendom when the nations go to war? (6) The Bible says that Christ's disciples would be no part of the world, and it warns that whoever wants to be a friend of the world makes himself an enemy of God; but the churches of Christendom and their members are deeply involved in the political affairs of the nations. (Jas. 4:4) In view of such a record, can it honestly be said that they really adhere to the Bible?

How do Jehovah's Witnesses arrive at their explanation of the Bible?

A key factor is that the Witnesses really believe that the Bible is God's Word and that what it contains is there for our instruction. (2 Tim. 3:16, 17; Rom. 15:4; 1 Cor. 10:11) So they do not resort to philosophical arguments to evade its clear statements of truth or to justify the way of life of people who have abandoned its moral standards.

In pointing out the meaning of symbolic language in the Bible, they let the Bible provide its own explanation, instead of giving their theories as to its significance. (1 Cor. 2:13) Indications as to the meaning of symbolic terms are usually found in other parts of the Bible. (As an example, see Revelation 21:1; then, regarding the meaning of "sea," read Isaiah 57:20. To identify "the Lamb" referred to in Revelation 14:1, see John 1:29 and 1 Peter 1:19.)

As for fulfillment of prophecy, they apply what Jesus said about being alert to events that correspond to what was foretold. (Luke 21:29-31; compare 2 Peter 1:16-19.) Conscientiously they point out those events and draw attention to what the Bible indicates they mean.

Jesus said that he would have on earth a "faithful and discreet slave" (his anointed followers viewed as a group), through which agency he would provide spiritual food to those making up the household of faith. (Matt. 24:45-47) Jehovah's Witnesses recognize that arrangement. As was true of first-century Christians, they look to the governing body of that "slave" class to resolve difficult questions—not on the basis of human wisdom, but by drawing on their knowledge of God's Word and his dealings with his servants, and with the help of God's spirit, for which they earnestly pray.—Acts 15:1-29; 16:4, 5.

Why have there been changes over the years in the teachings of Jehovah's Witnesses?

The Bible shows that Jehovah enables his servants to understand his purpose in a progressive manner. (Prov. 4:18; John 16:12) Thus, the prophets who were divinely inspired to write portions of the Bible did not understand the meaning of everything that they wrote. (Dan. 12:8, 9; 1 Pet. 1:10-12) The apostles of Jesus Christ realized that there was much they did not understand in their time. (Acts 1:6, 7; 1 Cor. 13:9-12) The Bible shows that there would be a great increase in knowledge of the truth during "the time of the end." (Dan. 12:4) Increased knowledge often requires adjustments in one's thinking. Jehovah's Witnesses are willing humbly to make such adjustments.

Why do Jehovah's Witnesses preach from house to house?

Jesus foretold for our day this work: "This good news of the kingdom will be preached in all the inhabited earth for a witness to all the nations; and then the end will come." He also instructed his followers: "Go . . . and make disciples of people of all the nations."—Matt. 24:14; 28:19.

When Jesus sent out his early disciples, he directed them to go to the homes of the people. (Matt. 10:7, 11-13) The apostle Paul said regarding his ministry: "I did not hold back from telling you any of the things that were profitable nor from teaching you publicly and *from house to house.*"—Acts 20:20, 21; see also Acts 5:42.

The message that the Witnesses proclaim involves the lives of people; they want to be careful to miss no one. (Zeph. 2:2, 3) Their calls are motivated by love—first for God, also for their neighbor.

A conference of religious leaders in Spain noted this: "Perhaps [the churches] are excessively neglectful about that which precisely constitutes the greatest preoccupation of the Witnesses—the home visit, which comes within the apostolic methodology of the primitive church. While the churches, on not a few occasions, limit themselves to constructing their temples, ringing their bells to attract the people and to preaching inside their places of worship, [the Witnesses] follow the apostolic tactic of going from house to house and of taking advantage of every occasion to witness."—*El Catolicismo,* Bogotá, Colombia, September 14, 1975, p. 14.

But why do the Witnesses call repeatedly even at homes of people who do not share their faith?

They do not force their message on others. But they know that people move to new residences and that the circumstances of people change. Today a person may be too busy to listen; another time he may gladly take the time. One member of a household may not be interested, but others may be. People themselves change; serious problems in life may stimulate an awareness of spiritual need.—See also Isaiah 6:8, 11, 12.

Why are Jehovah's Witnesses persecuted and spoken against?

Jesus said: "If the world hates you, you know that it has hated me before it hated you. If you were part of the world, the world would be fond of what is its own. Now because you are no part of the world, but I have chosen you out of the world, on this account the world hates you." (John 15:18, 19; see also 1 Peter 4:3, 4.) The Bible shows that the whole world lies under Satan's control; he is the principal instigator of the persecution.—1 John 5:19; Rev. 12:17.

Jesus also told his disciples: "You will be objects of hatred by all people on account of my name." (Mark 13:13) The word "name" here means what Jesus officially is, the Messianic King. Persecution comes because Jehovah's Witnesses put his commands ahead of those of any earthly ruler.

If Someone Says—

'Why don't you people get involved in doing things to help make the world (the community) a better place to live?'

You might reply: 'Conditions in the community are obviously important to you, and they are to me too. May I ask, What problem do you feel should be among the first that gets attention?' **Then perhaps add:** 'Why do you feel that this has become such a major need? . . . Obviously, immediate action on the matter can be beneficial, but I'm sure you'll agree that we would like to see improvement on a long-term basis. That is the approach that we as Jehovah's Witnesses take to the matter. (Explain what we do to help people to apply Bible principles in their lives in order to get to the root of the matter on a personal basis; also, what God's Kingdom will do, and why this will permanently solve the problem for humankind.)'

Or you could say: '(After covering some of the points in the preceding reply . . .) Some people contribute toward community improvement by providing money; others do it by volunteering their services. Jehovah's Witnesses do both. Let me explain.' **Then perhaps add:** (1) 'To be one of

Jehovah's Witnesses, a person must conscientiously pay his taxes; that provides money for the government to supply needed services.' (2) 'We go beyond that, calling at the homes of people, offering to study the Bible with them free of charge. When they become acquainted with what the Bible says, they learn to apply Bible principles and so cope with their problems.'

Another possibility: 'I'm glad you brought the matter up. Many people have never inquired to find out what the Witnesses are actually doing about community affairs. Obviously there is more than one way to offer help.' **Then perhaps add:** (1) 'Some do it by establishing institutions —hospitals, homes for the elderly, rehabilitation centers for drug addicts, and so forth. Others may volunteer to go right to the homes of people and offer appropriate help as they are able. That is what Jehovah's Witnesses do.' (2) 'We have observed that there is something that can transform a person's entire outlook on life, and that is knowledge of what the Bible shows to be the real purpose of life and what the future holds.'

An additional suggestion: 'I appreciate your raising that question. We would like to see conditions improve, would we not? May I ask, How do you feel about what Jesus Christ himself did? Would you say that the way he went about helping people was practical? . . . We try to follow his example.'

'Christians are supposed to be witnesses for Jesus, not for Jehovah'

You might reply: 'That's an interesting point you have brought up. And you are right that we do have a responsibility to be witnesses for Jesus. That's why Jesus' role in God's purpose is emphasized in our publications. (You may want to use a current book or a magazine to demonstrate this.) But here is something that may be a new thought to you. (Rev. 1:5) . . . Of whom was Jesus "the Faithful Witness"? (John 5:43; 17:6) . . . Jesus set the example that we should imitate, did he not? . . . Why is it so important to get to know both Jesus and his Father? (John 17:3)'

Jesus Christ

Definition: The only-begotten Son of God, the only Son produced by Jehovah alone. This Son is the firstborn of all creation. By means of him all other things in heaven and on earth were created. He is the second-greatest personage in the universe. It is this Son whom Jehovah sent to the earth to give his life as a ransom for mankind, thus opening the way to eternal life for those of Adam's offspring who would exercise faith. This same Son, restored to heavenly glory, now rules as King, with authority to destroy all the wicked and to carry out his Father's original purpose for the earth. The Hebrew form of the name *Jesus* means "Jehovah Is Salvation"; *Christ* is the equivalent of the Hebrew *Ma·shi'ach* (Messiah), meaning "Anointed One."

Was Jesus Christ a real, historical person?

The Bible itself is the principal evidence that Jesus Christ is a historical person. The record in the Gospels is not a vague narrative of events at some unspecified time and in an unnamed location. It clearly states time and place in great detail. For an example, see Luke 3:1, 2, 21-23.

The first-century Jewish historian Josephus referred to the stoning of "James, the brother of Jesus who was called the Christ." (*The Jewish Antiquities,* Josephus, Book XX, sec. 200) A direct and very favorable reference to Jesus, found in Book XVIII, sections 63, 64, has been challenged by some who claim that it must have been either added later or embellished by Christians; but it is acknowledged that the vocabulary and the style are basically those of Josephus, and the passage is found in all available manuscripts.

Tacitus, a Roman historian who lived during the latter part of the first century C.E., wrote: "Christus [Latin for "Christ"], from whom the name [Christian] had its origin, suffered the extreme penalty during the reign of Tiberius at the hands of one of our procurators, Pontius Pilatus."—*The Complete Works of Tacitus* (New York, 1942), "The Annals," Book 15, par. 44.

With reference to early non-Christian historical references to Jesus, *The New Encyclopædia Britannica* states: "These independent accounts prove that in ancient times

even the opponents of Christianity never doubted the histo-
ricity of Jesus, which was disputed for the first time and on
inadequate grounds by several authors at the end of the
18th, during the 19th, and at the beginning of the 20th
centuries."—(1976), Macropædia, Vol. 10, p. 145.

Was Jesus Christ simply a good man?

Interestingly, Jesus rebuked a man who addressed him
with the title "Good Teacher," because Jesus recognized not
himself but his Father to be the standard of goodness. (Mark
10:17, 18) However, to measure up to what people generally
mean when they say that someone is good, Jesus surely must
have been truthful. Indeed, even his enemies acknowledged
that he was. (Mark 12:14) He himself said that he had a
prehuman existence, that he was the unique Son of God, that
he was the Messiah, the one whose coming was foretold
throughout the Hebrew Scriptures. Either he was what he
said or he was a gross impostor, but neither option allows for
the view that he was simply a good man.—John 3:13; 10:36;
4:25, 26; Luke 24:44-48.

Was Jesus merely a prophet whose authority was similar to that of Moses, Buddha, Muhammad, and other religious leaders?

Jesus himself taught that he was the unique Son of God
(John 10:36; Matt. 16:15-17), the foretold Messiah (Mark
14:61, 62), that he had a prehuman existence in heaven
(John 6:38; 8:23, 58), that he would be put to death and then
would be raised to life on the third day and would thereafter
return to the heavens. (Matt. 16:21; John 14:2, 3) Were
these claims true, and was he thus really different from all
other true prophets of God and in sharp contrast to all
self-styled religious leaders? The truth of the matter would
be evident on the third day from his death. Did God then
resurrect him from the dead, thus confirming that Jesus
Christ had spoken the truth and was indeed God's unique
Son? (Rom. 1:3, 4) Over 500 witnesses actually saw Jesus
alive following his resurrection, and his faithful apostles
were eyewitnesses as he began his ascent back to heaven and

then disappeared from their view in a cloud. (1 Cor. 15:3-8; Acts 1:2, 3, 9) So thoroughly were they convinced that he had been raised from the dead that many of them risked their lives to tell others about it.—Acts 4:18-33.

Why did the Jews in general not accept Jesus as the Messiah?

The *Encyclopaedia Judaica* says: "The Jews of the Roman period believed [the Messiah] would be raised up by God to break the yoke of the heathen and to reign over a restored kingdom of Israel." (Jerusalem, 1971, Vol. 11, col. 1407) They wanted liberation from the yoke of Rome. Jewish history testifies that on the basis of the Messianic prophecy recorded at Daniel 9:24-27 there were Jews who expected the Messiah during the first century C.E. (Luke 3:15) But that prophecy also connected his coming with 'making an end of sin,' and Isaiah chapter 53 indicated that Messiah himself would die in order to make this possible. However, the Jews in general felt no need for anyone to die for their sins. They believed that they had a righteous standing with God on the basis of their descent from Abraham. Says *A Rabbinic Anthology,* "So great is the [merit] of Abraham that he can atone for all the vanities committed and lies uttered by Israel in this world." (London, 1938, C. Montefiore and H. Loewe, p. 676) By their rejection of Jesus as Messiah, the Jews fulfilled the prophecy that had foretold regarding him: "He was despised, and we esteemed him not." —Isaiah 53:3, *JP.*

Before his death, Moses foretold that the nation would turn aside from true worship and that, as a result, calamity would befall them. (Read Deuteronomy 31:27-29.) The book of Judges testifies that this occurred repeatedly. In the days of the prophet Jeremiah, national unfaithfulness led to the nation's being taken into exile in Babylon. Why did God also allow the Romans to destroy Jerusalem and its temple in 70 C.E.? Of what unfaithfulness had the nation been guilty so that God did not protect them as he had done when they had put their trust in him? It was shortly before this that they had rejected Jesus as the Messiah.

Is Jesus Christ actually God?

John 17:3, *RS:* "[Jesus prayed to his Father:] This is eternal life, that they know thee the only true God ["who alone art truly God," *NE*], and Jesus Christ whom thou hast sent." (Notice that Jesus referred not to himself but to his Father in heaven as "the only true God.")

John 20:17, *RS:* "Jesus said to her [Mary Magdalene], 'Do not hold me, for I have not yet ascended to the Father; but go to my brethren and say to them, I am ascending to my Father and your Father, to my God and your God.'" (So to the resurrected Jesus, the Father was God, just as the Father was God to Mary Magdalene. Interestingly, not once in Scripture do we find the Father addressing the Son as "my God.")

See also pages 411, 416, 417, under the heading "Trinity."

Does John 1:1 prove that Jesus is God?

John 1:1, *RS:* "In the beginning was the Word, and the Word was with God, and the Word was God [also *KJ, JB, Dy, Kx, NAB*]." *NE* reads "what God was, the Word was." *Mo* says "the Logos was divine." *AT* and *Sd* tell us "the Word was divine." The interlinear rendering of *ED* is "a god was the Word." *NW* reads "the Word was a god"; *NTIV* uses the same wording.

What is it that these translators are seeing in the Greek text that moves some of them to refrain from saying "the Word was God"? The definite article (the) appears before the first occurrence of *the·os'* (God) but not before the second. The articular (when the article appears) construction of the noun points to an identity, a personality, whereas a singular anarthrous (without the article) predicate noun before the verb (as the sentence is constructed in Greek) points to a quality about someone. So the text is not saying that the Word (Jesus) was the same as the God *with whom* he was but, rather, that the Word was godlike, divine, a god. (See 1984 Reference edition of *NW,* p. 1579.)

What did the apostle John mean when he wrote John 1:1? Did he mean that Jesus is himself God or perhaps that Jesus is one God with the Father? In the same chapter, verse 18,

John wrote: "No one ["no man," *KJ, Dy*] has ever seen God; the only Son ["the only-begotten god," *NW*], who is in the bosom of the Father, he has made him known." (*RS*) Had any human seen Jesus Christ, the Son? Of course! So, then, was John saying that Jesus was God? Obviously not. Toward the end of his Gospel, John summarized matters, saying: "These are written that you may believe that Jesus is the Christ, [not God, but] the Son of God."—John 20:31, *RS*.

Does Thomas' exclamation at John 20:28 prove that Jesus is truly God?

John 20:28 (*RS*) reads: "Thomas answered him, 'My Lord and my God!'"

There is no objection to referring to Jesus as "God," if this is what Thomas had in mind. Such would be in harmony with Jesus' own quotation from the Psalms in which powerful men, judges, were addressed as "gods." (John 10:34, 35, *RS;* Ps. 82:1-6) Of course, Christ occupies a position far higher than such men. Because of the uniqueness of his position in relation to Jehovah, at John 1:18 (*NW*) Jesus is referred to as "the only-begotten god." (See also *Ro, By*.) Isaiah 9:6 (*RS*) also prophetically describes Jesus as "Mighty God," but not as the Almighty God. All of this is in harmony with Jesus' being described as "a god," or "divine," at John 1:1 (*NW, AT*).

The context helps us to draw the right conclusion from this. Shortly before Jesus' death, Thomas had heard Jesus' prayer in which he addressed his Father as "the only true God." (John 17:3, *RS*) After Jesus' resurrection Jesus had sent a message to his apostles, including Thomas, in which he had said: "I am ascending . . . to my God and your God." (John 20:17, *RS*) After recording what Thomas said when he actually saw and touched the resurrected Christ, the apostle John stated: "These are written that you may believe that Jesus is the Christ, the Son of God, and that believing you may have life in his name." (John 20:31, *RS*) So, if anyone has concluded from Thomas' exclamation that Jesus is himself "the only true God" or that Jesus is a Trinitarian "God the Son," he needs to look again at what Jesus himself said (vs. 17) and at the conclusion that is clearly stated by the apostle John (vs. 31).

Does Matthew 1:23 indicate that Jesus when on earth was God?

Matt. 1:23, *RS:* "'Behold, a virgin shall conceive and bear a son, and his name shall be called Emman'u-el' (which means, God with us ["God is with us," *NE*])."

In announcing Jesus' coming birth, did Jehovah's angel say that the child would be God himself? No, the announcement was: "He will be great, and will be called the *Son* of the Most High." (Luke 1:32, 35, *RS;* italics added.) And Jesus himself never claimed to be God but, rather, "the *Son* of God." (John 10:36, *RS;* italics added.) Jesus was sent into the world by God; so by means of this only-begotten Son, God was with mankind.—John 3:17; 17:8.

It was not unusual for Hebrew names to include within them the word for God or even an abbreviated form of God's personal name. For example, Eli'athah means "God Has Come"; Jehu means "Jehovah Is He"; Elijah means "My God Is Jehovah." But none of these names implied that the possessor was himself God.

What is the meaning of John 5:18?

John 5:18, *RS:* "This was why the Jews sought all the more to kill him, because he not only broke the sabbath but also called God his Father, making himself equal with God."

It was the unbelieving Jews who reasoned that Jesus was attempting to make himself equal with God by claiming God as his Father. While properly referring to God as his Father, Jesus never claimed equality with God. He straightforwardly answered the Jews: "Truly, truly, I say to you, the Son can do nothing of his own accord, but only what he sees the Father doing." (John 5:19, *RS;* see also John 14:28; John 10:36.) It was those unbelieving Jews, too, who claimed that Jesus broke the Sabbath, but they were wrong also about that. Jesus kept the Law perfectly, and he declared: "It is lawful to do good on the sabbath."—Matt. 12:10-12, *RS.*

Does the fact that worship is given to Jesus prove that he is God?

At Hebrews 1:6, the angels are instructed to "worship" Jesus, according to the rendering of *RS, TEV, KJ, JB,* and

NAB. *NW* says "do obeisance to." At Matthew 14:33, Jesus' disciples are said to have "worshiped" him, according to *RS, TEV, KJ;* other translations say that they "showed him reverence" (*NAB*), "bowed down before him" (*JB*), "fell at his feet" (*NE*), "did obeisance to him" (*NW*).

The Greek word rendered "worship" is *pro·sky·ne'o,* which *A Greek-English Lexicon of the New Testament and Other Early Christian Literature* says was also "used to designate the custom of prostrating oneself before a person and kissing his feet, the hem of his garment, the ground." (Chicago, 1979, Bauer, Arndt, Gingrich, Danker; second English edition; p. 716) This is the term used at Matthew 14:33 to express what the disciples did toward Jesus; at Hebrews 1:6 to indicate what the angels are to do toward Jesus; at Genesis 22:5 in the Greek *Septuagint* to describe what Abraham did toward Jehovah and at Genesis 23:7 to describe what Abraham did, in harmony with the custom of the time, toward people with whom he was doing business; at 1 Kings 1:23 in the *Septuagint* to describe the prophet Nathan's action on approaching King David.

At Matthew 4:10 (*RS*), Jesus said: "You shall worship [from *pro·sky·ne'o*] the Lord your God and him only shall you serve." (At Deuteronomy 6:13, which Jesus is evidently here quoting, appears the personal name of God, the Tetragrammaton.) In harmony with that, we must understand that it is *pro·sky·ne'o* with a particular attitude of heart and mind that should be directed only toward God.

Do the miracles performed by Jesus prove that he is God?

Acts 10:34, 38, *RS:* "Peter opened his mouth and said: '. . . God anointed Jesus of Nazareth with the Holy Spirit and with power; . . . he went about doing good and healing all that were oppressed by the devil, for God was with him.'" (So Peter did not conclude from the miracles that he observed that Jesus was God but, rather, that God was *with* Jesus. Compare Matthew 16:16, 17.)

John 20:30, 31, *RS:* "Now Jesus did many other signs ["miracles," *TEV, Kx*] in the presence of the disciples, which are not written in this book; but these are written that you may believe that Jesus is the Christ, the Son of God, and that believing you may have life in his name." (So the conclusion we should properly draw from the miracles is that Jesus is "the Christ," the Messiah, "the Son of God." The expression "Son of God" is very different from "God the Son.")

Pre-Christian prophets such as Elijah and Elisha performed miracles similar to those of Jesus. Yet that certainly is no proof that they were God.

Is Jesus the same as Jehovah in the "Old Testament"?

See pages 197, 198, under the main heading "Jehovah."

Is believing in Jesus Christ all that is required for salvation?

Acts 16:30-32, *RS:* "'Men, what must I do to be saved?' And they [Paul and Silas] said, 'Believe in the Lord Jesus, and you will be saved, you and your household.' And they spoke the word of the Lord ["God," *NAB,* also *JB* and *NE* footnotes; "God's message," *AT*] to him and to all that were in his house." (Was that man's 'believing in the Lord Jesus' just a matter of his saying sincerely that he believed? Paul showed that more was required—namely, knowledge and acceptance of the Word of God, as Paul and Silas now proceeded to preach it to the jailer. Would a person's belief in Jesus be genuine if he did not worship the God whom Jesus worshiped, if he did not apply what Jesus taught as to the kind of persons his disciples should be, or if he did not do the work that Jesus commanded his followers to perform? We cannot *earn* salvation; it is possible only on the basis of faith in the value of the sacrifice of Jesus' human life. But our lives must be consistent with the faith that we profess, even though that may involve hardship. At Matthew 10:22 [*RS*] Jesus said: "He who endures to the end will be saved.")

Did Jesus have a heavenly existence before he became a human?

Col. 1:15-17, *RS:* "He [Jesus] is the image of the invisible

God, the first-born of all creation . . . All things were created through him and for him. He is before all things."

John 17:5, *RS:* "[In prayer Jesus said:] Father, glorify thou me in thy own presence with the glory which I had with thee before the world was made." (Also John 8:23)

Does Jesus have his fleshly body in heaven?

1 Cor. 15:42-50, *RS:* "So is it with the resurrection of the dead. What is sown is perishable, what is raised is imperishable. . . . It is sown a physical body, it is raised a spiritual body. . . . Thus it is written, 'The first man Adam became a living being'; the last Adam [Jesus Christ, who was a perfect human as Adam had been at the start] became a life-giving *spirit*. . . . I tell you this, brethren: flesh and blood cannot inherit the kingdom of God, nor does the perishable inherit the imperishable." (Italics added.)

1 Pet. 3:18, *RS:* "Christ also died for sins once for all, . . . being put to death in the flesh but made alive in the spirit [*"in* the spirit," *NE, AT, JB, Dy*]." (See page 334.)

Illustration: If a man pays a debt for a friend but then promptly takes back the payment, obviously the debt continues. Likewise, if, when he was resurrected, Jesus had taken back his human body of flesh and blood, which had been given in sacrifice to pay the ransom price, what effect would that have had on the provision he was making to relieve faithful persons of the debt of sin?

It is true that Jesus appeared in physical form to his disciples after his resurrection. But on certain occasions, why did they not at first recognize him? (Luke 24:15-32; John 20:14-16) On one occasion, for the benefit of Thomas, Jesus appeared with the physical evidence of nail prints in his hands and a spear wound in his side. But how was it possible on that occasion for him suddenly to appear in their midst even though the doors were locked? (John 20:26, 27) Jesus evidently materialized bodies on these occasions, as angels had done in the past when appearing to humans. Disposing of Jesus' physical body at the time of his resurrection presented no problem for God. Interestingly, although the physical body was not left by God in the tomb (evidently to strengthen the conviction of the disciples that Jesus had actually been raised), the linen cloths in which it had been wrapped were left there; yet, the resurrected Jesus always appeared fully clothed.—John 20:6, 7.

Is Jesus Christ the same person as Michael the archangel?

The name of this Michael appears only five times in the Bible. The glorious spirit person who bears the name is referred to as "one of the chief princes," "the great prince who has charge of your [Daniel's] people," and as "the archangel." (Dan. 10:13; 12:1; Jude 9, *RS*) Michael means "Who Is Like God?" The name evidently designates Michael as the one who takes the lead in upholding Jehovah's sovereignty and destroying God's enemies.

At 1 Thessalonians 4:16 (*RS*), the command of Jesus Christ for the resurrection to begin is described as "the archangel's call," and Jude 9 says that the archangel is Michael. Would it be appropriate to liken Jesus' commanding call to that of someone lesser in authority? Reasonably, then, the archangel Michael is Jesus Christ. (Interestingly, the expression "archangel" is never found in the plural in the Scriptures, thus implying that there is only one.)

Revelation 12:7-12 says that Michael and his angels would war against Satan and hurl him and his wicked angels out of heaven in connection with the conferring of kingly authority on Christ. Jesus is later depicted as leading the armies of heaven in war against the nations of the world. (Rev. 19:11-16) Is it not reasonable that Jesus would also be the one to take action against the one he described as "ruler of this world," Satan the Devil? (John 12:31) Daniel 12:1 (*RS*) associates the 'standing up of Michael' to act with authority with "a time of trouble, such as never has been since there was a nation till that time." That would certainly fit the experience of the nations when Christ as heavenly executioner takes action against them. So the evidence indicates that the Son of God was known as Michael before he came to earth and is known also by that name since his return to heaven where he resides as the glorified spirit Son of God.

If Someone Says—

'You don't believe in Jesus'

You might reply: 'Evidently *you* are a person who believes in Jesus. And so do I; otherwise I would not be at your door today.' **Then perhaps add:** 'In fact, the importance of faith in Jesus is prominently featured in our publications. (Turn to an appropriate chapter in whatever book you are offering and use this as a basis for discussion, highlighting his role as King. Or read what is stated on page 2 of *The Watchtower,* regarding the purpose of the magazine.)'

Or you could say: 'Do you mind if I ask you why you feel that way?'

Another possibility: 'Apparently someone has told you that, but may I say that such is not really the case, because we have very strong faith in Jesus Christ.' **Then perhaps add:** (1) 'But we do not believe everything that people say about Jesus. For example, some say that he was just a good man, not the Son of God. We do not believe that, do you? . . . That is not what the Bible teaches.' (2) 'And we do not believe the teachings of groups that contradict what Jesus himself said about his relationship with his Father. (John 14:28) His Father has given him ruling authority that affects the lives of all of us today. (Dan. 7:13, 14)'

'Do you accept Jesus as your personal Savior?'

You might reply: 'The Bible clearly says . . . (quote Acts 4:12). I believe that. But I have also learned that serious responsibilities go with it. How is that? Well, if I really believe in Jesus, then I can't believe in him just as far as it seems convenient.' **Then perhaps add:** 'His perfect life given in sacrifice makes it possible for us to have forgiveness of sins. But I know that it is also vital to pay attention to his instructions regarding our responsibilities as Christians. (Acts 1:8; Matt. 28:19, 20)'

Or you could say: '(After confirming the fact that you do believe in Jesus as Savior, not only of yourself, but of all who exercise faith in him . . .) It is important that we

respond appreciatively not only to what he did in the past
but also to what he is doing now. (Matt. 25:31-33)'

'I have accepted Jesus as my personal Savior'

You might reply: 'I am glad to hear that you believe in
Jesus, because there are so many people today who give no
thought to what Jesus did for us. You no doubt know well
the scripture at John 3:16, don't you? . . . But where will
such people live forever? Some will be with Christ in heaven.
But does the Bible show that all good people go there? (Matt.
6:10; 5:5)'

Jews

Definition: As commonly used today, the term refers to people
of Hebrew descent and others who have been converted to
Judaism. The Bible also draws attention to the fact that there
are Christians who are Jews spiritually and who make up "the
Israel of God."

Are the natural Jews today God's chosen people?

That is the belief of many Jews. Says the *Encyclopaedia
Judaica* (Jerusalem, 1971, Vol. 5, col. 498): "CHOSEN PEO-
PLE, a common designation for the people of Israel, expressing the idea that the people of Israel stands in a special
and unique relationship to the universal deity. This idea has
been a central one throughout the history of Jewish
thought."—See Deuteronomy 7:6-8; Exodus 19:5.

Many in Christendom hold similar views. The "Religion"
section of the Atlanta *Journal and Constitution* (January 22,
1983, p. 5-B) reported: "Contrary to the churches' centuries-
old teachings that God had 'cast off his people Israel' and
replaced them with a 'new Israel,' he [Paul M. Van Buren,
theologian at Temple University in Philadelphia] says
churches now affirm that 'the covenant between God and the

Jewish people is eternal. This amazing reversal has been made by Protestants and Catholics, on both sides of the Atlantic.'" *The New York Times* (February 6, 1983, p. 42) added: "'There is a fascination on the part of the evangelical right with Israel and a belief that everything Israel does must be supported, because God is on Israel's side,' said Timothy Smith, a professor of theology at Johns Hopkins University and a Wesleyan evangelical." Some in Christendom expect the conversion and ultimate salvation of all natural Israel. Others take the view that there has always been an inseparable bond between God and Israel, so they reason that it is only the Gentiles who are to be reconciled through Christ.

Consider: Following the Babylonian exile, when Israel was restored to its land, the people were to restore true worship in their God-given land. One of the first projects undertaken was the rebuilding of Jehovah's temple in Jerusalem. However, since the destruction of Jerusalem by the Romans in 70 C.E., the temple has never been rebuilt. Instead, in the former temple area stands an Islamic shrine. If the Jews, who say they are under the Mosaic Law, were today in Jerusalem *as God's chosen people,* would not the temple devoted to his worship have been rebuilt?

Matt. 21:42, 43: "Jesus said to them [the chief priests and the older men of the Jews in Jerusalem]: 'Did you never read in the Scriptures, "The stone that the builders rejected is the one that has become the chief cornerstone. From Jehovah this has come to be, and it is marvelous in our eyes"? This is why I say to you, The kingdom of God will be taken from you and be given to a nation producing its fruits.'"

Matt. 23:37, 38: "Jerusalem, Jerusalem, the killer of the prophets and stoner of those sent forth to her,—how often I wanted to gather your children together, the way a hen gathers her chicks together under her wings! But you people did not want it. Look! Your house is abandoned to you."

Does God's covenant with Abraham give assurance that the Jews continue to be the chosen people of God?

Gal. 3:27-29: "All of you who were baptized into Christ

have put on Christ. There is neither Jew nor Greek, there is neither slave nor freeman, there is neither male nor female; for you are all one person in union with Christ Jesus. Moreover, *if you belong to Christ, you are really Abraham's seed,* heirs with reference to a promise." (So, from God's standpoint, it is no longer natural descent from Abraham that determines who are Abraham's seed.)

Will all the Jews be converted to faith in Christ and attain to eternal salvation?

Rom. 11:25, 26: "I do not want you, brothers, to be ignorant of this sacred secret, in order for you not to be discreet in your own eyes: that a dulling of sensibilities has happened in part to Israel until the full number of people of the nations has come in, and in this manner ["this is how," *TEV;* "thus," *CC, By;* Greek, *hou'tos*] all Israel will be saved." (Notice that the saving of "all Israel" is accomplished, not by conversion of all the Jews, but by the 'coming in' of people from Gentile nations. Some translators render verse 26: "And then *after this* the rest of Israel will be saved." But *A Manual Greek Lexicon of the New Testament* [Edinburgh, 1937, G. Abbott-Smith, p. 329] defines *hou'tos* as meaning "in this way, so, thus.")

To arrive at a correct understanding of what is recorded at Romans 11:25, 26, we should also take into account these earlier statements in Romans: "He is not a Jew who is one on the outside, nor is circumcision that which is on the outside upon the flesh. But he is a Jew who is one on the inside, and his circumcision is that of the heart by spirit, and not by a written code." (2:28, 29) "Not all who spring from Israel are really 'Israel.'"—9:6.

Is it necessary for Jews to put faith in Jesus Christ in order to be saved?

Isaiah 53:1-12 foretold the death of the Messiah 'to bear the sins of many and to make intercession for the transgressors.' Daniel 9:24-27 connected the coming of the Messiah and his death with 'making an end of sin and forgiving iniquity.' (*JP*) Both passages show that the Jews were in need of such intercession and forgiveness. Could they expect to reject the Messiah and have the approval of the One who sent him?

Acts 4:11, 12: "[Regarding Jesus Christ, the apostle Peter was moved by holy spirit to say to the Jewish rulers and older men in Jerusalem:] This is 'the stone that was treated by you builders as of no account that has become the head of the corner.' Furthermore, there is no salvation in anyone else, for there is not another name under heaven that has been given among men by which we must get saved." (Although the nation of natural Israel no longer enjoys special divine favor, the way is open to individual Jews, as it is to people of all nations, to benefit from the salvation that is made possible through Jesus the Messiah.)

Are the events taking place in Israel today in fulfillment of Bible prophecy?

Ezek. 37:21, 22, *JP:* "Thus saith the Lord GOD: Behold, I will take the children of Israel from among the nations, whither they are gone, and will gather them on every side, and bring them into their own land; and I will make them one nation in the land, upon the mountains of Israel, and one king shall be king to them all." (Israel today is not a nation under a king of the royal line of David. Theirs is a republic.)

Isa. 2:2-4, *JP:* "It shall come to pass in the end of days, that the mountain of the LORD'S house shall be established as the top of the mountains, and shall be exalted above the hills; and all nations shall flow unto it. And many peoples shall go and say: 'Come ye, and let us go up to the mountain of the LORD, to the house of the God of Jacob; and He will teach us of His ways, and we will walk in His paths.' . . . And they shall beat their swords into plowshares, and their spears into pruning-hooks; nation shall not lift up sword against nation, neither shall they learn war any more." (In Jerusalem today, where the temple was formerly located there is no "house of the God of Jacob," but, instead, an Islamic shrine. And there is no move on the part of Israel or its neighbors to "beat their swords into plowshares." They depend for survival on military preparedness.)

Isa. 35:1, 2, *JP:* "The wilderness and the parched land

shall be glad; and the desert shall rejoice, and blossom as the rose. It shall blossom abundantly, and rejoice, even with joy and singing; the glory of Lebanon shall be given unto it, the excellency of Carmel and Sharon; they shall see the glory of the LORD, the excellency of our God." (Remarkable reforestation and irrigation projects have been successfully undertaken in Israel. But its leaders do not give credit to the Lord God. As a former premier, David Ben-Gurion, said: "Israel is determined . . . to conquer the desert and make it flourish by the power of science and the pioneering spirit, and to transform the country into a bastion of democracy.")

Zech. 8:23, *JP:* "In those days it shall come to pass, that ten men shall take hold, out of all the languages of the nations, shall even take hold of the skirt of him that is a Jew, saying: We will go with you, for we have heard that God is with you." (To what God does the prophecy refer? In the Hebrew language his name [יהוה, commonly translated Jehovah] appears over 130 times in this one book of the Holy Scriptures. Today when someone uses that name, do people conclude that the person must be a Jew? No; for many centuries, superstition has caused the Jewish people as a whole to refrain from ever uttering God's personal name. The upsurge of religious interest concerning natural Israel today does not fit this prophecy.)

How, then, are events in modern-day Israel to be viewed? Merely as part of global developments foretold in the Bible. These include war, lawlessness, cooling off of love for God, and the love of money.—Matt. 24:7, 12; 2 Tim. 3:1-5.

Among whom do the prophecies about restoration of Israel have fulfillment today?

Gal. 6:15, 16: "Neither is circumcision anything nor is uncircumcision, but a new creation is something. And all those who will walk orderly by this rule of conduct, upon them be peace and mercy, even upon the Israel of God." (So "the Israel of God" is no longer determined on the basis of conforming to the requirement laid upon Abraham for all the males of his household to be circumcised. Rather, as stated at Galatians 3:26-29, those who belong to Christ and who are spirit-begotten sons of God "are really Abraham's seed.")

Jer. 31:31-34: "'Look! There are days coming,' is the utterance of Jehovah, 'and I will conclude with the house of Israel and with the house of Judah a new covenant . . . And they will no more teach each one his companion and each one his brother, saying, "Know Jehovah!" for they will all of them know me, from the least one of them even to the greatest one of them,' is the utterance of Jehovah." (That new covenant was made, not with the nation of natural Israel, but with the loyal followers of Jesus Christ to whom hope of heavenly life was being extended. When instituting the Memorial of his death, Jesus gave them a cup of wine and said: "This cup means the new covenant by virtue of my blood." [1 Cor. 11:25])

Rev. 7:4: "I heard the number of those who were sealed, a hundred and forty-four thousand, sealed out of every tribe of the sons of Israel." (But in the verses that follow, mention is made of "the tribe of Levi" and "the tribe of Joseph." These were not included in lists of the 12 tribes of natural Israel. Interestingly, while it is said that people would be "sealed out of every tribe," the tribes of Dan and Ephraim are not mentioned. [Compare Numbers 1:4-16.] Reference must here be made to the spiritual Israel of God, to those whom Revelation 14:1-3 shows will share with Christ in his heavenly Kingdom.)

Heb. 12:22: "You have approached a Mount Zion and a city of the living God, heavenly Jerusalem, and myriads of angels." (Thus it is not to earthly Jerusalem but to "heavenly Jerusalem" that true Christians look for fulfillment of the promises of God.)

Kingdom

Definition: The Kingdom of God is the expression of Jehovah's universal sovereignty toward his creatures, or the means used by him to express that sovereignty. This term is used particularly to designate the manifestation of God's sovereignty through the royal government headed by his Son, Jesus Christ. "Kingdom" may refer to the rulership of the one anointed as King or to the earthly realm ruled by that heavenly government.

Is God's Kingdom a real government?

Or is it, instead, a condition in the hearts of men?

Luke 17:21, *KJ:* "Neither shall they say, Lo here! or, lo there! for, behold, the kingdom of God is within you [also *TEV, Dy;* but "among you," *KJ* margin, *NE, JB;* "in the midst of you," *RS;* "in your midst," *NW*]." (Notice that, as shown by verse 20, Jesus was speaking to the Pharisees, whom he also denounced as hypocrites, so he could not have meant that the Kingdom was in *their* hearts. But the Kingdom as represented by Christ was in their midst. Thus *The Emphatic Diaglott* reads: "God's royal majesty is among you.")

Does the Bible actually speak of God's Kingdom as being a government?

Isa. 9:6, 7, *RS:* "To us a child is born, to us a son is given; and the government [also *KJ, AT, Dy;* "dominion," *JB, NE;* "princely rule," *NW*] will be upon his shoulder, and his name will be called 'Wonderful Counselor, Mighty God, Everlasting Father, Prince of Peace.' Of the increase of his government and of peace there will be no end."

Who are the rulers in the Kingdom?

Rev. 15:3: "Great and wonderful are your works, Jehovah God, the Almighty. Righteous and true are your ways, King of eternity."

Dan. 7:13, 14: "With the clouds of the heavens someone like a son of man [Jesus Christ; see Mark 14:61, 62] happened to be coming; and to the Ancient of Days [Jehovah God] he gained access, and they brought him up close even before that One. And to him [to Jesus Christ] there were given rulership and dignity and kingdom, that the peoples, national groups and languages should all serve even him."

Rev. 5:9, 10: "You [Jesus Christ] were slaughtered and with your blood you bought persons for God out of every tribe and tongue and people and nation, and you made them to be a kingdom and priests to our God, and they are to rule as kings over the earth." (At Revelation 14:1-3 these "bought from the earth" to be rulers with the Lamb on heavenly Mount Zion are said to number 144,000.)

What effect will this Kingdom have on human governments?

Dan. 2:44: "In the days of those kings the God of heaven will set up a kingdom that will never be brought to ruin. And the kingdom itself will not be passed on to any other people. It will crush and put an end to all these kingdoms, and it itself will stand to times indefinite."

Ps. 2:8, 9: "Ask of me, that I may give nations as your inheritance and the ends of the earth as your own possession. You will break them with an iron scepter, as though a potter's vessel you will dash them to pieces."

What will God's Kingdom accomplish?

Sanctify Jehovah's name and uphold his sovereignty

Matt. 6:9, 10: "You must pray, then, this way: 'Our Father in the heavens, let your name be sanctified. Let your kingdom come.'" (Here the sanctifying of God's name is closely associated with the coming of his Kingdom.)

Ezek. 38:23: "I shall certainly magnify myself and sanctify myself and make myself known before the eyes of many nations; and they will have to know that I am Jehovah." (God's name will be cleansed of all reproach; it will be treated as holy and deserving of respect, and all who live will be persons who willingly uphold Jehovah's sovereignty, delighting to do his will. Upon such sanctification of Jehovah's name the peace and well-being of all the universe depend.)

Put an end to Satan's tolerated rulership over the world

Rev. 20:2, 3: "He [the heavenly King, Jesus Christ] seized the dragon, the original serpent, who is the Devil and Satan, and bound him for a thousand years. And he hurled him into the abyss and shut it and sealed it over him, that he might not mislead the nations anymore until the thousand years were ended. After these things he must be let loose for a little while." (Thus mankind will be freed from the satanic influence that has made life very difficult for people who want to do what is right. Gone will be the diabolic influence that has caused acts of extreme inhumanity and the demonic influence that has filled the lives of many with fear.)

Unify all creation in worship of the one true God

Rev. 5:13; 15:3, 4: "And every creature that is in heaven and on earth and underneath the earth and on the sea, and all the things in them, I heard saying: 'To the One sitting on the throne [Jehovah God] and to the Lamb [Jesus Christ] be the blessing and the honor and the glory and the might forever and ever.'" "Great and wonderful are your works, Jehovah God, the Almighty. Righteous and true are your ways, King of eternity. Who will not really fear you, Jehovah, and glorify your name, because you alone are loyal? For all the nations will come and worship before you, because your righteous decrees have been made manifest."

Bring mankind back into harmonious relationship with God

Rom. 8:19-21: "The eager expectation of the creation [humankind] is waiting for the revealing of the sons of God [the evidence that those raised to heavenly life with Jesus Christ have gone into action as rulers]. For the creation was subjected to futility, not by its own will but through him that subjected it, on the basis of hope that the creation itself [mankind in general] also will be set free from enslavement to corruption and have the glorious freedom of the children of God."

Free mankind from all threat of war

Ps. 46:8, 9: "Come, you people, behold the activities of Jehovah, how he has set astonishing events on the earth. He is making wars to cease to the extremity of the earth."

Isa. 2:4: "They will have to beat their swords into plowshares and their spears into pruning shears. Nation will not lift up sword against nation, neither will they learn war anymore."

Rid the earth of corrupt rulers and oppression

Ps. 110:5: "Jehovah himself at your right hand will certainly break kings to pieces on the day of his anger."

Ps. 72:12-14: "He [Jehovah's Messianic King] will deliver the poor one crying for help, also the afflicted one and whoever has no helper. He will feel sorry for the lowly one and the poor one, and the souls of the poor ones he will save. From oppression and from violence he will redeem their soul, and their blood will be precious in his eyes."

Provide an abundance of food for all mankind

Ps. 72:16: "There will come to be plenty of grain on the earth; on the top of the mountains there will be an overflow."

Isa. 25:6: "Jehovah of armies will certainly make for all the peoples, in this mountain [in heavenly Mount Zion, the seat of God's Kingdom, provision for its earthly subjects will be made], a banquet of well-oiled dishes, a banquet of wine kept on the dregs, of well-oiled dishes filled with marrow, of wine kept on the dregs, filtered."

Remove sickness and disabilities of all kinds

Luke 7:22; 9:11: "Go your way, report to John what you saw and heard: the blind are receiving sight, the lame are walking, the lepers are being cleansed and the deaf are hearing, the dead are being raised up, the poor are being told the good news." "He [Jesus Christ] received them kindly and began to speak to them about the kingdom of God, and he healed those needing a cure." (Thus Jesus demonstrated what he as heavenly King will do for mankind.)

Provide suitable homes for everyone

Isa. 65:21, 22: "They will certainly build houses and have occupancy; and they will certainly plant vineyards and eat their fruitage. They will not build and someone else have occupancy; they will not plant and someone else do the eating."

Assure satisfying employment for all

Isa. 65:23: "They will not toil for nothing, nor will they bring to birth for disturbance; because they are the offspring made up of the blessed ones of Jehovah, and their descendants with them."

Guarantee security, freedom from danger to one's person or property

Mic. 4:4: "They will actually sit, each one under his vine and under his fig tree, and there will be no one making them tremble; for the very mouth of Jehovah of armies has spoken it."

Ps. 37:10, 11: "Just a little while longer, and the wicked one will be no more; and you will certainly give attention to his place, and he will not be. But the meek ones themselves will possess the earth, and they will indeed find their exquisite delight in the abundance of peace."

Cause righteousness and justice to prevail

2 Pet. 3:13: "There are new heavens and a new earth that we are awaiting according to his promise, and in these righteousness is to dwell."

Isa. 11:3-5: "He [the Messianic King] will not judge by any mere appearance to his eyes, nor reprove simply according to the thing heard by his ears. And with righteousness he must judge the lowly ones, and with uprightness he must give reproof in behalf of the meek ones of the earth. . . . And righteousness must prove to be the belt of his hips, and faithfulness the belt of his loins."

Safeguard mankind from any injury due to natural forces

Mark 4:37-41: "Now a great violent windstorm broke out, and the waves kept dashing into the boat, so that the boat was close to being swamped. . . . With that he [Jesus] roused himself and rebuked the wind and said to the sea: 'Hush! Be quiet!' And the wind abated, and a great calm set in. . . . But they felt an unusual fear, and they would say to one another: 'Who really is this, because even the wind and the sea obey him?'" (Thus Christ demonstrated the power that he as heavenly King will exercise over such natural elements.)

Resurrect the dead

John 5:28, 29: "Do not marvel at this, because the hour is

coming in which all those in the memorial tombs will hear his voice [the voice of Christ the King] and come out.'"

Rev. 20:12: "I saw the dead, the great and the small, standing before the throne, and scrolls were opened. But another scroll was opened; it is the scroll of life. And the dead were judged out of those things written in the scrolls according to their deeds [those done following their resurrection; compare Romans 6:7]."

Remove all death due to inheritance of Adamic sin

Isa. 25:8: "He will actually swallow up death forever, and the Sovereign Lord Jehovah will certainly wipe the tears from all faces."

Rev. 21:4: "He will wipe out every tear from their eyes, and death will be no more, neither will mourning nor outcry nor pain be anymore. The former things have passed away."

Provide a world in which people genuinely love one another

John 13:35: "By this all will know that you are my disciples [hence, in line to be Jesus' associates in the heavenly Kingdom or earthly subjects of that Kingdom], if you have love among yourselves."

Bring animals and humans into harmonious relationship with one another

Isa. 11:6-9: "The wolf will actually reside for a while with the male lamb, and with the kid the leopard itself will lie down, and the calf and the maned young lion and the well-fed animal all together; and a mere little boy will be leader over them. And the cow and the bear themselves will feed; together their young ones will lie down. And even the lion will eat straw just like the bull. And the sucking child will certainly play upon the hole of the cobra; and upon the light aperture of a poisonous snake will a weaned child actually put his own hand. They will not do any harm or cause any ruin in all my holy mountain." (Also Isaiah 65:25)

Hos. 2:18: "For them I shall certainly conclude a covenant in that day in connection with the wild beast of the field and with the flying creature of the heavens and the creeping thing of the ground, . . . and I will make them lie down in security."

Make the earth a paradise

Luke 23:43: "Truly I tell you today, You will be with me in Paradise."

Ps. 98:7-9: "Let the sea thunder and that which fills it, the productive land and those dwelling in it. Let the rivers themselves clap their hands; all together let the very mountains cry out joyfully before Jehovah, for he has come to judge the earth. He will judge the productive land with righteousness and the peoples with uprightness."

Compare Genesis 1:28; 2:15; Isaiah 55:11.

When was God's Kingdom to begin to rule?

Was it in the first century?

Col. 1:1, 2, 13: "Paul, an apostle of Christ Jesus through God's will, and Timothy our brother to the holy ones [those who were heirs of the heavenly Kingdom] . . . He [God] delivered us from the authority of the darkness and transferred us [the holy ones, members of the Christian congregation] into the kingdom of the Son of his love." (So Christ had, indeed, begun to rule over the Christian congregation in the first century, before this was written, but the establishment of the Kingdom to rule over all the earth was yet future.)

1 Cor. 4:8: "You men already have your fill, do you? You are rich already, are you? You have begun ruling as kings without us, have you? And I wish indeed that you had begun ruling as kings, that we also might rule with you as kings." (It is obvious that the apostle Paul is reproving them for having the wrong viewpoint.)

Rev. 12:10, 12: "Now have come to pass the salvation and the power and *the kingdom of our God and the authority of his Christ,* because the accuser of our brothers has been hurled down, who accuses them day and night before our God! On this account be glad, you heavens and you who reside in them! Woe for the earth and for the sea, because the Devil has come down to you, having great anger, knowing he has a short period of time." (The establishment of God's Kingdom is here associated with the hurling of Satan out of heaven. This had not occurred at the time of the rebellion in Eden, as is shown in Job chapters 1, 2. Revelation was recorded in 96 C.E., and Revelation 1:1 shows that it deals with events then future.)

Must the coming to power of God's Kingdom await the conversion of the world?

Ps. 110:1, 2: "The utterance of Jehovah to my Lord [Jesus Christ] is: 'Sit at my right hand until I place your enemies as a stool for your feet.' The rod of your strength Jehovah will send out of Zion, saying: 'Go subduing in the midst of your enemies.'" (So there would be enemies for him to subdue; not all would submit to his rule.)

Matt. 25:31-46: "When the Son of man [Jesus Christ] arrives in his glory, and all the angels with him, then he will sit down on his glorious throne. And all the nations will be gathered before him, and he will separate people one from another, just as a shepherd separates the sheep from the goats. . . . And these [who showed no love for his anointed brothers] will depart into everlasting cutting-off, but the righteous ones into everlasting life." (Obviously, not all mankind were to be converted before Christ would take his throne; not all would prove to be righteous ones.)

Does the Bible indicate when the Kingdom would begin its rule?

See pages 95-97, under the main heading "Dates," and pages 234-239, under "Last Days."

If Someone Says—

'It won't come in my lifetime'

You might reply: 'But it is going to come in someone's lifetime, isn't it? . . . Would anyone be able to know that his generation was the one to see it? Jesus' own apostles wanted to know that, and the answer he gave them is very significant for us today. (Matt. 24:3-14; Luke 21:29-32)'

Or you could say: 'That view is a very common one. But Jehovah's Witnesses firmly believe, on the basis of the Bible, that God's Kingdom is already ruling in the heavens and that it is up to us to show whether we want to continue to live on earth under God's righteous government or not. That is why I came to your door today. Notice what is stated here at Matthew 25:31-33.'

Last Days

Definition: The Bible uses the expression "last days" to refer to the concluding time period leading up to a divinely appointed execution that marks the end of a system of things. The Jewish system with its worship built around the temple in Jerusalem experienced its last days from 33 to 70 C.E. What occurred then was pictorial of what would be experienced in a greatly intensified way and on a global scale at a time when all nations would be facing the execution of judgment decreed by God. The present wicked system of things, which extends worldwide, entered its last days in 1914, and some of the generation alive then will also be on hand to witness its complete end in the "great tribulation."

What indicates that we today are living in "the last days"?

The Bible describes events and conditions that mark this significant time period. "The sign" is a composite one made up of many evidences; thus its fulfillment requires that all aspects of the sign be clearly in evidence during one generation. The various aspects of the sign are recorded at Matthew chapters 24, 25, Mark 13, and Luke 21; there are further details at 2 Timothy 3:1-5, 2 Peter 3:3, 4, and Revelation 6:1-8. By way of illustration, we will consider a few outstanding portions of the sign.

"Nation will rise against nation and kingdom against kingdom" (Matt. 24:7)

War has marred life on the earth for thousands of years.

International wars and wars within nations have been fought. But beginning in 1914 the first *world* war was fought. This was not merely a conflict between two armies on the battlefield. For the first time, all the major powers were at war. Entire nations—including civilian populations—were mobilized to support the war effort. It is estimated that by the end of the war 93 percent of the population of the world was involved. (Regarding the historical significance of 1914, see pages 239, 240.)

As foretold at Revelation 6:4, 'peace was taken away from the earth.' Thus the world has continued to be in a state of upheaval ever since 1914. World War II was fought from 1939 to 1945. According to retired Admiral Gene La Rocque, as of 1982 there had been another 270 wars since 1945. Upwards of 100 million persons have been slaughtered in warfare during this century. Also, according to the 1982 edition of *World Military and Social Expenditures,* there were in that year 100 million people engaged directly or indirectly in military activities.

Is more required in order to fulfill this aspect of the prophecy? There are tens of thousands of nuclear weapons deployed for immediate use. Leading scientists have said that if the nations were to use even a fraction of their nuclear arsenals, civilization and possibly the entire human species would be destroyed. But that is not the outcome to which Bible prophecy points.

"There will be food shortages ... in one place after another" (Matt. 24:7)

There have been many famines in human history. To what extent has the 20th century been afflicted by them? World war led to widespread starvation in Europe and Asia. Africa has been stricken by drought, resulting in extensive food shortages. Late in 1980 the Food and Agriculture Organization estimated that 450 million people were hungry to the point of starvation, and up to a billion did not have enough to eat. Of these, some 40 million a year actually die—in some years as many as 50 million—because of the shortage of food.

Is anything different about these food shortages? Revelation 6:6 indicated that a small quantity of such staples as wheat or barley would be selling for a day's wage (a denarius; see Matthew 20:2) but that supplies of such items as olive oil and wine used by people who are well-to-do would not be harmed. So apparently many would suffer shortage while others could still get what they wanted. This situation is no longer local, but *global.* In 1981 *The New York Times* reported: "The improvement in living standards and the growing demand for food around the world have put pressure on food prices, making it harder for the poorest countries to import their food needs." In many lands the production of food, *even with the aid of modern science,* has not been able to keep pace with the increase in total population. Modern food experts see no real solution to the problem.

"There will be great earthquakes" (Luke 21:11)

It is true that there were major quakes in centuries past; furthermore, with their sensitive equipment scientists now detect more than a million quakes a year. But no special instruments are needed for people to know when there is a *great* earthquake.

Has there actually been a significant number of major earthquakes since 1914? With data obtained from the National Geophysical Data Center in Boulder, Colorado, supplemented by a number of standard reference works, a tabulation was made in 1984 that included only earthquakes that measured 7.5 or more on the Richter scale, or that resulted in destruction of five million dollars (U.S.) or more in property, or that caused 100 or more deaths. It was calculated that there had been 856 of such earthquakes during the 2,000 years before 1914. The same tabulation showed that in *just 69 years* following 1914 there were 605 of such quakes. That means that, in comparison with the previous 2,000 years, the average per year has been 20 times as great since 1914.

"In one place after another pestilences" (Luke 21:11)

At the close of the first world war the Spanish flu swept around the globe, claiming upwards of 20 million lives and at a rate unparalleled in the history of disease. Despite advances in medical science, a heavy toll is exacted every year by cancer, heart disease, numerous sexually transmitted diseases, multiple sclerosis, malaria, river blindness, and Chagas' disease.

'Increased lawlessness accompanied by a cooling off of love on the part of the greater number' (Matt. 24:11, 12)

A leading criminologist says: "The one thing that hits you in the eye when you look at crime on the world scale is a pervasive and persistent increase everywhere. Such exceptions as there are stand out in splendid isolation, and may soon be swamped in the rising tide." (*The Growth of Crime,* New York, 1977, Sir Leon Radzinowicz and Joan King, pp. 4, 5) The increase is real; it is not merely a matter of better reporting. It is true, past generations had criminals too, but never before has crime been as pervasive as it is now. Persons who are up in years know that from personal experience.

The lawlessness referred to in the prophecy includes contempt for the known laws of God, a placing of self instead of God at the center of one's life. As a result of this attitude, divorce rates are skyrocketing, sex outside of marriage and homosexuality are widely accepted, and tens of millions of abortions are performed every year. Such lawlessness is associated (in Matthew 24:11, 12) with the influence of false prophets, those who set aside God's Word in favor of their own teachings. Heeding their philosophies instead of holding to the Bible contributes toward a loveless world. (1 John 4:8) Read the description of it at 2 Timothy 3:1-5.

"Men become faint out of fear and expectation of the things coming upon the inhabited earth" (Luke 21:25, 26)

"The fact is that today the biggest single emotion which dominates our lives is fear," said *U.S. News & World Report.* (October 11, 1965, p. 144) "Never before has mankind been as fearful as at present," reported the German magazine *Hörzu.*—No. 25, June 20, 1980, p. 22.

Many factors contribute to this global atmosphere of fear: violent crime, unemployment, economic instability because so many nations are hopelessly in debt, worldwide pollution of the environment, lack of strong and loving family ties, and the overwhelming feeling that mankind is in imminent danger of nuclear annihilation. Luke 21:25 mentions 'signs in sun, moon, and stars, and roaring of the seas' in connection with the anguish felt by the nations. The rising of the sun often causes, not happy anticipation, but fear of what the day may bring; when the moon and stars shine, fear of crime makes people stay behind locked doors. In the 20th century, but not before, planes and missiles have been used to send destruction streaking down from the heavens. Submarines carrying deadly loads of missiles prowl the seas, just one such submarine being equipped to annihilate 160 cities. No wonder the nations are in anguish!

'Christ's true followers to be objects of hatred by all nations on account of his name' (Matt. 24:9)

This persecution is not because of political meddling but 'on account of the name of Jesus Christ,' because his followers adhere to him as Jehovah's Messianic King, because of their obeying Christ ahead of any earthly ruler, because of their loyally adhering to his Kingdom and not becoming involved in the affairs of human governments. As modern-day history testifies, that has been the experience of Jehovah's Witnesses in all parts of the earth.

'This good news of the kingdom preached in all the inhabited earth for a witness' (Matt. 24:14)

The message that would be preached is that God's Kingdom in the hands of Jesus Christ has begun to rule in the heavens, that soon it will put an end to the entire wicked system of things, that under its rule mankind will be brought to perfection and earth will become a paradise. That good news is being preached today in over 200 lands and island groups, to the most distant parts of the earth. Jehovah's Witnesses devote hundreds of millions of hours to this activity each year, making repeated house-to-house visits so that everyone possible is given the opportunity to hear.

To what do all these events of "the last days" point?

Luke 21:31, 32: "When you see these things occurring, know that the kingdom of God is near [that is, the time when it will destroy the present wicked world and itself take full charge of earth's affairs]. Truly I say to you, This generation will by no means pass away until all things occur." (The "generation" that was alive at the beginning of fulfillment of the sign in 1914 is now well along in years. The time remaining must be very short. World conditions give every indication that this is the case.)

Why do Jehovah's Witnesses say that it was in 1914 that "the last days" began?

The year 1914 is marked by Bible prophecy. For details regarding the chronology, see pages 95-97, under the main heading "Dates." The correctness of the date is shown by the fact that world conditions foretold to mark this time period have come to pass since 1914 exactly as foretold. The facts set out above illustrate this.

How do secular historians view the year 1914?

"Looking back from the vantage point of the present we see clearly today that the outbreak of World War I ushered in a twentieth-century 'Time of Troubles'—in the expressive term of the British historian Arnold Toynbee—from which our civilization has by no means yet emerged. Directly or indirectly all the convulsions of the last half century stem back to 1914."—*The Fall of the Dynasties: The Collapse of the Old Order* (New York, 1963), Edmond Taylor, p. 16.

"People of the World War II generation, my generation, will always think of their conflict as the great modern watershed of change. . . . We should be allowed our vanity, our personal rendezvous with history. But we should know that, in social terms, a far more decisive change came with World War I. It was then that political and social systems, centuries in the building, came apart—sometimes in a matter of weeks. And others were permanently transformed. It was in World War I that the age-old certainties were lost.

. . . World War II continued, enlarged and affirmed this change. In social terms World War II was the last battle of World War I."—*The Age of Uncertainty* (Boston, 1977), John K. Galbraith, p. 133.

"Half a century has gone by, yet the mark that the tragedy of the Great War [World War I, which started in 1914] left on the body and soul of the nations has not faded . . . The physical and moral magnitude of this ordeal was such that nothing left was the same as before. Society in its entirety: systems of government, national borders, laws, armed forces, interstate relations, but also ideologies, family life, fortunes, positions, personal relations—everything was changed from top to bottom. . . . Humanity finally lost its balance, never to recover it to this day."—General Charles de Gaulle, speaking in 1968 (*Le Monde,* Nov. 12, 1968, p. 9).

Will anyone at all be alive on earth after the end of the present world system?

Definitely yes. The end of the present global system will come, not as a result of indiscriminate slaughter in nuclear war, but in a great tribulation that includes "the war of the great day of God the Almighty." (Rev. 16:14, 16) That war will not destroy the earth, nor will it bring all mankind to ruin.

Matt. 24:21, 22: "Then there will be great tribulation such as has not occurred since the world's beginning until now, no, nor will occur again. In fact, unless those days were cut short, no flesh would be saved; but on account of the chosen ones those days will be cut short." (So some "flesh," some of humankind, will survive.)

Prov. 2:21, 22: "The upright are the ones that will reside in the earth, and the blameless are the ones that will be left over in it. As regards the wicked, they will be cut off from the very earth; and as for the treacherous, they will be torn away from it."

Ps. 37:29, 34: "The righteous themselves will possess the earth, and they will reside forever upon it. Hope in Jehovah and keep his way, and he will exalt you to take possession of the earth. When the wicked ones are cut off, you will see it."

Why does God allow so much time to pass before destroying the wicked?

2 Pet. 3:9: "Jehovah is not slow respecting his promise, as some people consider slowness, but he is patient with you because he does not desire any to be destroyed but desires all to attain to repentance."

Mark 13:10: "In all the nations the good news has to be preached first."

Matt. 25:31, 32, 46: "When the Son of man [Jesus Christ] arrives in his glory, and all the angels with him, then he will sit down on his glorious throne. And all the nations will be gathered before him, and he will separate people one from another, just as a shepherd separates the sheep from the goats. And these [who fail to recognize Christ's spiritual brothers as representatives of the King himself] will depart into everlasting cutting-off, but the righteous ones into everlasting life."

See also pages 363, 364 and 428-430.

If Someone Says—

'Conditions are no worse today; there have always been wars, famines, earthquakes, crime'

You might reply: 'I can understand why you feel that way. We were born into a world where these things are everyday news. But historians explain that there is something drastically different about the 20th century. (Read quotations on pages 239, 240.)'

Or you could say: 'It is not merely the fact that there have been wars, famines, earthquakes, and crime that is significant. Did you realize that the sign Jesus gave was a composite one?' **Then perhaps add:** 'He did not say that any one event by itself would prove that we were in "the last days." But when the entire sign is in evidence, that is significant—and especially when it appears on a global scale and beginning with a year that is fixed by Bible chronology.' (See pages 234-239, also pages 95-97.)

'How do you know that some future generation won't fit the prophecy even better than this one?'

You might reply: 'That's an interesting question, and the answer highlights the fact that we really are living in "the last days." How? Well, part of the sign given by Jesus involves war between nations and kingdoms. But what would happen today if fulfillment of the sign required that we wait until another all-out war were to break out between the superpowers? Such a war would leave few if any survivors. So, you see, God's purpose that there be survivors indicates that we are now very close to the end of this old system.'

Or you could say: 'Matching world events to this prophecy is like matching a fingerprint to its owner. There will not be someone else with the identical print. Likewise, the pattern of events that began in 1914 will not be repeated in some future generation.' **Then perhaps add:** (1) 'Everything that goes to make up the sign is clearly in evidence.' (2) 'Surely we do not want to be like the people in Noah's day. (Matt. 24:37-39)'

'We won't see the end in our lifetime'

You might reply: 'But you do believe that God is going to intervene at some time, don't you?' **Then perhaps add:** (1) 'The only way that any of us could know when that will be is if He made that information available to us. Now, Jesus stated plainly that no man knows the day or the hour, but he did describe in detail the things that would happen during the generation when it would occur.' (2) 'That description deals with events with which you personally are familiar. (If possible, discuss details of the sign, using the facts provided on the preceding pages.)'

'I don't worry about these things; I live just one day at a time'

You might reply: 'It certainly is good not to be overly anxious about the future. But we all do try to plan our lives in such a way as to protect ourselves and our loved ones. Realistic planning is practical. The Bible shows that there are wonderful things ahead, and we are wise if we plan so as to benefit from them. (Prov. 1:33; 2 Pet. 3:13)'

'I don't dwell on all these bad conditions; I like to be optimistic about the future'

You might reply: 'Interestingly, Jesus said that there would be good reason for his followers to be optimistic in our day. (Luke 21:28, 31)' **Then perhaps add:** 'But notice that he is not telling them to close their eyes to what is happening in the world and be happy. He is saying that their optimism would be well founded; it would be because they understood the meaning of world events and knew what the outcome would be.'

Life

Definition: An active condition that distinguishes plants, animals, humans, and spirit beings from inanimate objects. Physical living things generally have the capabilities of growth, metabolism, response to external stimuli, and reproduction. Vegetation has active life but not life as a sense-possessing soul. In earthly souls, animal and human, there are both active life-force to animate them and breath to sustain that life-force.

Life in the fullest sense, as applied to intelligent persons, is perfect existence with the right to it. The human soul is not immortal. But faithful servants of God have the prospect of everlasting life in perfection—on earth for many, in heaven for a "little flock" as heirs of the Kingdom of God. Upon their resurrection to spirit life, members of the Kingdom class are also granted immortality, a quality of life that does not need to be sustained by any created thing.

What is the purpose of human life?

Basic to having purpose in our lives is recognition of the Source of life. If life were the product of mindless chance, our existence would, of necessity, be without purpose, and there would be no dependable future for which we could plan. But Acts 17:24, 25, 28 informs us: "The God that made the world and all the things in it . . . gives to all persons life and breath and all things. For by him we have life and move and exist." Revelation 4:11, which is addressed to God, adds: "You are worthy, Jehovah, even our God, to receive the glory and the honor and the power, because you created all things, and because of your will they existed and were created." (See also pages 145-151, under the main heading "God.")

Frustration results from a life course that conflicts with the Creator's requirements and his guidelines for happiness. Galatians 6:7, 8 warns: "Do not be misled: God is not one to be mocked. For whatever a man is sowing, this he will also reap; because he who is sowing with a view to his flesh will reap corruption from his flesh."—Also Galatians 5:19-21. (See also the main heading "Independence.")

The inheritance of sin from Adam prevents humans from having at present full enjoyment of life as God purposed at the beginning. Romans 8:20 states that, as a result of divine judgment following Adam's sin, "the creation [humankind] was subjected to futility." Regarding his own situation as a sinful human, the apostle Paul wrote: "I am fleshly, sold under sin. For the good that I wish I do not do, but the bad that I do not wish is what I practice. I really delight in the law of God according to the man I am within, but I behold in my members another law warring against the law of my mind and leading me captive to sin's law that is in my members. Miserable man that I am!"—Rom. 7:14, 19, 22-24.

We find the greatest happiness possible now and our lives take on richness of meaning when we apply Bible principles and put first the doing of God's will. We do not enrich God by serving him; he teaches us 'to benefit ourselves.' (Isa. 48:17) The Bible counsels: "Become steadfast, unmovable, always having plenty to do in the work of the Lord, knowing that your labor is not in vain in connection with the Lord." —1 Cor. 15:58.

The Bible sets before us *the prospect of eternal life in perfection* if we put faith in Jehovah's provisions for life and walk in his ways. That hope is solidly based; it will not lead to disappointment; activity in harmony with that hope can fill our lives with real meaning even now.—John 3:16; Titus 1:2; 1 Pet. 2:6.

Were humans made simply to live for a few years and then die?

Gen. 2:15-17: "Jehovah God proceeded to take the man [Adam] and settle him in the garden of Eden to cultivate it and to take care of it. And Jehovah God also laid this command upon the man: 'From every tree of the garden you may eat to satisfaction. But as for the tree of the knowledge of good and bad you must not eat from it, for in the day you eat from it you will positively die.'" (God here spoke of death, not as an unavoidable circumstance, but as what would result from sin. He was urging Adam to avoid it. Compare Romans 6:23.)

Gen. 2:8, 9: "Jehovah God planted a garden in Eden, toward the east, and there he put the man whom he had formed. Thus Jehovah God made to grow out of the ground every tree desirable to one's sight and good for food and also the tree of life in the middle of the garden." (After Adam's sin the human pair were driven out of Eden so that they would not eat from the tree of life, according to Genesis 3: 22, 23. So it seems that if Adam had remained obedient to his Creator, God would in time have permitted him to eat from that tree as a symbol of his having proved worthy to live forever. The presence of the tree of life in Eden pointed to such a prospect.)

Ps. 37:29: "The righteous themselves will possess the earth, and they will reside forever upon it." (This promise makes it clear that God's basic purpose regarding the earth and mankind has not changed.)

See also page 98, under the main heading "Death."

But in our own case today, is a brief existence, often marred by suffering, what life is meant to be?

Rom. 5:12: "Through one man [Adam] sin entered into the world and death through sin, and thus death spread to all men because they had all sinned." (That is what all of us inherited, not because God purposed it, but because of Adam's sin.) (See also the main heading "Fate.")

Job 14:1: "Man, born of woman, is short-lived and glutted with agitation." (To a large extent that characterizes life in this imperfect system of things.)

However, even under these circumstances our lives can be richly rewarding, filled with meaning. See the material on pages 243, 244 on the purpose of human life.

Is life on earth simply a proving ground to determine who will go to heaven?

See pages 162-168, under the main heading "Heaven."

Do we have an immortal soul that continues to live after death of the fleshly body?

See pages 375-380, under the main heading "Soul."

On what basis can anyone hope to have more than his present brief human existence?

Matt. 20:28: "The Son of man [Jesus Christ] came, not to be ministered to, but to minister and to give his soul a ransom in exchange for many."

John 3:16: "God loved the world so much that he gave his only-begotten Son, in order that everyone *exercising faith* in him might not be destroyed but have everlasting life."

Heb. 5:9: "After he [Jesus Christ] had been made perfect he became responsible for everlasting salvation to all those *obeying* him." (Also John 3:36)

How will the prospects for future life be realized?

Acts 24:15: "I have hope toward God, which hope these men themselves also entertain, that there is going to be a resurrection of both the righteous and the unrighteous." (This will include persons who faithfully served God in the past as well as the large number who never knew enough about the true God to accept or to reject his ways.)

John 11:25, 26: "Jesus said to her [the sister of a man whom he thereafter restored to life]: 'I am the resurrection and the life. He that exercises faith in me, even though he dies, will come to life; and everyone that is living and exercises faith in me will never die at all. Do you believe this?'" (So, besides the hope of resurrection, Jesus held out something else for persons living when the present wicked world comes to its end. Those with the hope of being earthly subjects of God's Kingdom have the prospect of surviving and never dying at all.)

Is there any evidence in the makeup of the human body that it was designed to live forever?

It is widely recognized that the capacity of the human brain far exceeds any use to which we put it during our present lifetime, whether we live to 70 or even 100 years of age. The *Encyclopædia Britannica* states that the human brain "is endowed with considerably more potential than is realizable in the course of one person's lifetime." (1976, Vol. 12, p. 998) Scientist Carl Sagan states that the human brain could hold information that "would fill some twenty million volumes, as many as in the world's largest libraries." (*Cosmos,* 1980, p. 278) Regarding the capacity of the human brain's "filing system," biochemist Isaac Asimov wrote that it is "perfectly capable of handling any load of learning and memory which the human being is likely to put upon it—and a billion times more than that quantity, too."—*The New York Times Magazine,* October 9, 1966, p. 146. (Why was the human brain endowed with such a capacity if it was not to be used? Is it not reasonable that humans, with the capacity for endless learning, were actually designed to live forever?)

Is there life on other planets?

The New York Times reports: "The search for intelligent life elsewhere in the universe . . . began 25 years ago . . . The awesome task, which involves scanning hundreds of billions of stars, has so far yielded no clear evidence that life exists beyond Earth."—July 2, 1984, p. A1.

The Encyclopedia Americana says: "No other planets

[outside our solar system] have definitely been detected. But for each planet that might exist outside the solar system, there is a chance that life began and evolved into an advanced civilization." (1977, Vol. 22, p. 176) (As reflected in this statement, could it be that a major motivation in the extremely costly search for life in outer space is the desire to find some proof for the theory of evolution, some evidence that man was not created by God and so is not accountable to Him?)

The Bible reveals that life on this earth is not the only life there is. There are spirit beings—God and the angels —that are vastly superior to man in intelligence and power. They have already communicated with humankind, explaining the origin of life and what the solution is to the overwhelming problems that confront the world. (See the main headings "Bible" and "God.")

Marriage

Definition: The union of a man and a woman to live together as husband and wife according to the standard set out in the Holy Scriptures. Marriage is a divine institution. It provides for intimate relationship between husband and wife along with a feeling of security because there is a climate of love and because a personal commitment has been made by each mate. When establishing marriage, Jehovah did so not only to provide a close companion who would be a complement of man but also to make provision for producing more humans and doing so within a family arrangement. Legally registering a marriage relationship that is acceptable to the Christian congregation is required wherever possible.

Is it really important to get married in accord with legal requirements?

Titus 3:1: "Continue reminding them to be in subjection and be obedient to governments and authorities as rulers." (When people heed these instructions, the name of each party to the union is kept above reproach, and any children are spared the reproach that falls on those whose parents are not married. Additionally, legal registration of the marriage safeguards the property rights of family members in the event of death of one of the mates.)

Heb. 13:4: "Let marriage be honorable among all, and the marriage bed be without defilement, for God will judge fornicators and adulterers." (Getting legally married plays an important part in having a marriage that is accepted as being "honorable." When defining "fornication" and "adultery," we should keep in mind what is stated at Titus 3:1, quoted above.)

1 Pet. 2:12-15: "Maintain your conduct fine among the nations, that, in the thing in which they are speaking against you as evildoers, they may as a result of your fine works of which they are eyewitnesses glorify God in the day for his inspection. For the Lord's sake subject yourselves to every human creation: whether to a king as being superior or to governors as being sent by him to inflict punishment on evildoers but to praise doers of good. For so the will of God is, that by doing good you may muzzle the ignorant talk of the unreasonable men."

Were there any "legal formalities" when Adam and Eve began to live together?

Gen. 2:22-24: "Jehovah God proceeded to build the rib that he had taken from the man [Adam] into a woman and to bring her to the man. Then the man said: 'This is at last bone of my bones and flesh of my flesh. This one will be called Woman, because from man this one was taken.' That is why a man will leave his father and his mother and he must stick to his wife and they must become one flesh." (Notice that it was Jehovah God himself, the Universal Sovereign, who brought Adam and Eve together. This was not a matter of a man and a woman deciding to live together without concerning themselves about legal authority. Observe, too, the emphasis that God placed on the permanence of the union.)

Gen. 1:28: "God blessed them [Adam and Eve] and God said to them: 'Be fruitful and become many and fill the earth and subdue it, and have in subjection the fish of the sea and the flying creatures of the heavens and every living creature that is moving upon the earth.'" (Here the blessing of the highest legal Authority was pronounced upon the union, they were authorized to have sex relations and were given an assignment that would fill their lives with meaning.)

May a person practice polygamy if local law allows for it?

1 Tim. 3:2, 12: "The overseer should therefore be irreprehensible, a husband of one wife . . . Let ministerial servants be husbands of one wife." (Not only were these men entrusted with responsibility but they were also examples to be imitated by others in the Christian congregation.)

1 Cor. 7:2: "Because of prevalence of fornication, let each man have his own wife and each woman have her own husband." (There is no allowance here for plurality of mates on either side.)

Why did God permit Abraham, Jacob, and Solomon each to have more than one wife?

Jehovah is not the originator of polygamy. He gave Adam just one wife. Later, Lamech, a descendant of Cain, took two wives for himself. (Gen. 4:19) In time others imitated his example, and some took slave girls as concubines. God tolerated the practice, and under the Mosaic Law he even instituted measures to assure proper treatment of women who had such a relationship. He did this until the Christian congregation was established, but then he required that his servants return to the standard that he himself had instituted in Eden.

As for *Abraham,* he took Sarai (Sarah) as his wife. When she was about 75 years of age and thought she would never bear a child, *she* requested her husband to have relations with her maidservant so that Sarai could have a legal child by means of her. Abraham did so, but it led to serious friction in his household. (Gen. 16:1-4) Jehovah fulfilled his promise to Abraham regarding a "seed" by later miraculously causing Sarah herself to become pregnant. (Gen. 18:9-14) It was not until after Sarah's death that Abraham took another wife.—Gen. 23:2; 25:1.

Jacob became a polygamist because of deception on the part of his father-in-law. It was not what Jacob had in mind when he went to seek a wife in Pad'dan-a'ram. The Bible record tells in considerable detail about the unhappy rivalry between his wives.—Gen. 29:18–30:24.

It is well known that *Solomon* had many wives as well as concubines. But not everyone is aware that, in doing so, he was violating Jehovah's clearly stated commandment that the king "should also *not* multiply wives for himself, that his heart may not turn aside." (Deut. 17:17) It should also be noted that, because of the influence of his foreign wives, Solomon turned to the worship of false gods and "began to do what was bad in the eyes of Jehovah . . . And Jehovah came to be incensed at Solomon."—1 Ki. 11:1-9.

If mates just cannot live together in peace, is separation permissible?

1 Cor. 7:10-16: "To the married people I give instructions, yet not I but the Lord, that a wife should not depart from her husband; but if she should actually depart, let her remain unmarried or else make up again with her husband; and a husband should not leave his wife. But to the others I say, yes, I, not the Lord [but, as verse 40 shows, Paul was directed by holy spirit]: If any brother has an unbelieving wife, and yet she is agreeable to dwelling with him, let him not leave her; and a woman who has an unbelieving husband, and yet he is agreeable to dwelling with her, let her not leave her husband. For the unbelieving husband is sanctified in relation to his wife, and the unbelieving wife is sanctified in relation to the brother; otherwise, your children would really be unclean, but now they are holy. But if the unbelieving one proceeds to depart, let him depart; a brother or a sister is not in servitude under such circumstances, but God has called you to peace. For, wife, how do you know but that you will save your husband? Or, husband, how do you know but that you will save your wife?" (Why would the believer put up with hardship and earnestly endeavor to hold the marriage together? Out of respect for the divine origin of marriage and in hope that the unbeliever may in time be helped to become a servant of the true God.)

What is the Bible's view regarding divorce with a view to remarriage?

Mal. 2:15, 16: "'You people must guard yourselves respecting your spirit, and with the wife of your youth may no one deal treacherously. For he has hated a divorcing,' Jehovah the God of Israel has said."

Matt. 19:8, 9: "[Jesus] said to them: 'Moses, out of regard for your hardheartedness, made the concession to you of divorcing your wives, but such has not been the case from the beginning. I say to you that whoever divorces his wife, *except on the ground of fornication* [extramarital intercourse], and marries another commits adultery.'" (So the innocent mate is permitted, but not required, to divorce a mate who commits "fornication.")

Rom. 7:2, 3: "A married woman is bound by law to her husband while he is alive; but if her husband dies, she is discharged from the law of her husband. So, then, while her husband is living, she would be styled an adulteress if she became another man's. But if her husband dies, she is free from his law, so that she is not an adulteress if she becomes another man's."

1 Cor. 6:9-11: "Do not be misled. Neither fornicators, nor idolaters, nor adulterers, nor men kept for unnatural purposes, nor men who lie with men . . . will inherit God's kingdom. And yet that is what some of you were. But you have been washed clean, but you have been sanctified, but you have been declared righteous in the name of our Lord Jesus Christ and with the spirit of our God." (This emphasizes the seriousness of the matter. Unrepentant adulterers will have no part in God's Kingdom. Yet, people who formerly committed adultery, perhaps even improperly getting remarried, can gain God's forgiveness and a clean standing with him if they are genuinely repentant and exercise faith in the sin-atoning value of Jesus' sacrifice.)

In the past why did God allow marriage between brother and sister?

The Bible record does indicate that Cain married one of his sisters (Gen. 4:17; 5:4) and that Abram married his half sister. (Gen. 20:12) But later, in the Law given through Moses, such marriage unions were specifically forbidden. (Lev. 18:9, 11) They are not permitted among Christians today. Marriage to a close relative results in a more-than-average probability that damaging hereditary factors will be passed on to their offspring.

Why was brother-and-sister marriage not inappropriate at the beginning of mankind's history? God created Adam and Eve perfect and purposed that all humankind descend from them. (Gen. 1:28; 3:20) Obviously some marrying of close relatives, especially within the first few generations, would occur. Even after sin made its appearance, there was relatively little danger of marked deformities in the children during early generations, because the human race was much closer to the perfection that had been enjoyed by Adam and Eve. This is attested to by the longevity of people then. (See Genesis 5:3-8; 25:7.) But about 2,500 years after Adam became a sinner, God prohibited incestuous marriage. This served to safeguard the offspring and it elevated the sexual morality of Jehovah's servants above that of people around them who were then engaging in all manner of depraved practices.—See Leviticus 18:2-18.

What can help to improve a marriage?

(1) Studying God's Word together regularly and praying to God for help in resolving problems.—2 Tim. 3:16, 17; Prov. 3:5, 6; Phil. 4:6, 7.

(2) Appreciating the principle of headship. This puts a heavy responsibility on the husband. (1 Cor. 11:3; Eph. 5:25-33; Col. 3:19) It also calls for earnest effort on the part of the wife.—Eph. 5:22-24, 33; Col. 3:18; 1 Pet. 3:1-6.

(3) Confining sexual interest to one's mate. (Prov. 5:15-21; Heb. 13:4) Loving concern for the needs of one's mate can help to safeguard that one against temptation to wrongdoing.—1 Cor. 7:2-5.

(4) Speaking in a kindly, considerate manner to each other; avoiding outbursts of anger, nagging, and harsh critical remarks.—Eph. 4:31, 32; Prov. 15:1; 20:3; 21:9; 31:26, 28.

(5) Being industrious and dependable in caring for the family's dwelling place and clothing, also in preparing wholesome meals.—Titus 2:4, 5; Prov. 31:10-31.

(6) Humbly applying Bible counsel whether you feel that the other one is doing everything he should or not.—Rom. 14:12; 1 Pet. 3:1, 2.

(7) Giving attention to the development of personal spiritual qualities.—1 Pet. 3:3-6; Col. 3:12-14; Gal. 5:22, 23.

(8) Providing needed love, training, and discipline for the children, if there are any.—Titus 2:4; Eph. 6:4; Prov. 13:24; 29:15.

Mary (Jesus' Mother)

Definition: The divinely chosen and highly favored woman who gave birth to Jesus. There are five other Marys mentioned in the Bible. This one was a descendant of King David, of the tribe of Judah, and a daughter of Heli. When she is first introduced to us in Scripture, she is engaged to Joseph, also of the tribe of Judah and a descendant of David.

What can we learn from the Bible record about Mary?

(1) A lesson in willingness to listen to what God says through his messengers even though what we hear may at first disturb us or seem impossible.—Luke 1:26-37.

(2) Courage to act in harmony with what one learns to be God's will, trusting fully in him. (See Luke 1:38. As shown at Deuteronomy 22:23, 24, there could be serious consequences for an unmarried Jewish girl who was found to be pregnant.)

(3) God's willingness to use a person regardless of that one's station in life.—Compare Luke 2:22-24 with Leviticus 12:1-8.

(4) Giving prominence to spiritual interests. (See Luke 2:41; Acts 1:14. It was not required that Jewish wives join their husbands for the long trip to Jerusalem at Passover time each year, but Mary did so.)

(5) Appreciation of moral purity.—Luke 1:34.

(6) Diligence in teaching one's children the Word of God. (This was reflected in what Jesus was doing at the age of 12. See Luke 2:42, 46-49.)

Was Mary truly a virgin when she gave birth to Jesus?

Luke 1:26-31 (*JB*) reports that it was to "a virgin" whose name was Mary that the angel Gabriel carried the news: "You are to conceive and bear a son, and you must name him Jesus." At this, verse 34 states, "Mary said to the angel, 'But how can this come about, since I am a virgin ["I do not know man: i.e., as husband," *NAB* footnote; "I am having no intercourse with a man," *NW*]?'" Matthew 1:22-25 (*JB*) adds: "Now all this took place to fulfil the words spoken by the Lord through the prophet: The virgin will conceive and give birth to a son and they will call him Immanuel, a name which means 'God-is-with-us'. When Joseph woke up he did what the angel of the Lord had told him to do: he took his wife to his home and, though he had not had intercourse with her, she gave birth to a son; and he named him Jesus."

Is this reasonable? Surely it was not impossible for the Creator, who designed the human reproductive organs, to bring about the fertilization of an egg cell in the womb of Mary by supernatural means. Marvelously, Jehovah transferred the life-force and the personality pattern of his first-born heavenly Son to the womb of Mary. God's own active force, his holy spirit, safeguarded the development of the child in Mary's womb so that what was born was a perfect human.—Luke 1:35; John 17:5.

Was Mary always a virgin?

Matt. 13:53-56, *JB:* "When Jesus had finished these parables he left the district; and, coming to his home town, he taught the people in their synagogue in such a way that they were astonished and said, 'Where did the man get this wisdom and these miraculous powers? This is the carpenter's son, surely? Is not his mother the woman called Mary, and his brothers [Greek, *a·del·phoi´*] James and Joseph and

Simon and Jude? His sisters [Greek, *a·del·phai'*], too, are they not all here with us?'" (On the basis of this text, would you conclude that Jesus was Mary's only child or that she had other sons as well as daughters?)

The *New Catholic Encyclopedia* (1967, Vol. IX, p. 337) admits regarding the Greek words *a·del·phoi'* and *a·del·phai',* used at Matthew 13:55, 56, that these "have the meaning of full blood brother and sister in the Greek-speaking world of the Evangelist's time and would naturally be taken by his Greek reader in this sense. Toward the end of the 4th century (*c.* 380) Helvidius in a work now lost pressed this fact in order to attribute to Mary other children besides Jesus so as to make her a model for mothers of larger families. St. Jerome, motivated by the Church's traditional faith in Mary's perpetual virginity, wrote a tract against Helvidius (A.D. 383) in which he developed an explanation ... that is still in vogue among Catholic scholars."

Mark 3:31-35, *JB:* "His mother and brothers now arrived and, standing outside, sent in a message asking for him. A crowd was sitting round him at the time the message was passed to him, 'Your mother and brothers and sisters are outside asking for you'. He replied, 'Who are my mother and my brothers?' And looking round at those sitting in a circle about him, he said, 'Here are my mother and my brothers. Anyone who does the will of God, that person is my brother and sister and mother.'" (Here a clear distinction is drawn between Jesus' natural brothers and his spiritual brothers, his disciples. No one claims that the reference to Jesus' mother means anything different from what it says. Is it consistent, then, to reason that his natural brothers were not that but were perhaps cousins? When what is meant is not brothers but relatives, a different Greek word [*syg·ge·non'*] is used, as at Luke 21:16.)

Was Mary the Mother of God?

The angel who informed her of the coming miraculous birth did not say that her son would be God. He said: "You are to conceive and bear a son, and you must name him Jesus. He will be great and will be called *Son* of the Most

High. . . . The child will be holy and will be called *Son* of God."
—Luke 1:31-35, *JB;* italics added.

Heb. 2:14, 17, *JB:* "Since all the children share the same blood and flesh, he [Jesus] too shared equally in it . . . It was essential that he should in this way become completely like his brothers." (But would he have been "completely like his brothers" if he had been a God-man?)

The *New Catholic Encyclopedia* says: "Mary is truly the mother of God if two conditions are fulfilled: that she is really the mother of Jesus and that Jesus is really God." (1967, Vol. X, p. 21) The Bible says that Mary was the mother of Jesus, but was Jesus God? In the fourth century, long after the writing of the Bible was completed, the Church formulated its statement of the Trinity. (*New Catholic Encyclopedia,* 1967, Vol. XIV, p. 295; see page 405, under the heading "Trinity.") At that time in the Nicene Creed the Church spoke of Jesus Christ as "very God." After that, at the Council of Ephesus in 431 C.E., Mary was proclaimed by the Church to be *The·o·to´kos,* meaning "God-bearer" or "Mother of God." However, neither that expression nor the idea is found in the text of any translation of the Bible. (See pages 212-216, under "Jesus Christ.")

Was Mary herself immaculately conceived, free from original sin when her mother conceived her?

The *New Catholic Encyclopedia* (1967, Vol. VII, pp. 378-381) acknowledges regarding the origin of the belief: " . . . the Immaculate Conception is not taught explicitly in Scripture . . . The earliest Church Fathers regarded Mary as holy but not as absolutely sinless. . . . It is impossible to give a precise date when the belief was held as a matter of faith, but by the 8th or 9th century it seems to have been generally admitted. . . . [In 1854 Pope Pius IX defined the dogma] 'which holds that the most Blessed Virgin Mary was preserved from all stain of original sin in the first instant of her Conception.'" This belief was confirmed by Vatican II (1962-1965).—*The Documents of Vatican II* (New York, 1966), edited by W. M. Abbott, S.J., p. 88.

The Bible itself says: "Well then, sin entered the world through one man [Adam], and through sin death, and thus death has spread through the whole human race because *everyone* has sinned." (Rom. 5:12, *JB;* italics added.) Does that include Mary? The Bible reports that in accord with the requirement of the Mosaic Law, 40 days after Jesus' birth Mary offered at the temple in Jerusalem a sin offering for purification from uncleanness. She, too, had inherited sin and imperfection from Adam.—Luke 2:22-24; Lev. 12:1-8.

Did Mary ascend to heaven with her body of flesh?

In commenting on the proclamation made by Pope Pius XII in 1950 that made this dogma an official article of Catholic faith, the *New Catholic Encyclopedia* (1967, Vol. I, p. 972) states: "There is no explicit reference to the Assumption in the Bible, yet the Pope insists in the decree of promulgation that the Scriptures are the ultimate foundation of this truth."

The Bible itself says: "Flesh and blood cannot inherit the kingdom of God: and the perishable cannot inherit what lasts for ever." (1 Cor. 15:50, *JB*) Jesus said that "God is spirit." At Jesus' resurrection he again became spirit, now "a life-giving spirit." The angels are spirits. (John 4:24; 1 Cor. 15:45; Heb. 1:13, 14, *JB*) Where is the *Scriptural* basis for saying that anyone would attain to heavenly life in a body that requires the physical surroundings of the earth to sustain it? (See pages 334-336, under "Resurrection.")

Is it proper to address prayers to Mary as intercessor?

Jesus Christ said: "You should pray like this: 'Our Father in heaven . . . '" He also said: "I am the Way, the Truth and the Life. No one can come to the Father except through me. . . . If you ask for anything in *my name,* I will do it."—Matt. 6:9; John 14:6, 14, *JB;* italics added.

Will prayers to the Father through Jesus Christ be received with as much understanding and compassion as they would if they were directed through someone who has shared the experiences of womankind? Concerning the Father, the Bible tells us: "As tenderly as a father treats his children, so Yahweh treats those who fear him; he knows what we are made of, he remembers we are dust." He is "a God of tenderness and compassion, slow to anger, rich in kindness and faithfulness." (Ps. 103:13, 14; Ex. 34:6, *JB*) And of Christ it is written: "It is not as if we had a high priest who was incapable of feeling our weaknesses with us; but we have one who has been tempted in every way that we are, though he is without sin. Let us be confident, then, in approaching the throne of grace, that we shall have mercy from him and find grace when we are in need of help."—Heb. 4:15, 16, *JB*.

Is the veneration of images of Mary in harmony with Bible Christianity?

The practice was definitely encouraged by Vatican II (1962-1965). "This most holy Synod . . . admonishes all the sons of the Church that the cult, especially the liturgical cult, of the Blessed Virgin, be generously fostered. It charges that practices and exercises of devotion toward her be treasured as recommended by the teaching authority of the Church in the course of centuries, and that those decrees issued in earlier times regarding the veneration of images of Christ, the Blessed Virgin, and the saints, be religiously observed."—*The Documents of Vatican II,* pp. 94, 95.

For the Bible's answer, see "Images," pages 183-187.

Was Mary specially honored in the first-century Christian congregation?

The apostle Peter makes no mention of her at all in his inspired writings. The apostle Paul did not use her name in his inspired letters but spoke of her only as "a woman." —Gal. 4:4.

What example did Jesus himself set in referring to his mother?

John 2:3, 4, *JB:* "When they ran out of wine [at a wedding feast in Cana], since the wine provided for the wedding was all finished, the mother of Jesus said to him, 'They have no wine'. Jesus said, 'Woman, why turn to me ["what is that to me and to thee," *Dy*]? My hour has not come yet.'" (When Jesus was a child he subjected himself to his mother and his adoptive father. But now that he was grown he kindly but firmly rejected Mary's direction. She humbly accepted the correction.)

Luke 11:27, 28, *JB:* "Now as he [Jesus] was speaking, a woman in the crowd raised her voice and said, 'Happy the womb that bore you and the breasts you sucked!' But he replied, 'Still happier those who hear the word of God and keep it!'" (This would certainly have been a fine opportunity for Jesus to pay special honor to his mother if that had been appropriate. He did not do so.)

What are the historical origins of the adoration of Mary?

Says Catholic priest Andrew Greeley: "Mary is one of the most powerful religious symbols in the history of the Western world . . . The Mary symbol links Christianity directly to the ancient religions of mother goddesses."—*The Making of the Popes 1978* (U.S.A., 1979), p. 227.

Of interest is the location where the teaching that Mary is the Mother of God was confirmed. "The Council of Ephesus assembled in the basilica of the Theotokos in 431. There, if anywhere, in the city so notorious for its devotion to Artemis, or Diana as the Romans called her, where her image was said to have fallen from heaven, under the shadow of the great temple dedicated to the Magna Mater since 330 B.C. and containing, according to tradition, a temporary residence of Mary, the title 'God-bearer' hardly could fail to be upheld."—*The Cult of the Mother-Goddess* (New York, 1959), E. O. James, p. 207.

If Someone Says—

'Do you believe in the Virgin Mary?'

You might reply: 'The Holy Scriptures clearly say that the mother of Jesus Christ was a virgin, and we believe that.

God was his Father. The child that was born was truly the Son of God, just as the angel told Mary. (Luke 1:35)' **Then perhaps add:** 'But have you ever wondered why it was so important that Jesus be born in that way? . . . Only in that way could a suitable ransom be provided that would make possible release from sin and death for us.—1 Tim. 2:5, 6; then perhaps John 3:16.'

Or you could say: 'Yes, we do. We believe everything the Sacred Scriptures say about her, and they definitely say that it was as a virgin that she gave birth to Jesus. I also find very heartwarming other things they tell us about Mary and the lessons that we can learn from her. (Use material on pages 254, 255.)'

'You don't believe in the Virgin Mary'

You might reply: 'I realize that there are people who do not believe that it was a virgin who gave birth to the Son of God. But we *do* believe that. (Open one of our books to a section that discusses this matter and show the householder.)' **Then perhaps add:** 'But is there anything more that is needed if we are to gain salvation? . . . Notice what Jesus said in prayer to his Father. (John 17:3)'

Mass

Definition: As stated by the Sacred Congregation of Rites of the Roman Catholic Church, the Mass is "—A sacrifice in which the Sacrifice of the Cross is perpetuated; —A memorial of the death and resurrection of the Lord, who said 'do this in memory of me' (*Luke* 22:19); —A sacred banquet in which, through the communion of the Body and Blood of the Lord, the People of God share the benefits of the Paschal Sacrifice, renew the New Covenant which God has made with man once for all through the Blood of Christ, and in faith and hope foreshadow and anticipate the eschatological banquet in the kingdom of the Father, proclaiming the Lord's death 'till His coming.'" (*Eucharisticum Mysterium,* May 25, 1967) It is the Catholic Church's way of doing what they understand that Jesus Christ did at the Last Supper.

Are the bread and the wine actually changed into Christ's body and blood?

In a "Solemn Profession of Faith" on June 30, 1968, Pope Paul VI declared: "We believe that as the bread and wine consecrated by the Lord at the Last Supper were changed into His Body and His Blood which were to be offered for us on the cross, so the bread and wine consecrated by the priest are changed into the Body and Blood of Christ enthroned gloriously in heaven, and We believe that the mysterious presence of the Lord, under the appearance of those elements which seem to our senses the same after as before the Consecration, is a true, real and substantial presence. . . . This mysterious change is very appropriately called by the Church *transubstantiation.*" (*Official Catholic Teachings —Christ Our Lord,* Wilmington, N.C.; 1978, Amanda G. Watlington, p. 411) Do the Holy Scriptures agree with that belief?

What did Jesus mean when he said, "This is my body," "This is my blood"?

Matt. 26:26-29, *JB:* "Now as they were eating, Jesus took some bread, and when he had said the blessing he broke it and gave it to the disciples. 'Take it and eat;' he said 'this is my body.' Then he took a cup, and when he had returned thanks he gave it to them. 'Drink all of you from this,' he said 'for this is my blood, the blood of the covenant, which is to be poured out for many for the forgiveness of sins. From now on, I tell you, I shall not drink wine until the day I drink the new wine with you in the kingdom of my Father.'"

Regarding the expressions "this is my body" and "this is my blood," the following is noteworthy: *Mo* reads, "it *means* my body," "this *means* my blood." (Italics added.) *NW* reads similarly. *LEF* renders the expressions, "this *represents* my body," "this *represents* my blood." (Italics added.) These renderings agree with what is stated in the context, in verse 29, in various Catholic editions. *Kx* reads: "I shall not drink of *this fruit of the vine* again, until I drink it with you, new wine, in the kingdom of my Father." (Italics added.) *CC, NAB, Dy* also show Jesus referring to what was in the cup as being "this fruit of the vine," and that was after Jesus had said, "This is my blood."

Consider the expressions "this is my body" and "this is my blood" in the light of other vivid language used in the Scriptures. Jesus also said, "I am the light of the world," "I am the gate of the sheepfold," "I am the true vine." (John 8:12; 10:7; 15:1, *JB*) None of these expressions implied a miraculous transformation, did they?

At 1 Corinthians 11:25 (*JB*), the apostle Paul wrote concerning the Last Supper and expressed the same ideas in slightly different words. Instead of quoting Jesus as saying regarding the cup, "Drink all of you from this . . . for this is my blood, the blood of the covenant," he worded it in this way: "This cup is the new covenant in my blood." Surely that did not mean that the cup was somehow miraculously transformed into the new covenant. Is it not more reasonable to conclude that what was in the cup *represented* Jesus' blood by means of which the new covenant was validated?

What did Jesus mean by his statement at John 6:53-57?

"Jesus replied: 'I tell you most solemnly, if you do not eat the flesh of the Son of Man and drink his blood, you will not have life in you. Anyone who does eat my flesh and drink my blood has eternal life, and I shall raise him up on the last day. For my flesh is real food and my blood is real drink. He who eats my flesh and drinks my blood lives in me and I live in him. As I, who am sent by the living Father, myself draw life from the Father, so whoever eats me will draw life from me.'"—John 6:53-57, *JB*.

Is this to be understood as meaning that they were literally to eat Jesus' flesh and drink his blood? If so, Jesus would have been advocating a violation of the Law that God had given Israel through Moses. That Law prohibited the consuming of any sort of blood. (Lev. 17:10-12) Contrary to advocating such a thing, Jesus spoke out strongly against breaking any of the requirements of the Law. (Matt. 5: 17-19) So what Jesus had in mind must have been eating and drinking in a figurative sense, by exercising faith in the value of his perfect human sacrifice.—Compare John 3:16; 4:14; 6:35, 40.

Did Jesus instruct his disciples to have not merely a memorial of his death but a rite that would actually renew his sacrifice?

According to *The Documents of Vatican II:* "At the Last Supper, on the night when He was betrayed, our Savior instituted the Eucharistic *Sacrifice* of His Body and Blood. He did this in order to perpetuate the sacrifice of the Cross . . . "—(New York, 1966), edited by W. M. Abbott, S.J., p. 154; italics added.

The Catholic Encyclopedia states: "The Church intends the Mass to be regarded as a 'true and proper sacrifice' . . . The chief source of our doctrine, however, is tradition, which from the earliest times declares the impetratory value of the Sacrifice of the Mass."—(1913), Vol. X, pp. 6, 17.

Jesus himself said: "Do this as a memorial of me." (Luke 22:19; 1 Cor. 11:24, *JB*) At Luke 22:19, *Kx* and *Dy* read: "Do this for a commemoration of me." *NAB* reads: "Do this as a remembrance of me." Jesus did not say that what he did at the Last Supper was a *sacrifice* of himself or that his disciples were to renew his sacrifice.

Heb. 9:25-28, *JB:* "He does not have to offer himself again and again, like the [Jewish] high priest going into the sanctuary year after year with the blood that is not his own, or else he would have had to suffer over and over again since the world began. Instead of that, he has made his appearance *once and for all* . . . to do away with sin by sacrificing himself. Since men only die once, and after that comes judgement, so Christ, too, offers himself *only once.*" (Italics added.)

Is it all simply "an unfathomable mystery"?

The Bible does refer to divine mysteries, or sacred secrets. But none of these conflict with clearly stated Scriptural truths. Concerning those who put their traditions ahead of the Scriptures, Jesus said: "Hypocrites! It was you Isaiah meant when he so rightly prophesied: This people honours me only with lip-service, while their hearts are far from me. The worship they offer me is worthless; the doctrines they teach are only human regulations."—Matt. 15: 7-9, *JB*.

Did Jesus mean for this memorial to be kept perhaps every day or every week?

Basic Catechism says: "Special Duties of Catholic Christians" include "participating in Mass every Sunday and holyday of obligation." (Boston, 1980, p. 21) "The faithful are in fact encouraged to participate in the Mass and to receive Communion frequently, even daily."—*The Teaching of Christ—A Catholic Catechism for Adults,* Abridged Edition (Huntington, Ind.; 1979), p. 281.

Do all Scriptural references to "breaking of bread" indicate that Christ's death was being commemorated? (Acts 2: 42, 46; 20:7, *JB*) Jesus 'broke bread' when food was being shared at a meal even before the Last Supper. (Mark 6:41; 8:6) The bread used by the Jews at that time was not what many people are accustomed to today. When eating it, they would often break or tear off a piece.

Jesus did not specifically state how often the Memorial of his death was to be kept. However, he instituted it on the date of the Jewish Passover, which was replaced among his disciples by the Memorial of Christ's death. The Passover was an annual event, celebrated on Nisan 14. Similarly, the Jewish Festival of Unfermented Cakes, the Festival of Weeks (Pentecost), the Festival of Booths, or Ingathering, and the Day of Atonement were all held once a year.

Does the saying of Mass bring relief to souls in purgatory?

The Teaching of Christ—A Catholic Catechism for Adults states: "The word 'purgatory' is not in the Bible, nor is the doctrine of purgatory explicitly taught there. . . . The works of the Fathers have many references not only to the existence of purgatory, but also the fact that the faithful departed can be helped by the prayers of the living, especially by the Sacrifice of the Mass."—Pp. 347, 348.

Regarding the condition of the dead, the Holy Scriptures say: "The living know at least that they will die, the dead know nothing." (Eccl. 9:5, *JB*) "The soul ["soul," *Kx;* "man," *JB*] that sinneth, the same shall die." (Ezek. 18:4, *Dy*) (See also pages 100-102, under the heading "Death.")

Memorial
(Lord's Evening Meal)

Definition: A meal commemorating the death of Jesus Christ; hence, a memorial of his death, the death that has had effects that are more far reaching than that of any other person. This is the only event that the Lord Jesus Christ commanded his disciples to memorialize. It is also known as the Lord's Supper, or the Lord's Evening Meal.—1 Cor. 11:20.

What is the significance of the Memorial?

To his faithful apostles Jesus said: "Keep doing this in remembrance of me." (Luke 22:19) When writing to members of the spirit-begotten Christian congregation, the apostle Paul added: "As often as you eat this loaf and drink this cup, you keep proclaiming the death of the Lord, until he arrives." (1 Cor. 11:26) So, the Memorial calls special attention to the significance of the death of Jesus Christ in the outworking of Jehovah's purpose. It highlights the meaning of Jesus' sacrificial death particularly in relation to the new covenant and to the way that his death affects those who will be heirs with him of the heavenly Kingdom.—John 14:2, 3; Heb. 9:15.

The Memorial is also a reminder that Jesus' death and the way it was accomplished, in harmony with God's purpose as expressed at Genesis 3:15 and thereafter, served to vindicate Jehovah's name. By maintaining integrity to Jehovah down till his death, Jesus proved that Adam's sin was not due to any flaw in the Creator's designing of man but that it is possible for a human to maintain perfect godly devotion even under severe pressure, and thus Jesus vindicated Jehovah God as Creator and Universal Sovereign. Besides that, Jehovah had purposed that Jesus' death would provide the perfect human sacrifice needed to ransom Adam's offspring, and thus make it possible for billions who would exercise faith to live forever in a paradise earth, in fulfillment of Jehovah's original purpose and in expression of his great love for mankind.—John 3:16; Gen. 1:28.

266

What a tremendous burden rested upon Jesus on his last night on earth as a man! He knew what his heavenly Father had purposed for him, but he also knew that he had to prove faithful under test. Had he failed, what a reproach it would have meant for his Father and what a loss to humankind! Because of all that would be accomplished by means of his death, it was most fitting that Jesus instructed that it be memorialized.

What is the meaning of the bread and the wine served at the Memorial?

Regarding the *unleavened bread* that Jesus gave to his apostles when instituting the Memorial, he said: "This means my body." (Mark 14:22) That bread symbolized his own sinless body of flesh. This he would give in behalf of the future life prospects of mankind, and on this occasion special attention is drawn to the life prospects that it makes possible for those who would be chosen to share with Jesus in the heavenly Kingdom.

When passing the *wine* to his faithful apostles, Jesus said: "This means my 'blood of the covenant,' which is to be poured out in behalf of many." (Mark 14:24) That wine symbolized his own lifeblood. By means of his shed blood, forgiveness of sins would be possible for those who put faith in it. On this occasion Jesus was highlighting the cleansing from sin that it would make possible for his prospective joint heirs. His words also indicate that by means of that blood the new covenant between Jehovah God and the spirit-anointed Christian congregation would be made operative.

See also pages 261-263, under the heading "Mass."

Who is to partake of the bread and the wine?

Who partook when Jesus instituted the Lord's Evening Meal shortly before he died? Eleven faithful followers to whom Jesus said: "I make a covenant with you, just as my Father has made a covenant with me, for a kingdom." (Luke 22:29) They were all persons who were being invited to share with Christ in his heavenly Kingdom. (John 14:2, 3) All who partake of the bread and wine today should also be persons whom Christ brings into that 'covenant for a kingdom.'

How many are there that partake? Jesus said that only a "little flock" would receive the heavenly Kingdom as their reward. (Luke 12:32) The full number would be 144,000. (Rev. 14:1-3) That group began to be selected in 33 C.E. Reasonably, there would be only a small number partaking now.

Does John 6:53, 54 indicate that only those who do partake will gain everlasting life?

John 6:53, 54: "Jesus said to them: 'Most truly I say to you, Unless you eat the flesh of the Son of man and drink his blood, you have no life in yourselves. He that feeds on my flesh and drinks my blood has everlasting life, and I shall resurrect him at the last day.'"

This eating and drinking would obviously have to be done figuratively; otherwise the one doing it would be violating God's law. (Gen. 9:4; Acts 15:28, 29) However, it should be noted that Jesus' statement at John 6:53, 54 was not made in connection with the inauguration of the Lord's Evening Meal. None who heard him had any idea of a celebration with bread and wine used to represent Christ's flesh and blood. That arrangement was not introduced until about a year later, and the apostle John's report about the Lord's Evening Meal does not begin until more than seven chapters later on (in John 14) in the Gospel bearing his name.

How, then, can a person "eat the flesh of the Son of man and drink his blood" in a figurative way if not by partaking of the bread and the wine at the Memorial? Notice that Jesus said that those thus eating and drinking would have "everlasting life." Earlier, in verse 40, when explaining what people must do to have everlasting life, what did he say was the will of his Father? That "everyone that beholds the Son and *exercises faith* in him should have everlasting life." Reasonably, then, 'eating his flesh and drinking his blood' in a figurative sense is done by *exercising faith* in the redeeming power of Jesus' flesh and blood laid down in sacrifice. This exercising of faith is required of all who will gain the fullness of life, whether in the heavens with Christ or in the earthly Paradise.

How often is the Memorial to be commemorated, and when?

Jesus did not specifically state how often it was to be done. He simply said: "Keep doing this in remembrance of me." (Luke 22:19) Paul said: "For as often as you eat this loaf and drink this cup, you keep proclaiming the death of the Lord, until he arrives." (1 Cor. 11:26) "As often" need not mean many times a year; it can mean annually over a period of many years. If you commemorate an important event, such as a wedding anniversary, or if a nation commemorates an important event in its history, how often is it done? Once a year on the anniversary date. This would also be consistent with the fact that the Lord's Evening Meal was instituted on the date of the Jewish Passover, a yearly celebration that no longer had to be kept by Jews who had become Christians.

Jehovah's Witnesses observe the Memorial after sundown on Nisan 14, according to the reckoning of the Jewish calendar that was common in the first century. The Jewish day begins at sundown and extends until the following sundown. So Jesus died on the same Jewish calendar day that he instituted the Memorial. The *beginning* of the month of Nisan was the sunset after the new moon nearest the spring equinox became *visible in Jerusalem*. The Memorial date is 14 days thereafter. (Thus the date for the Memorial may not coincide with that of the Passover kept by modern-day Jews. Why not? The start of their calendar months is set to coincide with the astronomical new moon, not the visible new moon over Jerusalem, which may come 18 to 30 hours later. Also, most Jews today keep the Passover on Nisan 15, not on the 14th as did Jesus in harmony with what was stated in the Mosaic Law.)

Neutrality

Definition: The position of those who do not take sides with or give support to either of two or more contending parties. It is a fact of ancient and modern-day history that in every nation and under all circumstances true Christians have endeavored to maintain complete neutrality as to conflicts between factions of the world. They do not interfere with what others do about sharing in patriotic ceremonies, serving in the armed forces, joining a political party, running for a political office, or voting. But they themselves worship only Jehovah, the God of the Bible; they have dedicated their lives unreservedly to him and give their full support to his Kingdom.

What scriptures have had a bearing on the attitude of Christians toward the authority of secular governments?

Rom. 13:1, 5-7: "Let every soul be in subjection to the superior authorities [governmental rulers], for there is no authority except by God . . . There is therefore compelling reason for you people to be in subjection, not only on account of that wrath but also on account of your conscience. . . . Render to all their dues, to him who calls for the tax, the tax; to him who calls for the tribute, the tribute; to him who calls for fear, such fear; to him who calls for honor, such honor." (No government could exist without God's permission. Regardless of the conduct of individual officials, true Christians have shown them respect because of the office they occupied. For example, regardless of the use that governments have made of tax money, worshipers of Jehovah have made honest payment of their taxes in return for those services from which everyone could benefit.)

Mark 12:17: "Jesus then said: 'Pay back Caesar's things to Caesar, but God's things to God.'" (So Christians have always recognized that they must not only "pay back" money in the form of taxes to the secular government but also fulfill the superior obligations they have toward God.)

Acts 5:28, 29: "[A spokesman for the Jewish high court] said: 'We positively ordered you [the apostles] not to keep teaching upon the basis of this name [of Jesus Christ], and yet, look! you have filled Jerusalem with your teaching, and you are determined to bring the blood of this man upon us.' In answer Peter and the other apostles said: 'We must obey God as ruler rather than men.'" (When there has been a direct conflict between the commands of human rulers and the requirements of God, true Christians have imitated the example of the apostles by putting obedience to God first.)

What scriptures have always had a bearing on the attitude of true Christians toward participation in carnal warfare?

Matt. 26:52: "Jesus said to him: 'Return your sword to its place, for all those who take the sword will perish by the sword.'" (Could there have been any higher cause for which to fight than to safeguard the Son of God? Yet, Jesus here indicated that those disciples were not to resort to weapons of physical warfare.)

Isa. 2:2-4: "It must occur in the final part of the days that the mountain of the house of Jehovah will become firmly established above the top of the mountains . . . And he will certainly render judgment among the nations and set matters straight respecting many peoples. And they will have to beat their swords into plowshares and their spears into pruning shears. Nation will not lift up sword against nation, neither will they learn war anymore." (Individuals out of all nations must personally decide what course they will pursue. Those who have heeded Jehovah's judgment give evidence that he is their God.)

2 Cor. 10:3, 4: "Though we walk in the flesh, we do not wage warfare according to what we are in the flesh. For the weapons of our warfare are not fleshly, but powerful by God for overturning strongly entrenched things." (Paul here states that he never resorted to fleshly weapons, such as trickery, high-sounding language, or carnal weapons, to protect the congregation against false teachings.)

Luke 6:27, 28: "I [Jesus Christ] say to you who are listening, Continue to love your enemies, to do good to those hating you, to bless those cursing you, to pray for those who are insulting you."

Is it not true that Jehovah allowed ancient Israel to engage in warfare?

Jehovah directed ancient Israel to use warfare to take possession of the land that he himself designated as their inheritance and to execute people whose depraved practices and defiance of the true God caused Jehovah to view them as being no longer fit to live. (Deut. 7:1, 2, 5; 9:5; Lev. 18:

24, 25) Nevertheless, mercy was shown to Rahab and to the Gibeonites because they demonstrated faith in Jehovah. (Josh. 2:9-13; 9:24-27) In the Law covenant God laid down rules for warfare that he would approve, stipulating exemptions and the manner in which this warfare was to be carried out. Such were truly holy wars of Jehovah. That is not true of the carnal warfare of any nation today.

With the establishing of the Christian congregation, a new situation came into existence. Christians are not under the Mosaic Law. Christ's followers were to make disciples of people of all nations; so worshipers of the true God would in time be found in all those nations. However, what is the motive of those nations when they go to war? Is it to carry out the will of the Creator of all the earth or is it to further some nationalistic interest? If true Christians in one nation were to go to war against another nation, they would be fighting against fellow believers, against people who prayed for help to the same God that they did. Appropriately, Christ directed his followers to lay down the sword. (Matt. 26:52) He himself, glorified in the heavens, would henceforth carry out the execution of those who showed defiance of the true God and His will.—2 Thess. 1:6-8; Rev. 19:11-21.

As to serving in the armed forces, what does secular history disclose about the attitude of early Christians?

"A careful review of all the information available goes to show that, until the time of Marcus Aurelius [Roman emperor from 161 to 180 C.E.], no Christian became a soldier; and no soldier, after becoming a Christian, remained in military service."—*The Rise of Christianity* (London, 1947), E. W. Barnes, p. 333.

"We who were filled with war, and mutual slaughter, and every wickedness, have each through the whole earth changed our warlike weapons,—our swords into ploughshares, and our spears into implements of tillage,—and we cultivate piety, righteousness, philanthropy, faith, and hope, which we have from the Father Himself through Him who was crucified."—Justin Martyr in "Dialogue With Trypho, a Jew" (2nd century C.E.), *The Ante-Nicene Fathers* (Grand

Rapids, Mich.; reprint of 1885 Edinburgh edition), edited by A. Roberts and J. Donaldson, Vol. I, p. 254.

"They refused to take any active part in the civil administration or the military defence of the empire. . . . it was impossible that the Christians, without renouncing a more sacred duty, could assume the character of soldiers, of magistrates, or of princes."—*History of Christianity* (New York, 1891), Edward Gibbon, pp. 162, 163.

What scriptures have always had a bearing on the attitude of true Christians toward involvement in political issues and activities?

John 17:16: "They are no part of the world, just as I [Jesus] am no part of the world."

John 6:15: "Jesus, knowing they [the Jews] were about to come and seize him to make him king, withdrew again into the mountain all alone." Later, he told the Roman governor: "My kingdom is no part of this world. If my kingdom were part of this world, my attendants would have fought that I should not be delivered up to the Jews. But, as it is, my kingdom is not from this source."—John 18:36.

Jas. 4:4: "Adulteresses, do you not know that the friendship with the world is enmity with God? Whoever, therefore, wants to be a friend of the world is constituting himself an enemy of God." (Why is the matter so serious? Because, as 1 John 5:19 says, "the whole world is lying in the power of the wicked one." At John 14:30, Jesus referred to Satan as being "the ruler of the world." So, no matter what worldly faction a person might support, under whose control would he really come?)

Regarding political involvement, what do secular historians report as being the attitude of those known as early Christians?

"Early Christianity was little understood and was regarded with little favor by those who ruled the pagan world. . . . Christians refused to share certain duties of Roman citizens. . . . They would not hold political office."—*On the Road to*

Civilization, A World History (Philadelphia, 1937), A. Heckel and J. Sigman, pp. 237, 238.

"The Christians stood aloof and distinct from the state, as a priestly and spiritual race, and Christianity seemed able to influence civil life only in that manner which, it must be confessed, is the purest, by practically endeavouring to instil more and more of holy feeling into the citizens of the state."—*The History of the Christian Religion and Church, During the Three First Centuries* (New York, 1848), Augustus Neander, translated from German by H. J. Rose, p. 168.

What scriptures have always had a bearing on the attitude of true Christians toward ceremonies involving flags and national anthems?

1 Cor. 10:14: "Flee from idolatry." (Also Exodus 20:4, 5)

1 John 5:21: "Little children, guard yourselves from idols."

Luke 4:8: "In reply Jesus said to him: 'It is written, "It is Jehovah your God you must worship, and it is to him alone you must render sacred service."'"

See also Daniel 3:1-28.

Do such patriotic symbols and ceremonies really have religious significance?

"[Historian] Carlton Hayes pointed out long ago that the ritual of flag-worship and oath-taking in an American school is a religious observance. . . . And that these daily rituals are religious has been at last affirmed by the Supreme Court in a series of cases."—*The American Character* (New York, 1956), D. W. Brogan, pp. 163, 164.

"Early flags were almost purely of a religious character. . . . The national banner of England for centuries—the red cross of St. George—was a religious one; in fact the aid of religion seems ever to have been sought to give sanctity to national flags, and the origin of many can be traced to a sacred banner."—*Encyclopædia Britannica* (1946), Vol. 9, p. 343.

"In a public ceremony presided over by the vice president of the [Military Supreme] Court, on the 19th of November, honors were shown to the Brazilian flag. . . . After the flag was hoisted, Minister General of the Army Tristao de Alencar Araripe expressed himself concerning the commemoration in this manner: '. . . flags have become a divinity of patriotic religion which imposes worship . . . The flag is venerated and worshiped . . . The flag is worshiped, just as the Fatherland is worshiped.'"—*Diario da Justiça* (Federal Capital, Brazil), February 16, 1956, p. 1906.

With reference to patriotic ceremonies, what does secular history say about the attitude of those known as early Christians?

"Christians refused to . . . sacrifice to the emperor's genius—roughly equivalent today to refusing to salute the flag or repeat the oath of allegiance. . . . Very few of the Christians recanted, although an altar with a fire burning on it was generally kept in the arena for their convenience. All a prisoner had to do was scatter a pinch of incense on the flame and he was given a Certificate of Sacrifice and turned free. It was also carefully explained to him that he was not worshiping the emperor; merely acknowledging the divine character of the emperor as head of the Roman state. Still, almost no Christians availed themselves of the chance to escape."—*Those About to Die* (New York, 1958), D. P. Mannix, pp. 135, 137.

"The act of emperor worship consisted in sprinkling a few grains of incense or a few drops of wine on an altar which stood before an image of the emperor. Perhaps at our long remove from the situation we see in the act nothing different from . . . lifting the hand in salute to the flag or to some distinguished ruler of state, an expression of courtesy, respect, and patriotism. Possibly a good many people in the first century felt just that way about it but not so the Christians. They viewed the whole matter as one of religious worship, acknowledging the emperor as a deity and therefore being disloyal to God and Christ, and they refused to do it."—*The Beginnings of the Christian Religion* (New Haven, Conn.; 1958), M. F. Eller, pp. 208, 209.

Has the neutrality of Christians meant that they are not interested in the welfare of their neighbors?

Certainly not. They know well and conscientiously endeavor to apply the command repeated by Jesus: "You must love your neighbor as yourself." (Matt. 22:39) Also the counsel recorded by the apostle Paul: "Let us work what is good toward all, but especially toward those related to us in the faith." (Gal. 6:10) They have been convinced that the greatest good that they can do for their neighbors is to share with them the good news of God's Kingdom, which will lastingly solve the problems facing mankind and which opens up to those who embrace it the marvelous prospect of eternal life.

New World Translation

Definition: A translation of the Holy Scriptures made directly from Hebrew, Aramaic, and Greek into modern-day English by a committee of anointed witnesses of Jehovah. These expressed themselves regarding their work as follows: "The translators of this work, who fear and love the Divine Author of the Holy Scriptures, feel toward Him a special responsibility to transmit his thoughts and declarations as accurately as possible. They also feel a responsibility toward the searching readers who depend upon a translation of the inspired Word of the Most High God for their everlasting salvation." This translation was originally released in sections, from 1950 to 1960. Editions in other languages have been based on the English translation.

On what is the "New World Translation" based?

As a basis for translating the Hebrew Scriptures, the text of Rudolf Kittel's *Biblia Hebraica,* editions of 1951-1955, was used. The 1984 revision of the *New World Translation* benefited from updating in harmony with the *Biblia Hebraica Stuttgartensia* of 1977. Additionally, the Dead Sea Scrolls and numerous early translations into other languages were consulted. For the Christian Greek Scriptures, the master Greek text of 1881 as prepared by Westcott and Hort was used primarily, but several other master texts were consulted as well as numerous early versions in other languages.

Who were the translators?

When presenting as a gift the publishing rights to their translation, the New World Bible Translation Committee requested that its members remain anonymous. The Watch Tower Bible and Tract Society of Pennsylvania has honored their request. The translators were not seeking prominence for themselves but only to honor the Divine Author of the Holy Scriptures.

Over the years other translation committees have taken a similar view. For example, the jacket of the Reference Edition (1971) of the *New American Standard Bible* states: "We have not used any scholar's name for reference or recommendations because it is our belief God's Word should stand on its merits."

Is it really a scholarly translation?

Since the translators have chosen to remain anonymous, the question cannot here be answered in terms of their educational background. The translation must be appraised on its own merits.

What kind of translation is this? For one thing, it is an accurate, largely literal translation from the original languages. It is not a loose paraphrase, in which the translators leave out details that they consider unimportant and add ideas that they believe will be helpful. As an aid to students, a number of editions provide extensive footnotes showing variant readings where expressions can legitimately be rendered in more than one way, also a listing of the specific ancient manuscripts on which certain renderings are based.

Some verses may not read the same as what a person is accustomed to. Which rendering is right? Readers are invited to examine manuscript support cited in footnotes of the Reference edition of the *New World Translation,* read explanations given in the appendix, and compare the rendering with a variety of other translations. They will generally find that some other translators have also seen the need to express the matter in a similar manner.

Why is the name Jehovah used in the Christian Greek Scriptures?

It should be noted that the *New World Translation* is not the only Bible that does this. The divine name appears in translations of the Christian Greek Scriptures into Hebrew, in passages where quotations are made directly from the inspired Hebrew Scriptures. *The Emphatic Diaglott* (1864) contains the name Jehovah 18 times. Versions of the Christian Greek Scriptures in at least 38 other languages also use a vernacular form of the divine name.

The emphasis that Jesus Christ put on the name of his Father indicates that he personally used it freely. (Matt. 6:9; John 17:6, 26) According to Jerome of the fourth century C.E., the apostle Matthew wrote his Gospel first in Hebrew, and that Gospel makes numerous quotations of passages from the Hebrew Scriptures that contain the divine name. Others of the Christian Greek Scripture writers quoted from the Greek *Septuagint* (a translation of the Hebrew Scriptures into Greek, begun about 280 B.C.E.), early copies of which contained the divine name in Hebrew characters, as shown by actual fragments that have been preserved.

Professor George Howard of the University of Georgia wrote: "Since the Tetragram [four Hebrew letters for the divine name] was still written in the copies of the Greek Bible which made up the Scriptures of the early church, it is reasonable to believe that the N[ew] T[estament] writers, when quoting from Scripture, preserved the Tetragram within the biblical text."—*Journal of Biblical Literature,* March 1977, p. 77.

Why are some verses apparently missing?

Those verses, found in some translations, are not in the oldest available Bible manuscripts. Comparison with other modern translations, such as *The New English Bible* and the Catholic *Jerusalem Bible,* shows that other translators have also recognized that the verses in question do not belong in the Bible. In some instances, they were taken from another part of the Bible and added to the text being copied by a scribe.

If Someone Says—

'You have your own Bible'

You might reply: 'Which translation of the Bible do you have? Is it . . . (list several in your language)? There are many translations, you know.' **Then perhaps add:** 'I'm glad to use whatever translation you prefer. But you may be interested in knowing why I especially like the *New World Translation*. It is because of its modern, understandable language, also because the translators held so closely to what is in the original Bible languages.'

Or you could say: 'What you say makes me feel that you must have a Bible in your home. What translation of the Bible do you use? . . . Would you be willing to get it?' **Then perhaps add:** 'For all of us, regardless of which translation we use, at John 17:3 Jesus stressed the important thing to keep in mind, as you can see here in your own Bible. . . . '

Another possibility: 'There are many translations of the Bible. Our Society encourages the use of a variety of them in order to make comparisons and to help students to grasp the real sense of the Scriptures. As you may know, the Bible was originally written in Hebrew, Aramaic, and Greek. So we appreciate what translators have done to put it into our language. Which Bible translation do you use?'

An additional suggestion: 'Evidently you are a person who loves God's Word. So I am sure you would be interested in knowing what one of the big differences is between the *New World Translation* and other versions. It involves the name of the most important person spoken of in the Scriptures. Do you know who that is?' **Then perhaps add:** (1) 'Did you know that his personal name appears in the Bible in the original Hebrew some 7,000 times—more than any other name?' (2) 'What difference does it make whether we use the personal name of God or not? Well, do you have any really close friends whose name you do not know? . . . If we want a personal relationship with God, knowing his name is an important start. Notice what Jesus said at John 17:3, 6. (Ps. 83:18)'

Organization

Definition: An association or society of persons whose efforts are coordinated for a particular work or purpose. Members of an organization are united by administrative arrangements and by standards or requirements. Persons who are dedicated and baptized witnesses of Jehovah come into Jehovah's organization as a result of personal choice, not by birth nor by any compulsion. They have been drawn to his earthly organization because of its teachings and practices and because they want to share in the work that it is doing.

Does Jehovah really have an organization here on earth?

To answer that question, consider the following:

Are God's heavenly creatures, the angels, organized?

Dan. 7:9, 10: "I kept on beholding until there were thrones placed and the Ancient of Days sat down. His clothing was white just like snow, and the hair of his head was like clean wool. His throne was flames of fire; its wheels were a burning fire. There was a stream of fire flowing and going out from before him. There were a thousand thousands that kept ministering to him, and ten thousand times ten thousand that kept standing right before him. The Court took its seat, and there were books that were opened."

Ps. 103:20, 21: "Bless Jehovah, O you angels of his, mighty in power, carrying out his word, by listening to the voice of his word. Bless Jehovah, all you armies of his, you ministers of his, doing his will." (An "army" is an organized group.)

How did God convey instructions to his servants on earth in times past?

When worshipers of Jehovah were few in number, he gave directions to family heads such as Noah and Abraham, and they then acted as Jehovah's spokesmen to their families. (Gen. 7:1, 7; 12:1-5) When Jehovah delivered the Israelites from Egypt, he gave them directions through Moses. (Ex. 3:10) At Mount Sinai, God organized the people into a nation, providing laws and regulations to govern their worship and their relations with one another. (Ex. 24:12) He established a priesthood to take the lead in matters of worship and to instruct the people in Jehovah's requirements; at times he also raised up prophets to deliver needed exhortation and warning to the people. (Deut. 33:8, 10; Jer. 7:24, 25) Thus, although Jehovah listened to the prayers of individual worshipers, he provided instruction for them through an organizational arrangement.

As the time neared for Jehovah to begin to unify true worshipers with himself by means of Jesus Christ, God sent him to earth to act as His spokesman. (Heb. 1:1, 2) Then with the outpouring of holy spirit at Pentecost of 33 C.E., the Christian congregation was brought into existence. After Jesus had returned to heaven, this congregation became Jehovah's arrangement for instructing and for coordinating the efforts of individual Christians. There were overseers to take the lead in local congregations, and a central governing body made necessary decisions and helped to coordinate activity. Clearly, Jehovah had brought into existence an organization on earth made up of true Christians.—Acts 14:23; 16:4, 5; Gal. 2:7-10.

Do Jehovah's works of physical creation indicate that he is a God of organization?

Isa. 40:26: "Raise your eyes high up and see. Who has created these things? It is the One who is bringing forth the army of them even by number, all of whom he calls even by name. Due to the abundance of dynamic energy, he also being vigorous in power, not one of them is missing." (The stars are grouped into galaxies and move in relation to one another, even though the characteristics of the individual stars differ. The planets move with precision timing, in assigned orbits. The electrons found in every atom of every element also have orbits. And the structure of all matter follows mathematical patterns that are so consistent that it was possible for scientists to predict the existence of certain elements before they actually discovered them. All of this gives evidence of extraordinary organization.)

Does the Bible show that true Christians would be an organized people?

Matt. 24:14; 28:19, 20: "This good news of the kingdom will be preached in all the inhabited earth for a witness to all the nations; and then the end will come." "Go therefore and make disciples of people of all the nations, baptizing them . . . teaching them." (How would this be accomplished without organization? When Jesus trained his early disciples for this work, He did not simply tell each one to go wherever he desired and to share his faith in whatever way he chose. He trained them, gave them instructions and sent them out in an organized manner. See Luke 8:1; 9:1-6; 10: 1-16.)

Heb. 10:24, 25: "Let us consider one another to incite to love and fine works, not forsaking the gathering of ourselves together, as some have the custom, but encouraging one another, and all the more so as you behold the day drawing near." (But to where would a person direct interested ones so they could obey this command if there were no organization with regular meetings where they could gather?)

1 Cor. 14:33, 40: "God is a God, not of disorder, but of peace. . . . Let all things take place decently and by arrangement." (The apostle Paul is here discussing orderly procedure at congregation meetings. Applying this inspired counsel requires respect for organization.)

1 Pet. 2:9, 17: "But you are 'a chosen race, a royal priesthood, a holy nation, a people for special possession, that you should declare abroad the excellencies' of the one that called you out of darkness into his wonderful light. . . . Have love for the whole association of brothers." (An association of people whose efforts are directed to accomplish a particular work is an organization.)

***Are those who are faithful servants of God simply
individuals who are scattered in the various
churches of Christendom?***

2 Cor. 6:15-18: "What portion does a faithful person have
with an unbeliever? . . . 'Therefore get out from among them,
and separate yourselves,' says Jehovah, 'and quit touching
the unclean thing'; 'and I will take you in.' 'And I shall be a
father to you, and you will be sons and daughters to me,' says
Jehovah the Almighty." (Is a person really a faithful servant
of God if he continues to share in worship with those who
show by their way of life that they really are unbelievers?
See the main heading "Babylon the Great.")

1 Cor. 1:10: "Now I exhort you, brothers, through the
name of our Lord Jesus Christ that you should all speak in
agreement, and that there should not be divisions among
you, but that you may be fitly united in the same mind and
in the same line of thought." (Such unity does not exist
among the varied churches of Christendom.)

John 10:16: "I have other sheep, which are not of this
fold; those also I must bring, and they will listen to my voice,
and they will become one flock, one shepherd." (Since Jesus
would bring such ones into "one flock," is it not obvious that
they could not be scattered in Christendom's religions?)

How can Jehovah's visible organization in our day be identified?

(1) It truly exalts Jehovah as the only true God, magni-
fying his name.—Matt. 4:10; John 17:3.

(2) It fully recognizes the vital role of Jesus Christ in
Jehovah's purpose—as the vindicator of Jehovah's sovereignty, the Chief Agent of life, the head of the Christian
congregation, the ruling Messianic King.—Rev. 19:11-13;
12:10; Acts 5:31; Eph. 1:22, 23.

(3) It adheres closely to God's inspired Word, basing all
its teachings and standards of conduct on the Bible.—2 Tim.
3:16, 17.

(4) It keeps separate from the world.—Jas. 1:27; 4:4.

(5) It maintains a high level of moral cleanness among its
members, because Jehovah himself is holy.—1 Pet. 1:15, 16;
1 Cor. 5:9-13.

(6) It devotes its principal efforts to doing the work that the Bible foretold for our day, namely, the preaching of the good news of God's Kingdom in all the world for a witness. —Matt. 24:14.

(7) Despite human imperfections, its members cultivate and produce the fruits of God's spirit—love, joy, peace, long-suffering, kindness, goodness, faith, mildness, self-control—doing so to such a degree that it sets them apart from the world in general.—Gal. 5:22, 23; John 13:35.

How can we show respect for Jehovah's organization?

1 Cor. 10:31: "Do all things for God's glory."

Heb. 13:17: "Be obedient to those who are taking the lead among you and be submissive, for they are keeping watch over your souls as those who will render an account."

Jas. 1:22: "Become doers of the word, and not hearers only."

Titus 2:11, 12: "The undeserved kindness of God which brings salvation to all sorts of men has been manifested, instructing us to repudiate ungodliness and worldly desires and to live with soundness of mind and righteousness and godly devotion."

1 Pet. 2:17: "Have love for the whole association of brothers."

Paradise

Definition: In the Greek *Septuagint* version of the Bible the translators appropriately used the term "paradise" (*pa·ra'dei·sos*) with reference to the garden of Eden, because it evidently was an enclosed park. After the account in Genesis, Bible texts that tell about paradise refer to (1) the garden of Eden itself, or (2) the earth as a whole when it will be transformed in the future to a condition like that of Eden, or (3) flourishing spiritual conditions among God's servants on earth, or (4) provisions in heaven that remind one of Eden.

Does the "New Testament" refer to a future earthly paradise or is that only in the "Old Testament"?

Separation of the Bible into two parts, appraising the value of statements on the basis of whether they are in the "Old" part or the "New" is not Scriptural. At 2 Timothy 3:16 we are told: *"All* Scripture is inspired of God and beneficial for teaching, for reproving, for setting things straight." Romans 15:4 refers to the pre-Christian inspired Scriptures when it says: "All the things that were written aforetime were written for our instruction." So, a sound answer to the question should consider the entire Bible.

Genesis 2:8 states: "Jehovah God planted a garden ["park," *Mo;* "paradise," *Dy; pa·ra′dei·son, LXX*] in Eden, toward the east, and there he put the man [Adam] whom he had formed." There was an abundance of varied and fascinating plant and animal life. Jehovah blessed the first human pair and said to them: "Be fruitful and become many and fill the earth and subdue it, and have in subjection the fish of the sea and the flying creatures of the heavens and every living creature that is moving upon the earth." (Gen. 1:28) God's original purpose for all the earth to be a paradise populated by those who appreciatively obey his laws will not go unfulfilled. (Isa. 45:18; 55:10, 11) That is why Jesus said: "Happy are the mild-tempered ones, since they will inherit *the earth."* That is also why he taught his disciples to pray: "Our Father in the heavens, let your name be sanctified. Let your kingdom come. Let your will take place, as in heaven, *also upon earth."* (Matt. 5:5; 6:9, 10) In harmony with that, Ephesians 1:9-11 explains God's purpose "to gather all things together again in the Christ, the things in the heavens *and the things on the earth."* Hebrews 2:5 refers to *"the inhabited earth to come."* Revelation 5:10 mentions those who, as joint heirs with Christ, are to "rule as kings *over the earth."* Revelation 21:1-5 and 22:1, 2 add delightful descriptions of conditions that will exist in the "new earth" and that remind one of the original Paradise in Eden with its tree of life.—Gen. 2:9.

Additionally, Jesus used the Greek expression *pa·ra′dei·sos* when referring to the future earthly Paradise.

"He said to him [an evildoer who was being impaled alongside Jesus and who expressed faith in Jesus' coming king-
ship]: 'Truly I tell you today, You will be with me in Paradise.'"—Luke 23:43.

How can we be sure what Jesus meant by Paradise in his statement to the evildoer, at Luke 23:43?

Was it a temporary abode for 'departed souls of the just,' a part of Hades?

What is the origin of that view? *The New International
Dictionary of New Testament Theology* states: "With the
infiltration of the G[ree]k doctrine of the immortality of the
soul paradise becomes the dwelling-place of the righteous
during the intermediate state." (Grand Rapids, Mich.; 1976,
edited by Colin Brown, Vol. 2, p. 761) Was that unscriptural
view common among the Jews when Jesus was on earth?
Hastings' *Dictionary of the Bible* indicates that this is
doubtful.—(Edinburgh, 1905), Vol. III, pp. 669, 670.

Even if that view were common among the Jews in the
first century, would Jesus have endorsed it by his promise to
the repentant evildoer? Jesus had forcefully condemned the
Jewish Pharisees and scribes for teaching traditions that
conflicted with God's Word.—Matt. 15:3-9; see also the main
heading "Soul."

Jesus did go to Hades when he died, as is shown at Acts
2:30, 31. (The apostle Peter, when referring there to Psalm
16:10, is quoted as using Hades as the equivalent of Sheol.)
But the Bible nowhere states that Sheol/Hades or any part
of it is a paradise that brings a person pleasure. Rather,
Ecclesiastes 9:5, 10 says that those who are there "are
conscious of nothing at all."

Was the Paradise of Luke 23:43 heaven or some part of heaven?

The Bible does not agree with the view that Jesus and the
evildoer went to heaven on the day that Jesus spoke to him.
Jesus had foretold that, after his being killed, he would not
be raised up until the third day. (Luke 9:22) During that

three-day period he was not in heaven, because following his resurrection he told Mary Magdalene: "I have not yet ascended to the Father." (John 20:17) It was 40 days after Jesus' resurrection that his disciples saw him lifted up from the earth and out of their sight as he began his ascent to heaven.—Acts 1:3, 6-11.

The evildoer did not meet the requirements to go to heaven even at some later time. He was not "born again" —being neither baptized in water nor begotten by God's spirit. Holy spirit was not poured out upon Jesus' disciples until more than 50 days after the evildoer's death. (John 3: 3, 5; Acts 2:1-4) On the day of his death, Jesus had made with those 'who had stuck with him in his trials' a covenant for a heavenly kingdom. The evildoer had no such record of faithfulness and was not included.—Luke 22:28-30.

What points to this Paradise as being earthly?

The Hebrew Scriptures had never led faithful Jews to expect a reward of heavenly life. Those Scriptures pointed to the restoration of Paradise here on earth. Daniel 7:13, 14 had foretold that when "rulership and dignity and kingdom" would be given to the Messiah, "the peoples, national groups and languages should all serve even him." Those subjects of the Kingdom would be here on the earth. By what he said to Jesus, the evildoer was evidently expressing the hope that Jesus would remember him when that time came.

How, then, would Jesus be *with* the evildoer? By raising him from the dead, making provision for his physical needs, and extending to him the opportunity to learn and conform to Jehovah's requirements for eternal life. (John 5:28, 29) Jesus saw in the evildoer's repentant and respectful attitude a basis for including him among the billions who will be resurrected to earthly life and the opportunity to prove their worthiness to live forever in Paradise.

When will the evildoer be in Paradise?

One's understanding of Luke 23:43 is influenced by the punctuation used by the translator. There was no punctuation in the original Greek Bible manuscripts. *The Encyclopedia Americana* (1956, Vol. XXIII, p. 16) states: "No attempt to punctuate is apparent in the earlier manuscripts and inscriptions of the Greeks." Not until the 9th century C.E. did such punctuation come into use. Should Luke 23:43 read, "Truly, I say to you, today you will be with me in Paradise" (*RS*), or should it be, 'Truly I say to you today, You will be with me in Paradise'? The teachings of Christ and the rest of the Bible must be the basis for determination, and not a comma inserted in the text centuries after Jesus said those words.

The Emphasised Bible translated by J. B. Rotherham agrees with the punctuation in the *New World Translation*. In a footnote on Luke 23:43, German Bible translator L. Reinhardt says: "The punctuation presently used [by most translators] in this verse is undoubtedly false and contradictory to the entire way of thinking of Christ and the evildoer. . . . [Christ] certainly did not understand paradise to be a subdivision of the realm of the dead, but rather the restoration of a paradise on earth."

When would Jesus 'get into his kingdom' and fulfill his Father's purpose to make the earth a paradise? The book of Revelation, written about 63 years after the statements recorded at Luke 23:42, 43 were made, indicates that these events were still in the future. (See pages 95-98, under "Dates," also the main heading "Last Days.")

Philosophy

Definition: The word philosophy is derived from Greek roots that mean "love of wisdom." As used here, philosophy is not built on acceptance of belief in God, but it tries to give people a unified view of the universe and endeavors to make them critical thinkers. It employs chiefly speculative means rather than observation in a search for truth.

How can any of us acquire true knowledge and wisdom?

Prov. 1:7; Ps. 111:10: "The fear of Jehovah is the beginning of knowledge . . . [and] of wisdom." (If the universe were not the product of an intelligent Creator but only of some blind, irrational force, then no unified view of the universe would be possible, would it? Nothing that would qualify as wisdom could result from a study of something that was itself irrational, could it? Those who attempt to understand the universe or life itself, while endeavoring to leave God and his purpose out of account, meet with constant frustration. They misinterpret what they learn and misuse facts that they glean. Leaving out of account belief in God destroys the key to accurate knowledge and makes impossible any truly consistent framework of thought.)

Prov. 2:4-7: "If you keep seeking for it as for silver, and as for hid treasures you keep searching for it, in that case you will understand the fear of Jehovah, and you will find the very knowledge of God. For Jehovah himself gives wisdom; out of his mouth there are knowledge and discernment. And for the upright ones he will treasure up practical wisdom." (Jehovah provides needed help through his written Word and his visible organization. An earnest desire and personal effort, including the use of one's thinking ability in a constructive manner, are also necessary.)

Is it realistic to expect to find absolute truth from this Source?

2 Tim. 3:16; John 17:17: "All Scripture is inspired of God." "[Jesus said to his heavenly Father:] Your word is truth." (Is it not reasonable that the Creator of the universe would have full understanding of it? In the Bible he has not told us everything about the universe, but what he has had recorded there is not speculation; it is truth. He has also stated in the Bible what his purpose is for the earth and for mankind and how he will accomplish it. His almighty power, superlative wisdom, flawless justice, and great love guarantee that this purpose will be fully accomplished, and in the best possible manner. His qualities thus assure us that his statement of purpose is completely dependable; it is truth.)

What is the origin of human philosophies?

They come from people who have limitations: The Bible informs us: "It does not belong to man who is walking even to direct his step." (Jer. 10:23) History testifies that trying to ignore that limitation has not produced good results. On one occasion, "Jehovah proceeded to answer Job out of the windstorm and say: 'Who is this that is obscuring counsel by words without knowledge? Gird up your loins, please, like an able-bodied man, and let me question you, and you inform me. Where did you happen to be when I founded the earth? Tell me, if you do know understanding.'" (Job 38:1-4) (Humans by nature have limitations. Additionally, their experience in life is relatively brief and is usually confined to one culture or one environment. The knowledge they possess is thus restricted, and everything is interconnected to such an extent that they constantly find aspects that they had not adequately considered. Any philosophy that they originate will reflect these limitations.)

They are developed by humans who are imperfect: "All have sinned and fall short of the glory of God." (Rom. 3:23) "There exists a way that is upright before a man, but the ways of death are the end of it afterward." (Prov. 14:12) (Because of such imperfection, human philosophies often reflect a basic selfishness that leads perhaps to momentary pleasure but also to frustration and much unhappiness.)

They are influenced by demonic spirits: "The whole world is lying in the power of the wicked one." (1 John 5:19) "The one called Devil and Satan . . . is misleading the entire inhabited earth." (Rev. 12:9) "You at one time walked according to the system of things of this world, according to the ruler of the authority of the air, the spirit that now operates in the sons of disobedience." (Eph. 2:2) (Philosophies that encourage people to disobey God's wholesome and upright requirements reflect such an influence. No wonder that, as history testifies, human philosophies and schemes have often brought grief to large segments of humankind.)

Why is it an evidence of clear thinking to study the teachings of Jesus Christ instead of human philosophy?

Col. 1:15-17: "He [Jesus Christ] is the image of the invisible God, the firstborn of all creation; because by means of him all other things were created in the heavens and upon the earth . . . All other things have been created through him and for him. Also, he is before all other things and by means of him all other things were made to exist." (His intimate relationship with God enables him to help us to learn the truth about God. Furthermore, as the one through whom all other things were made, Jesus has a full knowledge of the entire created universe. No human philosopher can offer any of this.)

Col. 1:19, 20: "God saw good for all fullness to dwell in him [Jesus Christ], and through him to reconcile again to himself all other things by making peace through the blood he shed on the torture stake." (Thus Jesus Christ is the one through whom God has purposed to bring all creation back into harmony with himself. To Jesus, God has also entrusted rulership over all the earth, as shown at Daniel 7:13, 14. So our life prospects for the future depend on getting to know him and responding favorably to his instruction.)

Col. 2:8: "Look out: perhaps there may be someone who will carry you off as his prey through the philosophy and empty deception according to the tradition of men, according to the elementary things of the world and not according to Christ." (What a sad mistake it would be to choose such deceptive human philosophy in preference to acquiring true wisdom as a disciple of Jesus Christ, the second-greatest person in the universe, next to God himself!)

How does God view the "wisdom" offered by human philosophy?

1 Cor. 1:19-25: "It is written: 'I will make the wisdom of the wise men perish, and the intelligence of the intellectual men I will shove aside.' Where is the wise man? Where the scribe? Where the debater of this system of things? Did not God make the wisdom of the world foolish? For since, in the wisdom of God, the world through its wisdom did not get to know God, God saw good through the foolishness [as it appears to the world] of what is preached to save those believing. . . . Because a foolish thing of God [as the world views it] is wiser than men, and a weak thing of God [as the world may see it] is stronger than men." (Such a viewpoint

on God's part is certainly not arbitrary or unreasonable. He has provided in the Bible, the most widely circulated book in the world, a clear statement of his purpose. He has sent his witnesses to discuss it with all who will listen. How foolish for any creature to think that he has wisdom greater than that of God!)

Prayer

Definition: Worshipful address, whether aloud or silently in one's thoughts, to the true God or to false gods.

Do you feel, as many do, that you get no answer to your prayers?

Whose prayers is God willing to hear?

Ps. 65:2; Acts 10:34, 35: "O Hearer of prayer, even to you people of all flesh will come." "God is not partial, but in every nation the man that fears him and works righteousness is acceptable to him." (One's nationality, the color of one's skin, or one's economic circumstances have no bearing on the matter. But the motivations of one's heart and one's way of life do.)

Luke 11:2: "Whenever you pray, say, 'Father, let your name be sanctified.'" (Are your prayers addressed to the Father, the one whose name the Bible says is Jehovah? Or, instead, do you address your prayers to "saints"?)

John 14:6, 14: "Jesus said to him: 'I am the way and the truth and the life. No one comes to the Father except through me. If you ask anything in my name, I will do it.'" (Do you pray in the name of Jesus Christ, recognizing that as a sinful human you need his intercession on your behalf?)

1 John 5:14: "This is the confidence that we have toward him, that, no matter what it is that we ask according to his will, he hears us." (To have such confidence, however, you must first know God's will. Then be sure that your requests are in harmony with it.)

1 Pet. 3:12: "The eyes of Jehovah are upon the righteous

ones, and his ears are toward their supplication; but the face of Jehovah is against those doing bad things." (Have you taken time to learn what Jehovah says through his Word as to what is righteous and what is bad?)

1 John 3:22: "Whatever we ask we receive from him, because we are observing his commandments and are doing the things that are pleasing in his eyes." (Is it truly your desire to be pleasing to God, and are you earnestly endeavoring to obey those of his commandments that you already know?)

Isa. 55:6, 7: "Search for Jehovah, you people, while he may be found. Call to him while he proves to be near. Let the wicked man leave his way, and the harmful man his thoughts; and let him return to Jehovah, who will have mercy upon him, and to our God, for he will forgive in a large way." (Mercifully, Jehovah invites even persons who have done bad things to call to him in prayer. But, to have God's approval, they must sincerely repent of their wrong ways and thoughts and change their course.)

What could make a person's prayers unacceptable to God?

Matt. 6:5: "When you pray, you must not be as the hypocrites; because they like to pray standing in the synagogues and on the corners of the broad ways to be visible to men. Truly I say to you, They are having their reward in full." (Also Luke 18:9-14)

Matt. 6:7: "When praying, do not say the same things over and over again, just as the people of the nations do, for they imagine they will get a hearing for their use of many words."

Prov. 28:9: "He that is turning his ear away from hearing the law [of God]—even his prayer is something detestable."

Mic. 3:4: "At that time they will call to Jehovah for aid, but he will not answer them. And he will conceal his face from them in that time, according as they committed badness in their dealings."

Jas. 4:3: "You do ask, and yet you do not receive, because you are asking for a wrong purpose, that you may expend it upon your cravings for sensual pleasure."

Isa. 42:8, *Dy;* Matt. 4:10, *JB:* "I, the Lord ["Yahweh," *JB;* "Jehovah," *NW*]: this is my name. I will not give my glory to another, nor my praise to graven things." "You must worship the Lord your God ["Jehovah your God," *NW*], and serve him alone." (Also Psalm 115:4-8, or 113:4-8 second set of numbers in *Dy*) (Prayer is a form of worship. If you pray before graven things, or images, is that going to please God?)

Isa. 8:19: "In case they should say to you people: 'Apply to the spiritistic mediums or to those having a spirit of prediction who are chirping and making utterances in low tones,' is it not to its God that any people should apply? Should there be application to dead persons in behalf of living persons?"

Jas. 1:6, 7: "Let him keep on asking in faith, not doubting at all, for he who doubts is like a wave of the sea driven by the wind and blown about. In fact, let not that man suppose that he will receive anything from Jehovah."

What are proper matters about which to pray?

Matt. 6:9-13: "You must pray, then, this way: '[1] Our Father in the heavens, let your name be sanctified. [2] Let your kingdom come. [3] Let your will take place, as in heaven, also upon earth. [4] Give us today our bread for this day; and [5] forgive us our debts, as we also have forgiven our debtors. And [6] do not bring us into temptation, but deliver us from the wicked one.'" (Notice that God's name and purpose should be given priority.)

Ps. 25:4, 5: "Make me know your own ways, O Jehovah; teach me your own paths. Make me walk in your truth and teach me, for you are my God of salvation."

Luke 11:13: "If you, although being wicked, know how to give good gifts to your children, how much more so will the Father in heaven give holy spirit to those asking him!"

1 Thess. 5:17, 18: "Pray incessantly. In connection with everything give thanks."

Matt. 14:19, 20: "[Jesus] took the five loaves and two fishes, and, looking up to heaven, he said a blessing and, after breaking the loaves, he distributed them to the disciples, the disciples in turn to the crowds. So all ate and were satisfied."

Jas. 5:16: "Pray for one another."

Matt. 26:41: "Keep on the watch and pray continually, that you may not enter into temptation."

Phil. 4:6: "Do not be anxious over anything, but in everything by prayer and supplication along with thanksgiving let your petitions be made known to God."

If Someone Says—

'Pray with me first, then give me your message'

You might reply: 'I'm glad to know that you are a person who appreciates the importance of prayer. Jehovah's Witnesses also pray regularly. But there is something that Jesus said about when and how to pray that may be new to you. Did you know that he told his disciples not to offer public prayers with a view to having others see that they were devout, praying persons? . . . (Matt. 6:5)' **Then perhaps add:** 'Notice what he went on to say should be of primary concern to us and what we should put first in our prayers. That is what I have come to share with you. (Matt. 6:9, 10)'

Or you could say: 'I know that representatives from some religious groups do that. But Jehovah's Witnesses do not, because Jesus instructed his disciples to go about their work of preaching in another manner. Instead of saying, "When you enter a house, first pray," notice what he said, as found here at Matthew 10:12, 13. . . . And see here in verse 7 what they were to talk about. . . . How can that Kingdom help people like you and me? (Rev. 21:4)'

Prophecy

Definition: An inspired message; a revelation of the divine will and purpose. Prophecy may be a prediction of something to come, inspired moral teaching, or an expression of a divine command or judgment.

What predictions recorded in the Bible have already been fulfilled?

For some samples, see the main headings "Bible," "Last Days," and "Dates," also the book *"All Scripture Is Inspired of God and Beneficial,"* pages 343-346.

What are some of the outstanding Bible prophecies that are yet to be fulfilled?

1 Thess. 5:3: "Whenever it is that they are saying: 'Peace and security!' then sudden destruction is to be instantly upon them just as the pang of distress upon a pregnant woman; and they will by no means escape."

Rev. 17:16: "The ten horns that you saw, and the wild beast, these will hate the harlot [Babylon the Great] and will make her devastated and naked, and will eat up her fleshy parts and will completely burn her with fire."

Ezek. 38:14-19: "You must say to Gog, 'This is what the Sovereign Lord Jehovah has said: "Will it not be in that day when my people [spiritual] Israel are dwelling in security that you will know it? And you will certainly come from your place, from the remotest parts of the north, you and many peoples with you . . . " "And it must occur in that day, in the day when Gog comes in upon the soil of Israel," is the utterance of the Sovereign Lord Jehovah, "that my rage will come up into my nose. And in my ardor, in the fire of my fury, I shall have to speak."'"

Dan. 2:44: "The kingdom [set up by God] . . . will crush and put an end to all these [human] kingdoms, and it itself will stand to times indefinite."

Ezek. 38:23: "I shall certainly magnify myself and sanctify myself and make myself known before the eyes of many nations; and they will have to know that I am Jehovah."

Rev. 20:1-3: "I saw an angel coming down out of heaven with the key of the abyss and a great chain in his hand. And he seized the dragon, the original serpent, who is the Devil and Satan, and bound him for a thousand years. And he hurled him into the abyss and shut it and sealed it over him, that he might not mislead the nations anymore until the thousand years were ended. After these things he must be let loose for a little while.'"

John 5:28, 29: "Do not marvel at this, because the hour is coming in which all those in the memorial tombs will hear his voice and come out, those who did good things to a resurrection of life, those who practiced vile things to a resurrection of judgment."

Rev. 21:3, 4: "I heard a loud voice from the throne say: 'Look! The tent of God is with mankind, and he will reside with them, and they will be his peoples. And God himself will be with them. And he will wipe out every tear from their eyes, and death will be no more, neither will mourning nor outcry nor pain be anymore. The former things have passed away.'"

1 Cor. 15:24-28: "Next, the end, when he hands over the kingdom to his God and Father . . . But when all things will have been subjected to him, then the Son himself will also subject himself to the One who subjected all things to him, that God may be all things to everyone."

Why should Christians be keenly interested in the Bible's predictions?

Matt. 24:42: "Keep on the watch, therefore, because you do not know on what day your Lord is coming."

2 Pet. 1:19-21: "We have the prophetic word made more sure [as a result of what occurred at the transfiguration of Jesus]; and you are doing well in paying attention to it . . . For prophecy was at no time brought by man's will, but men spoke from God as they were borne along by holy spirit."

Prov. 4:18: "The path of the righteous ones is like the bright light that is getting lighter and lighter until the day is firmly established."

Matt. 4:4: "Man must live, not on bread alone, but on every utterance coming forth through Jehovah's mouth." (That includes his grand prophetic promises.)

2 Tim. 3:16: "*All* Scripture is inspired of God and beneficial for teaching, for reproving, for setting things straight, for disciplining in righteousness." (Thus the *entire* written Word of God deserves our earnest study.)

If Someone Says—

'You put too much emphasis on prophecy. All that is needed is to accept Christ as your Savior and to lead a good Christian life'

You might reply: 'Appreciation of the role of Jesus Christ is certainly vital. But did you know that one reason why the Jews in the first century failed to accept him was that they did not pay sufficient attention to prophecy?' **Then perhaps add:** (1) 'The prophecies in the Hebrew Scriptures had foretold when the Messiah (Christ) would appear and what he would do. But the Jews in general did not pay heed to what those prophecies said. They had their own ideas as to what the Messiah should do, and as a result they rejected the Son of God. (See page 211, under "Jesus Christ.")' (2) 'We today live at the time when Christ has begun to rule as heavenly King and is separating people of all nations, with a view to life or destruction. (Matt. 25:31-33, 46) But most people are looking for something else.'

Or you could say: 'I agree that being a good Christian is important. But would I be a good Christian if I did *some* of the things that Jesus taught but ignored what he said we should put first in life? . . . Notice what he said as recorded here at Matthew 6:33.' **Then perhaps add:** 'Isn't it true that Jesus taught us to pray for that Kingdom, even putting it ahead of our asking for forgiveness because of our faith in him as Savior? (Matt. 6:9-12)'

Purgatory

Definition: "According to the teaching of the [Roman Catholic] Church, the state, place, or condition in the next world . . . where the souls of those who die in the state of grace, but not yet free from all imperfection, make expiation for unforgiven venial sins or for the temporal punishment due to venial and mortal sins that have already been forgiven and, by so doing, are purified before they enter heaven." (*New Catholic Encyclopedia*, 1967, Vol. XI, p. 1034) *Not a Bible teaching.*

On what is the teaching of purgatory based?

After reviewing what Catholic writers have said regarding such texts as 2 Maccabees 12:39-45, Matthew 12:32, and 1 Corinthians 3:10-15, the *New Catholic Encyclopedia* (1967, Vol. XI, p. 1034) acknowledges: "In the final analysis, the Catholic doctrine on purgatory is based on tradition, not Sacred Scripture."

"The church has relied on tradition to support a middle ground between heaven and hell."—*U.S. Catholic,* March 1981, p. 7.

Regarding the nature of purgatory, what do Catholic spokesmen say?

"Many think that the total suffering of purgatory is identified with the awareness of the temporary postponement of the beatific vision, although the more common view holds that, in addition to this, there is some positive punishment . . . In the Latin Church it has been generally maintained that this pain is imposed through real fire. This is not, however, essential to belief in purgatory. It is not even certain. . . . Even if one chooses, with the theologians of the East, to reject the idea of suffering induced by fire, one should be careful not to exclude all positive suffering from purgatory. There are still real affliction, sorrow, chagrin, shame of conscience, and other spiritual sorrows capable of inflicting true pain on the soul. . . . One should remember, at any rate, that in the midst of their sufferings these souls also experience great joy over the certainty of salvation."—*New Catholic Encyclopedia* (1967), Vol. XI, p. 1036, 1037.

"What goes on in purgatory is anyone's guess."—*U.S. Catholic,* March 1981, p. 9.

Does the soul survive the death of the body?

Ezek. 18:4, *Dy:* "The soul [Hebrew, *ne'phesh;* "man," *JB;* "one," *NAB;* "soul," *Kx*] that sinneth, the same shall die."

Jas. 5:20, *JB:* "Anyone who can bring back a sinner from the wrong way that he has taken will be saving a *soul* from *death* and covering up a great number of sins." (Italics added.) (Notice that this speaks of the death of the *soul*.)

For more details, see the headings "Death" and "Soul."

Is further punishment for sin exacted after one's death?

Rom. 6:7, *NAB:* "A man who is dead has been freed from sin." (*Kx:* "Guilt makes no more claim on a man who is dead.")

Are the dead able to experience joy because of confidence in the prospect of salvation?

Eccl. 9:5, *JB:* "The living know at least that they will die, the dead know nothing."

Isa. 38:18, *JB:* "Sheol does not praise you [Yahweh], death does not extol you; those who go down to the pit do not go on trusting in your faithfulness." (So how can any of them "experience great joy over the certainty of salvation"?)

According to the Bible, by what means is purification from sins accomplished?

1 John 1:7, 9, *JB:* "If we live our lives in the light, as he [God] is in the light, we are in union with one another, and the blood of Jesus, his Son, purifies us from all sin. . . . If we acknowledge our sins, then God who is faithful and just will forgive our sins and purify us from everything that is wrong ["all our wrong-doing is purged away," *Kx*]."

Rev. 1:5, *JB:* "Jesus Christ . . . loves us and has washed away our sins with his blood."

Races of Mankind

Definition: As used here, race means a division of mankind possessing in characteristic proportions certain combinations of physical traits that can be inherited and that are sufficient to set the group apart as a distinct human type. It should be noted, however, that the fact that the races are capable of intermarriage and reproduction shows that they are actually of one "kind," all being members of the human family. So the various races are merely facets of the total variation possible in humankind.

From where did the various races come?

Gen. 5:1, 2; 1:28: "In the day of God's creating Adam he made him in the likeness of God. Male and female he created them. After that he blessed them and called their name Man [or, Mankind] in the day of their being created." "God blessed them and God said to them: 'Be fruitful and become many and fill the earth.'" (Thus all mankind are descendants of that first human pair, Adam and Eve.)

Acts 17:26: "[God] made out of one man [Adam] every nation of men, to dwell upon the entire surface of the earth." (So, regardless of what races make up a nation, they all are offspring of Adam.)

Gen. 9:18, 19: "Noah's sons who came out of the ark were Shem and Ham and Japheth. . . . These three were Noah's sons, and from these was all the earth's population spread abroad." (After God destroyed the ungodly world by means of a global flood in Noah's day, the earth's new population, including all the races known today, developed from the offspring of Noah's three sons and their wives.)

Were Adam and Eve merely allegorical (fictional) persons?

The Bible does not support that view; see the main heading "Adam and Eve."

Where did Cain get his wife if there was just one family?

Gen. 3:20: "Adam called his wife's name Eve, because she had to become the mother of everyone living." (So all humans were to be the offspring of Adam and Eve.)

Gen. 5:3, 4: "Adam lived on for a hundred and thirty years. Then he became father to a son in his likeness, in his image, and called his name Seth. And the days of Adam after his fathering Seth came to be eight hundred years. Meanwhile he became father to sons and daughters." (One of Adam's sons was Cain, and one of Adam's daughters must have become Cain's wife. At that time in human history when humans still had outstanding physical health and vitality, as indicated by the length of their lives, the likelihood of passing on defects as a result of marrying a close relative was not great. After some 2,500 years of human history, however, when mankind's physical condition had greatly deteriorated, Jehovah gave to Israel laws forbidding incest.)

Gen. 4:16, 17: "Cain went away from the face of Jehovah and took up residence in the land of Fugitiveness [or, Nod] to the east of Eden. Afterward Cain had intercourse with his wife ["knew his wife," that is, intimately so, *KJ, RS;* "lay with his wife," *NE*] and she became pregnant and gave birth to Enoch." (Notice that Cain did not first *meet* his wife in the land to which he fled, as if she were from another family. Rather, it was there that he had sexual relations with her to produce a son.)

What explains the development of the various racial characteristics?

"All men living today belong to a single species, *Homo sapiens,* and are derived from a common stock. . . . Biological differences between human beings are due to differences in hereditary constitution and to the influence of the environment on this genetic potential. In most cases, those differences are due to the interaction of these two sets of factors. . . . Differences between individuals within a race or within a population are often greater than the average differences between races or populations."—An international body of scientists convened by UNESCO, quoted in *Statement on Race* (New York, 1972, third ed.), Ashley Montagu, pp. 149, 150.

"A race is simply one of the partially isolated gene pools into which the human species came to be divided during and following its early geographical spread. Roughly one race has developed on each of the five major continental areas of the earth. . . . Man did indeed diverge genetically during this phase of history and we can measure and study the results of this divergence in what remains today of the old geographical races. As we would expect, divergence appears to be correlated with the degree of isolation. . . . When race formation took place on the continents, with the bottlenecking of thousands of populations in isolated gene pools all over the world, the gene-frequency differences we now see were established. . . . The paradox which faces us is that each group of humans appears to be externally different yet underneath these differences there is fundamental similarity." (*Heredity and Human Life*, New York, 1963, H. L. Carson, pp. 151, 154, 162, 163) (Thus, early in human history, when a group of people were isolated from others and married within the group, certain distinctive combinations of genetic traits were emphasized in their offspring.)

Does the Bible teach that blacks are cursed?

That idea is based on a misunderstanding of Genesis 9:25, where Noah is quoted as saying: "Cursed be Canaan. Let him become the lowest slave to his brothers." Read it carefully; it says nothing about skin color. The curse was because Ham's son Canaan had evidently performed some shocking act deserving of a curse. But who were Canaan's descendants? Not blacks, but lighter-skinned peoples living to the east of the Mediterranean Sea. Because of their depraved practices, demonistic rites, idolatry, and child sacrifice, they came under divine judgment, and God gave to Israel the land occupied by the Canaanites. (Gen. 10:15-19) Not all the Canaanites were destroyed; some were put at forced labor, in fulfillment of the curse.—Josh. 17:13.

From which of Noah's offspring did the blacks descend? "The sons of Cush [another one of Ham's sons] were Seba and Havilah and Sabtah and Raamah and Sabteca." (Gen. 10:6, 7) Later Biblical references to Cush are usually equivalent to Ethiopia. Seba is later used when referring to another people in the eastern part of Africa and evidently close to Ethiopia.—Isa. 43:3, footnote in *NW* Reference edition.

Are all humans children of God?

Being children of God is not something that we imperfect humans are entitled to by birth. But we are all the offspring

of Adam, who when created in perfection was a "son of God."
—Luke 3:38.

Acts 10:34, 35: "God is not partial, but in every nation the
man that fears him and works righteousness is acceptable
to him."

John 3:16: "God loved the world so much that he gave his
only-begotten Son, in order that *everyone* exercising faith
in him might not be destroyed but have everlasting life."
(Exercising genuine faith in him is necessary in order for
any of us to attain to the kind of relationship with God that
Adam lost. That privilege is open to people of all races.)

1 John 3:10: "The children of God and the children of the
Devil are evident by this fact: Everyone who does not carry
on righteousness does not originate with God, neither does
he who does not love his brother." (So God does not view all
humans as his children. From a spiritual standpoint, those
who deliberately practice what God condemns have the
Devil as their father. See John 8:44. However, true Christians reflect godly qualities. From among these, God has
selected a limited number to rule as kings with Christ in
heaven. These are referred to by God as his "children" or his
"sons." For further details, see the main heading "Born
Again.")

Rom. 8:19-21: "The eager expectation of the creation is
waiting for the revealing of the sons of God . . . The creation
itself also will be set free from enslavement to corruption
and have the glorious freedom of the children of God."
(Relief for mankind will come when "the sons of God," after
receiving heavenly life, are 'revealed' as taking positive
action on behalf of mankind under the direction of Christ.
After faithful ones on earth [referred to as "the creation" in
this scripture] have attained to human perfection and have
demonstrated unshakable loyalty to Jehovah as Universal
Sovereign, then they too will enjoy the fine relationship of
children of God. People of all races will share in this.)

Will people of all races ever truly be united as brothers and sisters?

To those who would be his true disciples, Jesus said: "All
you are brothers." (Matt. 23:8) Later he added: "By this all

will know that you are my disciples, if you have love among yourselves."—John 13:35.

Despite human imperfections, that sense of oneness was a reality among early Christians. The apostle Paul wrote: "There is neither Jew nor Greek, there is neither slave nor freeman, there is neither male nor female; for you are all one person in union with Christ Jesus."—Gal. 3:28.

Christian brotherhood unmarred by racial distinctions is a reality among Jehovah's Witnesses in the 20th century. Writer William Whalen said in *U.S. Catholic:* "I believe that one of the most attractive characteristics of [the organization of Jehovah's Witnesses] has been its traditional policy of racial equality." After making an extensive study of Jehovah's Witnesses in Africa, Oxford University sociologist Bryan Wilson stated: "The Witnesses are perhaps more successful than any other group in the speed with which they eliminate tribal discrimination among their own recruits." Reporting on an international gathering of Witnesses from 123 lands, *The New York Times Magazine* said: "The Witnesses impressed New Yorkers not only with their numbers, but with their diversity (they include people from all walks of life), their racial unself-consciousness (many Witnesses are Negroes) and their quiet, orderly behavior."

Soon God's Kingdom will destroy the present ungodly system of things, including all who do not genuinely love both Jehovah God and their fellowman. (Dan. 2:44; Luke 10: 25-28) God's Word promises that the survivors will be persons "out of all nations and tribes and peoples and tongues." (Rev. 7:9) Drawn together by worship of the true God, by faith in Jesus Christ, and by love for one another, they will truly make up a united human family.

Ransom

Definition: A price paid to buy back or to bring about release from some obligation or undesirable circumstance. The most significant ransom price is that of the shed blood of Jesus Christ. By paying over the value of that ransom in heaven, Jesus opened the way for Adam's offspring to be delivered from the sin and death that we all inherit because of the sin of our forefather Adam.

How was the death of Jesus Christ different from that of others who have become martyrs?

Jesus was a perfect human. He was born without any blemish of sin and he maintained that perfection throughout his life. "He committed no sin." He was "undefiled, separated from the sinners."—1 Pet. 2:22; Heb. 7:26.

He was the unique Son of God. God himself testified to this audibly from the heavens. (Matt. 3:17; 17:5) This Son had lived previously in heaven; through him God had brought into existence all other created persons and things in the entire universe. To carry out His will, God had miraculously transferred the life of this Son to the womb of a virgin girl so that he might be born as a human. To emphasize that he truly had become a human, Jesus referred to himself as the Son of man.—Col. 1:15-20; John 1:14; Luke 5:24.

He was not powerless before his executioners. He said: "I surrender my soul . . . No man has taken it away from me, but I surrender it of my own initiative." (John 10:17, 18) He declined to appeal for angelic forces to intervene on his behalf. (Matt. 26:53, 54) Though wicked men were permitted to carry out their schemes in having him put to death, his death was truly sacrificial.

His shed blood has value to provide deliverance for others. "The Son of man came, not to be ministered to, but to minister and to give his soul a ransom in exchange for many." (Mark 10:45) So his death was far more than a case of martyrdom because of refusal to compromise his beliefs.

See also pages 266, 267, under the heading "Memorial."

Why was it necessary for the ransom to be provided in the manner that it was in order for us to have eternal life?

Rom. 5:12: "Through one man [Adam] sin entered into the world and death through sin, and thus death spread to all men because they had all sinned." (No matter how uprightly we may live, all of us are sinners from birth. [Ps. 51:5] There is no way that we can *earn* the right to live forever.)

Rom. 6:23: "The wages sin pays is death."

Ps. 49:6-9: "Those who are trusting in their means of maintenance, and who keep boasting about the abundance of their riches, not one of them can by any means redeem even a brother, nor give to God a ransom for him; (and the redemption price of their soul is so precious that it has ceased to time indefinite) that he should still live forever and not see the pit." (No imperfect human can provide the means to deliver someone else from sin and death. His money cannot buy eternal life, and his soul laid down in death, being the wages that are to come to him anyway because of sin, has no value toward delivering anyone.)

Why did God not simply decree that, although Adam and Eve must die for their rebellion, all of their offspring who would obey God could live forever?

Because Jehovah is "a lover of righteousness and justice." (Ps. 33:5; Deut. 32:4; Jer. 9:24) So, the way he dealt with the situation upheld his righteousness, met the demands of absolute justice, and, at the same time, magnified his love and mercy. How is that so?

(1) Adam and Eve had produced no children before they sinned, so none were born perfect. All of Adam's offspring were brought forth in sin, and sin leads to death. If Jehovah had simply ignored this, that would have been a denial of his own righteous standards. God could not do that and so become a party to unrighteousness. He did not sidestep the requirements of absolute justice; so no intelligent creature could ever legitimately find fault in this respect.—Rom. 3: 21-26.

(2) Without ignoring the requirements of justice, how could provision be made to deliver those of Adam's offspring who would demonstrate loving obedience to Jehovah? If a *perfect* human was to die sacrificially, justice could allow for that perfect life to provide a covering for the sins of those

who would in faith accept the provision. Since one man's sin (that of Adam) had been responsible for causing the entire human family to be sinners, the shed blood of another perfect human (in effect, a second Adam), being of corresponding value, could balance the scales of justice. Because Adam was a willful sinner, he could not benefit; but because the penalty that all mankind was due to pay for sin would in this way be paid by someone else, Adam's offspring could be delivered. But there was no such perfect human. Humankind could never meet those demands of absolute justice. So, as an expression of marvelous love and at great personal cost, Jehovah himself made the provision. (1 Cor. 15:45; 1 Tim. 2:5, 6; John 3:16; Rom. 5:8) God's only-begotten Son was willing to do his part. Humbly leaving behind his heavenly glory and becoming a perfect human, Jesus died on behalf of mankind.—Phil. 2:7, 8.

Illustration: A family head may become a criminal and be sentenced to death. His children may be left destitute, hopelessly in debt. Perhaps their kindly grandfather intervenes on their behalf, making provision through a son who is living with him to pay their debts and to open up for them the possibility of a new life. Of course, to benefit, the children must accept the arrangement, and the grandfather may reasonably require certain things as assurance that the children will not imitate the course of their father.

To whom first was the merit of Jesus' sacrifice applied, and with what objective?

Rom. 1:16: "The good news [regarding Jesus Christ and his role in Jehovah's purpose] . . . is, in fact, God's power for salvation to everyone having faith, to the Jew first and also to the Greek." (The invitation to benefit from the provision for salvation through Christ was extended first to the Jews, then to non-Jews.)

Eph. 1:11-14: "In union with [Christ] we [Jews, including the apostle Paul] were also assigned as heirs [Heirs of what? Of the heavenly Kingdom] . . . that we should serve for the praise of his glory, we who have been first to hope in the Christ. But you also [Christians taken out of the Gentile nations, as were many in Ephesus] hoped in him after you heard the word of truth, the good news about your salvation. By means of him also, after you believed, you were sealed with the promised holy spirit, which is a token in advance of our inheritance, for the purpose of releasing by a ransom God's own possession, to his glorious praise." (That inheritance, as shown at 1 Peter 1:4, is reserved in the heavens. Revelation 14:1-4 indicates that those who share in it number 144,000. Along with Christ, these will serve as kings and priests over mankind for 1,000 years, during which God's purpose for the earth to be a paradise populated by perfect offspring of the first human pair will be accomplished.)

Who else in our day are experiencing benefits from Jesus' sacrifice?

1 John 2:2: "He [Jesus Christ] is a propitiatory sacrifice for our sins [those of the apostle John and other spirit-anointed Christians], yet not for ours only but also for the whole world's [others of mankind, those for whom the prospect of eternal life on earth is thus made possible]."

John 10:16: "I have other sheep, which are not of this fold; those also I must bring, and they will listen to my voice, and they will become one flock, one shepherd." (These "other sheep" come under the loving care of Jesus Christ while the remnant of the "little flock" of Kingdom heirs is still on earth; thus the "other sheep" can be associated with the Kingdom heirs as part of the "one flock." They all enjoy many of the same benefits from Jesus' sacrifice, but not identically so, because they have different destinies.)

Rev. 7:9, 14: "After these things I saw, and, look! a great crowd, which no man was able to number, out of all nations and tribes and peoples and tongues . . . 'These are the ones that come out of the great tribulation, and they have washed their robes and made them white in the blood of the Lamb.'" (So, the members of this great crowd are living when the great tribulation begins, and they have a clean standing before God because they exercise faith in the ransom. The righteousness counted to them as a result of this is sufficient for them to be preserved alive on earth through the great tribulation.)

What future blessings will be enjoyed as a result of the ransom?

Rev. 5:9, 10: "They sing a new song, saying: 'You [the Lamb, Jesus Christ] are worthy to take the scroll and open its seals, because you were slaughtered and with your blood you bought persons for God out of every tribe and tongue and people and nation, and you made them to be a kingdom and priests to our God, and they are to rule as kings over the earth.'" (The ransom was a vital factor in opening the way to heavenly life for those who are to rule with Christ. Soon all the rulers in earth's new government will be on their heavenly thrones.)

Rev. 7:9, 10: "Look! a great crowd, which no man was able to number, out of all nations and tribes and peoples and tongues, standing before the throne and before the Lamb [Jesus Christ, who died as if a sacrificial lamb], dressed in white robes; and there were palm branches in their hands. And they keep on crying with a loud voice, saying: 'Salvation we owe to our God, who is seated on the throne, and to the Lamb.'" (Faith in Christ's sacrifice is a key factor in the survival of this great crowd through the great tribulation.)

Rev. 22:1, 2: "And he showed me a river of water of life, clear as crystal, flowing out from the throne of God *and of the Lamb* down the middle of its broad way. And on this side of the river and on that side there were trees of life producing twelve crops of fruit, yielding their fruits each month. And the leaves of the trees were for the curing of the nations." (Thus, application of the value of the sacrifice of the Lamb of God, Jesus Christ, is an important part of the provision made by God to cure mankind of all the effects of sin and to enable them to enjoy eternal life.)

Rom. 8:21: "The creation itself [mankind] also will be set free from enslavement to corruption and have the glorious freedom of the children of God."

What is required of us in order to benefit lastingly from Jesus' perfect sacrifice?

John 3:36: "He that exercises faith in the Son has everlasting life; he that disobeys the Son will not see life, but the wrath of God remains upon him."

Heb. 5:9: "After he [Jesus Christ] had been made perfect he became responsible for everlasting salvation to all those obeying him."

What does the provision of the ransom reveal as to how God feels about mankind?

1 John 4:9, 10: "By this the love of God was made manifest in our case, because God sent forth his only-begotten Son into the world that we might gain life through him. The love is in this respect, not that we have loved God, but that he loved us and sent forth his Son as a propitiatory sacrifice for our sins."

Rom. 5:7, 8: "Hardly will anyone die for a righteous man; indeed, for the good man, perhaps, someone even dares to die. But God recommends his own love to us in that, while we were yet sinners, Christ died for us."

What effect should this provision have on how we use our lives?

1 Pet. 2:24: "He himself bore our sins in his own body upon the stake, in order that we might be done with sins and live to righteousness." (In view of all that Jehovah and his Son have done to cleanse us from sin, we should strive diligently to overcome sinful tendencies. It should be completely unthinkable for us deliberately to do anything that we know is sinful!)

Titus 2:13, 14: "Christ Jesus . . . gave himself for us that he might deliver us from every sort of lawlessness and cleanse for himself a people peculiarly his own, zealous for fine works." (Appreciation for this marvelous provision should move us to have a zealous share in those works that Christ assigned to his true followers.)

2 Cor. 5:14, 15: "The love the Christ has compels us, because this is what we have judged, that one man died for all; so, then, all had died; and he died for all that those who live might live no longer for themselves, but for him who died for them and was raised up."

Rapture

Definition: The belief that faithful Christians will be bodily caught up from the earth, suddenly taken out of the world, to be united with the Lord "in the air." The word "rapture" is understood by some persons, but not by all, to be the meaning of 1 Thessalonians 4:17. The word "rapture" does not occur in the inspired Scriptures.

When the apostle Paul said that Christians would be "caught up" to be with the Lord, what subject was being discussed?

1 Thess. 4:13-18, *RS:* "We would not have you ignorant, brethren, concerning those who are asleep ["those who sleep in death," *NE;* "those who have died," *TEV, JB*], that you may not grieve as others do who have no hope. For since we believe that Jesus died and rose again, even so, through Jesus, God will bring with him those who have fallen asleep. For this we declare to you by the word of the Lord, that we who are alive, who are left until the coming of the Lord, shall not precede those who have fallen asleep. For the Lord himself will descend from heaven with a cry of command, with the archangel's call, and with the sound of the trumpet of God. And the dead in Christ will rise first; then we who are alive, who are left, shall be caught up together with them in the clouds to meet the Lord in the air; and so we shall always be with the Lord. Therefore comfort one another with these words." (Evidently some members of the Christian congregation in Thessalonica had died. Paul encouraged the survivors to comfort one another with the *resurrection hope*. He reminded them that Jesus was resurrected after his death; so, too, at the coming of the Lord, those faithful Christians among them who had died would be raised to be with Christ.)

Who are the ones that will be 'caught up in the clouds,' as stated at 1 Thessalonians 4:17?

Verse 15 explains that they are faithful ones "who are left until the coming of the Lord," that is, they are still living at the time of Christ's coming. Will they ever die? According to Romans 6:3-5 and 1 Corinthians 15:35, 36, 44 (quoted on pages 314, 315), they must die before they can gain heavenly life. But there is no need for them to remain in the death state awaiting Christ's return. They will instantly be "caught up," "in the twinkling of an eye," to be with the Lord. —1 Cor. 15:51, 52, *RS;* also Revelation 14:13.

Will Christ appear visibly on a cloud and then take away faithful Christians into the heavens while the world looks on?

Did Jesus say whether the world would see him again with their physical eyes?

John 14:19, *RS:* "Yet a little while, and *the world will see me no more,* but you [his faithful disciples] will see me; because I live, you will live also." (Italics added.) (Compare 1 Timothy 6:16.)

What is the meaning of the Lord's 'descending from heaven'?

Could the Lord "descend from heaven," as stated at 1 Thessalonians 4:16, without being visible to physical eyes? In the days of ancient Sodom and Gomorrah, Jehovah said that he was going to "go down to see" what the people were doing. (Gen. 18:21, *RS*) But when Jehovah made that inspection, no human saw him, although they did see the angelic representatives that he sent. (John 1:18) Similarly, without having to return in the flesh, Jesus could turn his attention to his faithful followers on earth to reward them.

In what sense, then, will humans "see" the Lord "coming in a cloud"?

Jesus foretold: "Then they will see the Son of man [Jesus Christ] coming in a cloud with power and great glory." (Luke 21:27, *RS*) In no way does this statement or similar ones in other texts contradict what Jesus said as recorded at John 14:19. Consider: At Mount Sinai, what occurred when God 'came to the people *in a thick cloud,*' as stated at Exodus 19:9? (*RS*) God was invisibly present; the people of Israel saw visible evidence of his presence, but none of them actually saw God with their eyes. So, too, when Jesus said that he would come "in a cloud," he must have meant that he would be *invisible* to human eyes but that humans would be aware of his presence. They would "see" him with their mental eyes, discerning the fact that he was present. (For further comments, see the main heading "Return of Christ.")

Is it possible for Christians to be taken to heaven with their physical bodies?

1 Cor. 15:50, *RS:* "I tell you this, brethren: flesh and blood cannot inherit the kingdom of God, nor does the perishable inherit the imperishable."

Does the experience of the prophet Elijah contradict this? Not at all. It must be understood in the light of Jesus' clear statement centuries later: "No one has ascended into heaven but he who descended from heaven, the Son of man." (John 3:13, *RS*) Although Elijah was seen as he "went up by a whirlwind into heaven," this does not mean that he went into the spirit realm. Why not? Because he is later reported as sending a letter of reproof to the king of Judah. (2 Ki. 2: 11, *RS;* 2 Chron. 21:1, 12-15) Before humans invented airplanes, Jehovah there used his own means (a fiery chariot and a whirlwind) to lift Elijah off the ground into the heaven where the birds fly and to transport him to another place. —Compare Genesis 1:6-8, 20.

Will faithful Christians perhaps be taken to heaven secretly, simply disappearing from the earth without dying?

Rom. 6:3-5, *RS:* "Do you not know that all of us who have been baptized into Christ Jesus were baptized into his death? . . . For if we have been united with him in a death like his, we shall certainly be united with him in a resurrection like his." (What occurred in the case of Jesus set the pattern. His disciples as well as others knew he had died. He was not restored to heavenly life until after his death and resurrection.)

1 Cor. 15:35, 36, 44, *RS:* "Some one will ask, 'How are the

dead raised? With what kind of body do they come?' You foolish man! What you sow does not come to life unless it dies. It is sown a physical body, it is raised a spiritual body." (So death comes before one receives that spiritual body, does it not?)

Will all faithful Christians be taken miraculously from the earth by the Lord before the great tribulation?

Matt. 24:21, 22: "Then there will be great tribulation such as has not occurred since the world's beginning until now, no, nor will occur again. In fact, unless those days were cut short, no flesh would be saved; but on account of the chosen ones those days will be cut short." (This does not say that "the chosen ones" will all have been taken to heaven before the great tribulation, does it? Rather, it holds out the prospect to them, along with associates in the flesh, of surviving that great tribulation on earth.)

Rev. 7:9, 10, 14, *RS:* "After this I looked, and behold, a great multitude which no man could number, from every nation, from all tribes and peoples and tongues, standing before the throne and before the Lamb, clothed in white robes, with palm branches in their hands, and crying out with a loud voice, 'Salvation belongs to our God who sits upon the throne, and to the Lamb!' . . . 'These are they who have come out of the great tribulation.'" (To "come out" of something a person must *go into* it or *be in* it. So this great multitude must be persons who actually experience the great tribulation and come out of it as survivors.) (Regarding their being on earth, see pages 167, 168.)

What protection will there be for true Christians during the great tribulation?

Rom. 10:13, *RS:* "Every one who calls upon the name of the Lord ["Jehovah," *NW*] will be saved."

Zeph. 2:3, *RS:* "Seek the LORD ["Jehovah," *NW, AS, Yg, By*], all you humble of the land, who do his commands; seek righteousness, seek humility; perhaps you may be hidden on the day of the wrath of the LORD." (Also Isaiah 26:20)

Will all true Christians perhaps be taken to heaven after the great tribulation?

Matt. 5:5, *RS:* "Blessed are the meek, for they shall inherit the earth."

Ps. 37:29, *RS:* "The righteous shall possess the land ["earth," *Ro, NW*], and dwell upon it for ever." (Also verses 10, 11, 34)

1 Cor. 15:50, *RS:* "Flesh and blood cannot inherit the kingdom of God."

See also the main heading "Heaven."

Why are some Christians taken to heaven to be with Christ?

Rev. 20:6, *RS:* "They shall be priests of God and of Christ, and they shall reign with him a thousand years." (Since they are to reign with Christ, there must be people over whom they reign. Who are these? See Matthew 5:5 and Psalm 37:29.)

See also the main heading "Born Again."

Will those who go to heaven be returned later to the earth to live forever here in Paradise?

Prov. 2:21, *RS:* "The upright will inhabit the land ["dwell on earth," *NE*], and men of integrity will remain in it." (Notice that the scripture does not say that such upright people will *return* to the earth but that they will *remain* there.)

1 Thess. 4:17, *RS:* "And so we [Christians caught away to heaven] shall *always* be with the Lord."

If Someone Says—

'Do you believe in the rapture?'

You might reply: 'I find that not everyone has the same idea as to what the rapture means. May I ask what your thoughts are about it? . . . On any matter, it is beneficial to compare our thoughts with what the Bible itself says. (Use the portions of the material above that are applicable.)'

Or you could say: 'The rapture has been explained to me as an escape plan for Christians. Many feel that this is the way they will escape the coming great tribulation. Is that how you feel?' **Then perhaps add:** (1) 'We certainly want God's protection at that time, and I find to be very encouraging some texts that show how we can benefit from it. (Zeph. 2:3)' (2) 'Interestingly, the Bible shows that God will safeguard some faithful ones right here on earth. (Prov. 2: 21, 22) That is in harmony with God's purpose when he first created Adam and put him in Paradise, is it not?'

Another possibility: 'By the rapture you mean that Christians living at the end of the system of things are to be taken to heaven, is that not right? . . . Have you wondered what they will do when they get to heaven? . . . Notice what Revelation 20:6 (and 5:9, 10) says. . . . But over whom will they rule? (Ps. 37:10, 11, 29)'

Reincarnation

Definition: The belief that one is reborn in one or more successive existences, which may be human or animal. Usually it is an intangible "soul" that is believed to be reborn in another body. *Not a Bible teaching.*

Does a strange feeling of being familiar with entirely new acquaintances and places prove reincarnation to be a fact?

Have you ever mistaken one man or woman who is alive for another who is *also now living?* Many have had that experience. Why? Because some people have similar mannerisms or may even look almost identical. So the feeling that you know a person even though you never met him before really does not prove that you were acquainted with him in a former life, does it?

Why might a house or a town seem familiar to you if you have never been there before? Is it because you lived there during a former life? Many houses are built according to similar designs. Furniture used in cities far apart may be produced from similar patterns. And is it not true that the scenery in some widely separated places looks very much alike? So, without resorting to reincarnation, your feeling of familiarity is quite understandable.

Do recollections of life at another time in another place, as drawn out under hypnosis, prove reincarnation?

Under hypnosis much information stored in the brain can be drawn out. Hypnotists tap the subconscious memory. But how did those memories get there? Perhaps you read a book, saw a motion picture, or learned about certain people on television. If you put yourself in the place of the people about whom you were learning, it might have made a vivid impression, almost as if the experience were your own. What you actually did may have been so long ago that you have forgotten it, but under hypnosis the experience may be recalled as if you were remembering "another life." Yet, if that were true, would not everyone have such memories? But not everyone does. It is noteworthy that an increasing number of state supreme courts in the United States do not accept hypnotically induced testimony. In 1980 the Minnesota Supreme Court declared that "the best expert testimony indicates that no expert can determine whether memory retrieved by hypnosis, or any part of that memory, is truth, falsehood, or confabulation—a filling of gaps with fantasy. Such results are not scientifically reliable as accurate." (*State v. Mack,* 292 N.W.2d 764) The influence of suggestions made by the hypnotist to the one hypnotized is a factor in this unreliability.

Does the Bible contain evidence of belief in reincarnation?

Does Matthew 17:12, 13 reflect a belief in reincarnation?

Matt. 17:12, 13: "[Jesus said:] 'Elijah has already come and they did not recognize him but did with him the things they wanted. In this way also the Son of man is destined to suffer at their hands.' Then the disciples perceived that he spoke to them about John the Baptist."

Did this mean that John the Baptist was a reincarnated Elijah? When Jewish priests asked John, "Are you Elijah?" he said, "I am not." (John 1:21) What, then, did Jesus mean? As Jehovah's angel foretold, John went before Jehovah's Messiah "with Elijah's spirit and power, to turn back the hearts of fathers to children and the disobedient ones to the practical wisdom of righteous ones, to get ready for Jehovah a prepared people." (Luke 1:17) So John the Baptist was fulfilling prophecy by *doing a work like that of the prophet Elijah.*—Mal. 4:5, 6.

Is reincarnation indicated by the account at John 9:1, 2?

John 9:1, 2: "Now as he [Jesus] was passing along he saw a man blind from birth. And his disciples asked him: 'Rabbi, who sinned, this man or his parents, so that he was born blind?'"

Is it possible that these disciples had been influenced by the belief of the Jewish Pharisees, who said that "the souls of good men only are removed into other bodies"? (*Wars of the Jews,* Josephus, Book II, chap. VIII, par. 14) It is not likely, since their question does not imply that they thought he was a 'good man.' It is more likely that as Jesus' disciples they believed the Scriptures and knew that the soul dies. Yet, since even a baby in the womb has life and was conceived in sin, they may have wondered whether such an unborn child could have sinned, resulting in his blindness. In any event, Jesus' answer did not support either reincarnation or the idea that a child yet in its mother's womb sins before birth. Jesus himself answered: "Neither this man sinned nor his parents." (John 9:3) Jesus knew that, because we are offspring of Adam, there is an inheritance of human defects and imperfections. Using the situation to magnify God, Jesus healed the blind man.

Does the Bible's teaching about the soul and death allow for reincarnation?

Genesis 2:7 states: "Jehovah God proceeded to form the man out of dust from the ground and to blow into his nostrils the breath of life, and the man came to be a living soul."

Notice that the man himself was the soul; the soul was not immaterial, separate and distinct from the body. "The soul that is sinning—it itself will die." (Ezek. 18:4, 20) And a deceased person is referred to as a "dead soul." (Num. 6:6) At death, "his spirit goes out, he goes back to his ground; in that day his thoughts do perish." (Ps. 146:4) So when someone dies, the complete person is dead; there is nothing that remains alive and that could pass into another body. (For further details, see the main headings "Soul" and "Death.")

Eccl. 3:19: "There is an eventuality as respects the sons of mankind and an eventuality as respects the beast, and they have the same eventuality. As the one dies, so the other dies." (As in the case of humans, nothing survives at the death of an animal. There is nothing that can experience rebirth in another body.)

Eccl. 9:10: "All that your hand finds to do, do with your very power, for there is no work nor devising nor knowledge nor wisdom in Sheol, the place to which you are going." (It is not into another body but into Sheol, the common grave of mankind, that the dead go.)

How much of a difference is there between reincarnation and the hope held out in the Bible?

Reincarnation: According to this belief, when a person dies, the soul, the "real self," passes on to a better existence if the individual has lived a good and proper life, but possibly to existence as an animal if his record has been more bad than good. Each rebirth, it is believed, brings the individual back into this same system of things, where he will face further suffering and eventual death. The cycles of rebirth are viewed as virtually endless. Is such a future really what awaits you? Some believe that the only way of escape is by extinguishing all desire for things pleasing to the senses. To what do they escape? To what some describe as unconscious life.

Bible: According to the Bible, the soul is the complete person. Even though a person may have done bad things in the past, if he repents and changes his ways, Jehovah God

will forgive him. (Ps. 103:12, 13) When a person dies, nothing survives. Death is like a deep, dreamless sleep. There will be a resurrection of the dead. This is not a reincarnation but a bringing back to life of the same personality. (Acts 24:15) For most people, the resurrection will be to life on earth. It will take place after God brings the present wicked system to its end. Sickness, suffering, even the necessity to die, will become things of the past. (Dan. 2:44; Rev. 21:3, 4) Does such a hope sound like something about which you would like to learn more, to examine the reasons for confidence in it?

If Someone Says—

'I believe in reincarnation'

You might reply: 'You hope that it will eventually result in a better life, is that right? . . . Tell me, would you like to live in a world like the one described here at Revelation 21: 1-5?'

Or you could say: 'I appreciate your telling me that. May I ask, Is this something that you have always believed? . . . What was it that made you leave behind your former beliefs?' (Then perhaps use the ideas under the heading on page 320.)

Another possibility: 'I have enjoyed conversations with others who share that belief. May I ask, Why do you feel that reincarnation is needed?' **Then perhaps add:** (1) 'Do you remember all the details of the earlier lives you believe you had? . . . But that would be necessary if a person were to correct his former errors and improve, would it not?' (2) If the person says that it is a kindness that we forget, you might ask: 'But do you view a bad memory as an advantage to a person in everyday life? Then, by forgetting every 70 years or so everything we have learned, would we be helped to improve our lot?' (3) If the person says that only the better people are born again as humans, you might ask: 'Why is it, then, that world conditions have continued to get worse? . . . The Bible shows how real improvement will be made in our day. (Dan. 2:44)'

Religion

Definition: A form of worship. It includes a system of religious attitudes, beliefs, and practices; these may be personal, or they may be advocated by an organization. Usually religion involves belief in God or in a number of gods; or it treats humans, objects, desires, or forces as objects of worship. Much religion is based on human study of nature; there is also revealed religion. There is true religion and false.

Why are there so many religions?

A recent tabulation concluded that there are 10 main religions and some 10,000 sects. Of these, some 6,000 exist in Africa, 1,200 in the United States, and hundreds in other lands.

Many factors have contributed to the development of new religious groups. Some have said that the various religions all represent different ways of presenting religious truth. But a comparison of their teachings and practices with the Bible indicates, rather, that the diversity of religions is because people have become followers of men instead of listening to God. It is noteworthy that, to a large extent, teachings they hold in common, but that differ from the Bible, originated in ancient Babylon. (See pages 50, 51, under the heading "Babylon the Great.")

Who is the instigator of such religious confusion? The Bible identifies Satan the Devil as "the god of this system of things." (2 Cor. 4:4) It warns us that "the things which the nations sacrifice they sacrifice to demons, and not to God." (1 Cor. 10:20) How vitally important, then, to make sure that we really are worshiping the true God, the Creator of heaven and earth, and that our worship is pleasing to him!

Are all religions acceptable to God?

Judg. 10:6, 7: "The sons of Israel again proceeded to do what was bad in the eyes of Jehovah, and they began to serve the Baals and the Ashtoreth images and the gods of Syria and the gods of Sidon and the gods of Moab and the gods of the sons of Ammon and the gods of the Philistines. So they left Jehovah and did not serve him. At this Jehovah's anger blazed against Israel." (If a person worships any thing or any person other than the true God, the Creator of heaven and earth, it is evident that his form of worship is not acceptable to Jehovah.)

Mark 7:6, 7: "He [Jesus] said to them [the Jewish Pharisees and scribes]: 'Isaiah aptly prophesied about you hypocrites, as it is written, "This people honor me with their lips, but their hearts are far removed from me. It is in vain that they keep worshiping me, because they teach as doctrines commands of men."'" (Regardless of whom a group *profess* to worship, if they hold to doctrines of men instead of the inspired Word of God, their worship is in vain.)

Rom. 10:2, 3: "I bear them witness that they have a zeal for God; but not according to accurate knowledge; for, because of not knowing the righteousness of God but seeking to establish their own, they did not subject themselves to the righteousness of God." (People may have God's written Word but lack accurate knowledge of what it contains, because they have not been taught properly. They may feel that they are zealous for God, but they may not be doing what he requires. Their worship is not going to please God, is it?)

Is it true that there is good in all religions?

Most religions do teach that a person should not lie or steal, and so forth. But is that sufficient? Would you be happy to drink a glass of poisoned water because someone assured you that *most* of what you were getting was water?

2 Cor. 11:14, 15: "Satan himself keeps transforming himself into an angel of light. It is therefore nothing great if his ministers also keep transforming themselves into ministers of righteousness." (Here we are cautioned that not everything that originates with Satan may appear hideous. One of his chief methods of deceiving mankind has been false religion of all kinds, to some of which he gives a righteous appearance.)

2 Tim. 3:2, 5: "Men will be . . . having a form of godly devotion but proving false to its power; and from these turn away." (Regardless of their outward professions of love for

God, if those with whom you worship do not sincerely apply his Word in their own lives, the Bible urges you to break off such association.)

Is it proper to leave the religion of one's parents?

If what our parents taught us is really from the Bible, we should hold on to it. Even if we learn that their religious practices and beliefs are out of harmony with God's Word, our parents deserve our respect. But what if you learned that a certain habit of your parents was harmful to health and could shorten a person's life? Would you imitate them and encourage your children to do so, or would you respectfully share with them what you learned? Similarly, knowledge of Bible truth brings responsibility. If possible, we should share with family members what we learn. We must make a decision: Do we really love God? Do we really want to obey God's Son? Our doing so may require that we leave the religion of our parents to take up true worship. It certainly would not be fitting to allow our devotion to our parents to be greater than our love for God and Christ, would it? Jesus said: "He that has greater affection for father or mother than for me is not worthy of me; and he that has greater affection for son or daughter than for me is not worthy of me."—Matt. 10:37.

Josh. 24:14: "Now fear Jehovah and serve him in fault-lessness and in truth, and remove the gods that your fore-fathers served on the other side of the River and in Egypt, and serve Jehovah." (That meant a change from the religion of their forefathers, did it not? To serve Jehovah acceptably, they had to get rid of any images used in such religion and cleanse their hearts of any desire for those things.)

1 Pet. 1:18, 19: "You know that it was not with corruptible things, with silver or gold, that you were delivered from your fruitless form of conduct received by tradition from your forefathers. But it was with precious blood, like that of an unblemished and spotless lamb, even Christ's." (So, early Christians turned away from those traditions of their fore-fathers, which traditions could never give them eternal life.

Gratitude for the sacrifice of Christ made them eager to get rid of anything that caused their lives to be fruitless, lacking real meaning because they did not honor God. Should not we have the same attitude?)

What is the Bible's viewpoint as to interfaith?

How did Jesus view religious leaders who pretended to be righteous but disrespected God? "Jesus said to them: 'If God were your Father, you would love me, for from God I came forth and am here. Neither have I come of my own initiative at all, but that One sent me forth. . . . You are from your father the Devil, and you wish to do the desires of your father. That one was a manslayer when he began, and he did not stand fast in the truth, because truth is not in him. When he speaks the lie, he speaks according to his own disposition, because he is a liar and the father of the lie. Because I, on the other hand, tell the truth, you do not believe me. . . . This is why you do not listen, because you are not from God.'"
—John 8:42-47.

Would it demonstrate loyalty to God and to his righteous standards if his servants were to embrace in religious brotherhood those who themselves practice what God condemns or who condone such practices? "Quit mixing in company with anyone called a brother that is a fornicator or a greedy person or an idolater or a reviler or a drunkard or an extortioner, not even eating with such a man. . . . Neither fornicators, nor idolaters, nor adulterers, nor men kept for unnatural purposes, nor men who lie with men, nor thieves, nor greedy persons, nor drunkards, nor revilers, nor extortioners will inherit God's kingdom." (1 Cor. 5:11; 6:9, 10) "Whoever . . . wants to be a friend of the world is constituting himself an enemy of God." (Jas. 4:4) "O you lovers of Jehovah, hate what is bad. He is guarding the souls of his loyal ones."—Ps. 97:10.

2 Cor. 6:14-17: "Do not become unevenly yoked with unbelievers. For what fellowship do righteousness and lawlessness have? Or what sharing does light have with darkness? Further, what harmony is there between Christ and Belial? Or what portion does a faithful person have with an

unbeliever? And what agreement does God's temple have with idols? . . . '"Therefore get out from among them, and separate yourselves," says Jehovah, "and quit touching the unclean thing"'; '"and I will take you in."'"

Rev. 18:4, 5: "I heard another voice out of heaven say: 'Get out of her, my people, if you do not want to share with her in her sins, and if you do not want to receive part of her plagues. For her sins have massed together clear up to heaven, and God has called her acts of injustice to mind.'" (For details, see the main heading "Babylon the Great.")

Is belonging to an organized religion necessary?

Most religious organizations have produced bad fruitage. It is not the fact that groups are organized that is bad. But many have promoted forms of worship that are based on false teachings and are largely ritualistic instead of providing genuine spiritual guidance; they have been misused to control the lives of people for selfish objectives; they have been overly concerned with money collections and ornate houses of worship instead of spiritual values; their members are often hypocritical. Obviously no one who loves righteousness would want to belong to such an organization. But true religion is a refreshing contrast to all of that. Nevertheless, to fulfill the Bible's requirements, it must be organized.

Heb. 10:24, 25: "Let us consider one another to incite to love and fine works, not forsaking the gathering of ourselves together, as some have the custom, but encouraging one another, and all the more so as you behold the day drawing near." (To carry out this Scriptural command, there must be Christian meetings that we can attend on a consistent basis. Such an arrangement encourages us to express love toward others, not only concern about self.)

1 Cor. 1:10: "Now I exhort you, brothers, through the name of our Lord Jesus Christ that you should all speak in agreement, and that there should not be divisions among you, but that you may be fitly united in the same mind and in the same line of thought." (Such unity would never be achieved if the individuals did not meet together, benefit

from the same spiritual feeding program, and respect the agency through which such instruction was provided. See also John 17:20, 21.)

1 Pet. 2:17: "Have love for the whole association of brothers." (Does that include only those who may meet together for worship in a particular private home? Not at all; it is an international brotherhood, as shown by Galatians 2:8, 9 and 1 Corinthians 16:19.)

Matt. 24:14: "This good news of the kingdom will be preached in all the inhabited earth for a witness to all the nations; and then the end will come." (For all nations to be given the opportunity to hear that good news, the preaching must be carried out in an orderly way, with suitable oversight. Love for God and for one's fellowman has caused people around the earth to unite their efforts to do this work.)

See also the main heading "Organization."

Is loving one's fellowman what really counts?

There is no doubt about it, such love is important. (Rom. 13:8-10) But being a Christian involves more than simply being kind to our neighbor. Jesus said that his true disciples would be outstandingly identified by their love for one another, for fellow believers. (John 13:35) The importance of that is emphasized repeatedly in the Bible. (Gal. 6:10; 1 Pet. 4:8; 1 John 3:14, 16, 17) However, Jesus showed that even more important is our love for God himself, which is shown by our obedience to his commandments. (Matt. 22:35-38; 1 John 5:3) To demonstrate such love, we need to study and apply God's Word and assemble with fellow servants of God for worship.

Is having a personal relationship with God the really important thing?

It certainly is important. Merely attending religious services in a formalistic way cannot take the place of it. But we need to be careful. Why? In the first century, there were people who thought they had a good relationship with God but whom Jesus showed to be badly mistaken. (John 8:41-44) The apostle Paul wrote about some who evidently were

zealous about their faith and obviously thought they had a
good relationship with God but who did not understand what
was really required in order to have God's approval.—Rom.
10:2-4.

Could we have a good personal relationship with God if we
treated as of little importance his commandments? One of
these is that we regularly assemble with fellow believers.
—Heb. 10:24, 25.

If we personally read the Bible, is that sufficient?

It is true that many people can learn a great deal by
reading the Bible personally. If their motive is to learn the
truth about God and his purposes, what they are doing is
highly commendable. (Acts 17:11) But, being honest with
ourselves, are we truly going to grasp the full significance
of it all without help? The Bible tells about a man who held
a prominent position but who was humble enough to acknowledge his need for help in understanding Bible prophecy. That help was provided by a member of the Christian
congregation.—Acts 8:26-38; compare other references to
Philip in Acts 6:1-6; 8:5-17.

Of course, if a person reads the Bible but does not apply
it in his life, it does him little good. If he believes it and acts
on it, he *will* associate with God's servants in regular congregation meetings. (Heb. 10:24, 25) He will also join with
them in sharing the "good news" with other people.—1 Cor.
9:16; Mark 13:10; Matt. 28:19, 20.

How can a person know which religion is right?

(1) On what are its teachings based? Are they from
God, or are they largely from men? (2 Tim. 3:16; Mark 7:7)
Ask, for example: Where does the Bible teach that God is a
Trinity? Where does it say that the human soul is immortal?

**(2) Consider whether it is making known the name
of God.** Jesus said in prayer to God: "I have made your name
manifest to the men you gave me out of the world." (John
17:6) He declared: "It is Jehovah your God you must worship, and it is to him alone you must render sacred service."

(Matt. 4:10) Has your religion taught you that 'it is Jehovah you must worship'? Have you come to know the Person identified by that name—his purposes, his activities, his qualities—so that you feel you can confidently draw close to him?

(3) Is true faith in Jesus Christ being demonstrated? This involves appreciation of the value of the sacrifice of Jesus' human life and of his position today as heavenly King. (John 3:36; Ps. 2:6-8) Such appreciation is shown by obeying Jesus—sharing personally and zealously in the work that he assigned to his followers. True religion has such faith that is accompanied by works.—Jas. 2:26.

(4) Is it largely ritualistic, a formality, or is it a way of life? God strongly disapproves of religion that is merely a formalism. (Isa. 1:15-17) True religion upholds the Bible's standard of morality and clean speech instead of weakly going along with popular trends. (1 Cor. 5:9-13; Eph. 5:3-5) Its members reflect the fruits of God's spirit in their lives. (Gal. 5:22, 23) So, those who adhere to true worship can be identified because they sincerely endeavor to apply Bible standards in their lives not only at their places of meeting but in their family life, at their secular work, in school, and in recreation.

(5) Do its members truly love one another? Jesus said: "By this all will know that you are my disciples, if you have love among yourselves." (John 13:35) Such love reaches across racial, social, and national boundaries, drawing people together in genuine brotherhood. So strong is this love that it sets them apart as being truly different. When the nations go to war, who have enough love for their Christian brothers in other lands that they refuse to take up arms and kill them? That is what early Christians did.

(6) Is it truly separate from the world? Jesus said that his true followers would be "no part of the world." (John 15:19) To worship God in a manner that he approves requires that we keep ourselves "without spot from the world." (Jas. 1:27) Can that be said of those whose clergy and other members are involved in politics, or whose lives are largely built around materialistic and fleshly desires?—1 John 2: 15-17.

(7) Are its members active witnesses concerning God's Kingdom? Jesus foretold: "This good news of the kingdom will be preached in all the inhabited earth for a witness to all the nations; and then the end will come." (Matt. 24:14) What religion is really proclaiming God's Kingdom as the hope of mankind instead of encouraging people to look to human rulership to solve their problems? Has your religion equipped you to share in this activity, and to do it from house to house as Jesus taught his apostles to do?—Matt. 10:7, 11-13; Acts 5:42; 20:20.

Do Jehovah's Witnesses believe that theirs is the only right religion?

See pages 203, 204, under "Jehovah's Witnesses."

Why do some people have faith while others do not?

See the main heading "Faith."

If Someone Says—

'I'm not interested in religion'

You might reply: 'That doesn't surprise me. Many people share your view. May I ask, Have you always felt that way?' **Then perhaps add:** 'One of the things that impressed me was finding out that almost every major doctrine taught in the churches today is *not* found in the Bible. (Perhaps use what is found on pages 203, 204, under "Jehovah's Witnesses," with special emphasis on the Kingdom. By way of contrast, point out what Jehovah's Witnesses believe, as outlined on pages 199, 200.)'

See also pages 16, 17.

'There is too much hypocrisy in religion'

You might reply: 'Yes, I agree with you. Many preach one thing and live another way. But tell me, How do you feel about the Bible? (Ps. 19:7-10)'

'I live a good life. I treat my neighbors right. That's enough religion for me'

You might reply: 'Since you say that you live a good life, you evidently enjoy life, is that right? . . . How would you like to live under the kind of conditions described here in Revelation 21:4? . . . Notice what John 17:3 says is necessary in order to have a part in it.'

See also page 327.

'I'm not interested in organized religion. I believe that a personal relationship with God is what counts'

You might reply: 'That interests me. Have you always felt that way? . . . Did you ever associate with a religious group in the past? . . . (Then perhaps use material on pages 326-328.)'

'I don't agree with everything my church teaches, but I don't see the need to change to another. I'd rather work for improvement within my own'

You might reply: 'I appreciate your telling me that. I am sure you will agree that what is really important to all of us is having God's approval, is it not?' **Then perhaps add:** (1) 'God gives us all something serious to think about here at Revelation 18:4, 5. . . . Even if we personally do not practice the wrong things, the Bible shows that we share the blame if we support these organizations. (See also the main heading "Babylon the Great.")' (2) (Perhaps also use material on pages 328-330.) (3) 'God is looking for people who love truth, and he is bringing them together for united worship. (John 4:23, 24)'

'All religions are good; you have yours, and I have mine'

You might reply: 'You evidently are a broad-minded person. But you also recognize that we all need the guidance

that God's Word provides, and that is why you have a
religion, is that not right?' **Then perhaps add:** 'Here at
Matthew 7:13, 14 the Bible provides us some very valuable
guidance in the words of Jesus. (Read it.) . . . Why might that
be so?'

See also pages 322, 323.

'As long as you believe in Jesus, it really does not matter what church you belong to'

You might reply: 'There is no question about it, belief in
Jesus is vital. And I assume that by that you mean accepting
everything that he taught. No doubt you have observed, as
I have, that many who say they are Christians really do not
live up to what that name represents.' **Then perhaps add:**
(1) 'Notice what Jesus said here at Matthew 7:21-23.'
(2) 'There is a wonderful future for those who care enough
to find out what God's will is and then do it. (Ps. 37:10, 11;
Rev. 21:4)'

'What makes you think there is only one religion that is right?'

You might reply: 'Without doubt, there are sincere people in almost every religion. But what really counts is what
God's Word says. How many true faiths does it refer to?
Notice what is written here at Ephesians 4:4, 5.' **Then
perhaps add:** (1) 'That agrees with what other texts state.
(Matt. 7:13, 14, 21; John 10:16; 17:20, 21)' (2) 'So, the
challenge that we must face is identifying that religion. How
can we do it? (Perhaps use material on pages 328-330.)'
(3) (See also what is on pages 199, 200, under the heading
"Jehovah's Witnesses.")

'I just read my Bible at home and pray to God for understanding'

You might reply: 'Have you succeeded in reading the
entire Bible as yet?' **Then perhaps add:** 'As you work on
that, you will find something very interesting at Matthew
28:19, 20. . . . This is significant because it shows that Christ

uses other humans to help us to understand what is involved in being a real Christian. In harmony with that, Jehovah's Witnesses offer to visit people in their home for an hour or so each week, free of charge, to discuss the Bible. May I take just a few minutes to show you how we go about it?'

See also page 328.

'I feel that religion is a private affair'

You might reply: 'That is a common view nowadays, and if folks are really not interested in the Bible's message, we gladly go on to other homes. But did you realize that the reason I came to see you was that this is what Jesus instructed his followers to do? ... (Matt. 24:14; 28:19, 20; 10:40)'

Resurrection

Definition: *A·na'sta·sis,* the Greek word translated "resurrection," literally means "a standing up again" and it refers to a rising up from death. The fuller expression "resurrection of (from) the dead" is used repeatedly in the Scriptures. (Matt. 22:31; Acts 4:2; 1 Cor. 15:12) The Hebrew is *techi·yath' ham·me·thim',* which means "revival of the dead." (Matt. 22:23, ftn, *NW* Reference edition) Resurrection involves a reactivating of the life pattern of the individual, which life pattern God has retained in his memory. According to God's will for the individual, the person is restored in either a human or a spirit body and yet retains his personal identity, having the same personality and memories as when he died. The provision for resurrection of the dead is a magnificent expression of Jehovah's undeserved kindness; it displays his wisdom and power and is a means by which his original purpose regarding the earth will be carried out.

Is the resurrection a reuniting of an immaterial soul with the physical body?

For this to be possible, of course, humans would have to have an immaterial soul that could separate from the physical body. The Bible does not teach such a thing. That notion was borrowed from Greek philosophy. The Bible teaching regarding the soul is set out on pages 375-378. For evidence as to the origin of Christendom's belief in an immaterial, immortal soul, see pages 379, 380.

Was Jesus raised in a body of flesh, and does he have such a body in heaven now?

1 Pet. 3:18: "Christ died once for all time concerning sins, a righteous person for unrighteous ones, that he might lead you to God, he being put to death in the flesh, but being made alive in the spirit ["by the Spirit," *KJ;* "in the spirit," *RS, NE, Dy, JB*]." (At his resurrection from the dead, Jesus was brought forth with a spirit body. In the Greek text the words "flesh" and "spirit" are put in contrast to each other, and both are in the dative case; so, if a translator uses the rendering *"by* the spirit" he should also consistently say *"by* the flesh," or if he uses *"in* the flesh" he should also say *"in* the spirit.")

Acts 10:40, 41: "God raised this One [Jesus Christ] up on the third day and granted him to become manifest, not to all the people, but to witnesses appointed beforehand by God." (Why did not others see him too? Because he was a spirit creature and when, as angels had done in the past, he materialized fleshly bodies to make himself visible, he did so only in the presence of his disciples.)

1 Cor. 15:45: "It is even so written: 'The first man Adam became a living soul.' The last Adam [Jesus Christ, who was perfect as was Adam when created] became a life-giving spirit."

What does Luke 24:36-39 mean regarding the body in which Jesus was resurrected?

Luke 24:36-39: "While they [the disciples] were speaking of these things he himself stood in their midst and said to them: 'May you have peace.' But because they were terrified, and had become frightened, they were imagining they beheld a spirit. So he said to them: 'Why are you troubled, and why is it doubts come up in your hearts? See my hands and my feet, that it is I myself; feel me and see, because a spirit does not have flesh and bones just as you behold that I have.'"

Humans cannot see spirits, so the disciples evidently

thought they were seeing an apparition or a vision. (Compare Mark 6:49, 50.) Jesus assured them that he was no apparition; they could see his body of flesh and could touch him, feeling the bones; he also ate in their presence. Similarly, in the past, angels had materialized in order to be seen by men; they had eaten, and some had even married and fathered children. (Gen. 6:4; 19:1-3) Following his resurrection, Jesus did not always appear in the same body of flesh (perhaps to reinforce in their minds the fact that he was then a spirit), and so he was not immediately recognized even by his close associates. (John 20:14, 15; 21:4-7) However, by his repeatedly appearing to them in materialized bodies and then saying and doing things that they would identify with the Jesus they knew, he strengthened their faith in the fact that he truly had been resurrected from the dead.

If the disciples had actually seen Jesus in the body that he now has in heaven, Paul would not later have referred to the glorified Christ as being "the exact representation of [God's] very being," because God is a Spirit and has never been in the flesh.—Heb. 1:3; compare 1 Timothy 6:16.

When reading the reports of Jesus' postresurrection appearances, we are helped to understand them properly if we keep in mind 1 Peter 3:18 and 1 Corinthians 15:45, quoted on page 334.

See also pages 217, 218, under "Jesus Christ."

Who will be resurrected to share heavenly life with Christ, and what will they do there?

Luke 12:32: "Have no fear, *little flock,* because your Father has approved of giving you the kingdom." (These do not include all who have exercised faith; the number is limited. Their being in heaven is for a purpose.)

Rev. 20:4, 6: "I saw thrones, and there were those who sat down on them, and power of judging was given them. . . . Happy and holy is anyone having part in the first resurrection; over these the second death has no authority, but they will be priests of God and of the Christ, and will rule as kings with him for the thousand years."

See also pages 162-168, under the heading "Heaven."

Will those raised to heavenly life eventually have glorified physical bodies there?

Phil. 3:20, 21: "The Lord Jesus Christ . . . will refashion our humiliated body to be conformed to his glorious body according to the operation of the power that he has." (Does this mean that it is their body of flesh that will eventually be made glorious in the heavens? Or does it mean that, instead of having a lowly body of flesh, they will be clothed with a glorious spirit body when raised to heavenly life? Let the following scripture answer.)

1 Cor. 15:40, 42-44, 47-50: "There are heavenly bodies, and earthly bodies; but the glory of the heavenly bodies is one sort, and that of the earthly bodies is a different sort. So also is the resurrection of the dead. . . . It is sown a physical body, it is raised up a spiritual body. . . . The first man [Adam] is out of the earth and made of dust; the second man [Jesus Christ] is out of heaven. As the one made of dust is, so those made of dust are also; and as the heavenly one is, so those who are heavenly are also. And just as we have borne the image of the one made of dust, we shall bear also the image of the heavenly one. However, this I say, brothers, that flesh and blood cannot inherit God's kingdom." (There is no allowance here for any mixing of the two sorts of bodies or the taking of a fleshly body to heaven.)

How did Jesus demonstrate what resurrection will mean for mankind in general?

John 11:11, 14-44: "[Jesus said to his disciples:] 'Lazarus our friend has gone to rest, but I am journeying there to awaken him from sleep.' . . . Jesus said to them outspokenly: 'Lazarus has died.' . . . When Jesus arrived, he found he [Lazarus] had already been four days in the memorial tomb. . . . Jesus said to her [Martha, a sister of Lazarus]: 'I am the resurrection and the life.' . . . He cried out with a loud voice: 'Lazarus, come on out!' The man that had been dead came out with his feet and hands bound with wrappings, and his countenance was bound about with a cloth. Jesus said to them: 'Loose him and let him go.'" (If Jesus had thus called

Lazarus back from a state of bliss in another life, that would have been no kindness. But Jesus' raising Lazarus up from a lifeless state was a kindness both to him and to his sisters. Once again Lazarus became a living human.)

Mark 5:35-42: "Some men from the home of the presiding officer of the synagogue came and said: 'Your daughter died! Why bother the teacher any longer?' But Jesus, overhearing the word being spoken, said to the presiding officer of the synagogue: 'Have no fear, only exercise faith.' . . . He took along the young child's father and mother and those with him, and he went in where the young child was. And, taking the hand of the young child, he said to her: *'Tal′i·tha cu′mi,'* which, translated, means: 'Maiden, I say to you, Get up!' And immediately the maiden rose and began walking, for she was twelve years old. And at once they were beside themselves with great ecstasy." (When the general resurrection takes place on earth during Christ's Millennial Reign, doubtless many millions of parents and their offspring will be overjoyed when they are reunited.)

What prospects will await those raised to life on earth?

Luke 23:43: "Truly I tell you today, You will be with me in Paradise." (All the earth will be transformed into a paradise under the rule of Christ as King.)

Rev. 20:12, 13: "I saw the dead, the great and the small, standing before the throne, and scrolls were opened. But another scroll was opened; it is the scroll of life. And the dead were judged out of those things written in the scrolls according to their deeds. . . . They were judged individually according to their deeds." (The opening of scrolls evidently points to a time of education in the divine will, in harmony with Isaiah 26:9. The fact that "the scroll of life" is opened indicates that there is opportunity for those who heed that education to have their names written in that scroll. Ahead of them will be the prospect of eternal life in human perfection.)

See also pages 227-232, under "Kingdom."

Will some be raised simply to have judgment pronounced and then be consigned to second death?

What is the meaning of John 5:28, 29? It says: "All those in the memorial tombs will hear his voice and come out, those who did good things to a resurrection of life, those who practiced vile things to a resurrection of judgment." What Jesus said here must be understood in the light of the later revelation that he gave to John. (See Revelation 20:12, 13, quoted on page 337.) Both those who formerly did good things and those who formerly practiced bad things will be "judged individually according to their deeds." What deeds? If we were to take the view that people were going to be condemned on the basis of deeds in their past life, that would be inconsistent with Romans 6:7: "He who has died has been acquitted from his sin." It would also be unreasonable to resurrect people simply for them to be destroyed. So, at John 5:28, 29a, Jesus was pointing ahead to the resurrection; then, in the remainder of verse 29, he was expressing the outcome after they had been uplifted to human perfection and been put on judgment.

What does Revelation 20:4-6 indicate as to those who will be resurrected on earth?

Rev. 20:4-6: "I saw thrones, and there were those who sat down on them, and power of judging was given them. Yes, I saw the souls of those executed with the ax for the witness they bore to Jesus and for speaking about God . . . And they came to life and ruled as kings with the Christ for a thousand years. (The rest of the dead did not come to life until the thousand years were ended.) This is the first resurrection. Happy and holy is anyone having part in the first resurrection; over these the second death has no authority, but they will be priests of God and of the Christ, and will rule as kings with him for the thousand years."

The parentheses are used in *NW* and *Mo* to help the reader to connect what follows the parenthetical statement with what precedes it. As clearly stated, it is not "the rest of the dead" who share in the first resurrection. That resurrection is for those who rule with Christ for the thousand years. Does this mean that no others of mankind will live during the thousand years except the ones who rule in heaven with Christ? No; because, if such were the case, it would mean that there was no one on behalf of whom they were serving as priests, and their domain would be a desolate globe.

Who, then, are "the rest of the dead"? They are all those of mankind who died as a result of Adamic sin and those who, though survivors of the great tribulation or those who may be born during the Millennium, need to be relieved of the death-dealing effects of such sin.—Compare Ephesians 2:1.

In what sense do they not "come to life" until the end of the thousand years? This does not mean their resurrection. This 'coming to life' involves much more than merely existing as humans. It means attaining to human perfection, free from all effects of Adamic sin. Notice that the reference to this in verse 5 occurs immediately after the preceding verse says that those who will be in heaven "came to life." In their case it means life free from all effects of sin; they are even specially favored with immortality. (1 Cor. 15:54) For "the rest of the dead," then, it must mean the fullness of life in human perfection.

Who will be included in the earthly resurrection?

John 5:28, 29: "Do not marvel at this, because the hour is coming in which all those in the memorial tombs will hear his voice [the voice of Jesus] and come out." (The Greek word translated "memorial tombs" is not the plural form of *ta'phos* [grave, an individual burial place] or *hai'des* [gravedom, the common grave of dead mankind] but is the plural dative form of *mne·mei'on* [remembrance, memorial tomb]. It lays stress on preserving memory of the deceased person. Not those whose memory was blotted out in Gehenna because of unforgivable sins but persons remembered by God will be resurrected with the opportunity to live forever. —Matt. 10:28; Mark 3:29; Heb. 10:26; Mal. 3:16.)

Acts 24:15: "I have hope toward God . . . that there is going to be a resurrection of both the righteous and the unrighteous." (Both those who lived in harmony with God's righteous ways and people who, out of ignorance, did unrighteous things will be resurrected. The Bible does not answer all our questions as to whether certain specific individuals who have died will be resurrected. But we can be confident that God, who knows all the facts, will act impartially, with justice tempered by mercy that does not ignore his righteous standards. Compare Genesis 18:25.)

Rev. 20:13, 14: "The sea gave up those dead in it, and death and Hades gave up those dead in them, and they were judged individually according to their deeds. And death and Hades were hurled into the lake of fire. This means the second death, the lake of fire." (So, those whose death was attributable to Adamic sin will be raised, whether they were buried at sea or in Hades, the common earthly grave of dead mankind.)

See also the main heading "Salvation."

If billions are to be raised from the dead, where will they all live?

A very liberal estimate of the number of people who have ever lived on earth is 20,000,000,000. As we have seen, not all of these will be resurrected. But, even if we assume that they would be, there would be ample room. The land surface of the earth at present is about 57,000,000 square miles (147,600,000 sq km). If half of that were set aside for other purposes, there would still be just a little less than an acre (c. 0.37 ha) per person, which can provide more than enough food. At the root of present food shortages is not any inability of the earth to produce sufficient but, rather, political rivalry and commercial greed.

See also page 116, under the heading "Earth."

Return of Christ

Definition: Before leaving the earth, Jesus Christ promised to return. Thrilling events in connection with God's Kingdom are associated with that promise. It should be noted that there is a difference between *coming* and *presence*. Thus, while a person's coming (associated with his arrival or return) occurs at a given time, his presence may thereafter extend over a period of years. In the Bible the Greek word *er·kho·mai* (meaning "to come") is also used with reference to Jesus' directing his attention to an important task at a specific time *during* his presence, namely, to his work as Jehovah's executioner at the war of the great day of God the Almighty.

Do the events associated with Christ's presence take place in a very brief time or over a period of years?

Matt. 24:37-39: "Just as the days of Noah were, so the presence ["coming," *RS, TEV;* "presence," *Yg, Ro, ED;* Greek, *pa·rou·si'a*] of the Son of man will be. For as they were in those days before the flood, eating and drinking, men marrying and women being given in marriage, until the day that Noah entered into the ark; and they took no note until the flood came and swept them all away, so the presence of the Son of man will be." (The events of "the days of Noah" that are described here took place over a period of many years. Jesus compared his presence with what occurred back then.)

At Matthew 24:37 the Greek word *pa·rou·si'a* is used. Literally it means a "being alongside." Liddell and Scott's *Greek-English Lexicon* (Oxford, 1968) gives *"presence, of persons,"* as its first definition of *pa·rou·si'a*. The sense of the word is clearly indicated at Philippians 2:12, where Paul contrasts his presence (*pa·rou·si'a*) with his absence (*a·pou·si'a*). On the other hand, in Matthew 24:30, which tells of the "Son of man *coming* on the clouds of heaven with power and great glory" as Jehovah's executioner at the war of Armageddon, the Greek word *er·kho'me·non* is used. Some translators use 'coming' for both Greek words, but those that are more careful convey the difference between the two.

Will Christ return in a manner visible to human eyes?

John 14:19: "A little longer and the world will behold me no more, but you [Jesus' faithful apostles] will behold me, because I live and you will live." (Jesus had promised his apostles that he would come again and take them to heaven to be with him. They could see him because they would be spirit creatures as he is. But the world would not see him again. Compare 1 Timothy 6:16.)

Acts 13:34: "He [God] resurrected him [Jesus] from the dead destined no more to return to corruption." (Human bodies are by nature corruptible. That is why 1 Corinthians 15:42, 44 uses the word "corruption" in parallel construction with "physical body." Jesus will never again have such a body.)

John 6:51: "I am the living bread that came down from heaven; if anyone eats of this bread he will live forever; and, for a fact, the bread that I shall give is my flesh in behalf of the life of the world." (Having given it, Jesus does not take it back again. He does not thereby deprive mankind of the benefits of the sacrifice of his perfect human life.)

See also pages 313, 314, under "Rapture."

What is the meaning of Jesus' coming "in the same manner" as he ascended to heaven?

Acts 1:9-11: "While they [Jesus' apostles] were looking on, he was lifted up and a cloud caught him up from their vision. And as they were gazing into the sky while he was on his way, also, look! two men in white garments stood alongside them, and they said: 'Men of Galilee, why do you stand looking into the sky? This Jesus who was received up from you into the sky will come thus in the same manner as you have beheld him going into the sky.'" (Notice that this says "the same manner," not the same body. What was the "manner" of his ascent? As verse 9 shows, he disappeared from view, his departure being observed only by his disciples. The world in general was not aware of what happened. The same would be true of Christ's return.)

What is meant by his 'coming on the clouds' and 'every eye seeing him'?

Rev. 1:7: "Look! He is coming with the clouds, and every eye will see him, and those who pierced him; and all the tribes of the earth will beat themselves in grief because of him." (Also Matthew 24:30; Mark 13:26; Luke 21:27)

What is indicated by "clouds"? Invisibility. When an airplane is in a thick cloud or above the clouds, people on the ground usually cannot see it, although they may hear the roar of the engines. Jehovah told Moses: "I am coming to you in a dark cloud." Moses did not see God, but that cloud indicated Jehovah's invisible presence. (Ex. 19:9; see also Leviticus 16:2; Numbers 11:25.) If Christ were to appear visibly in the heavens, it is obvious that not "every eye" would see him. If he appeared over Australia, for example, he would not be visible in Europe, Africa, and the Americas, would he?

In what sense will 'every eye see him'? They will discern from events on earth that he is invisibly present. Also referring to sight that is not physical, John 9:41 reports: "Jesus said to [the Pharisees]: 'If you were blind, you would have no sin. But now you say, "We see." Your sin remains.'" (Compare Romans 1:20.) Following Christ's return, some persons show faith; they recognize the sign of his presence. Others reject the evidence, but when Christ goes into action as God's executioner of the wicked, even they will discern from the manifestation of his power that the destruction is not from men but from heaven. They will know what is happening because they were warned in advance. Because of what is overtaking them, they will "beat themselves in grief."

Who are "those who pierced him"? Literally, Roman soldiers did this at the time of Jesus' execution. But they have long been dead. So this must refer to people who similarly mistreat, or 'pierce,' Christ's true followers during "the last days."—Matt. 25:40, 45.

Can it really be said that a person has 'come' or that he is 'present' if he is not visible?

The apostle Paul spoke of his being "absent in body but *present* in spirit" with the congregation in Corinth.—1 Cor. 5:3.

Jehovah spoke of his 'going down' to confuse the language of the builders of the tower of Babel. (Gen. 11:7) He also said that he would "go down" to deliver Israel from bondage to Egypt. And God assured Moses, "My own person will go along" to lead Israel to the Promised Land. (Ex. 3:8; 33:14) But no human ever saw God.—Ex. 33:20; John 1:18.

What are some of the events with which the Bible associates the presence of Christ?

Dan. 7:13, 14: "With the clouds of the heavens someone like a son of man [Jesus Christ] happened to be coming; and to the Ancient of Days [Jehovah God] he gained access, and they brought him up close even before that One. And to him there were given rulership and dignity and kingdom, that the peoples, national groups and languages should all serve even him."

1 Thess. 4:15, 16: "This is what we tell you by Jehovah's word, that we the living who survive to the presence of the Lord shall in no way precede those who have fallen asleep in death; because the Lord himself will descend from heaven with a commanding call, with an archangel's voice and with God's trumpet, and those who are dead in union with Christ will rise first." (So, those who will rule with Christ would be resurrected to be with him in heaven—first those who had died in years past and then those who would die following the Lord's return.)

Matt. 25:31-33: "When the Son of man arrives in his glory, and all the angels with him, then he will sit down on his glorious throne. And all the nations will be gathered before him, and he will separate people one from another, just as a shepherd separates the sheep from the goats. And he will put the sheep on his right hand, but the goats on his left."

2 Thess. 1:7-9: "To you who suffer tribulation, relief along with us at the revelation of the Lord Jesus from heaven with his powerful angels in a flaming fire, as he brings vengeance upon those who do not know God and those who do not obey the good news about our Lord Jesus. These very ones will undergo the judicial punishment of everlasting destruction from before the Lord and from the glory of his strength."

Luke 23:42, 43: "He [the sympathetic evildoer impaled alongside Jesus] went on to say: 'Jesus, remember me when you get into your kingdom.' And he said to him: 'Truly I tell you today, You will be with me in Paradise.'" (Under Jesus' rule, all the earth will become a paradise; the dead who are in God's memory will be raised with an opportunity to enjoy perfect life on earth forever.)

See also pages 234-239, under the heading "Last Days."

Sabbath

Definition: Sabbath is taken from the Hebrew *sha·vath'*, meaning "rest, cease, desist." The sabbatical system prescribed in the Mosaic Law included a weekly Sabbath day, a number of additional specified days throughout each year, the seventh year, and the fiftieth year. The weekly Sabbath of the Jews, the seventh day of their calendar week, is from sunset on Friday until sunset on Saturday. Many professed Christians have traditionally kept Sunday as their day of rest and of worship; others have adhered to the day set aside on the Jewish calendar.

Are Christians under obligation to keep a weekly sabbath day?

Ex. 31:16, 17: "The sons of Israel must keep the sabbath, so as to carry out the sabbath during their generations. It is a covenant to time indefinite ["a perpetual covenant," *RS*]. Between me and the sons of Israel it is a sign to time indefinite." (Notice that sabbath observance was a sign between Jehovah and Israel; this would not be the case if everyone else were also obligated to keep the Sabbath. The Hebrew word rendered "perpetual" in *RS* is *'oh·lam'*, which basically means a period of time that, from the standpoint of the present, is indefinite or hidden from sight but of long duration. That can mean forever, but not necessarily so. At Numbers 25:13 the same Hebrew word is applied to the priesthood, which later ended, according to Hebrews 7:12.)

Rom. 10:4: "Christ is the end of the Law, so that everyone exercising faith may have righteousness." (Sabbath keeping was a part of that Law. God used Christ to bring that Law to its end. Our having a righteous standing with God depends on faith in Christ, not on keeping a weekly sabbath.) (Also Galatians 4:9-11; Ephesians 2:13-16)

Col. 2:13-16: "[God] kindly forgave us all our trespasses and blotted out the handwritten document against us, which consisted of decrees and which was in opposition to us . . . Therefore let no man judge you in eating and drinking or in respect of a festival or of an observance of the new moon or of a sabbath." (If a person was under the Mosaic Law and was judged guilty of profaning the Sabbath, he was to be stoned to death by the whole congregation, according to Exodus 31:14 and Numbers 15:32-35. Many who argue for sabbath keeping have reason to be glad that we are not under that Law. As shown in the scripture here quoted, an approved standing with God no longer requires observance of the sabbath requirement given to Israel.)

How did Sunday come to be the principal day of worship for much of Christendom?

Although Christ was resurrected on the first day of the week (now called Sunday), the Bible contains no instruction to set aside that day of the week as sacred.

"The retention of the old Pagan name of 'Dies Solis,' or 'Sunday,' for the weekly Christian festival, is, in great measure, owing to the union of Pagan and [so-called] Christian sentiment with which the first day of the week was recommended by Constantine [in an edict in 321 C.E.] to his subjects, Pagan and Christian alike, as the 'venerable day of the Sun.' . . . It was his mode of harmonizing the discordant religions of the Empire under one common institution."
—Lectures on the History of the Eastern Church (New York, 1871), A. P. Stanley, p. 291.

Was the requirement of sabbath keeping given to Adam and thus made binding on all of his offspring?

Jehovah God proceeded to rest as to his works of material, earthly creation after preparing the earth for human habitation. This is stated at Genesis 2:1-3. But nothing in the Bible record says that God directed Adam to keep the seventh day of each week as a sabbath.

Deut. 5:15: "You must remember that you [Israel] became a slave in the land of Egypt and Jehovah your God proceeded to bring you out from there with a strong hand and an outstretched arm. That is why Jehovah your God commanded you to carry on the sabbath day." (Here Jehovah connects his giving of the sabbath law with Israel's deliverance from slavery in Egypt, not with events in Eden.)

Ex. 16:1, 23-29: "The entire assembly of the sons of Israel finally came to the wilderness of Sin . . . on the fifteenth day of the second month after their coming out of the land of Egypt. . . . [Moses] said to them: 'It is what Jehovah has spoken. Tomorrow there will be a sabbath observance of a holy sabbath to Jehovah. . . . Six days you will pick [the manna] up, but on the seventh day is a sabbath. On it none will form.' . . . Jehovah said to Moses: . . . 'Mark the fact that Jehovah has given you the sabbath.'" (Prior to this, there had been a marking off of weeks of seven days each, but this is the first reference to a sabbath observance.)

Is the Mosaic Law divided into "ceremonial" and "moral" parts, and is the "moral law" (the Ten Commandments) binding on Christians?

Did Jesus refer to the Law in a manner that indicated division of it into two parts?

Matt. 5:17, 21, 23, 27, 31, 38: "Do not think I came to destroy the Law or the Prophets. I came, not to destroy, but to fulfill." Now, notice what Jesus included in his further comments. "You heard that it was said to those of ancient times, 'You must not murder [Ex. 20:13; the Sixth Commandment]' . . . If, then, you are bringing your gift to the altar [Deut. 16:16, 17; no part of the Ten Commandments] . . . You heard that it was said, 'You must not commit adultery [Ex. 20:14; the Seventh Commandment].' Moreover it was said, 'Whoever divorces his wife, let him give her a certificate of divorce [Deut. 24:1; no part of the Ten Commandments].' You heard that it was said, 'Eye for eye and tooth for tooth [Ex. 21:23-25; no part of the Ten Commandments].'" (So, Jesus mixed together references to the Ten Commandments and other parts of the Law, making no distinction between them. Should we treat them differently?)

When Jesus was asked, "Teacher, which is the greatest commandment in the Law?" did he isolate the Ten Commandments? Instead, he replied: "'You must love Jehovah your God with your whole heart and with your whole soul and with your whole mind.' This is the greatest and first commandment. The second, like it, is this, 'You must love your neighbor as yourself.' On these two commandments the whole Law hangs, and the Prophets." (Matt. 22:35-40) If some cling to the Ten Commandments (Deut. 5:6-21), saying that they are binding on Christians but that the rest are not, are they not actually rejecting what Jesus said (quoting Deut. 6:5; Lev. 19:18) as to which commandments are the greatest?

When referring to the passing away of the Mosaic Law, does the Bible directly say that the Ten Commandments were included in what came to an end?

Rom. 7:6, 7: "Now we have been *discharged from the Law,* because we have died to that by which we were being held fast . . . What, then, shall we say? Is the Law sin? Never may that become so! Really I would not have come to know sin if it had not been for the Law; and, for example, I would not have known covetousness if the Law had not said: *'You must not covet.'*" (Here, immediately after writing that Jewish Christians had been "discharged from the Law," what example from the Law does Paul cite? The Tenth Commandment, thus showing that it was included in the Law from which they had been discharged.)

2 Cor. 3:7-11: "If the code which administers death and which was *engraved in letters in stones* came about in a glory, so that the sons of Israel could not gaze intently at the face of Moses because of the glory of his face, a glory that was to be done away with, why should not the administering of the spirit be much more with glory? . . . For if that which *was to be done away with* was brought in with glory, much more would that which remains be with glory." (Reference is made here to a code that was "engraved in letters in stones" and it is said that "the sons of Israel could not gaze

intently at the face of Moses" on the occasion when it was delivered to them. What is this describing? Exodus 34:1, 28-30 shows that it is the giving of the Ten Commandments; these were the commandments engraved on stone. Obviously these are included in what the scripture here says "was to be done away with.")

Does doing away with the Mosaic Law, including the Ten Commandments, imply the taking away of all moral restraint?

Not at all; many of the moral standards set out in the Ten Commandments were restated in the inspired books of the Christian Greek Scriptures. (There was, however, no restating of the sabbath law.) But no matter how good a law is, as long as sinful inclinations dominate a person's desires, there will be lawlessness. However, regarding the new covenant, which has replaced the Law covenant, Hebrews 8:10 states: "'For this is the covenant that I shall covenant with the house of Israel after those days,' says Jehovah. 'I will put my laws in their mind, and in their hearts I shall write them. And I will become their God, and they themselves will become my people.'" How much more effective such laws are than those engraved on stone tablets!

Rom. 6:15-17: "Shall we commit a sin because we are not under law but under undeserved kindness? Never may that happen! Do you not know that if you keep presenting yourselves to anyone as slaves to obey him, you are slaves of him because you obey him, either of sin with death in view or of obedience with righteousness in view? But thanks to God that you were the slaves of sin but you became obedient from the heart to that form of teaching to which you were handed over." (See also Galatians 5:18-24.)

Of what significance to Christians is the weekly Sabbath?

There is "a sabbath resting" that Christians share in every day

Hebrews 4:4-11 says: "In one place [Genesis 2:2] he [God] has said of the seventh day as follows: 'And God rested on the seventh day from all his works,' and again in this place

[Psalm 95:11]: 'They shall not enter into my rest.' Since, therefore, it remains for some to enter into it, and those to whom the good news was first declared did not enter in because of disobedience, he again marks off a certain day by saying after so long a time in David's psalm [Psalm 95:7, 8] 'Today'; just as it has been said above: 'Today if you people listen to his own voice, do not harden your hearts.' For if Joshua had led them into a place of rest, God would not afterward have spoken of another day. *So there remains a sabbath resting for the people of God.* For the man that has entered into God's rest has also himself rested from his own works, just as God did from his own. Let us therefore do our utmost to enter into that rest, for fear anyone should fall in the same pattern of disobedience."

From what are Christians here urged to rest? From their "own works." What works? Works by means of which they formerly sought to prove themselves righteous. No longer do they believe that they can earn God's approval and gain eternal life by complying with certain rules and observances. That was the error of faithless Jews who, by 'seeking to establish their own righteousness, did not subject themselves to the righteousness of God.' (Rom. 10:3) True Christians recognize that all of us were born sinners and that it is only by faith in the sacrifice of Christ that anyone can have a righteous standing with God. They endeavor to take to heart and apply all the teachings of God's Son. They humbly accept counsel and reproof from God's Word. This does not mean that they think they can *earn* God's approval in this way; instead, what they do is an expression of their love and faith. By such a course of life they avoid the "pattern of disobedience" of the Jewish nation.

The "seventh day," referred to in Genesis 2:2, was not merely a 24-hour day. (See page 88, under the heading "Creation.") Similarly, the "sabbath resting" that true Christians share is not limited to a 24-hour day. By exercising faith and obeying the Bible's counsel, they can enjoy it every day, and especially will they do so in God's new system.

There is a thousand-year "sabbath" rest that lies ahead for mankind

Mark 2:27, 28: "[Jesus] went on to say to them: 'The

sabbath came into existence for the sake of man, and not man for the sake of the sabbath; hence the Son of man is Lord even of the sabbath.'"

Jesus knew that Jehovah had instituted the Sabbath as a sign between God and Israel, and that it was meant to bring them relief from their labors. Jesus also was aware that his own death would provide the basis for setting aside the Mosaic Law as having found its fulfillment in him. He appreciated that the Law, with its sabbath requirement, provided "a shadow of the good things to come." (Heb. 10:1; Col. 2:16, 17) In connection with those "good things" there is a "sabbath" of which he is to be Lord.

As Lord of lords, Christ will rule all the earth for a thousand years. (Rev. 19:16; 20:6; Ps. 2:6-8) While on earth, Jesus mercifully performed some of his most amazing works of healing on the Sabbath, thus demonstrating the kind of relief that he will bring to people out of all nations during his Millennial Reign. (Luke 13:10-13; John 5:5-9; 9:1-14) Those who appreciate the real meaning of the Sabbath will have opportunity also to benefit from that "sabbath" rest.

If Someone Says—

'Christians must keep the Sabbath'

You might reply: 'May I ask why you feel that way?' **Then perhaps add:** 'What the Bible says about it definitely should govern our thinking on the matter, should it not? . . . There are some Bible texts that I have found helpful on this subject. Please let me share them with you. (Then use appropriate portions of the material on the preceding pages.)'

'Why don't you keep the Sabbath?'

You might reply: 'My answer would depend on which sabbath you have in mind. Did you know that the Bible tells about more than one sabbath? . . . God gave sabbath laws to the Jews. But did you know that the Bible speaks of a different kind of sabbath that Christians are to keep?' **Then perhaps add:** (1) 'We do not keep one day a week as the Sabbath because the Bible says that requirement "was to be done away with." (2 Cor. 3:7-11; see comments regarding this on pages 348, 349.)' (2) 'But there is a sabbath that we do keep regularly. (Heb. 4:4-11; see pages 349, 350.)'

Saints

Definition: According to Roman Catholic teaching, saints are those who died and are now with Christ in heaven and who have been given recognition by the Church for outstanding holiness and virtue. The Tridentine profession of faith states that the saints are to be invoked as intercessors with God and that both the relics of saints and images of the saints are to be venerated. Other religions, too, invoke the help of saints. Certain religions teach that all of their members are saints and are free from sin. The Bible makes many references to saints, or holy ones. It refers to Christ's 144,000 spirit-anointed followers as being such.

Does the Bible teach that a person must have attained to heavenly glory before he is recognized as a saint?

The Bible definitely does refer to holy ones, or saints, that are in heaven. Jehovah is spoken of as "the Holy One [Greek, *ha'gi·on*]." (1 Pet. 1:15, 16; see Leviticus 11:45.) Jesus Christ is described as "the Holy One [*ha'gi·os*] of God" when on earth and as "holy [*ha'gi·os*]" in heaven. (Mark 1:24; Rev. 3:7, *JB*) The angels too are "holy." (Acts 10:22, *JB*) The same basic term in the original Greek is applied to a considerable number of persons on earth.

Acts 9:32, 36-41, *JB:* "Peter visited one place after another and eventually came to the saints [*ha·gi'ous*] living down in Lydda. At Jaffa there was a woman disciple called Tabitha [who died] . . . [Peter] turned to the dead woman and said, 'Tabitha, stand up'. She opened her eyes, looked at Peter and sat up. Peter helped her to her feet, then he called in the saints and widows and showed them she was alive." (Clearly, these saints were not yet in heaven, nor was just an outstanding individual such as Peter viewed as a saint.)

2 Cor. 1:1; 13:12, *JB:* "From Paul, appointed by God to be an apostle of Christ Jesus, and from Timothy, one of the brothers, to the church of God at Corinth and to all the saints [*ha·gi′ois*] in the whole of Achaia." "Greet one another with the holy kiss. All the saints send you greetings." (All these early Christians who were cleansed by the blood of Christ and set apart for God's service as prospective joint heirs with Christ were referred to as saints, or holy ones. Recognition of their being saints was obviously not deferred until after they had died.)

Is it Scriptural to pray to "saints" for them to act as intercessors with God?

Jesus Christ said: "You should pray like this: 'Our Father in heaven, . . . '" So prayers are to be addressed to the Father. Jesus also said: "I am the Way, the Truth and the Life. No one can come to the Father except through me. If you ask for anything in my name, I will do it." (Matt. 6:9; John 14: 6, 14, *JB*) Thus Jesus ruled out the idea that anyone else could fill the role of intercessor. The apostle Paul added regarding Christ: "He not only died for us—he rose from the dead, and there at God's right hand he stands and pleads for us." "He is living for ever to intercede for all who come to God through him." (Rom. 8:34; Heb. 7:25, *JB*) If we truly want our prayers to be heard by God, would it not be wise to approach God in the way that his Word directs? (See also pages 258, 259, under the heading "Mary.")

Eph. 6:18, 19, *JB:* "Never get tired of staying awake to pray *for* all the saints; and pray for me to be given an opportunity to open my mouth and speak without fear and give out the mystery of the gospel." (Italics added.) (Here encouragement is given to pray *for* the saints but not *to* them or *through* them. The *New Catholic Encyclopedia,* 1967, Vol. XI, p. 670, acknowledges: "Usually in the N[ew] T[estament], all prayer, private as well as public liturgical prayer, is addressed to God the Father through Christ.")

Rom. 15:30, *JB:* "I beg you, brothers, by our Lord Jesus Christ and the love of the Spirit, to help me through my dangers by praying to God for me." (The apostle Paul, himself a saint, asked fellow Christians who were also saints to pray for him. But notice that Paul did not address his prayers *to* those fellow saints, nor did their prayers on his behalf replace the personal intimacy that Paul himself enjoyed with the Father by means of prayer. Compare Ephesians 3:11, 12, 14.)

How should the practice of venerating relics and images of "saints" be viewed?

The *New Catholic Encyclopedia* admits: "It is thus vain to seek a justification for the cult of relics in the Old Testament; nor is much attention paid to relics in the New Testament. . . . [The Church "father"] Origen seems to have regarded the practice as a pagan sign of respect for a material object."—(1967), Vol. XII, pp. 234, 235.

It is noteworthy that God buried Moses, and no human ever found out where his grave was. (Deut. 34:5, 6) But Jude 9 informs us that the archangel Michael disputed with the Devil about Moses' body. Why? God's purpose to dispose of it in such a manner that humans would not know where to find it was clearly stated. Did the Adversary want to direct humans to that body so that it might be put on display and perhaps become an object of veneration?

Regarding the veneration of *images* of the "saints," see the main heading "Images."

Why are Catholic "saints" depicted with halos?

The *New Catholic Encyclopedia* acknowledges: "The most common attribute, applied to all saints, is the nimbus (cloud), a luminous defined shape surrounding the head of the saint. Its origins are pre-Christian, and examples are found in Hellenistic art of pagan inspiration; the halo was used, as evidenced in mosaics and coins, for demigods and divinities such as Neptune, Jupiter, Bacchus, and in particular Apollo (god of the sun)."—(1967), Vol. XII, p. 963.

The New Encyclopædia Britannica says: "In Hellenistic and Roman art the sun-god Helios and Roman emperors often appear with a crown of rays. Because of its pagan origin, the form was avoided in Early Christian art, but a simple circular nimbus was adopted by Christian emperors for their official portraits. From the middle of the 4th century, Christ was also shown with this imperial attribute . . . it was not until the 6th century that the halo became customary for the Virgin Mary and other saints."—(1976), Micropædia, Vol. IV, p. 864.

Is it proper to mix Christianity with pagan symbolism?

"Light and darkness have nothing in common. Christ is not the ally of Beliar [Belial; Satan], nor has a believer anything to share with an unbeliever. The temple of God has no common ground with idols, and that is what we are—the temple of the living God. . . . Then come away from them and keep aloof, says the Lord. Touch nothing that is unclean, and I will welcome you and be your father, and you shall be my sons and daughters, says the Almighty Lord."—2 Cor. 6: 14-18, *JB*.

Might all the members of a religious group be saints and thus free from sin?

It certainly was true that all who made up the first-century Christian congregation were saints. (1 Cor. 14: 33, 34; 2 Cor. 1:1; 13:13, *RS, KJ*) They are described as ones that received "forgiveness of sins" and were "sanctified" by God. (Acts 26:18; 1 Cor. 1:2, *RS, KJ*) Nevertheless, they did not claim to be free from all sin. They were born as descendants of the sinner Adam. This inheritance often made it a struggle for them to do what was right, as the apostle Paul humbly acknowledged. (Rom. 7:21-25) And the apostle John pointedly said: "If we say we have no sin, we deceive ourselves, and the truth is not in us." (1 John 1:8, *RS*) So, being a saint in the sense that the term is used regarding Christ's true followers does not mean that in the flesh they are free from all sin.

As to whether all true Christians today are saints with heavenly life before them, see pages 164-168.

If Someone Says—

'Do you believe in the saints?'

You might reply: 'Which ones do you have in mind?' If the person mentions Mary and/or the apostles, you might **possibly add:** (1) 'Yes, they are referred to in the Holy Scriptures, and I believe what is written there. But I am especially interested in what they are doing today and how it affects us, aren't you? . . . I have found something very interesting about them here in the Holy Scriptures, and I would like to share it with you. (Rev. 5:9, 10)' [Note, for use if a question is raised about the wording in the text: *JB* says "rule the world." *CC* reads "reign over the earth." *Kx* states "reign as kings over the earth." But *NAB* and *Dy* read "reign on the earth." For comments on the Greek grammar, see page 168, under "Heaven."] (2) 'What will life under such a government be like? (Rev. 21:2-4)'

Or you could say (if you were once a Catholic): 'For many years I shared in the festivals for the saints and regularly prayed to them. But then I read something in the Holy Scriptures that caused me to reconsider what I was doing. Please, let me show it to you. (See page 353.)'

Salvation

Definition: Preservation or deliverance from danger or destruction. That deliverance may be from the hands of oppressors or persecutors. For all true Christians, Jehovah provides through his Son deliverance from the present wicked system of things as well as salvation from bondage to sin and death. For a great crowd of faithful servants of Jehovah living during "the last days," salvation will include preservation through the great tribulation.

Will God, in his great mercy, eventually save all humankind?

Does 2 Peter 3:9 indicate that there will be universal salvation? It says: "The Lord is not slow about his promise as some count slowness, but is forbearing toward you, not wishing that any should perish ["he does not want anyone to be destroyed," *TEV*], but that all should reach repentance." (*RS*) It is God's merciful desire that all of Adam's offspring repent, and he has generously made provision for forgiveness of the sins of those who do. But he does not force anyone to accept that provision. (Compare Deuteronomy 30:15-20.) Many reject it. They are like a drowning man who pushes away a life preserver when it is thrown to him by someone who desires to help. It should be noted, however, that the alternative to repentance is not an eternity in hellfire. As 2 Peter 3:9 shows, those who do not repent will perish, or "be destroyed." Verse 7 (*RS*) also refers to *"destruction* of ungodly men." There is no thought of universal salvation here.—See also the main heading "Hell."

Does 1 Corinthians 15:22 prove that all humans will eventually be saved? It says: "As in Adam all die, so also in Christ shall all be made alive." (*RS*) As shown in the surrounding verses, what is under discussion here is resurrection. Who will be resurrected? All whose death is attributable to Adamic sin (see verse 21) but who have not also personally committed the willful transgressions set forth in Hebrews 10:26-29. As Jesus was raised from Hades (Acts 2:31), so all others who are in Hades will be "made alive" by means of the resurrection. (Rev. 1:18; 20:13) Will all of these gain eternal salvation? That opportunity will be open to them, but not everyone will take hold of it, as is indicated at John 5:28, 29, which shows that the outcome to some will be adverse "judgment."

What about texts such as Titus 2:11, which refers to "the salvation of all men," according to the rendering of RS? Other texts, such as John 12:32, Romans 5:18, and 1 Timothy 2:3, 4, convey a similar thought in *RS, KJ, NE, TEV,* etc. The Greek expressions rendered "all" and "everyone" in these verses are inflected forms of the word *pas.* As shown in Vine's *Expository Dictionary of New Testament Words* (London, 1962, Vol. I, p. 46), *pas* can also mean "every kind or variety." So, in the above verses, instead of "all," the expression "every kind of" could be used; or "all sorts of," as is done in *NW*. Which is correct—"all" or the thought conveyed by "all sorts of"? Well, which rendering is also harmonious with the rest of the Bible? The latter one is. Consider Acts 10:34, 35; Revelation 7:9, 10; 2 Thessalonians 1:9. (Note: Other translators also recognize this sense of the Greek word, as is shown by their renderings of it at Matthew 5:11—"all kinds of," *RS, TEV;* "every kind of," *NE;* "all manner of," *KJ.*)

Are there scriptures that definitely show that some will never be saved?

2 Thess. 1:9, *RS:* "They shall suffer the punishment of *eternal destruction* and exclusion from the presence of the Lord and from the glory of his might." (Italics added.)

Rev. 21:8, *RS:* "As for the cowardly, the faithless, the polluted, as for murderers, fornicators, sorcerers, idolaters, and all liars, their lot shall be in the lake that burns with fire and sulphur, which is the second death."

Matt. 7:13, 14, *RS:* "Enter by the narrow gate; for the gate is wide and the way is easy, that leads to destruction, and those who enter by it are many. For the gate is narrow and the way is hard, that leads to life, and those who find it are few."

Once a person is saved, is he always saved?

Jude 5, *RS:* "I desire to remind you, though you were once for all fully informed, that he who *saved* a people out of the land of Egypt, *afterward destroyed* those who did not believe." (Italics added.)

Matt. 24:13, *RS:* "He who endures to the end will be saved." (So a person's final salvation is not determined at the moment that he begins to put faith in Jesus.)

Phil. 2:12, *RS:* "As you have always obeyed, so now, not only as in my presence but much more in my absence, work out your own salvation with fear and trembling." (This was addressed to "the saints," or holy ones, at Philippi, as stated in Philippians 1:1. Paul urged them not to be overly confident but to realize that their final salvation was not yet assured.)

Heb. 10:26, 27, *RS:* "If we sin deliberately after receiving the knowledge of the truth, there no longer remains a sacrifice for sins, but a fearful prospect of judgment, and a fury of fire which will consume the adversaries." (Thus the Bible does not go along with the idea that no matter what sins a person may commit after he is "saved" he will not lose his salvation. It encourages faithfulness. See also Hebrews 6:4-6, where it is shown that even a person anointed with holy spirit can lose his hope of salvation.)

Is anything more than faith needed in order to gain salvation?

Eph. 2:8, 9, *RS:* "By grace ["undeserved kindness," *NW*] you have been saved through faith; and this is not your own doing, it is the gift of God—not because of works, lest any man should boast." (The entire provision for salvation is an expression of God's undeserved kindness. There is no way that a descendant of Adam can gain salvation on his own, no matter how noble his works are. Salvation is a gift from God given to those who put faith in the sin-atoning value of the sacrifice of his Son.)

Heb. 5:9, *RS:* "He [Jesus] became the source of eternal salvation to all who *obey* him." (Italics added.) (Does this conflict with the statement that Christians are "saved through faith"? Not at all. Obedience simply demonstrates that their faith is genuine.)

Jas. 2:14, 26, *RS:* "What does it profit, my brethren, if a man says he has faith but has not works? Can his faith save him? For as the body apart from the spirit is dead, so faith apart from works is dead." (A person does not *earn* salvation by his works. But anyone who has genuine faith *will* have works to go with it—works of obedience to the commands of God and Christ, works that demonstrate his faith and love. Without such works, his faith is dead.)

Acts 16:30, 31, *RS:* "'Men, what must I do to be saved?' And they [Paul and Silas] said, 'Believe in the Lord Jesus, and you will be saved, you and your household.'" (If that man and his household truly believed, would they not act in harmony with their belief? Certainly.)

If Someone Says—

'I'm saved'

You might reply: 'I am glad to know that, because it tells me that you believe in Jesus Christ. The work in which I am sharing is one that Jesus assigned his followers to do, that is, to tell others about the establishment of his Kingdom. (Matt. 24:14)' **Then perhaps add:** (1) 'What is that Kingdom? What will its coming mean to the world? (Dan. 2:44)' (2) 'What conditions will there be here on earth under that heavenly government? (Ps. 37:11; Rev. 21:3, 4)'

Or you could say: 'Then you appreciate what the apostle Peter said, here at Acts 4:12, don't you? . . . Have you ever wondered *by whom* the name of Jesus was *given* for us to put faith in it?' **Then perhaps add:** (1) 'Jesus himself tells us. (John 17:3)' (2) 'Notice that Jesus said he had made his Father's name known. (John 17:6) What is His personal name? What associations does it convey to your mind? (Ex. 3:15; 34:5-7)'

'Are you saved?'

You might reply: 'So far, I am. I say that because I am also aware of the Bible's counsel not to be overconfident of our standing. Are you acquainted with this text? (1 Cor. 10:12)' **Then perhaps add:** 'What is the reason for that? To persons who had been born again and had the hope of heavenly life (Heb. 3:1), the apostle Paul wrote . . . (Heb. 3:12-14) It is by growing in knowledge of God's Word that we fortify our faith.'

Or you could say: 'I could answer that by simply saying, Yes. But did you know that the Bible speaks of more than one salvation? For instance, have you ever considered the significance of Revelation 7:9, 10, 14? . . . So, there will be people who will be saved through the coming great tribulation, to live right here on earth. (Matt. 5:5)'

'Do you accept Jesus as your personal Savior?'

See pages 219, 220, under the heading "Jesus Christ."

'You say that only 144,000 are going to be saved'

You might reply: 'I am glad that you brought that up so I can tell you what we *really* believe. Salvation is open to just as many people as will demonstrate true faith in the provision that God has made through Jesus. But the Bible says that only 144,000 will go to heaven to be with Christ. Have you ever seen that in the Bible? . . . It is here at Revelation 14:1, 3.' **Then perhaps add:** (1) 'What will they do in heaven? (Rev. 20:6)' (2) 'It is obvious that they will be ruling *over* someone. Who might that be? . . . (Matt. 5:5; 6:10)'

Satan the Devil

Definition: The spirit creature who is the chief adversary of Jehovah God and of all who worship the true God. The name Satan was given to him because of his becoming a resister of Jehovah. Satan is also known as the Devil, because he is the foremost slanderer of God. Satan is described as the original serpent, evidently because of his using a serpent in Eden to deceive Eve, and for this reason "serpent" came to signify "deceiver." In the book of Revelation, the symbolism of a devouring dragon is also applied to Satan.

How can we know whether such a spirit person really exists?

The Bible is the chief source of evidence. There he is repeatedly referred to by name (Satan 52 times, Devil 33 times). Eyewitness testimony as to Satan's existence is also recorded there. Who was the eyewitness? Jesus Christ, who lived in heaven before coming to earth, repeatedly spoke of that wicked one by name.—Luke 22:31; 10:18; Matt. 25:41.

What the Bible says about Satan the Devil makes sense. The evil that mankind experiences is far out of proportion to the malice of the humans involved. The Bible's explanation of Satan's origin and his activities makes clear why, despite the desire of the majority to live in peace, mankind has been plagued with hatred, violence, and war for thousands of years and why this has reached such a level that it now threatens to destroy all mankind.

If there really were no Devil, accepting what the Bible says about him would not bring lasting benefits to a person. In many instances, however, persons who formerly dabbled in the occult or who belonged to groups practicing spiritism report that they were at that time greatly distressed because of hearing "voices" from unseen sources, being "possessed" by superhuman beings, etc. Genuine relief was gained when they learned what the Bible says about Satan and his demons, applied the Bible's counsel to shun spiritistic practices, and sought Jehovah's help in prayer.—See pages 384-389, under the heading "Spiritism."

Believing that Satan exists does not mean accepting the idea that he has horns, a pointed tail, and a pitchfork and that he roasts people in a fiery hell. The Bible gives no such description of Satan. That is the product of the minds of medieval artists who were influenced by representations of the mythological Greek god Pan and by the *Inferno* written by the Italian poet Dante Alighieri. Instead of teaching a fiery hell, the Bible clearly says that "the dead . . . are conscious of nothing at all."—Eccl. 9:5.

Is Satan perhaps only the evil within people?

Job 1:6-12 and 2:1-7 tell about conversations between Jehovah God and Satan. If Satan were the evil in a person, the evil in this case would have to be in Jehovah. But that is in complete disagreement with what the Bible tells us about Jehovah as being One "in whom there is no unrighteousness." (Ps. 92:15; Rev. 4:8) It is noteworthy that the Hebrew text uses the expression *has·Sa·tan'* (*the* Satan) in the accounts in Job, showing that reference is being made to the one who is outstandingly the resister of God.—See also Zechariah 3:1, 2, footnote in *NW* Reference edition.

Luke 4:1-13 reports that the Devil endeavored to tempt Jesus to do his bidding. The account relates statements made by the Devil and answers given by Jesus. Was Jesus there being tempted by evil within himself? Such a view does not harmonize with the Bible's description of Jesus as being sinless. (Heb. 7:26; 1 Pet. 2:22) Although at John 6:70 the Greek word *di·a'bo·los'* is used to describe a bad quality that had developed in Judas Iscariot, in Luke 4:3 the expression *ho di·a'bo·los* (*the* Devil) is used, thus designating a particular person.

Is blaming the Devil just a device used in an effort to escape from responsibility for bad conditions?

Some people blame the Devil for what they themselves do. In contrast, the Bible shows that humans often bear much of the blame for the badness they experience, whether at the hands of other humans or as a result of their own conduct. (Eccl. 8:9; Gal. 6:7) Yet, the Bible does not leave us ignorant of the existence and devices of the superhuman foe who has brought so much grief to mankind. It shows how we can get out from under his control.

From where did Satan come?

All of Jehovah's works are perfect; he is not the author of unrighteousness; so he did not create anyone wicked. (Deut. 32:4; Ps. 5:4) The one who became Satan was originally a perfect spirit son of God. When saying that the Devil "did not stand fast in the truth," Jesus indicated that at one time that one was "in the truth." (John 8:44) But, as is true of all of God's intelligent creatures, this spirit son was endowed with free will. He abused his freedom of choice, allowed feelings of self-importance to develop in his heart, began to crave worship that belonged only to God, and so enticed Adam and Eve to listen to him rather than obey God. Thus by his course of action he made himself Satan, which means "adversary."—Jas. 1:14, 15; see also page 372, under the heading "Sin."

Why did not God destroy Satan promptly after he rebelled?

Serious issues were raised by Satan: (1) *The righteousness and rightfulness of Jehovah's sovereignty.* Was Jehovah withholding from mankind freedom that would contribute to their happiness? Were mankind's ability to govern their affairs successfully and their continued life truly dependent on their obedience to God? Had Jehovah been dishonest in giving a law that stated that disobedience would lead to their death? (Gen. 2:16, 17; 3:3-5) So, did Jehovah really have the right to rule? (2) *The integrity of intelligent creatures toward Jehovah.* By the deflection of Adam and Eve the question was raised: Did Jehovah's servants really obey him out of love or might *all* of them abandon God and follow the lead being given by Satan? This latter issue was further developed by Satan in the days of Job. (Gen. 3:6; Job 1:8-11; 2:3-5; see also Luke 22:31.) These issues could not be settled by merely executing the rebels.

Not that God needed to prove anything to himself. But so that these issues would never again disrupt the peace and well-being of the universe, Jehovah has allowed ample time for them to be settled beyond all doubt. That Adam and Eve died following disobedience to God became evident in due time. (Gen. 5:5) But more was at issue. So, God has permitted both Satan and humans to try every form of government of their own making. None have brought lasting happiness. God has let mankind go to the limit in pursuing ways of life that ignore His righteous standards. The fruitage speaks for itself. As the Bible truthfully says: "It does not belong to man who is walking even to direct his step." (Jer. 10:23) At the same time God has given his servants opportunity to prove their loyalty to him by their acts of loving obedience, and this in the face of enticements and persecution instigated by Satan. Jehovah exhorts his servants, saying: "Be wise, my son, and make my heart rejoice, that I may make a reply to him that is taunting me." (Prov. 27:11) Those proving faithful reap great benefits now and have the prospect of eternal life in perfection. They will use such life in doing the will of Jehovah, whose personality and ways they truly love.

How powerful a figure is Satan in today's world?

Jesus Christ referred to him as being *"the ruler of the world,"* the one whom mankind in general obeys by heeding his urgings to ignore God's requirements. (John 14:30; Eph. 2:2) The Bible also calls him *"the god of this system of things,"* who is honored by the religious practices of people who adhere to this system of things.—2 Cor. 4:4; 1 Cor. 10:20.

When endeavoring to tempt Jesus Christ, the Devil "brought him up and showed him all the kingdoms of the inhabited earth in an instant of time; and the Devil said to him: 'I will give you all this authority and the glory of them, because it has been delivered to me, and to whomever I wish I give it. You, therefore, if you do an act of worship before me, it will all be yours.'" (Luke 4:5-7) Revelation 13:1, 2 reveals that Satan gives 'power, throne and great authority' to the global political system of rulership. Daniel 10:13, 20 discloses that Satan has had demonic princes over principal kingdoms of the earth. Ephesians 6:12 refers to these as constituting 'governments, authorities, world rulers of this darkness, wicked spirit forces in heavenly places.'

No wonder that 1 John 5:19 says: "The whole world is lying in the power of the wicked one." But his power is only for a limited period of time and is only by the toleration of Jehovah, who is God Almighty.

How long will Satan be allowed to mislead mankind?

For evidence that we now live in the last days of Satan's wicked system of things, see pages 95-98, under "Dates," and the main heading "Last Days."

The provision for relief from Satan's wicked influence is symbolically described in this way: "I saw an angel coming down out of heaven with the key of the abyss and a great chain in his hand. And he seized the dragon, the original serpent, who is the Devil and Satan, and bound him for a thousand years. And he hurled him into the abyss and shut it and sealed it over him, that he might not mislead the nations anymore until the thousand years were ended. After these things he must be let loose for a little while." (Rev. 20: 1-3) Then what? "The Devil who was misleading them was hurled into the lake of fire and sulphur." (Rev. 20:10) What does that mean? Revelation 21:8 answers: "This means the second death." He will be gone forever!

Does the 'abyssing' of Satan mean that he will be confined to a desolate earth with no one for him to tempt for 1,000 years?

Some persons refer to *Revelation 20:3* (quoted on page 365) to support this idea. They say that the "abyss," or "bottomless pit" (*KJ*), represents the earth in a state of desolation. Does it? Revelation 12:7-9, 12 (*KJ*) shows that at some time before his abyssing Satan is "cast out" of heaven down to the earth, where he brings increased woe upon mankind. So, when Revelation 20:3 (*KJ*) says that Satan is "cast . . . into the bottomless pit," he surely is not simply left where he already is—invisible but confined to the vicinity of the earth. He is removed far from there, "that he should deceive the nations no more, till the thousand years should be fulfilled." Notice that Revelation 20:3 says that, at the end of the thousand years, it is Satan, not the nations, that are loosed from the abyss. When Satan is loosed, people who formerly made up those nations will already be on hand.

Isaiah 24:1-6 and *Jeremiah 4:23-29* (*KJ*) are sometimes referred to in support of this belief. These say: "Behold, the LORD maketh the earth empty, and maketh it waste . . . The land shall be utterly emptied, and utterly spoiled: for the LORD hath spoken this word." "I beheld the earth, and, lo, it was without form, and void . . . I beheld, and, lo, there was no man . . . For thus hath the LORD said, The whole land shall be desolate . . . . Every city shall be forsaken, and not a man dwell therein." What do these prophecies mean? They had their first fulfillment upon Jerusalem and the land of Judah. In execution of divine judgment, Jehovah permitted the Babylonians to overrun the land. Eventually it was all left desolate and waste. (See Jeremiah 36:29.) But God did not then depopulate the entire globe, nor will he do so now. (See pages 112-115, under "Earth," also the main heading "Heaven.") However, he will completely desolate both the modern counterpart of unfaithful Jerusalem, Christendom, which reproaches the name of God by its unholy conduct, and all the rest of Satan's visible organization.

Instead of being a desolate waste, during Christ's Thousand Year Reign, and while Satan is in the abyss, all the earth will become a paradise. (See "Paradise.")

Sex

Definition: The characteristics of earthly creatures that serve as a means of reproduction by two interacting parents. The differences between the male and female sexes have far-reaching effects in human life. Since God himself is the Source of life and since humans are meant to reflect his qualities, the ability to transmit life by sexual relations is to be treated with great respect.

Does the Bible teach that sexual relations are sinful?

Gen. 1:28: "God blessed them [Adam and Eve] and God said to them: 'Be fruitful and become many and fill the earth.'" (Fulfilling this divine command would require that they have sexual relations, would it not? Doing so would not be sinful but would be in harmony with God's purpose for the populating of the earth. Some persons have thought that the 'forbidden fruit' in Eden was perhaps a symbolic reference to a divine restriction or even a prohibition of sexual relations on the part of Adam and Eve. But that conflicts with God's command quoted above. It also conflicts with the fact that, although Adam and Eve ate of the forbidden fruit in Eden, the first mention of their having sexual intercourse was after they had been expelled from there.—Gen. 2:17; 3: 17, 23; 4:1.)

Gen. 9:1: "God went on to bless Noah and his sons and to say to them: 'Be fruitful and become many and fill the earth.'" (This further blessing, together with a restatement of the divine command to procreate, was given after the global Flood in Noah's day. God's viewpoint toward lawful sexual relations had not changed.)

1 Cor. 7:2-5: "Because of prevalence of fornication, let each man have his own wife and each woman have her own husband. Let the husband render to his wife her due; but let the wife also do likewise to her husband. . . . Do not be depriving each other of it, except by mutual consent for an appointed time, . . . that Satan may not keep tempting you for your lack of self-regulation." (What is wrong is thus

shown to be fornication, not proper sexual relations between husband and wife.)

Are sexual relations before marriage wrong?

1 Thess. 4:3-8: "This is what God wills ... that you abstain from fornication; that each one of you should know how to get possession of his own vessel in sanctification and honor, not in covetous sexual appetite such as also those nations have which do not know God; that no one go to the point of harming and encroach upon the rights of his brother in this matter, because Jehovah is one who exacts punishment for all these things, just as we told you beforehand and also gave you a thorough witness. For God called us, not with allowance for uncleanness, but in connection with sanctification. So, then, the man that shows disregard is disregarding, not man, but God, who puts his holy spirit in you." (The Greek word *por·nei'a,* translated "fornication," refers to sexual intercourse between unmarried persons, also to extramarital relations on the part of married persons.)

Eph. 5:5: "No fornicator or unclean person or greedy person—which means being an idolater—has any inheritance in the kingdom of the Christ and of God." (This does not mean that anyone who *in the past* was a fornicator cannot enjoy the blessings of God's Kingdom, but he must cease that way of life in order to have God's approval. See 1 Corinthians 6:9-11.)

Does the Bible approve of living together as husband and wife without legal marriage?

See pages 248-250, under the heading "Marriage."

What does the Bible say about homosexuality?

Rom. 1:24-27: "God, in keeping with the desires of their hearts, gave them up to uncleanness, that their bodies might be dishonored among them ... God gave them up to disgraceful sexual appetites, for both their females changed the natural use of themselves into one contrary to nature; and likewise even the males left the natural use of the female and became violently inflamed in their lust toward one another, males with males, working what is obscene and receiving in themselves the full recompense, which was due for their error."

1 Tim. 1:9-11: "Law is promulgated, not for a righteous man, but for persons lawless and unruly, ungodly and sinners, . . . fornicators, men who lie with males, . . . and whatever other thing is in opposition to the healthful teaching according to the glorious good news of the happy God." (Compare Leviticus 20:13.)

Jude 7: "Sodom and Gomorrah and the cities about them, after they . . . [had] gone out after flesh for unnatural use, are placed before us as a warning example by undergoing the judicial punishment of everlasting fire." (The name Sodom has become the basis for the word "sodomy," which usually designates a homosexual practice. Compare Genesis 19:4, 5, 24, 25.)

What is the attitude of true Christians toward those who have a history of homosexuality?

1 Cor. 6:9-11: "Neither fornicators, nor idolaters, nor adulterers, nor men kept for unnatural purposes, nor men who lie with men . . . will inherit God's kingdom. And yet that is what some of you were. But you have been washed clean, but you have been sanctified, but you have been declared righteous in the name of our Lord Jesus Christ and with the spirit of our God." (Regardless of such a background, if persons now abandon their former unclean practices, apply Jehovah's righteous standards, and exercise faith in his provision for forgiveness of sins through Christ, they can enjoy a clean standing before God. After reforming, they may be welcomed in the Christian congregation.)

True Christians know that even deeply rooted wrong desires, including those that may have a genetic basis or that involve physical causes or environmental factors, are not insurmountable for persons who truly want to please Jehovah. Some people are by nature highly emotional. Perhaps in the past they gave free rein to fits of anger; but knowledge of God's will, the desire to please him, and the help of his spirit enable them to develop self-control. A person may be an alcoholic, but, with proper motivation, he can refrain from drinking and thus avoid becoming a drunkard. Likewise, a person may feel strongly attracted to others of the same sex, but by heeding the counsel of God's Word he can remain clean from homosexual practices. (See Ephesians 4: 17-24.) Jehovah does not allow us to go on thinking that wrong conduct really makes no difference; he kindly but firmly warns us of the consequences and provides abundant help for those who want to "strip off the old personality with its practices, and clothe [themselves] with the new personality."—Col. 3:9, 10.

Is the Bible's view regarding sex perhaps old-fashioned and needlessly restrictive?

1 Thess. 4:3-8: "This is what God wills . . . that you abstain from fornication . . . So, then, the man that shows disregard is disregarding, not man, but God, who puts his holy spirit in you." (The Bible's view regarding sex is not simply something that was developed by certain humans who lived many years ago. It comes from mankind's Creator; it makes clear what is required in order to have his approval; it also provides guidelines that contribute to stable families and wholesome, happy relationships outside the family. Those who apply this counsel safeguard themselves against the deep emotional scars and loathsome diseases that go with immoral conduct. The Bible's counsel is very much up to date in meeting the needs of those who want a clean conscience before God and a life free from needless frustration.)

If Someone Says—

'What is your attitude toward homosexuality?'

You might reply: 'It is the viewpoint that is expressed here in the Bible. I believe that what it says is more important than any human opinion, because this gives us the thoughts of mankind's Creator. (1 Cor. 6:9-11) You will notice that some of these who became Christians were formerly practicing homosexuality. But because of their love for God, and with the help of his spirit, they changed.'

Or you could say: 'In answering that, I might say that I've noticed that many who feel that no stigma should be attached to a homosexual life-style do not believe that the Bible is God's Word. May I ask how you view the Bible?' If the person *does* profess faith in the Bible, **you might perhaps add:** 'Homosexuality is not an issue that is new. The Bible sets out Jehovah God's unchanging viewpoint in very clear language. (Perhaps use material on pages 368, 369.)' If the person expresses doubts about the existence of God or about the Bible, **you could add:** 'If there were no God, we logically would not be accountable to him and so could live as we pleased. So the real question is, Is there a God and do I owe my existence to him [also, perhaps, Is the Bible inspired by God]? (Use thoughts from pages 145-151 or 58-68.)'

Sin

Definition: Literally, a missing of the mark, according to the Hebrew and Greek Bible texts. God himself sets the "mark" that his intelligent creatures are to reach. Missing that mark is sin, which is also unrighteousness, or lawlessness. (Rom. 3:23; 1 John 5:17; 3:4) Sin is anything not in harmony with God's personality, standards, ways, and will, all of which are holy. It may involve wrong conduct, failure to do what should be done, ungodly speech, unclean thoughts, or desires or motives that are selfish. The Bible differentiates between inherited sin and willful sin, between an act of sin over which a person is repentant and the practice of sin.

How was it possible for Adam to sin if he was perfect?

As to Adam's being perfect, read Genesis 1:27, 31 and Deuteronomy 32:4. When Jehovah God pronounced his earthly creation, including man and woman, to be "very good," what did it mean? For One whose activity is perfect to have said that what he made was "very good," it must have measured up to his perfect standards.

Did perfection require that Adam and Eve be unable to do wrong? The maker of a robot expects it to do exactly what he has programmed it to do. But a perfect robot would not be a perfect human. The qualities viewed as essential are not the same. Adam and Eve were humans, not robots. To humankind, God gave the ability to choose between right and wrong, between obedience and disobedience, to make moral decisions. Since this is the way humans were designed, the inability to make such decisions (and not an unwise decision) is what would have indicated imperfection.—Compare Deuteronomy 30:19, 20; Joshua 24:15.

For Adam and Eve to qualify as being created perfect, must all their decisions thereafter be right? That would be the same as saying that they had no choice. But God did not make them in such a way that their obedience would be automatic. God granted them the ability to choose, so that they could obey because they loved him. Or, if they allowed their hearts to become selfish, they would become disobedient. Which means more to you—when someone does something for you because he is *forced* to do it or because he *wants* to?—Compare Deuteronomy 11:1; 1 John 5:3.

How could such perfect humans become selfish, leading to acts of sin? Although created perfect, their physical bodies would not continue to function perfectly if not provided with proper food. So, too, if they let the mind feed on wrong thoughts, this would cause moral deterioration, unholiness. James 1:14, 15 explains: "Each one is tried by being drawn out and enticed by his own desire. Then the desire, when it has become fertile, gives birth to sin." In the case of Eve, the wrong desires began to develop when she listened with interest to Satan, who used a serpent as his mouthpiece. Adam heeded the urging of his wife to join her in eating the forbidden fruit. Instead of rejecting the wrong thoughts, both nourished selfish desires. Acts of sin resulted.—Gen. 3:1-6.

Was Adam's sin part of "God's plan"?

See page 29, under the heading "Adam and Eve," also page 142, under the heading "Fate."

Is there really such a thing as "sin" nowadays?

Illustrations: If a sick man was to break the thermometer, would that prove that he did not have a fever? If a thief said that he did not believe what is written in the lawbooks, would that make him innocent of crime? Similarly, the fact that many people do not believe it is necessary to live according to Bible standards does not put an end to sin.—See 1 John 1:8.

Some people may choose to do what God's Word forbids. But that does not prove the Bible wrong. Galatians 6:7, 8 warns: "Do not be misled: God is not one to be mocked. For whatever a man is sowing, this he will also reap; because he who is sowing with a view to his flesh will reap corruption from his flesh." The epidemic of sexually transmitted diseases, broken homes, and so forth, gives evidence of the truthfulness of what the Bible says. God made man; He knows what will bring us lasting happiness; He tells us in the Bible. Does it not make sense to listen to Him? (For evidence of God's existence, see the main heading "God.")

Is not much of what is called sin simply doing what is natural for humans?

Is sex sinful? Did Adam and Eve sin by having sexual relations with each other? That is not what the Bible says. Genesis 1:28 says that God himself told Adam and Eve to "be fruitful and become many and fill the earth." That would involve sexual relations between them, would it not? And Psalm 127:3 says that "sons are an inheritance from Jehovah," "a reward." It should be noted that Eve ate first of the forbidden fruit and did so when she was by herself; only later did she give some to Adam. (Gen. 3:6) Obviously, the tree on which the forbidden fruit grew was a literal one. What the Bible forbids is not normal sexual relations between husband and wife but practices such as fornication, adultery, homosexuality, and bestiality. The bad fruitage of such practices shows that the prohibition is an evidence of loving concern on the part of the One who knows how we are made.

Gen. 1:27: "God proceeded to create the man [Adam] in his image, in God's image he created him." (The *normal* thing, therefore, was for Adam to reflect God's holy qualities, to respond appreciatively to God's direction. To fall short of this was to miss the mark, to sin. See Romans 3:23, also 1 Peter 1:14-16.)

Eph. 2:1-3: "It is you [Christians] God made alive though you were dead in your trespasses and sins, in which you at one time walked according to the system of things of this world, according to the ruler of the authority of the air, the spirit that now operates in the sons of disobedience. Yes, among them we all at one time conducted ourselves in harmony with the desires of our flesh, doing the things willed by the flesh and the thoughts, and we were naturally children of wrath even as the rest." (As offspring of sinner Adam, we were born in sin. From birth on, the inclination of our heart is toward badness. If we do not curb those wrong tendencies, we may in time become accustomed to such a way of life. It may even seem "normal" because others around us are doing similar things. But the Bible identifies what is right and what is wrong from God's viewpoint, in view of how he made man and his purpose for mankind. If we listen to our Creator and lovingly obey him, life will take on a richness of meaning that we never knew before, and we will have an eternal future. Warmly our Creator invites us to taste and see how good it is.—Ps. 34:8.)

How does sin affect a person's relationship with God?

1 John 3:4, 8: "Everyone who practices sin is also practicing lawlessness, and so sin is lawlessness. He who carries on sin originates with the Devil." (How forceful this is! Those who deliberately choose a course of sin, making a practice of it, are viewed by God as criminals. The course they have chosen is the one that Satan himself first took.)

Rom. 5:8, 10: "While we were yet sinners, Christ died for us. . . . When we were enemies, we became reconciled to God through the death of his Son." (Notice that sinners are referred to as enemies of God. How wise, then, to avail ourselves of the provision that God has made for reconciliation to him!)

1 Tim. 1:13: "I was shown mercy [says the apostle Paul], because I was ignorant and acted with a lack of faith." (But when he was shown the right way by the Lord, he did not hold back from following it.)

2 Cor. 6:1, 2: "Working together with him, we also entreat you not to accept the undeserved kindness of God and miss its purpose. For he says: 'In an acceptable time I heard you, and in a day of salvation I helped you.' Look! Now is the especially acceptable time. Look! Now is the day of salvation." (Now is the time when the opportunity for salvation is available. God will not forever extend toward sinful humans such undeserved kindness. So, care needs to be exercised in order that we do not miss its purpose.)

How is relief from our sinful state possible?

See the main heading "Ransom."

Soul

Definition: In the Bible, "soul" is translated from the Hebrew *ne'phesh* and the Greek *psy·khe'*. Bible usage shows the soul to be a person or an animal or the life that a person or an animal enjoys. To many persons, however, "soul" means the immaterial or spirit part of a human being that survives the death of the physical body. Others understand it to be the principle of life. But these latter views are not Bible teachings.

What does the Bible say that helps us to understand what the soul is?

Gen. 2:7: "Jehovah God proceeded to form the man out of dust from the ground and to blow into his nostrils the breath of life, and the man came to be a living soul." (Notice that this does not say that man *was given* a soul but that he *became* a soul, a living person.) (The part of the Hebrew word here rendered "soul" is *ne'phesh*. KJ, AS, and Dy agree with that rendering. RS, JB, NAB read "being." NE says "creature." Kx reads "person.")

1 Cor. 15:45: "It is even so written: 'The first man Adam became a living soul.' The last Adam became a life-giving spirit." (So the Christian Greek Scriptures agree with the Hebrew Scriptures as to what the soul is.) (The Greek word here translated "soul" is the accusative case of *psy·khe'*. *KJ, AS, Dy, JB, NAB,* and *Kx* also read "soul." *RS, NE,* and *TEV* say "being.")

1 Pet. 3:20: "In Noah's days . . . a few people, that is, eight souls, were carried safely through the water." (The Greek word here translated "souls" is *psy·khai',* the plural form of *psy·khe'. KJ, AS, Dy,* and *Kx* also read "souls." *JB* and *TEV* say "people"; *RS, NE,* and *NAB* use "persons.")

Gen. 9:5: "Besides that, your blood of your souls [or, "lives"; Hebrew, from *ne'phesh*] shall I ask back." (Here the soul is said to have blood.)

Josh. 11:11: "They went striking every soul [Hebrew, *ne'phesh*] that was in it with the edge of the sword." (The soul is here shown to be something that can be touched by the sword, so these souls could not have been spirits.)

Where does the Bible say that animals are souls?

Gen. 1:20, 21, 24, 25: "God went on to say: 'Let the waters swarm forth a swarm of living souls* . . .' And God proceeded to create the great sea monsters and every living soul that moves about, which the waters swarmed forth according to their kinds, and every winged flying creature according to its kind. . . . And God went on to say: 'Let the earth put forth living souls according to their kinds . . .' And God proceeded to make the wild beast of the earth according to its kind and the domestic animal according to its kind and every moving animal of the ground according to its kind." (*In Hebrew the word here is *ne'phesh. Ro* reads "soul." Some translations use the rendering "creature[s].")

Lev. 24:17, 18: "In case a man strikes any soul [Hebrew, *ne'phesh*] of mankind fatally, he should be put to death without fail. And the fatal striker of the soul [Hebrew, *ne'phesh*] of a domestic animal should make compensation for it, soul for soul." (Notice that the same Hebrew word for soul is applied to both mankind and animals.)

Rev. 16:3: "It became blood as of a dead man, and every

living soul* died, yes, the things in the sea." (Thus the Christian Greek Scriptures also show animals to be souls.) (*In Greek the word here is *psy·khe'*. KJ, AS, and Dy render it "soul." Some translators use the term "creature" or "thing.")

Do other scholars who are not Jehovah's Witnesses acknowledge that this is what the Bible says the soul is?

"There is no dichotomy [division] of body and soul in the O[ld] T[estament]. The Israelite saw things concretely, in their totality, and thus he considered men as persons and not as composites. The term *nepeš* [*ne'phesh*], though translated by our word soul, never means soul as distinct from the body or the individual person. . . . The term [*psy·khe'*] is the N[ew] T[estament] word corresponding with *nepeš*. It can mean the principle of life, life itself, or the living being."—*New Catholic Encyclopedia* (1967), Vol. XIII, pp. 449, 450.

"The Hebrew term for 'soul' (*nefesh,* that which breathes) was used by Moses . . . , signifying an 'animated being' and applicable equally to nonhuman beings. . . . New Testament usage of *psychē* ('soul') was comparable to *nefesh.*"—*The New Encyclopædia Britannica* (1976), Macropædia, Vol. 15, p. 152.

"The belief that the soul continues its existence after the dissolution of the body is a matter of philosophical or theological speculation rather than of simple faith, and is accordingly nowhere expressly taught in Holy Scripture."—*The Jewish Encyclopedia* (1910), Vol. VI, p. 564.

Can the human soul die?

Ezek. 18:4: "Look! All the souls—to me they belong. As the soul of the father so likewise the soul of the son—to me they belong. The soul* that is sinning—it itself will die." (*Hebrew reads "the *ne'phesh.*" KJ, AS, RS, NE, and Dy render it "the soul." Some translations say "the man" or "the person.")

Matt. 10:28: "Do not become fearful of those who kill the

body but cannot kill the soul [or, "life"]; but rather be in fear of him that can destroy both soul* and body in Gehenna." (*Greek has the accusative case of *psy·khe'*. *KJ, AS, RS, NE, TEV, Dy, JB,* and *NAB* all render it "soul.")

Acts 3:23: "Indeed, any soul [Greek, *psy·khe'*] that does not listen to that Prophet will be completely destroyed from among the people."

Is it possible for human souls (people) to live forever?

See pages 243-247, under the heading "Life."

Is the soul the same as the spirit?

Eccl. 12:7: "Then the dust returns to the earth just as it happened to be and the spirit [or, life-force; Hebrew, *ru'ach*] itself returns to the true God who gave it." (Notice that the Hebrew word for spirit is *ru'ach;* but the word translated soul is *ne'phesh.* The text does not mean that at death the spirit travels all the way to the personal presence of God; rather, any prospect for the person to live again rests with God. In similar usage, we may say that, if required payments are not made by the buyer of a piece of property, the property "returns" to its owner.) (*KJ, AS, RS, NE,* and *Dy* all here render *ru'ach* as "spirit." *NAB* reads "life breath.")

Eccl. 3:19: "There is an eventuality as respects the sons of mankind and an eventuality as respects the beast, and they have the same eventuality. As the one dies, so the other dies; and they all have but one spirit [Hebrew, *ru'ach*]." (Thus both mankind and beasts are shown to have the same *ru'ach,* or spirit. For comments on verses 20, 21, see page 383.)

Heb. 4:12: "The word of God is alive and exerts power and is sharper than any two-edged sword and pierces even to the dividing of soul [Greek, *psy·khes';* "life," *NE*] and spirit [Greek, *pneu'ma·tos*], and of joints and their marrow, and is able to discern thoughts and intentions of the heart." (Observe that the Greek word for "spirit" is not the same as the word for "soul.")

Does conscious life continue for a person after the spirit leaves the body?

Ps. 146:4: "His spirit [Hebrew, from *ru'ach*] goes out, he goes back to his ground; in that day his thoughts do perish." (*NAB, Ro, Yg,* and *Dy* [145:4] here render *ru'ach* as "spirit." Some translations say "breath.") (Also Psalm 104:29)

What is the origin of Christendom's belief in an immaterial, immortal soul?

"The Christian concept of a spiritual soul created by God and infused into the body at conception to make man a living whole is the fruit of a long development in Christian philosophy. Only with Origen [died c. 254 C.E.] in the East and St. Augustine [died 430 C.E.] in the West was the soul established as a spiritual substance and a philosophical concept formed of its nature.... His [Augustine's] doctrine ... owed much (including some shortcomings) to Neoplatonism."—*New Catholic Encyclopedia* (1967), Vol. XIII, pp. 452, 454.

"The concept of immortality is a product of Greek thinking, whereas the hope of a resurrection belongs to Jewish thought.... Following Alexander's conquests Judaism gradually absorbed Greek concepts."—*Dictionnaire Encyclopédique de la Bible* (Valence, France; 1935), edited by Alexandre Westphal, Vol. 2, p. 557.

"Immortality of the soul is a Greek notion formed in ancient mystery cults and elaborated by the philosopher Plato."—*Presbyterian Life,* May 1, 1970, p. 35.

"Do we believe that there is such a thing as death? ... Is it not the separation of soul and body? And to be dead is the completion of this; when the soul exists in herself, and is released from the body and the body is released from the soul, what is this but death? ... And does the soul admit of death? No. Then the soul is immortal? Yes."—Plato's "Phaedo," Secs. 64, 105, as published in *Great Books of the Western World* (1952), edited by R. M. Hutchins, Vol. 7, pp. 223, 245, 246.

"The problem of immortality, we have seen, engaged the serious attention of the Babylonian theologians.... Neither the people nor the leaders of religious thought ever faced the possibility of the total annihilation of what once was called into existence. Death was a passage to another kind of life." —*The Religion of Babylonia and Assyria* (Boston, 1898), M. Jastrow, Jr., p. 556.

See also pages 100-102, under the heading "Death."

Spirit

Definition: The Hebrew word *ru'ach* and the Greek *pneu'ma*, which are often translated "spirit," have a number of meanings. All of them refer to that which is invisible to human sight and which gives evidence of force in motion. The Hebrew and Greek words are used with reference to (1) wind, (2) the active life-force in earthly creatures, (3) the impelling force that issues from a person's figurative heart and that causes him to say and do things in a certain way, (4) inspired utterances originating with an invisible source, (5) spirit persons, and (6) God's active force, or holy spirit. Several of these usages are here discussed in relation to topics that may arise in the field ministry.

What is the holy spirit?

A comparison of Bible texts that refer to the holy spirit shows that it is spoken of as 'filling' people; they can be 'baptized' with it; and they can be "anointed" with it. (Luke 1:41; Matt. 3:11; Acts 10:38) None of these expressions would be appropriate if the holy spirit were a person.

Jesus also referred to the holy spirit as a "helper" (Greek, *pa·ra'kle·tos*), and he said that this helper would "teach," "bear witness," "speak," and 'hear.' (John 14:16, 17, 26; 15:26; 16:13) It is not unusual in the Scriptures for something to be personified. For example, wisdom is said to have "children." (Luke 7:35) Sin and death are spoken of as being kings. (Rom. 5:14, 21) While some texts say that the spirit "spoke," other passages make clear that this was done through angels or humans. (Acts 4:24, 25; 28:25; Matt. 10:19, 20; compare Acts 20:23 with 21:10, 11.) At 1 John 5:6-8, not only the spirit but also "the water and the blood" are said to 'bear witness.' So, none of the expressions found in these texts in themselves prove that the holy spirit is a person.

The correct identification of the holy spirit must fit *all the scriptures* that refer to that spirit. With this viewpoint, it is logical to conclude that the holy spirit is the active force of God. It is not a person but is a powerful force that God causes to emanate from himself to accomplish his holy will.—Ps. 104:30; 2 Pet. 1:21; Acts 4:31.

See also pages 406, 407, under the heading "Trinity."

What gives evidence that a person really has the holy spirit, or "the Holy Ghost" (*KJ*)?

Luke 4:18, 31-35: "[Jesus read from the scroll of the prophet Isaiah:] 'Jehovah's spirit is upon me, because he anointed me to declare good news' . . . And he went down to Capernaum, a city of Galilee. And he was teaching them on the sabbath; and they were astounded at his way of teaching, because his speech was with authority. Now in the synagogue there was a man with a spirit, an unclean demon, and he shouted with a loud voice . . . But Jesus rebuked it, saying: 'Be silent, and come out of him.' So, after throwing the man down in their midst, the demon came out of him without hurting him." (What gave evidence that Jesus had God's spirit? The account does not say that he trembled or shouted or moved about in a fervor. Rather, it says he spoke with authority. It is noteworthy, however, that on that occasion a *demonic* spirit did move a man to shout and fall onto the floor.)

Acts 1:8 says that when Jesus' followers received holy spirit they would be witnesses about him. According to Acts 2:1-11, when they did receive that spirit, observers were impressed by the fact that, although the ones speaking were all Galileans, they were speaking about the magnificent things of God in languages that were familiar to the many foreigners who were present. But the record does not say that there were any emotional outbursts on the part of those who received the spirit.

It is noteworthy that when Elizabeth received the holy spirit and then gave voice to "a loud cry" she was not in a meeting for worship but was greeting a visiting relative. (Luke 1:41, 42) When, as reported at Acts 4:31, holy spirit came upon an assembly of disciples, *the place* was shaken, but the effect of that spirit on the disciples was, not that they trembled or rolled about, but that they 'spoke the word of God with boldness.' Likewise today, boldness in speaking the word of God, zealously engaging in the work of witnessing —these are what give evidence that a person has holy spirit.

Gal. 5:22, 23: "The fruitage of the spirit is love, joy, peace, long-suffering, kindness, goodness, faith, mildness, self-control." (It is this fruitage, rather than outbursts of religious fervor, that one should look for when seeking to find people who truly have God's spirit.)

Does ability to speak with great emotion in a tongue that a person never studied prove that he has God's spirit?

See the main heading "Tongues, Speaking in."

Is miraculous healing being done in our day by means of the spirit of God?

See the main heading "Healing."

Who is baptized with holy spirit?

See page 56, under "Baptism," also the main heading "Born Again."

Is there a spirit part of man that survives the death of the body?

Ezek. 18:4: "The soul that is sinning—it itself will die." (*RS, NE, KJ,* and *Dy* all render the Hebrew word *ne'phesh* in this verse as "soul," thus saying that it is *the soul* that dies. Some translations that render *ne'phesh* as "soul" in other passages use the expression "the man" or "the one" in this verse. So, the *ne'phesh,* the soul, is the person, not an immaterial part of him that survives when his body dies.) (See the main heading "Soul" for further details.)

Ps. 146:4: "His spirit goes out, he goes back to his ground;

in that day his thoughts do perish." (The Hebrew word here translated "spirit" is a derivative of *ru'ach.* Some translators render it "breath." When that *ru'ach,* or active life-force, leaves the body, the person's thoughts perish; they do not continue in another realm.)

Eccl. 3:19-21: "There is an eventuality as respects the sons of mankind and an eventuality as respects the beast, and they have the same eventuality. As the one dies, so the other dies; and they all have but one spirit, so that there is no superiority of the man over the beast, for everything is vanity. All are going to one place. They have all come to be from the dust, and they are all returning to the dust. Who is there knowing the spirit of the sons of mankind, whether it is ascending upward; and the spirit of the beast, whether it is descending downward to the earth?" (Because of the inheritance of sin and death from Adam, humans all die and return to the dust, as animals do. But does each human have a spirit that goes on living as an intelligent personality after it ceases to function in the body? No; verse 19 answers that humans and beasts "all have but one spirit." Based merely on human observation, no one can authoritatively answer the question raised in verse 21 regarding the spirit. But God's Word answers that there is nothing that humans have as a result of birth that gives them superiority over beasts when they die. However, because of God's merciful provision through Christ, the prospect of living forever has been opened up to humans who exercise faith, but not to animals. For many of mankind, that will be made possible by resurrection, when active life-force from God will invigorate them again.)

Luke 23:46: "Jesus called with a loud voice and said: 'Father, into your hands I entrust my spirit [Greek, *pneu'ma'*].' When he had said this, he expired." (Notice that Jesus expired. When his spirit went out he was not on his way to heaven. Not until the third day from this was Jesus resurrected from the dead. Then, as Acts 1:3, 9 shows, it was 40 more days before he ascended to heaven. So, what is the meaning of what Jesus said at the time of his death? He was saying that he knew that, when he died, his future life prospects rested entirely with God. For further comments regarding the 'spirit that returns to God,' see page 378, under the heading "Soul.")

If Someone Says—

'Do you have the holy spirit (or the Holy Ghost)?'

You might reply: 'Yes, and that is why I have come to your door today. (Acts 2:17, 18)'

Or you could say: 'That is what makes it possible for me to share in the Christian ministry. But I find that not everyone has the same idea as to what gives evidence that a person really has God's spirit. What do you look for?' **Then perhaps add:** (Discussion of some of the material on pages 381, 382.)

Spiritism

Definition: Belief that a spirit part of humans survives death of the physical body and can communicate with the living, usually through a person who serves as a medium. Some people believe that every material object and all natural phenomena have indwelling spirits. Sorcery is the use of power that is acknowledged to be from evil spirits. *All forms of spiritism are strongly condemned in the Bible.*

Is it really possible for a human to communicate with the "spirit" of a dead loved one?

Eccl. 9:5, 6, 10: "The living are conscious that they will die; but as for the dead, they are conscious of nothing at all . . . Also, their love and their hate and their jealousy have already perished, and they have no portion anymore to time indefinite in anything that has to be done under the sun. All that your hand finds to do, do with your very power, for there is no work nor devising nor knowledge nor wisdom in Sheol [the grave], the place to which you are going."

Ezek. 18:4, 20: "The soul that is sinning—it itself will die." (So the soul is not something that survives the death of the body and with which living humans can thereafter communicate.)

Ps. 146:4: "His spirit goes out, he goes back to his ground; in that day his thoughts do perish." (When the spirit is said to 'go out' of the body, this is merely another way of saying that the life-force has ceased to be active. Thus, after a person dies, his spirit does not exist as an immaterial being that can think and carry out plans apart from the body. It is not something with which the living can communicate after a person's death.)

See also pages 100-102, under the heading "Death."

Does not the Bible indicate that King Saul communicated with the prophet Samuel after Samuel's death?

The account is found at 1 Samuel 28:3-20. Verses 13, 14 show that Saul himself did not see Samuel but only assumed from the description given by the spirit medium that she saw Samuel. Saul desperately wanted to believe that it was Samuel and so let himself be deceived. Verse 3 says that Samuel was dead and buried. The scriptures quoted under the preceding subheading make clear that there was no part of Samuel that was alive in another realm and able to communicate with Saul. The voice that pretended to be that of Samuel was that of an impostor.

With whom are those who endeavor to speak with the dead actually communicating?

The truth about the condition of the dead is clearly stated in the Bible. But who tried to deceive the first human pair about death? Satan contradicted God's warning that disobedience would bring death. (Gen. 3:4; Rev. 12:9) In time, of course, it became obvious that humans did die as God said they would. Reasonably, then, who was responsible for inventing the idea that humans really do not die but that some spirit part of man survives the death of the body? Such a deception fits Satan the Devil, whom Jesus described as "the father of the lie." (John 8:44; see also 2 Thessalonians 2:

9, 10.) Belief that the dead are really alive in another realm and that we can communicate with them has not benefited mankind. On the contrary, Revelation 18:23 says that, by means of the spiritistic practices of Babylon the Great, "all the nations were misled." The spiritistic practice of 'talking with the dead' is actually a fraudulent deception that can put people in contact with the demons (angels that became selfish rebels against God) and often leads to a person's hearing unwanted voices and being harassed by those wicked spirits.

Is there harm in seeking healing or protection by spiritistic means?

Gal. 5:19-21: "The works of the flesh are manifest, and they are fornication, uncleanness, loose conduct, idolatry, practice of spiritism . . . As to these things I am forewarning you, the same way as I did forewarn you, that those who practice such things will not inherit God's kingdom." (Resorting to spiritism for help means that a person believes Satan's lies about death; he is seeking advice from people who endeavor to draw power from Satan and his demons. Such a person thus identifies himself with those who are avowed enemies of Jehovah God. Instead of being truly helped, anyone persisting in such a course suffers lasting harm.)

Luke 9:24: "Whoever wants to save his soul [or, life] will lose it; but whoever loses his soul for my sake [because he is a follower of Jesus Christ] is the one that will save it." (If a person deliberately violates the clearly stated commands of God's Word in an endeavor to safeguard or preserve his present life, he will lose out on the prospect of eternal life. How foolish!)

2 Cor. 11:14, 15: "Satan himself keeps transforming himself into an angel of light. It is therefore nothing great if his ministers also keep transforming themselves into ministers of righteousness." (So we should not be misled when some of the things done by spiritistic means seem to be temporarily of benefit.)

See also pages 156-160, under "Healing."

Is it wise to resort to spiritistic means to learn what the future holds or to assure oneself of success in some undertaking?

Isa. 8:19: "In case they should say to you people: 'Apply to the spiritistic mediums or to those having a spirit of prediction who are chirping and making utterances in low tones,' is it not to its God that any people should apply?"

Lev. 19:31: "Do not turn yourselves to the spirit mediums, and do not consult professional foretellers of events, so as to become unclean by them. I am Jehovah your God."

2 Ki. 21:6: "[King Manasseh] practiced magic and looked for omens and made spirit mediums and professional foretellers of events. He did on a large scale what was bad in Jehovah's eyes, to offend him." (Such spiritistic practices actually involved turning to Satan and his demons for help. No wonder it was "bad in Jehovah's eyes," and he brought severe punishment upon Manasseh for it. But when he repented and gave up these bad practices, he was blessed by Jehovah.)

What harm can there be in playing games that involve a form of divination or in seeking the meaning of something that seems to be an omen of good?

Deut. 18:10-12: "There should not be found in you anyone who . . . employs divination, a practicer of magic or anyone who looks for omens or a sorcerer, or one who binds others with a spell or anyone who consults a spirit medium or a professional foreteller of events or anyone who inquires of the dead. For everybody doing these things is something detestable to Jehovah." (Divination seeks to disclose hidden knowledge or to foretell events, not as a result of research, but by the interpretation of omens or by the help of supernatural powers. Jehovah prohibited such practices among his servants. Why? All these practices are an invitation to communication with or possession by unclean spirits, or demons. Engaging in such things would be gross unfaithfulness toward Jehovah.)

Acts 16:16-18: "A certain servant girl with a spirit, a

demon of divination, met us. She used to furnish her masters with much gain by practicing the art of prediction." (Obviously, no one who loves righteousness would consult such a source of information, whether with serious intent or as a game. Paul tired of her crying out, and he ordered the spirit to come out of her.)

Are wicked spirits able to take on human form?

In the days of Noah, disobedient angels did take on human form. They actually married, and they fathered children. (Gen. 6:1-4) However, when the Flood came, those angels were forced back into the spirit realm. Regarding them, Jude 6 says: "The angels that did not keep their original position but forsook their own proper dwelling place he has reserved with eternal bonds under dense darkness for the judgment of the great day." Not only did God abase them from their former heavenly privileges and consign them to dense darkness regarding Jehovah's purposes, but the reference to bonds indicates that he has restrained them. From what? Evidently, from taking on physical bodies so they could have relations with women, as they had done before the Flood. The Bible reports that faithful angels, as messengers of God, did materialize in the performance of their duties down until the first century C.E. But following the Flood, those angels that had misused their gifts were deprived of the ability to take on human form.

It is of interest, however, that demons apparently can cause humans to see visions, and what they see may appear to be real. When the Devil tempted Jesus, he evidently made use of such means in order to show Jesus "all the kingdoms of the world and their glory."—Matt. 4:8.

How can a person be freed from spiritistic influence?

Prov. 18:10: "The name of Jehovah is a strong tower. Into it the righteous runs and is given protection." (This does not mean that use of God's personal name serves as a charm to ward off evil. The "name" of Jehovah represents the Person himself. We are protected when we come to know him and put our full trust in him, submitting to his authority and obeying his commands. If we do this, then when we call out to him for help, using his personal name, he provides the protection that he has promised in his Word.)

Matt. 6:9-13: "You must pray, then, this way: '... Do not bring us into temptation, but deliver us from the wicked one.'" You must also "persevere in prayer." (Rom. 12:12) (God hears such prayers from those who truly desire to know the truth and to worship him in a manner that is pleasing to him.)

1 Cor. 10:21: "You cannot be partaking of 'the table of Jehovah' and the table of demons." (Those who want Jehovah's friendship and protection must break off all participation in spiritistic meetings. In harmony with the example recorded at Acts 19:19, it is also important to destroy or properly dispose of all objects in one's possession that relate to spiritism.)

Jas. 4:7: "Subject yourselves, therefore, to God; but oppose the Devil, and he will flee from you." (To do this, be diligent to learn God's will and to apply it in your life. With love for God fortifying you against fear of man, firmly refuse to share in any customs related to spiritism or to obey any rules laid down by a spiritist.)

Put on "the complete suit of armor from God" that is described in Ephesians 6:10-18 and be zealous about keeping every part of it in good condition.

Spirit of the World

Definition: The impelling force that influences human society made up of those who are not servants of Jehovah God, causing such people to say and do things according to a characteristic pattern. Although people act on individual preferences, those who manifest the spirit of the world give evidence of certain basic attitudes, ways of doing things, and aims in life that are common to the present system of things of which Satan is ruler and god.

Why is being tainted by the spirit of the world a matter of serious concern?

1 John 5:19: "The whole world is lying in the power of the wicked one." (Satan has fostered a spirit that dominates the thinking and activities of those of mankind who are not Jehovah's approved servants. It is a spirit of selfishness and pride that is so pervasive that it is like the air that humans breathe. We need to exercise great care not to submit to Satan's power by letting that spirit mold our lives.)

Rev. 12:9: "Down the great dragon was hurled, the original serpent, the one called Devil and Satan, who is misleading the entire inhabited earth; he was hurled down to the earth, and his angels were hurled down with him." (Ever since this took place, following the birth of the Kingdom in 1914, the influence of Satan and his demons has intensified greatly among mankind. His spirit has goaded people to acts of increased selfishness and violence. Especially do those who seek to serve Jehovah come under great pressure to be a part of the world, to do what others do, and to abandon true worship.)

What are some of the characteristics of the spirit of the world against which we need to be on guard?

1 Cor. 2:12: "Now we received, not the spirit of the world, but the spirit which is from God, that we might know the things that have been kindly given us by God." (If the spirit of the world takes root in a person's thinking and desires, its fruitage is soon seen in actions that manifest that spirit. So, breaking free from the spirit of the world requires not only avoiding unchristian activities and excesses but also getting to the root of the matter by cultivating attitudes that reflect *God's* spirit and genuine love for his ways. This you should keep in mind as you consider the following manifestations of the spirit of the world.)

Doing what a person wants to do, without regard for the will of God

Satan urged Eve to decide for herself what was good and

what was bad. (Gen. 3:3-5; in contrast see Proverbs 3:5, 6.) Many who follow Eve's course do not know what God's will for mankind is, nor are they interested in finding out. They just "do their own thing," as they say. Those who know God's requirements and try to conform to them need to be careful that the world's spirit does not cause them deliberately to ignore the counsel of God's Word in what they may view as "little things."—Luke 16:10; see also "Independence."

Reacting to situations on the basis of pride

It was Satan who first allowed an overestimation of self to corrupt his heart. (Compare Ezekiel 28:17; Proverbs 16:5.) Pride is a divisive force in the world of which he is ruler, causing people to consider themselves better than those of other races, nations, language groups, and economic status. Even those serving God may need to root out remnants of such feelings. They also need to be on guard so that pride does not cause them to make major issues of minor matters, or become a barrier to their acknowledging their own faults and accepting counsel and thus benefiting from much loving help that Jehovah provides through his organization.—Rom. 12:3; 1 Pet. 5:5.

Manifesting a rebellious attitude toward authority

Rebellion began with Satan, whose name means "Resister." By his defiance of Jehovah, Nimrod, whose name may mean "Let Us Rebel," demonstrated that he was a child of Satan. Avoiding that spirit will prevent God-fearing persons from becoming defiant of secular rulers (Rom. 13:1); it will help minors to submit to the God-given authority of their parents (Col. 3:20); it will be a safeguard against sympathizing with apostates, who disrespect those whom Jehovah has entrusted with responsibility in his visible organization. —Jude 11; Heb. 13:17.

Giving free rein to the desires of the fallen flesh

The influence of this can be seen and heard everywhere. There is a need constantly to be on guard against it. (1 John 2:16; Eph. 4:17, 19; Gal. 5:19-21) The thinking and the desires that may lead to more serious evidences of it may be manifest in a person's conversation, the jokes he tells, the lyrics of music to which he listens, the kind of dancing he does, or in his watching shows that feature immoral sex. This aspect of the world's spirit shows itself in drug abuse, drunkenness, adultery, fornication, and homosexuality. It also is manifest when a person unscripturally, but perhaps legally, divorces one mate and takes another.—Mal. 2:16.

Allowing one's life to be dominated by the desire to possess what one sees

It was such a desire that Satan cultivated in Eve, enticing her to do something that ruined her relationship with God. (Gen. 3:6; 1 John 2:16) Jesus firmly rejected such a temptation. (Matt. 4:8-10) Those who want to please Jehovah need to be on guard so that they do not allow the commercial world to develop such a spirit in them. Much grief and spiritual ruin result to those ensnared by it.—Matt. 13:22; 1 Tim. 6:7-10.

Showing off one's possessions and supposed attainments

This practice, too, "originates with the world" and needs to be abandoned by those who become servants of God. (1 John 2:16) It is rooted in pride, and instead of building up others spiritually, it dangles material enticements and visions of worldly achievement before them.—Rom. 15:2.

Giving vent to one's emotions in abusive speech and violent acts

These are "works of the flesh" against which many persons have to put up a hard fight. With genuine faith and the help of God's spirit they can conquer the world rather than let its spirit dominate them.—Gal. 5:19, 20, 22, 23; Eph. 4:31; 1 Cor. 13:4-8; 1 John 5:4.

Basing one's hopes and fears on what humans are able to do

A physical man considers what he can see and touch to be what really counts. His hopes and fears revolve around the promises and threats of other men. He looks to human rulers for help and is disillusioned when they fail. (Ps. 146:3, 4; Isa.

8:12, 13) To him, this life is all there is. Threats of death easily enslave him. (In contrast, see Matthew 10:28; Hebrews 2:14, 15.) But a new force actuates the minds of people who get to know Jehovah, those who fill their minds and hearts with his promises and who learn to turn to him for help in every time of need.—Eph. 4:23, 24; Ps. 46:1; 68:19.

Giving to humans and things the worshipful honor that belongs to God

"The god of this system of things," Satan the Devil, encourages all sorts of practices that misdirect man's God-given inclination to worship. (2 Cor. 4:4) Some rulers have been treated as gods. (Acts 12:21-23) Millions bow before idols. Millions more idolize actors and outstanding athletes. Celebrations frequently give undue honor to individual humans. So common is this spirit that those who truly love Jehovah and want to give him exclusive devotion need to be alert to its influence every day.

Suffering

Definition: The experience undergone by a person when enduring pain or distress. The suffering may be physical, mental, or emotional. Many things can cause suffering; for example, the damage done as a result of war and of commercial greed, adverse hereditary factors, illness, accidents, "natural disasters," unkind things said or done by others, demonic pressures, an awareness of impending calamity, or one's own foolishness. Suffering that results from these various causes will be considered here. However, suffering may also be experienced because of a person's sensitivity to the plight of other people or his grief at observing ungodly conduct.

Why does God permit suffering?

Who really is to blame for it?

Humans are to blame for much of the suffering. They fight wars, commit crimes, pollute the environment, often carry on business in a manner motivated by greed rather than concern for their fellowman, and sometimes indulge in habits that they know can be harmful to their health. When they do these things, they hurt others and themselves. Should it be expected that humans would be immune to the consequences of what they do? (Gal. 6:7; Prov. 1:30-33) Is it reasonable to blame God for these things that humans themselves do?

Satan and his demons also share responsibility. The Bible discloses that much suffering is because of the influence of wicked spirits. The suffering for which so many people blame God does not come from him at all.—Rev. 12:12; Acts 10:38; see also pages 363, 364, under the heading "Satan the Devil."

How did suffering get started? Examination of the causes focuses attention on our first human parents, Adam and Eve. Jehovah God created them perfect and put them in paradise surroundings. If they had obeyed God, they would never have got sick or died. They could have enjoyed perfect human life forever. Suffering was not part of Jehovah's purpose for mankind. But Jehovah clearly told Adam that continued enjoyment of what He had given them depended on obedience. Obviously, they had to breathe, eat, drink, and sleep in order to continue living. And they had to keep God's moral requirements in order to enjoy life fully and to be favored with such life forever. But they chose to go their own way, to set their own standards of good and bad, and thus they turned away from God, the Life-Giver. (Gen. 2: 16, 17; 3:1-6) Sin led to death. It was as sinners that Adam and Eve produced children, and they could not pass on to their children what they no longer had. All were born in sin, with inclinations toward wrongdoing, weaknesses that could lead to illness, a sinful inheritance that would eventually result in death. Because everyone on earth today was born in sin, all of us experience suffering in various ways.—Gen. 8:21; Rom. 5:12.

Ecclesiastes 9:11 says that *"time and unforeseen occurrence"* also have a bearing on what happens to us. We may get hurt, not because the Devil directly causes it or because any human does it, but because by chance we are in a place at the wrong moment.

Why does God not do something to bring relief to mankind? Why should we all suffer for something that Adam did?

In the Bible, God tells us how we can avoid much suffering. He has provided the very best counsel on living. When applied, this fills our lives with meaning, results in happy family life, brings us into close association with people who really love one another, and safeguards us against practices that can bring much needless physical suffering. If we ignore that help, is it fair to blame God for the trouble that we bring upon ourselves and others?—2 Tim. 3:16, 17; Ps. 119:97-105.

Jehovah has made provision to end all suffering. He created the first human pair perfect, and he lovingly made every provision so that life would be pleasant for them. When they deliberately turned their backs on God, was God obligated to intervene so as to shield their children from the effects of what the parents had done? (Deut. 32:4, 5; Job 14:4) As we well know, married couples may have the joys that go with producing children, but they also have responsibilities. The attitudes and actions of parents affect their children. Nevertheless, Jehovah, as an expression of marvelous undeserved kindness, sent his own dearly loved Son to earth to lay down his life as a ransom, to provide relief for those of Adam's offspring who would appreciatively exercise faith in this provision. (John 3:16) As a result, the opportunity is open to people living today to have what Adam lost —perfect human life, free from suffering, in a paradise earth. What a generous provision that is!

See also pages 306-308, under "Ransom."

But why would a God of love allow the suffering to continue so long?

Have we benefited because he has allowed it until now? "Jehovah is not slow respecting his promise, as some people consider slowness, but he is patient with you because he does not desire any to be destroyed but desires all to attain to repentance." (2 Pet. 3:9) If God had immediately executed Adam and Eve, following their sin, none of us would be in existence today. Surely that is not what we would want. Moreover, had God at some later time destroyed all who were sinners, we would not have been born. The fact that God has allowed this sinful world to exist until now has afforded us the opportunity to be alive and learn his ways, to make needed changes in our lives, and to avail ourselves of his loving provisions for eternal life. That Jehovah has granted us this opportunity is an evidence of great love on his part. The Bible shows that God has a set time to destroy this wicked system and will do so soon.—Hab. 2:3; Zeph. 1:14.

God can and will undo all the harm that may come upon his servants in this system of things. God is not the one who is causing the suffering. But by means of Jesus Christ, God will raise the dead, heal obedient ones of all their illnesses, root out every trace of sin, and even cause former grief to fade from our minds.—John 5:28, 29; Rev. 21:4; Isa. 65:17.

The time that has elapsed has been needed to settle the issues that were raised in Eden. For details, see pages 363, 364, also 428-430.

We personally are anxious to have relief. But when God takes action, it must be in behalf of *all* who love what is right, not just a few. God is not partial.—Acts 10:34.

Illustrations: Is it not true that a loving parent may allow a child to undergo a painful operation because of beneficial results that can come from it? Also, is it not true that "quick solutions" to painful ailments are often only superficial? More time is frequently needed in order to eliminate the cause.

Why did God not forgive Adam and so prevent the terrible suffering experienced by mankind?

Would that really have prevented suffering or would it, instead, have made God responsible for it? What happens when a father simply overlooks deliberate wrongdoing on the part of his children rather than take firm disciplinary measures? The children often get involved in first one form of wrongdoing and then another, and much of the responsibility lies with the father.

Similarly, if Jehovah had forgiven Adam's deliberate sin, it would really have made God a party to the wrongdoing. That would not have improved conditions on earth at all. (Compare Ecclesiastes 8:11.) Furthermore, it would have resulted in disrespect for God on the part of his angelic sons, and it would mean that there was no real basis for hope of anything better. But such a situation could never have occurred, because righteousness is an unalterable foundation of Jehovah's rulership.—Ps. 89:14.

Why does God allow children to be born with serious physical and mental defects?

God does not cause such defects. He created the first human pair perfect, with the ability to bring forth perfect children in their own likeness.—Gen. 1:27, 28.

We have inherited sin from Adam. That inheritance carries with it the potential for physical and mental defects. (Rom. 5:12; for further details see page 394.) This inheritance of sin is with us from the time of conception in the womb. It is for that reason that King David wrote: "In sin my mother conceived me." (Ps. 51:5) If Adam had not sinned, there would be only desirable traits to transmit. (For comments on John 9:1, 2, see page 319.)

Parents can harm their unborn offspring—for example, by drug abuse or by smoking during pregnancy. Of course, it is not true that in every case the mother or the father is responsible for birth defects or poor health of their child.

Jehovah lovingly extends to children the benefits of Christ's ransom sacrifice. Out of consideration for parents who faithfully serve God, he views their young children as holy. (1 Cor. 7:14) This motivates God-fearing parents to be careful about their own standing with God, out of loving concern for their offspring. To young ones who are old enough to exercise faith and demonstrate obedience to God's commands, Jehovah extends the privilege of having an approved standing as his servants. (Ps. 119:9; 148:12, 13; Acts 16:1-3) It is noteworthy that Jesus, who was a perfect reflection of his Father, showed special interest in the welfare of young ones, even raising a child from the dead. Surely he will continue to do that as Messianic King.—Matt. 19:13-15; Luke 8:41, 42, 49-56.

Why does God permit "natural disasters," which cause extensive damage to property and life?

God is not causing the earthquakes, hurricanes, floods, droughts, and volcanic eruptions that are so often in today's news. He is not using these to bring punishment on certain peoples. To a large extent, these are caused by natural forces that have been operating since the earth's creation. The Bible foretold great earthquakes and food shortages for our day, but that does not mean that either God or Jesus is responsible for them, any more than a meteorologist is responsible for the weather that he forecasts. Because these are occurring along with all the other things foretold in the composite sign of the conclusion of this system of things, they are part of the evidence that the blessings of God's Kingdom are near.—Luke 21:11, 31.

Humans often bear heavy responsibility for harm done. In what way? Even when given ample warning, many people refuse to get out of the danger area or fail to take needed precautions.—Prov. 22:3; compare Matthew 24:37-39.

God can control such natural forces. He empowered Jesus Christ to calm a storm on the Sea of Galilee, as an example of what He will do for mankind under His Messianic Kingdom. (Mark 4:37-41) By turning his back on God, Adam rejected such divine intervention on behalf of himself and his offspring. Those who are granted life during Christ's Messianic Reign will experience such loving care, the kind of care that only a government empowered by God can give. —Isa. 11:9.

Are people who suffer adversity being punished by God because of wickedness?

Those who violate godly standards of living do experience bad effects. (Gal. 6:7) Sometimes they reap a bitter harvest quickly. In other instances, they may seem to prosper for a long time. In contrast, Jesus Christ, who never did wrong, was cruelly mistreated and put to death. So, in this system of things prosperity should not be viewed as proof of God's blessing, nor should adversity be considered proof of his disapproval.

When Job lost his possessions and was afflicted with loathsome disease, that was not because of God's disapproval. The Bible clearly says that Satan was responsible. (Job 2:3, 7, 8) But companions who came to visit Job argued that Job's plight must prove that he had done something wicked. (Job 4:7-9; 15:6, 20-24) Jehovah reproved them, saying: "My anger has grown hot against you . . . for you men have not spoken concerning me what is truthful as has my servant Job."—Job 42:7.

Wicked ones may, in fact, prosper for a while. Asaph wrote: "I became envious of the boasters, when I would see the very peace of wicked people. They are not even in the trouble of mortal man, and they are not plagued the same as other men. They scoff and speak about what is bad; about defrauding they speak in an elevated style. Look! These are the wicked, who are at ease indefinitely. They have increased their means of maintenance."—Ps. 73:3, 5, 8, 12.

The day of accounting with God will come. At that time he will punish the wicked, destroying them forever. Proverbs 2:21, 22 says: "The upright are the ones that will reside in the earth, and the blameless are the ones that will be left over in it. As regards the wicked, they will be cut off from the very earth; and as for the treacherous, they will be torn away from it." Then the upright ones, many of whom have suffered adversity, will enjoy perfect health and a generous share of earth's abundant produce.

If Someone Says—

'Why does God permit all this suffering?'

You might reply: 'That is a matter that deeply concerns all of us. May I ask, What makes you bring it up today?' **Then perhaps add:** (1) '(Use material from pages 393-396.)' (2) '(Bring in other scriptures that hold out relief from the specific kind of situation that has brought suffering to the individual personally.)'

Or you could say (if their concern is because of the injustices of the world): 'The Bible shows why these conditions exist today. (Eccl. 4:1; 8:9) Did you know that it also shows what God is going to do to bring us relief? (Ps. 72: 12, 14; Dan. 2:44)'

Another possibility: 'Evidently you are a person who believes in God. Do you believe that God is love? . . . Do you believe that he is wise and that he is almighty? . . . Then he must have some good reasons for permitting suffering. The Bible shows what those reasons are. (See page 393-396.)'

Tongues, Speaking in

Definition: A special ability given through the holy spirit to some disciples in the early Christian congregation that enabled them to preach or otherwise glorify God in a language other than their own.

Does the Bible say that all who would have God's spirit would "speak in tongues"?

1 Cor. 12:13, 30: "Truly by one spirit we were all baptized into one body . . . Not all have gifts of healings, do they? Not all speak in tongues, do they?" (Also 1 Corinthians 14:26)

1 Cor. 14:5: "Now I would like for all of you to speak in tongues, but I prefer that you prophesy. Indeed, he that prophesies is greater than he that speaks in tongues, unless, in fact, he translates, that the congregation may receive upbuilding."

Does ecstatic speech in a language that a person never learned prove that he has holy spirit?

Can the ability to "speak in tongues" come from a source other than the true God?

1 John 4:1: "Beloved ones, do not believe every inspired

expression ["every spirit," *KJ, RS*], but test the inspired expressions to see whether they originate with God." (See also Matthew 7:21-23; 2 Corinthians 11:14, 15.)

Among those 'speaking in tongues' today are Pentecostals and Baptists, also Roman Catholics, Episcopalians, Methodists, Lutherans, and Presbyterians. Jesus said that the holy spirit would 'guide his disciples into all the truth.' (John 16:13) Do the members of each of these religions believe that the others who also "speak in tongues" have been guided into "all the truth"? How could that be, since they are not all in agreement? What spirit is making it possible for them to "speak in tongues"?

A joint statement by the Fountain Trust and the Church of England Evangelical Council admitted: "We are also aware that a similar phenomenon can occur under occult/demonic influence." (*Gospel and Spirit,* April 1977, published by the Fountain Trust and the Church of England Evangelical Council, p. 12) The book *Religious Movements in Contemporary America* (edited by Irving I. Zaretsky and Mark P. Leone, quoting L. P. Gerlach) reports that in Haiti 'speaking in tongues' is characteristic of both Pentecostal and Voodoo religions.—(Princeton, N.J.; 1974), p. 693; see also 2 Thessalonians 2:9, 10.

Is the 'speaking in tongues' that is done today the same as that done by first-century Christians?

In the first century, the miraculous gifts of the spirit, including the ability to "speak in tongues," verified that God's favor had shifted from the Jewish system of worship to the newly established Christian congregation. (Heb. 2: 2-4) Since that objective was accomplished in the first century, is it necessary to prove the same thing again and again in our day?

In the first century, the ability to "speak in tongues" gave impetus to the international work of witnessing that Jesus had commissioned his followers to do. (Acts 1:8; 2:1-11; Matt. 28:19) Is that how those who "speak in tongues" use that ability today?

In the first century, when Christians 'spoke in tongues,' what they said had meaning to people who knew those languages. (Acts 2:4, 8) Today, is it not true that 'speaking in tongues' usually involves an ecstatic outburst of unintelligible sounds?

In the first century, the Bible shows, congregations were to limit the 'speaking in tongues' to two or three persons who might do that at any given meeting; they were to do it "each in turn," and if there was no interpreter present they were to keep silent. (1 Cor. 14:27, 28, *RS*) Is that what is being done today?

See also pages 381, 382, under the heading "Spirit."

Might the holy spirit be directing charismatics into practices that reach beyond what is found in the Scriptures?

2 Tim. 3:16, 17: "All Scripture is inspired of God and beneficial for teaching, for reproving, for setting things straight, for disciplining in righteousness, that the man of God may be fully competent, completely equipped for every good work." (If someone claims to have an inspired message that conflicts with revelations made by God's spirit through Jesus and his apostles, could it possibly be from the same source?)

Gal. 1:8: "Even if we or an angel out of heaven were to declare to you as good news something beyond ["at variance with," *NE*] what we declared to you as good news, let him be accursed."

Does the way of life of members of organizations that look with favor on 'speaking in tongues' give evidence that they have God's spirit?

As a group do they outstandingly manifest such fruits of the spirit as mildness and self-control? Are these qualities readily evident to persons who attend their meetings for worship?—Gal. 5:22, 23.

Are they truly "no part of the world"? Because of this do they give full devotion to the Kingdom of God or are they involved in the world's political affairs? Have they remained clean of bloodguilt during wartime? As a group do they have a fine reputation because of avoiding the world's immoral conduct?—John 17:16; Isa. 2:4; 1 Thess. 4:3-8.

Are true Christians today identified by the ability to "speak in tongues"?

John 13:35: "By this all will know that you are my disciples, if you have love among yourselves."

1 Cor. 13:1, 8: "If I speak in the tongues of men and of angels but do not have love, I have become a sounding piece of brass or a clashing cymbal. Love never fails. But whether there are gifts of prophesying, they will be done away with; whether there are tongues, they will cease."

Jesus said that holy spirit would come upon his followers and that they would be witnesses of him to the most distant part of the earth. (Acts 1:8) He instructed them to "make disciples of people of all the nations." (Matt. 28:19) He also foretold that 'this good news of the kingdom would be preached in all the inhabited earth for a witness to all nations.' (Matt. 24:14) Who today, both as a group and individually, are doing this work? In harmony with what Jesus said, should we not look for this as an evidence that a group has holy spirit?

Is 'speaking in tongues' to continue until that which is "perfect" comes?

At 1 Corinthians 13:8 reference is made to several miraculous gifts—prophecy, tongues, and knowledge. Verse 9 again refers to two of these gifts—knowledge and prophecy —saying: "For we know in part, and we prophesy in part." (*KJ*) Or, as *RS* reads: "For our knowledge is imperfect and our prophecy is imperfect." Then verse 10 states: "But when that which is perfect is come, then that which is in part shall be done away." (*KJ*) The word "perfect" is translated from the Greek *te'lei·on,* which conveys the thought of being full grown, complete, or perfect. *Ro, By,* and *NW* here render it "complete." Notice that it is not the gift of tongues that is said to be "imperfect," "in part," or partial. That is said of "prophecy" and "knowledge." In other words, even with those miraculous gifts, the early Christians had only an imperfect or partial understanding of God's purpose. But when the prophecies would come to fulfillment, when God's purpose would be accomplished, then "that which is perfect," or complete, would come. So, this is obviously not discussing how long the 'gift of tongues' would continue.

However, the Bible does indicate how long the 'gift of tongues' would be a part of Christian experience. According to the record, this gift and the other gifts of the spirit were always conveyed to persons by the laying on of hands of the apostles of Jesus Christ or in their presence. (Acts 2:4, 14, 17; 10:44-46; 19:6; see also Acts 8:14-18.) Thus, after their death and when the individuals who in that way had received the gifts died, the miraculous gifts resulting from the operation of God's spirit must have come to their end. Such a view agrees with the purpose of those gifts as stated at Hebrews 2:2-4.

Does not Mark 16:17, 18 (KJ) show that the ability to "speak with new tongues" would be a sign identifying believers?

It should be noted that these verses refer not only to 'speaking with new tongues' but also to handling serpents and drinking deadly poison. Are all who "speak in tongues" also encouraging these practices?

For comments on the reasons why these verses are not accepted by all Bible scholars, see pages 158, 159, under the heading "Healing."

If Someone Says—

'Do you believe in speaking in tongues?'

You might reply: 'Jehovah's Witnesses do speak many languages, but we do not engage in ecstatic speaking in "unknown tongues." But may I ask, Do you believe that the "speaking in tongues" that is done today is the same as what was practiced by first-century Christians?' **Then perhaps add:** 'Here are some points of comparison that I found to be very interesting. (Perhaps use material from pages 401, 402.)'

Or you could say: 'We do believe that first-century Christians "spoke in tongues" and that this filled definite needs back then. Do you know what those needs were?'

Then perhaps add: (1) 'It served as a sign that God had shifted his favor from the Jewish system to the newly formed Christian congregation. (Heb. 2:2-4)' (2) 'It was a practical means to spread the good news on an international scale in a short time. (Acts 1:8)'

Trinity

Definition: The central doctrine of religions of Christendom. According to the Athanasian Creed, there are three divine Persons (the Father, the Son, the Holy Ghost), each said to be eternal, each said to be almighty, none greater or less than another, each said to be God, and yet together being but one God. Other statements of the dogma emphasize that these three "Persons" are not separate and distinct individuals but are three modes in which the divine essence exists. Thus some Trinitarians emphasize their belief that Jesus Christ is God, or that Jesus and the Holy Ghost are Jehovah. *Not a Bible teaching.*

What is the origin of the Trinity doctrine?

The New Encyclopædia Britannica says: "Neither the word Trinity, nor the explicit doctrine as such, appears in the New Testament, nor did Jesus and his followers intend to contradict the Shema in the Old Testament: 'Hear, O Israel: The Lord our God is one Lord' (Deut. 6:4). . . . The doctrine developed gradually over several centuries and through many controversies. . . . By the end of the 4th century . . . the doctrine of the Trinity took substantially the form it has maintained ever since."—(1976), Micropædia, Vol. X, p. 126.

The *New Catholic Encyclopedia* states: "The formulation 'one God in three Persons' was not solidly established, certainly not fully assimilated into Christian life and its profession of faith, prior to the end of the 4th century. But it is precisely this formulation that has first claim to the title *the Trinitarian dogma.* Among the Apostolic Fathers, there had been nothing even remotely approaching such a mentality or perspective."—(1967), Vol. XIV, p. 299.

In *The Encyclopedia Americana* we read: "Christianity derived from Judaism and Judaism was strictly Unitarian [believing that God is one person]. The road which led from Jerusalem to Nicea was scarcely a straight one. Fourth century Trinitarianism did not reflect accurately early Christian teaching regarding the nature of God; it was, on the contrary, a deviation from this teaching."—(1956), Vol. XXVII, p. 294L.

According to the *Nouveau Dictionnaire Universel,* "The Platonic trinity, itself merely a rearrangement of older trinities dating back to earlier peoples, appears to be the rational philosophic trinity of attributes that gave birth to the three hypostases or divine persons taught by the Christian churches. . . . This Greek philosopher's [Plato, fourth century B.C.E.] conception of the divine trinity . . . can be found in all the ancient [pagan] religions."—(Paris, 1865-1870), edited by M. Lachâtre, Vol. 2, p. 1467.

John L. McKenzie, S.J., in his *Dictionary of the Bible,* says: "The trinity of persons within the unity of nature is defined in terms of 'person' and 'nature' which are G[ree]k philosophical terms; actually the terms do not appear in the Bible. The trinitarian definitions arose as the result of long controversies in which these terms and others such as 'essence' and 'substance' were erroneously applied to God by some theologians."—(New York, 1965), p. 899.

Even though, as Trinitarians acknowledge, neither the word "Trinity" nor a statement of the Trinitarian dogma is found in the Bible, are the concepts that are embodied in that dogma found there?

Does the Bible teach that the "Holy Spirit" is a person?

Some individual texts that refer to the holy spirit ("Holy Ghost," *KJ*) might seem to indicate personality. For example, the holy spirit is referred to as a helper (Greek, *pa·ra'kle·tos;* "Comforter," *KJ;* "Advocate," *JB, NE*) that 'teaches,' 'bears witness,' 'speaks' and 'hears.' (John 14:

16, 17, 26; 15:26; 16:13) But other texts say that people were "filled" with holy spirit, that some were 'baptized' with it or "anointed" with it. (Luke 1:41; Matt. 3:11; Acts 10:38) These latter references to holy spirit definitely do not fit a person. To understand what the Bible as a whole teaches, all these texts must be considered. What is the reasonable conclusion? That the first texts cited here employ a figure of speech personifying God's holy spirit, his active force, as the Bible also personifies wisdom, sin, death, water, and blood. (See also pages 380, 381, under the heading "Spirit.")

The Holy Scriptures tell us the personal name of the Father—Jehovah. They inform us that the Son is Jesus Christ. But nowhere in the Scriptures is a *personal* name applied to the holy spirit.

Acts 7:55, 56 reports that Stephen was given a vision of heaven in which he saw "Jesus standing at God's right hand." But he made no mention of seeing the holy spirit. (See also Revelation 7:10; 22:1, 3.)

The *New Catholic Encyclopedia* admits: "The majority of N[ew] T[estament] texts reveal God's spirit as something, not someone; this is especially seen in the parallelism between the spirit and the power of God." (1967, Vol. XIII, p. 575) It also reports: "The Apologists [Greek Christian writers of the second century] spoke too haltingly of the Spirit; with a measure of anticipation, one might say too impersonally."—Vol. XIV, p. 296.

Does the Bible agree with those who teach that the Father and the Son are not separate and distinct individuals?

Matt. 26:39, *RS:* "Going a little farther he [Jesus Christ] fell on his face and prayed, 'My Father, if it be possible, let this cup pass from me; nevertheless, not as I will, but as thou wilt.'" (If the Father and the Son were not distinct individuals, such a prayer would have been meaningless. Jesus would have been praying to himself, and his will would *of necessity* have been the Father's will.)

John 8:17, 18, *RS:* "[Jesus answered the Jewish Pharisees:] In your law it is written that the testimony of two men is true; I bear witness to myself, and the Father who sent me bears witness to me." (So, Jesus definitely spoke of himself as being an individual separate and distinct from the Father.)

See also pages 197, 198, under "Jehovah."

Does the Bible teach that all who are said to be part of the Trinity are eternal, none having a beginning?

Col. 1:15, 16, *RS:* "He [Jesus Christ] is the image of the invisible God, the first-born of all creation; for in him all things were created, in heaven and on earth." In what sense is Jesus Christ "the first-born of all creation"? (1) Trinitarians say that "first-born" here means prime, most excellent, most distinguished; thus Christ would be understood to be, not part of creation, but the most distinguished in relation to those who were created. If that is so, and if the Trinity doctrine is true, why are the Father and the holy spirit not also said to be the firstborn of all creation? But the Bible applies this expression only to the Son. According to the customary meaning of "firstborn," it indicates that Jesus is the eldest in Jehovah's family of sons. (2) Before Colossians 1:15, the expression "the firstborn of" occurs upwards of 30 times in the Bible, and in each instance that it is applied to living creatures the same meaning applies—the firstborn is part of the group. "The firstborn of Israel" is one of the sons of Israel; "the firstborn of Pharaoh" is one of Pharaoh's family; "the firstborn of beast" are themselves animals. What, then, causes some to ascribe a different meaning to it at Colossians 1:15? Is it Bible usage or is it a belief to which they already hold and for which they seek proof? (3) Does Colossians 1:16, 17 (*RS*) exclude Jesus from having been created, when it says "in him all things were created . . . all things were created through him and for him"? The Greek word here rendered "all things" is *pan′ta,* an inflected form of *pas.* At Luke 13:2, *RS* renders this "all . . . other"; *JB* reads "any other"; *NE* says "anyone else." (See also Luke 21:29 in *NE* and Philippians 2:21 in *JB.*) In harmony with everything else that the Bible says regarding the Son, *NW* assigns the same meaning to *pan′ta* at Colossians 1:16, 17 so that it reads, in part, "by means of him *all other things* were created . . . *All other things* have been created through him and for him." Thus he is shown to be a created being, part of the creation produced by God.

Rev. 1:1; 3:14, *RS:* "The revelation of Jesus Christ, which God gave him . . . 'And to the angel of the church in La-odicea write: "The words of the Amen, the faithful and true witness, the beginning [Greek, *ar·khe'*] of God's creation."'" (*KJ, Dy, CC,* and *NW,* as well as others, read similarly.) Is that rendering correct? Some take the view that what is meant is that the Son was 'the beginner of God's creation,' that he was its 'ultimate source.' But Liddell and Scott's *Greek-English Lexicon* lists "beginning" as its first meaning of *ar·khe'*. (Oxford, 1968, p. 252) The logical conclusion is that the one being quoted at Revelation 3:14 is a creation, the first of God's creations, that he had a beginning. Compare Proverbs 8:22, where, as many Bible commentators agree, the Son is referred to as wisdom personified. According to *RS, NE,* and *JB,* the one there speaking is said to be "created.")

Prophetically, with reference to the Messiah, Micah 5:2 (*KJ*) says his "goings forth have been from of old, from everlasting." *Dy* reads: "his going forth is from the beginning, from the days of eternity." Does that make him the same as God? It is noteworthy that, instead of saying "days of eternity," *RS* renders the Hebrew as "ancient days"; *JB,* "days of old"; *NW,* "days of time indefinite." Viewed in the light of Revelation 3:14, discussed above, Micah 5:2 does not prove that Jesus was without a beginning.

Does the Bible teach that none of those who are said to be included in the Trinity is greater or less than another, that all are equal, that all are almighty?

Mark 13:32, *RS:* "Of that day or that hour no ones knows, not even the angels in heaven, nor the Son, but only the Father." (Of course, that would not be the case if Father, Son, and Holy Spirit were coequal, comprising one Godhead. And if, as some suggest, the Son was limited by his human nature from knowing, the question remains, Why did the Holy Spirit not know?)

Matt. 20:20-23, *RS:* "The mother of the sons of Zebedee . . . said to him [Jesus], 'Command that these two sons of mine may sit, one at your right hand and one at your left, in your kingdom.' But Jesus answered, . . . 'You will drink my cup, but to sit at my right hand and at my left is not mine to grant, but it is for those for whom it has been prepared by my Father.'" (How strange, if, as claimed, Jesus is God! Was Jesus here merely answering according to his "human nature"? If, as Trinitarians say, Jesus was truly "God-man" —*both* God and man, not one or the other—would it truly be consistent to resort to such an explanation? Does not Matthew 20:23 rather show that the Son is not equal to the Father, that the Father has reserved some prerogatives for himself?)

Matt. 12:31, 32, *RS:* "Every sin and blasphemy will be forgiven men, but the blasphemy against the Spirit will not be forgiven. And whoever says a word against the Son of man will be forgiven; but whoever speaks against the Holy Spirit will not be forgiven, either in this age or in the age to come." (If the Holy Spirit were a person and were God, this text would flatly contradict the Trinity doctrine, because it would mean that in some way the Holy Spirit was greater than the Son. Instead, what Jesus said shows that the Father, to whom the "Spirit" belonged, is greater than Jesus, the Son of man.)

John 14:28, *RS:* "[Jesus said:] If you loved me, you would have rejoiced, because I go to the Father; for the Father is greater than I."

1 Cor. 11:3, *RS:* "I want you to understand that the head of every man is Christ, the head of a woman is her husband, and the head of Christ is God." (Clearly, then, Christ is not God, and God is of superior rank to Christ. It should be noted that this was written about 55 C.E., some 22 years after Jesus returned to heaven. So the truth here stated applies to the relationship between God and Christ in heaven.)

1 Cor. 15:27, 28 *RS:* "'God has put all things in subjection under his [Jesus'] feet.' But when it says, 'All things are put in subjection under him,' it is plain that he is excepted who put all things under him. When all things are subjected to him, then the Son himself will also be subjected to him who

put all things under him, that God may be everything to every one."

The Hebrew word *Shad·dai'* and the Greek word *Pan·to·kra'tor* are both translated "Almighty." Both original-language words are repeatedly applied to Jehovah, the Father. (Ex. 6:3; Rev. 19:6) Neither expression is ever applied to either the Son or the holy spirit.

Does the Bible teach that each of those said to be part of the Trinity is God?

Jesus said in prayer: "Father, . . . this is eternal life, that they know thee *the only true God,* and Jesus Christ whom thou hast sent." (John 17:1-3, *RS;* italics added.) (Most translations here use the expression "the only true God" with reference to the Father. *NE* reads "who alone art truly God." He cannot be "the only true God," the one "who alone [is] truly God," if there are two others who are God to the same degree as he is, can he? Any others referred to as "gods" must be either false or merely a reflection of the true God.)

1 Cor. 8:5, 6, *RS:* "Although there may be so-called gods in heaven or on earth—as indeed there are many 'gods' and many 'lords'—yet for us there is one God, the Father, from whom are all things and for whom we exist, and one Lord, Jesus Christ, through whom are all things and through whom we exist." (This presents the Father as the "one God" of Christians and as being in a class distinct from Jesus Christ.)

1 Pet. 1:3, *RS:* "Blessed be the God and Father of our Lord Jesus Christ!" (Repeatedly, even following Jesus' ascension to heaven, the Scriptures refer to the Father as "the God" of Jesus Christ. At John 20:17, following Jesus' resurrection, he himself spoke of the Father as "my God." Later, when in heaven, as recorded at Revelation 3:12, he again used the same expression. But never in the Bible is the Father reported to refer to the Son as "my God," nor does either the Father or the Son refer to the holy spirit as "my God.")

For comments on scriptures used by some in an effort to prove that Christ is God, see pages 212-216, under the heading "Jesus Christ."

In *Theological Investigations,* Karl Rahner, S.J., admits: "Θεός [God] is still never used of the Spirit," and: "ὁ θεός [literally, the God] is never used in the New Testament to speak of the πνεῦμα ἅγιον [holy spirit]."—(Baltimore, Md.; 1961), translated from German, Vol. I, pp. 138, 143.

Do any of the scriptures that are used by Trinitarians to support their belief provide a solid basis for that dogma?

A person who is really seeking to know the truth about God is not going to search the Bible hoping to find a text that he can construe as fitting what he already believes. He wants to know what God's Word itself says. He may find some texts that he feels can be read in more than one way, but when these are compared with other Biblical statements on the same subject their meaning will become clear. It should be noted at the outset that *most of the texts* used as "proof" of the Trinity actually mention only two persons, not three; so even if the Trinitarian explanation of the texts were correct, these would not prove that the Bible teaches the Trinity. Consider the following:

(Unless otherwise indicated, all the texts quoted in the following section are from RS.)

Texts in which a title that belongs to Jehovah is applied to Jesus Christ or is claimed to apply to Jesus

Alpha and Omega: To whom does this title properly belong? (1) At Revelation 1:8, its owner is said to be God, the Almighty. In verse 11 according to *KJ,* that title is applied to one whose description thereafter shows him to be Jesus Christ. But scholars recognize the reference to Alpha and Omega in verse 11 to be spurious, and so it does not appear in *RS, NE, JB, NAB, Dy.* (2) Many translations of Revelation into Hebrew recognize that the one described in verse 8 is Jehovah, and so they restore the personal name of God there. See *NW,* 1984 Reference edition. (3) Revelation 21:6, 7 indicates that Christians who are spiritual conquerors are to be 'sons' of the one known as the Alpha and the Omega. That is never said of the relationship of spirit-anointed Christians to Jesus Christ. Jesus spoke of them as his 'brothers.' (Heb. 2:11; Matt. 12:50; 25:40) But those 'brothers' of Jesus are referred to as "sons of God." (Gal. 3:26; 4:6) (4) At Revelation 22:12, *TEV* inserts the name Jesus, so the reference to Alpha and Omega in verse 13 is made to appear to apply to him. But the name Jesus does not appear there in Greek, and other translations do not include it. (5) At Revelation 22:13, the Alpha and Omega is also said to be "the first and the last," which expression is applied to Jesus at Revelation 1:17, 18. Similarly, the expression "apostle" is applied both to Jesus Christ and to certain ones of his followers. But that does not prove that they are the same person or are of equal rank, does it? (Heb. 3:1) So the evidence points to the conclusion that the title "Alpha and Omega" applies to Almighty God, the Father, not to the Son.

Savior: Repeatedly the Scriptures refer to God as Savior. At Isaiah 43:11 God even says: "Besides me there is no savior." Since Jesus is also referred to as Savior, are God and Jesus the same? Not at all. Titus 1:3, 4 speaks of "God our Savior," and then of both "God the Father and Christ Jesus our Savior." So, both persons are saviors. Jude 25 shows the relationship, saying: "God, our Savior *through* Jesus Christ our Lord." (Italics added.) (See also Acts 13:23.) At Judges 3:9, the same Hebrew word (*moh·shi´a'*, rendered "savior" or "deliverer") that is used at Isaiah 43:11 is applied to Othniel, a judge in Israel, but that certainly did not make Othniel Jehovah, did it? A reading of Isaiah 43:1-12 shows that verse 11 means that Jehovah alone was the One who provided salvation, or deliverance, for Israel; that salvation did not come from any of the gods of the surrounding nations.

God: At Isaiah 43:10 Jehovah says: "Before me no god was formed, nor shall there be any after me." Does this mean that, because Jesus Christ is prophetically called "Mighty God" at Isaiah 9:6, Jesus must be Jehovah? Again, the context answers, No! None of the idolatrous Gentile nations formed a god before Jehovah, because no one existed before Jehovah. Nor would they at a future time form any real, live god that was able to prophesy. (Isa. 46:9, 10) But that does not mean that *Jehovah* never caused to exist anyone who is properly referred to as a god. (Ps. 82:1, 6; John 1:1, *NW*) At

Isaiah 10:21 Jehovah is referred to as "mighty God," just as Jesus is in Isaiah 9:6; but only Jehovah is ever called "God *Almighty.*"—Gen. 17:1.

If a certain title or descriptive phrase is found in more than one location in the Scriptures, it should never hastily be concluded that it must always refer to the same person. Such reasoning would lead to the conclusion that Nebuchadnezzar was Jesus Christ, because both were called "king of kings" (Dan. 2:37; Rev. 17:14); and that Jesus' disciples were actually Jesus Christ, because both were called "the light of the world." (Matt. 5:14; John 8:12) We should always consider the context and any other instances in the Bible where the same expression occurs.

Application to Jesus Christ by inspired Bible writers of passages from the Hebrew Scriptures that clearly apply to Jehovah

Why does John 1:23 quote Isaiah 40:3 and apply it to what John the Baptizer did in preparing the way for *Jesus Christ,* when Isaiah 40:3 is clearly discussing preparing the way before *Jehovah?* Because Jesus *represented* his Father. He came in his Father's name and had the assurance that his Father was always with him because he did the things pleasing to his Father.—John 5:43; 8:29.

Why does Hebrews 1:10-12 quote Psalm 102:25-27 and apply it to the Son, when the psalm says that it is addressed to God? Because the Son is the one *through whom* God performed the creative works there described by the psalmist. (See Colossians 1:15, 16; Proverbs 8:22, 27-30.) It should be observed in Hebrews 1:5b that a quotation is made from 2 Samuel 7:14 and applied to the Son of God. Although that text had its first application to Solomon, the later application of it to Jesus Christ does not mean that Solomon and Jesus are the same. Jesus is "greater than Solomon" and carries out a work foreshadowed by Solomon.—Luke 11:31.

Scriptures that mention together the Father, the Son, and the Holy Spirit

Matthew 28:19 and 2 Corinthians 13:14 are instances of this. Neither of these texts says that Father, Son, and Holy

Spirit are coequal or coeternal or that all are God. The Scriptural evidence already presented on pages 408-412 argues against reading such thoughts into the texts.

McClintock and Strong's *Cyclopedia of Biblical, Theological, and Ecclesiastical Literature,* though advocating the Trinity doctrine, acknowledges regarding Matthew 28: 18-20: "This text, however, taken by itself, would not prove decisively either the *personality* of the three subjects mentioned, or their *equality* or *divinity*." (1981 reprint, Vol. X, p. 552) Regarding other texts that also mention the three together, this *Cyclopedia* admits that, taken by themselves, they are "insufficient" to prove the Trinity. (Compare 1 Timothy 5:21, where God and Christ and the angels are mentioned together.)

Texts in which the plural form of nouns is applied to God in the Hebrew Scriptures

At Genesis 1:1 the title "God" is translated from *'Elo·him',* which is plural in Hebrew. Trinitarians construe this to be an indication of the Trinity. They also explain Deuteronomy 6:4 to imply the unity of members of the Trinity when it says, "The LORD our God [from *'Elo·him'*] is one LORD."

The plural form of the noun here in Hebrew is the plural of majesty or excellence. (See *NAB,* St. Joseph Edition, Bible Dictionary, p. 330; also, *New Catholic Encyclopedia,* 1967, Vol. V, p. 287.) It conveys no thought of plurality of persons within a godhead. In similar fashion, at Judges 16:23 when reference is made to the false god Dagon, a form of the title *'elo·him'* is used; the accompanying verb is singular, showing that reference is to just the one god. At Genesis 42:30, Joseph is spoken of as the "lord" (*'adho·neh',* the plural of excellence) of Egypt.

The Greek language does not have a 'plural of majesty or excellence.' So, at Genesis 1:1 the translators of *LXX* used *ho The·os'* (God, singular) as the equivalent of *'Elo·him'.* At Mark 12:29, where a reply of Jesus is reproduced in which he quoted Deuteronomy 6:4, the Greek singular *ho The·os'* is similarly used.

At Deuteronomy 6:4, the Hebrew text contains the Tetragrammaton twice, and so should more properly read: "Jehovah our God is one Jehovah." (*NW*) The nation of Israel, to whom that was stated, did not believe in the Trinity. The Babylonians and the Egyptians worshiped triads of gods, but it was made clear to Israel that Jehovah is different.

Texts from which a person might draw more than one conclusion, depending on the Bible translation used

If a passage can grammatically be translated in more than one way, what is the correct rendering? One that is in agreement with the rest of the Bible. If a person ignores other portions of the Bible and builds his belief around a favorite rendering of a particular verse, then what he believes really reflects, not the Word of God, but his own ideas and perhaps those of another imperfect human.

John 1:1, 2:

RS reads: "In the beginning was the Word, and the Word was with God, and the Word was God. He was in the beginning with God." (*KJ, Dy, JB, NAB* use similar wording.) However, *NW* reads: "In the beginning the Word was, and the Word was with God, and the Word was a god. This one was in the beginning with God."

Which translation of John 1:1, 2 agrees with the context? John 1:18 says: "No one has ever seen God." Verse 14 clearly says that "the Word became flesh and dwelt among us . . . we have beheld his glory." Also, verses 1, 2 say that in the beginning he was *"with* God." Can one be *with* someone and at the same time *be* that person? At John 17:3, Jesus addresses the Father as "the only true God"; so, Jesus as "a god" merely reflects his Father's divine qualities.—Heb. 1:3.

Is the rendering "a god" consistent with the rules of Greek grammar? Some reference books argue strongly that the Greek text must be translated, "The Word was God." But not all agree. In his article "Qualitative Anarthrous Predicate Nouns: Mark 15:39 and John 1:1," Philip B. Harner said that such clauses as the one in John 1:1, "with an anarthrous predicate preceding the verb, are primarily qualitative in meaning. They indicate that the *logos* has the nature of *theos.*" He suggests: "Perhaps the clause could be translated, 'the Word had the same nature as God.'" (*Journal of Biblical Literature,* 1973, pp. 85, 87) Thus, in this text, the fact that the word *the·os'* in its second occurrence is without the definite article (*ho*) and is placed before the verb in the sentence in Greek is significant. Interestingly, translators that insist on rendering John 1:1, "The Word was God," do not hesitate to use the indefinite article (a, an) in their rendering of other passages where a singular anarthrous predicate noun occurs before the verb. Thus at John 6:70, *JB* and *KJ* both refer to Judas Iscariot as "a devil," and at John 9:17 they describe Jesus as "a prophet."

John L. McKenzie, S.J., in his *Dictionary of the Bible,* says: "Jn 1:1 should rigorously be translated 'the word was with the God [= the Father], and the word was a divine being.'"—(Brackets are his. Published with nihil obstat and imprimatur.) (New York, 1965), p. 317.

In harmony with the above, *AT* reads: "the Word was divine"; *Mo,* "the Logos was divine"; *NTIV,* "the word was a god." In his German translation Ludwig Thimme expresses it in this way: "God of a sort the Word was." Referring to the Word (who became Jesus Christ) as "a god" is consistent with the use of that term in the rest of the Scriptures. For example, at Psalm 82:1-6 human judges in Israel were referred to as "gods" (Hebrew, *'elo·him';* Greek, *the·oi',* at John 10:34) because they were representatives of Jehovah and were to speak his law.

See also *NW* appendix, 1984 Reference edition, p. 1579.

John 8:58:

RS reads: "Jesus said to them, 'Truly, truly, I say to you, before Abraham was, I am [Greek, *e·go' ei·mi'*].'" (*NE, KJ, TEV, JB, NAB* all read "I am," some even using capital letters to convey the idea of a title. Thus they endeavor to connect the expression with Exodus 3:14, where, according to their rendering, God refers to himself by the title "I Am.") However, in *NW* the latter part of John 8:58 reads: "Before Abraham came into existence, I have been." (The same idea is conveyed by the wording in *AT, Mo, CBW,* and *SE.*)

Which rendering agrees with the context? The question of the Jews (verse 57) to which Jesus was replying had to do with age, not identity. Jesus' reply logically dealt with his age, the length of his existence. Interestingly, no effort is ever made to apply *e·go' ei·mi'* as a title to the holy spirit.

Says *A Grammar of the Greek New Testament in the Light of Historical Research,* by A. T. Robertson: "The verb [*ei·mi'*] . . . Sometimes it does express existence as a predicate like any other verb, as in [*e·go' ei·mi'*] (Jo. 8:58)." —Nashville, Tenn.; 1934, p. 394.

See also *NW* appendix, 1984 Reference edition, pp. 1582, 1583.

Acts 20:28:

JB reads: "Be on your guard for yourselves and for all the flock of which the Holy Spirit has made you the overseers, to feed the Church of God which he bought with his own blood." (*KJ, Dy, NAB* use similar wording.) However, in *NW* the latter part of the verse reads: "the blood of his own [Son]." (*TEV* reads similarly. Although the 1953 printing of *RS* reads "with his own blood," the 1971 edition reads "with the blood of his own Son." *Ro* and *Da* simply read "the blood of his own.")

Which rendering(s) agree with 1 John 1:7, which says: "The blood of Jesus his [God's] Son cleanses us from all sin"? (See also Revelation 1:4-6.) As stated in John 3:16, did God send his only-begotten Son, or did he himself come as a man, so that we might have life? It was the blood, not of God, but of his Son that was poured out.

See also *NW* appendix, 1984 Reference edition, p. 1580.

Romans 9:5:

JB reads: "They are descended from the patriarchs and from their flesh and blood came Christ who is above all, God for ever blessed! Amen." (*KJ, Dy* read similarly.) However, in *NW* the latter part of the verse reads: "from whom the Christ sprang according to the flesh: God, who is over all, be blessed forever. Amen." (*RS, NE, TEV, NAB, Mo* all use wording similar to *NW*.)

Is this verse saying that Christ is "over all" and that he is therefore God? Or does it refer to God and Christ as distinct individuals and say that God is "over all"? Which rendering of Romans 9:5 agrees with Romans 15:5, 6, which first distinguishes God from Christ Jesus and then urges the reader to "glorify the God and Father of our Lord Jesus Christ"? (See also 2 Corinthians 1:3 and Ephesians 1:3.) Consider what follows in Romans chapter 9. Verses 6-13 show that the outworking of God's purpose depends not on inheritance according to the flesh but on the will of *God*. Verses 14-18 refer to God's message to Pharaoh, as recorded at Exodus 9:16, to highlight the fact that *God* is over all. In verses 19-24 *God's* superiority is further illustrated by an analogy with a potter and the clay vessels that he makes. How appropriate, then, in verse 5, the expression: "God, who is over all, be blessed forever. Amen"!—*NW*.

The New International Dictionary of New Testament Theology states: "Rom. 9:5 is disputed. . . . It would be easy, and linguistically perfectly possible to refer the expression to Christ. The verse would then read, 'Christ who is God over all, blessed for ever. Amen.' Even so, Christ would not be equated absolutely with God, but only described as a being of divine nature, for the word *theos* has no article. . . . The much more probable explanation is that the statement is a doxology directed to God."—(Grand Rapids, Mich.; 1976), translated from German, Vol. 2, p. 80.

See also *NW* appendix, 1984 Reference edition, pp. 1580, 1581.

Philippians 2:5, 6:

KJ reads: "Let this mind be in you, which was also in Christ Jesus: Who, being in the form of God, thought it not robbery to be equal with God." (*Dy* has the same wording. *JB* reads: "he did not cling to his equality with God.") However, in *NW* the latter portion of that passage reads: "who, although he was existing in God's form, gave no consideration to a seizure [Greek, *har·pag·mon*´], namely, that he should be equal to God." (*RS, NE, TEV, NAB* convey the same thought.)

Which thought agrees with the context? Verse 5 counsels

Christians to imitate Christ in the matter here being discussed. Could they be urged to consider it "not robbery," but their right, "to be equal with God"? Surely not! However, they can imitate one who "gave no consideration to a seizure, namely, that he should be equal to God." (*NW*) (Compare Genesis 3:5.) Such a translation also agrees with Jesus Christ himself, who said: "The Father is greater than I." —John 14:28.

The Expositor's Greek Testament says: "We cannot find any passage where [*har·pa'zo*] or any of its derivatives [including *har·pag·mon'*] has the sense of 'holding in possession,' 'retaining'. It seems invariably to mean *'seize,' 'snatch violently'*. Thus it is not permissible to glide from the true sense 'grasp at' into one which is totally different, 'hold fast.'"—(Grand Rapids, Mich.; 1967), edited by W. Robertson Nicoll, Vol. III, pp. 436, 437.

Colossians 2:9:

KJ reads: "In him [Christ] dwelleth all the fulness of the Godhead [Greek, *the·o'te·tos*] bodily." (A similar thought is conveyed by the renderings in *NE, RS, JB, NAB, Dy*.) However, *NW* reads: "It is in him that all the fullness of the divine quality dwells bodily." (*AT, We*, and *CKW* read "God's nature," instead of "Godhead." Compare 2 Peter 1:4.)

Admittedly, not everyone offers the same interpretation of Colossians 2:9. But what is in agreement with the rest of the inspired letter to the Colossians? Did Christ have in himself something that is his because he is God, part of a Trinity? Or is "the fullness" that dwells in him something that became his because of the decision of someone else? Colossians 1:19 (*KJ, Dy*) says that all fullness dwelt in Christ because it "pleased the Father" for this to be the case. *NE* says it was "by God's own choice."

Consider the immediate context of Colossians 2:9: In verse 8, readers are warned against being misled by those who advocate philosophy and human traditions. They are also told that in Christ "are hid all the treasures of wisdom and knowledge" and are urged to "live in him" and to be "rooted and built up in him and established in the faith." (Verses 3, 6, 7) It is in him, and not in the originators or the teachers of human philosophy, that a certain precious "fulness" dwells. Was the apostle Paul there saying that the "fulness" that was in Christ made Christ God himself? Not according to Colossians 3:1, where Christ is said to be "seated at the right hand of God."—See *KJ, Dy, TEV, NAB*.

According to Liddell and Scott's *Greek-English Lexicon,* *the·o′tes* (the nominative form, from which *the·o′te·tos* is derived) means "divinity, divine nature." (Oxford, 1968, p. 792) Being truly "divinity," or of "divine nature," does not make Jesus as the Son of God coequal and coeternal with the Father, any more than the fact that all humans share "humanity" or "human nature" makes them coequal or all the same age.

Titus 2:13:

RS reads: "Awaiting our blessed hope, the appearing of the glory of our great God and Savior Jesus Christ." (Similar wording is found in *NE, TEV, JB*.) However, *NW* reads: "while we wait for the happy hope and glorious manifestation of the great God and of the Savior of us, Christ Jesus." (*NAB* has a similar rendering.)

Which translation agrees with Titus 1:4, which refers to "God the Father and Christ Jesus our Savior"? Although the Scriptures also refer to God as being a Savior, this text clearly differentiates between him and Christ Jesus, the one through whom God provides salvation.

Some argue that Titus 2:13 indicates that Christ is both God and Savior. Interestingly, *RS, NE, TEV, JB* render Titus 2:13 in a way that might be construed as allowing for that view, but they do not follow the same rule in their translation of 2 Thessalonians 1:12. Henry Alford, in *The Greek Testament,* states: "I would submit that [a rendering that clearly differentiates God and Christ, at Titus 2:13] satisfies all the grammatical requirements of the sentence: that it is both structurally and contextually more probable, and more agreeable to the Apostle's way of writing."—(Boston, 1877), Vol. III, p. 421.

See also *NW* appendix, 1984 Reference edition, pp. 1581, 1582.

Hebrews 1:8:

RS reads: "Of the Son he says, 'Thy throne, O God, is for ever and ever.'" (*KJ, NE, TEV, Dy, JB, NAB* have similar renderings.) However, *NW* reads: "But with reference to the Son: 'God is your throne forever and ever.'" (*AT, Mo, TC, By* convey the same idea.)

Which rendering is harmonious with the context? The preceding verses say that *God* is speaking, not that he is being addressed; and the following verse uses the expression "God, thy God," showing that the one addressed is not the Most High God but is a worshiper of that God. Hebrews 1:8 quotes from Psalm 45:6, which originally was addressed to a human king of Israel. Obviously, the Bible writer of this psalm did not think that this human king was Almighty God. Rather, Psalm 45:6, in *RS,* reads "Your divine throne." (*NE* says, "Your throne is like God's throne." *JP* [verse 7]: "Thy throne given of God.") Solomon, who was possibly the king originally addressed in Psalm 45, was said to sit "upon Jehovah's throne." (1 Chron. 29:23, *NW*) In harmony with the fact that God is the "throne," or Source and Upholder of Christ's kingship, Daniel 7:13, 14 and Luke 1:32 show that God confers such authority on him.

Hebrews 1:8, 9 quotes from Psalm 45:6, 7, concerning which the Bible scholar B. F. Westcott states: "The LXX. admits of two renderings: [*ho the·os'*] can be taken as a vocative in both cases (*Thy throne, O God, . . . therefore, O God, Thy God . . .*) or it can be taken as the subject (or the predicate) in the first case (*God is Thy throne,* or *Thy throne is God . . .*), and in apposition to [*ho the·os' sou*] in the second case (*Therefore God, even Thy God . . .*). . . . It is scarcely possible that [*'Elo·him'*] in the original can be addressed to the king. The presumption therefore is against the belief that [*ho the·os'*] is a vocative in the LXX. Thus on the whole it seems best to adopt in the first clause the rendering: *God is Thy throne* (or, *Thy throne is God*), that is 'Thy kingdom is founded upon God, the immovable Rock.'"—*The Epistle to the Hebrews* (London, 1889), pp. 25, 26.

1 John 5:7, 8:

KJ reads: "For there are three that bear record in heaven, the Father, the Word, and the Holy Ghost: and these three are one. And there are three that bear witness in earth, the spirit, and the water, and the blood: and these three agree in one." (*Dy* also includes this Trinitarian passage.) However, *NW* does not include the words "in heaven, the Father, the Word, and the Holy Ghost: and these three are one. And there are three that bear witness in earth." (*RS, NE, TEV, JB, NAB* also leave out the Trinitarian passage.)

Regarding this Trinitarian passage, textual critic F. H. A. Scrivener wrote: "We need not hesitate to declare our conviction that the disputed words were not written by St. John: that they were originally brought into Latin copies in Africa from the margin, where they had been placed as a pious and orthodox gloss on ver. 8: that from the Latin they crept into two or three late Greek codices, and thence into the printed Greek text, a place to which they had no rightful claim."—*A Plain Introduction to the Criticism of the New Testament* (Cambridge, 1883, third ed.), p. 654.

See also footnote on these verses in *JB,* and *NW* appendix, 1984 Reference edition, p. 1580.

Other scriptures that are said by Trinitarians to express elements of their dogma

Notice that the first of these texts refers to only the Son; the other refers to both Father and Son; neither refers to Father, Son, and Holy Spirit and says that they comprise one God.

John 2:19-22:

By what he here said, did Jesus mean that he would resurrect himself from the dead? Does that mean that Jesus is God, because Acts 2:32 says, "This Jesus God raised up"? Not at all. Such a view would conflict with Galatians 1:1, which ascribes the resurrection of Jesus to *the Father,* not to the Son. Using a similar mode of expression, at Luke 8:48 Jesus is quoted as saying to a woman: "Your faith has made you well." Did she heal herself? No; it was power from God through Christ that healed her *because* she had faith. (Luke 8:46; Acts 10:38) Likewise, by his perfect obedience as a human, Jesus provided the moral basis for the Father to raise him from the dead, thus acknowledging Jesus as God's Son. Because of Jesus' faithful course of life, it could properly be said that Jesus himself was responsible for his resurrection.

Says A. T. Robertson in *Word Pictures in the New Testament:* "Recall [John] 2:19 where Jesus said: 'And in three days I will raise it up.' He did not mean that he will raise himself from the dead independently of the Father as the active agent (Rom. 8:11)."—(New York, 1932), Vol. V, p. 183.

John 10:30:

When saying, "I and the Father are one," did Jesus mean that they were equal? Some Trinitarians say that he did. But at John 17:21, 22, Jesus prayed regarding his followers: "That they may all be one," and he added, "that they may be one even as we are one." He used the same Greek word (*hen*) for "one" in all these instances. Obviously, Jesus' disciples do not all become part of the Trinity. But they do come to share a oneness of purpose with the Father and the Son, the same sort of oneness that unites God and Christ.

In what position does belief in the Trinity put those who cling to it?

It puts them in a very dangerous position. The evidence is indisputable that the dogma of the Trinity is not found in the Bible, nor is it in harmony with what the Bible teaches. (See the preceding pages.) It grossly misrepresents the true God. Yet, Jesus Christ said: "The hour is coming, and now is, when the true worshipers will worship the Father in spirit and truth, for such the Father seeks to worship him. God is spirit, and those who worship him must worship in spirit and truth." (John 4:23, 24, *RS*) Thus Jesus made it clear that those whose worship is not 'in truth,' not in harmony with the truth set out in God's own Word, are not "true worshipers." To Jewish religious leaders of the first century, Jesus said: "For the sake of your tradition, you have made void the word of God. You hypocrites! Well did Isaiah prophesy of you, when he said: 'This people honors me with their lips, but their heart is far from me; in vain do they worship me, teaching as doctrines the precepts of men.'" (Matt. 15:6-9, *RS*) That applies with equal force to those in Christendom today who advocate human traditions in preference to the clear truths of the Bible.

Regarding the Trinity, the Athanasian Creed (in English) says that its members are "incomprehensible." Teachers of the doctrine often state that it is a "mystery." Obviously such a Trinitarian God is not the one that Jesus had in mind when he said: "We worship what we know." (John 4:22, *RS*) Do you really know the God you worship?

Serious questions confront each one of us: Do we sincerely love the truth? Do we really want an approved relationship with God? Not everyone genuinely loves the truth. Many have put having the approval of their relatives and associates above love of the truth and of God. (2 Thess. 2: 9-12; John 5:39-44) But, as Jesus said in earnest prayer to his heavenly Father: "This means everlasting life, their taking in knowledge of you, the only true God, and of the one whom you sent forth, Jesus Christ." (John 17:3, *NW*) And Psalm 144:15 truthfully states: "Happy is the people whose God is Jehovah!"—*NW*.

When Someone Says—

'Do you believe in the Trinity?'

You might reply: 'That is a very popular belief in our time. But did you know that this is not what was taught by Jesus and his disciples? So, we worship the One that Jesus said to worship.' **Then perhaps add:** (1) 'When Jesus was teaching, here is the commandment that he said was greatest . . . (Mark 12:28-30).' (2) 'Jesus never claimed to be equal to God. He said . . . (John 14:28).' (3) 'Then what is the origin of the Trinity doctrine? Notice what well-known encyclopedias say about that. (See pages 405, 406.)'

Or you could say: 'No, I do not. You see, there are Bible texts that I could never fit in with that belief. Here is one of them. (Matt. 24:36) Perhaps you can explain it to me.' **Then perhaps add:** (1) 'If the Son is equal to the Father, how is it that the Father knows things that the Son does not?' If they answer that this was true only regarding his human nature, then ask: (2) 'But why does the holy spirit not know?' (If the person shows a sincere interest in the truth, show him what the Scriptures do say about God. [Ps. 83:18; John 4:23, 24])

Another possibility: 'We do believe in Jesus Christ but not in the Trinity. Why? Because we believe what the apostle Peter believed about Christ. Notice what he said . . . (Matt. 16:15-17).'

An additional suggestion: 'I find that not everyone has the same thing in mind when he refers to the Trinity. Perhaps I could answer your question better if I knew what you mean.' **Then perhaps add:** 'I appreciate that explanation. But what I believe is only what the Bible teaches. Have you ever seen the word "Trinity" in the Bible? . . . (Refer to the concordance in your Bible.) But is Christ referred to in the Bible? . . . Yes, and we believe in him. Notice here in the concordance under "Christ" one of the references is to Matthew 16:16. (Read it.) That is what I believe.'

Or you might answer (if the person draws particular attention to John 1:1): 'I am acquainted with that verse. In some Bible translations it says that Jesus is "God," and others say that he is "a god." Why is that?' (1) 'Could it be because the next verse says that he was *"with* God"?' (2) 'Might it also be because of what is found here in John 1:18?' (3) 'Have you ever wondered whether Jesus himself worships someone as God? (John 20:17)'

'Do you believe in the divinity of Christ?'

You might reply: 'Yes, I certainly do. But perhaps I do not have in mind the same thing that you do when you refer to "the divinity of Christ."' **Then perhaps add:** (1) 'Why do I say that? Well, at Isaiah 9:6 Jesus Christ is described as "Mighty God," but only his Father is ever referred to in the Bible as the *Almighty* God.' (2) 'And notice that at John 17:3 Jesus speaks of his Father as "the *only* true God." So, at most, Jesus is just a reflection of the true God.' (3) 'What is required on our part to be pleasing to God? (John 4:23, 24)'

Wickedness

Definition: That which is very bad morally. It often denotes that which is injurious, malevolent, or destructive in influence.

Why is there so much wickedness?

God is not to blame. He gave mankind a perfect start, but humans have chosen to ignore God's requirements and decide for themselves what is good and what is bad. (Deut. 32: 4, 5; Eccl. 7:29; Gen. 3:5, 6) By doing this, they have come under the influence of wicked superhuman forces.—Eph. 6: 11, 12.

1 John 5:19: "The whole world is lying in the power of the wicked one."

Rev. 12:7-12: "War broke out in heaven . . . the dragon and its angels battled but it did not prevail, neither was a place found for them any longer in heaven. So down the great dragon was hurled, the original serpent, the one called Devil and Satan, who is misleading the entire inhabited earth; he was hurled down to the earth, and his angels were hurled down with him. . . . 'On this account be glad, you heavens and you who reside in them! Woe for the earth and for the sea, because the Devil has come down to you, having great anger, knowing he has a short period of time.'" (This increased woe to the world has occurred since Satan was hurled out of heaven following the birth of the Kingdom. See verse 10.)

2 Tim. 3:1-5: "Know this, that in the last days critical times hard to deal with will be here. For men will be lovers of themselves, lovers of money, self-assuming, haughty, blasphemers, disobedient to parents, unthankful, disloyal, having no natural affection, not open to any agreement, slanderers, without self-control, fierce, without love of goodness, betrayers, headstrong, puffed up with pride, lovers of pleasures rather than lovers of God, having a form of godly devotion but proving false to its power." (This is the fruitage of centuries of apostasy from true worship. These conditions have developed because people who have professed to be religious have ignored what God's Word really says. They

427

have proved false to the power for good that true godly
devotion can have in one's life.)

Why does God permit it?

At times it may seem to us that the best thing would be
simply to get rid of everyone who is wicked. We long for an
end to wickedness, and yet we have experienced it for
relatively few years when compared with the time that
wickedness has existed. *How must Jehovah God feel?* For
thousands of years people have blamed him, even cursed
him, for the bad conditions they have endured. Yet, these are
caused, not by him, but by Satan and by wicked men. Jehovah has the power to destroy the wicked. Surely there must
be good reasons why he has exercised such restraint. If
Jehovah's way of handling the situation is different from
what we would recommend, should that surprise us? His
experience is much greater than man's, and his view of the
situation is much broader than that of any human.—Compare Isaiah 55:8, 9; Ezekiel 33:17.

*There would be no wickedness if God had not endowed
intelligent creatures with free will.* But God has given us the
capacity to choose to obey him because we love him or to
disobey. (Deut. 30:19, 20; Josh. 24:15) Do we wish it were
otherwise? If we are parents, which makes us happier
—when our children obey us because they love us or when
we make them do it? Should God have forced Adam to be
obedient? Would we really be happier if we lived in a world
where we were forced to obey God? Before destroying this
wicked system, God is allowing opportunity for people to
demonstrate whether they really want to live in harmony
with his righteous laws or not. At his appointed time, he will
without fail destroy the wicked.—2 Thess. 1:9, 10.

Wisely he is allowing time for the settling of vital issues:
(1) The righteousness and rightfulness of Jehovah's rule was
challenged in Eden. (Gen. 2:16, 17; 3:1-5) (2) The integrity
of all of God's servants in heaven and on earth was called
into question. (Job 1:6-11; 2:1-5; Luke 22:31) God could
have destroyed the rebels (Satan, Adam, and Eve) immediately, but that would not have settled matters. Might does

not prove that one's cause is right. The issues raised were moral ones. God's allowing of time was, not to prove any point to himself, but to permit all creatures with free will to see for themselves the bad fruitage produced by rebellion against his rulership, also to afford them opportunity to demonstrate where they personally stand on these vital matters. With these issues settled, never again would anyone be permitted to disrupt the peace. The good order, harmony, and well-being of the entire universe depend upon the sanctifying of Jehovah's name, the treating of him with heartfelt honor by all intelligent creatures. (See also pages 363, 364, under the heading "Satan the Devil.")

Illustration: If someone made a charge before the whole community that you abused your position as family head, that your children would be better off if they made their own decisions independent of you, and that all of them obeyed you, not because of love, but because of material benefits you provided, what would be the best way to settle the matter? Would shooting the false accuser put the charges to rest in the minds of the community? Instead, what a fine answer it would be if you gave your children opportunity to be your witnesses to show that you are a just and loving family head and that they live with you because they love you! If some of your children believed your adversary, left home, and ruined their lives by adopting other life-styles, it would only make honest observers realize that the children would have been better off if they had heeded your direction.

Have we in any way benefited by God's permission of wickedness down till the present?

2 Pet. 3:9: "Jehovah is not slow respecting his promise, as some people consider slowness, but he is patient with you because he does not desire any to be destroyed but desires all to attain to repentance." (Because his patience has extended down till our day, we have the opportunity to demonstrate that we are repentant and that, instead of making our own decisions as to good and bad, we want to submit to Jehovah's righteous rulership.)

Rom. 9:14-24: "What shall we say, then? Is there injustice with God? Never may that become so! . . . If, now, God, although having the will to demonstrate his wrath and to make his power known, tolerated with much long-suffering vessels of wrath made fit for destruction [that is, he tolerated the existence of wicked people for a time], in order that he might make known the riches of his glory upon vessels of mercy, which he prepared beforehand for glory [that is, he would use the time to extend mercy to certain ones, in harmony with his purpose], namely, us, whom he called not only from among Jews but also from among nations, what of it?" (Thus God put off the destruction of the wicked so as to allow time to select people whom he would glorify with Christ as members of the heavenly Kingdom. Has God's doing that been an injustice to anyone? No; it is part of Jehovah's arrangement for blessing people of all sorts who will be favored with the opportunity to live forever on a paradise earth. Compare Psalm 37:10, 11.)

If Someone Says—

'Why does God permit such wickedness?'

You might reply: 'Your question is a good one. Many faithful servants of God have been disturbed by the wickedness around them. (Hab. 1:3, 13)' **Then perhaps add:** (1) 'It is not because of any indifference on God's part. He assures us that he has a set time when he will call the wicked to account. (Hab. 2:3)' (2) 'But what is required on our part if we are to be among the survivors when that time comes? (Hab. 2:4b; Zeph. 2:3)'

Or you could say: 'I am glad that you brought that question up. It is one that disturbs many honest-hearted people. I have here some very helpful information that answers your question. (Then read together some of the information on pages 428-430.)

'After all these years, I don't believe that God is going to do anything to change matters'

You might reply: 'I'm glad to hear that you do believe in God. It certainly is true that there is a lot of wickedness, and it began long before our time. But have you considered this . . . ? (Use the thoughts in paragraph 1 on page 428, regarding the length of time that God has endured it.)'

Or you could say: 'I'm sure you'll agree with me when I say that anyone who has the ability to build a house certainly is capable of cleaning it too. . . . Since God created the earth, it would not be a difficult matter for him to clean it up. Why has he waited so long? I found this answer very satisfying. Tell me what you think. (Then read together the material on pages 428-430.)'

Women

Definition: Adult human females. In Hebrew, the word for woman is *'ish·shah'*, which literally means "a female man."

Does the Bible downgrade women or treat them as if they were inferior persons?

Gen. 2:18: "Jehovah God went on to say: 'It is not good for the man to continue by himself. I am going to make a helper for him, as a complement of him.'" (The man is not here described by God as being a better person than the woman. Rather, God indicated that woman would possess qualities that would complement those of man within God's arrangement. A complement is one of two mutually completing parts. Thus women as a group are outstanding in certain qualities and abilities; men, in others. Compare 1 Corinthians 11:11, 12.)

Gen. 3:16: "To the woman [God] said: ' . . . your craving will be for your husband, and he will dominate you.'" (This declaration after Adam and Eve had sinned was not a statement of what men *should* do but of what Jehovah foreknew they *would* do now that selfishness had become part of human life. A number of Bible accounts thereafter tell of the very unhappy situations that developed because of such selfish domination by men. But the Bible does not say that God approved of such conduct or that it is an example for others to follow.)

Is the assigning of headship to men demeaning to women?

Being under headship is not in itself demeaning. Headship contributes to the handling of matters in an orderly arrangement, and Jehovah is "a God, not of disorder, but of peace." (1 Cor. 14:33) Jesus Christ is under the headship of Jehovah God, and he finds great satisfaction in that relationship. —John 5:19, 20; 8:29; 1 Cor. 15:27, 28.

A relative headship is also assigned to man, particularly in the family and in the Christian congregation. God has not given to man absolute authority over woman; man must answer to his head, Jesus Christ, and to God for the way that he exercises such headship. (1 Cor. 11:3) Furthermore, husbands are commanded "to be loving their wives as their own bodies" and to 'assign honor' to their wives. (Eph. 5:28; 1 Pet. 3:7) The sexual needs of a husband are not put above those of his wife in God's arrangement for married couples. (1 Cor. 7:3, 4) The role of a capable wife, as outlined in the Bible, emphasizes her value to the household and the community. It allows a broad field in which she can use initiative while demonstrating her appreciation for her husband's headship. (Prov. 31:10-31) The Bible commands children to honor not only their father but their mother as well. (Eph. 6:1-3) It also gives special attention to caring for the needs of widows. (Jas. 1:27) Thus among true Christians, women can find great security, true appreciation for themselves as individuals, and personal satisfaction in their activity.

The dignity of woman's position in God's arrangement is further shown by the fact that Jehovah refers to his own organization of loyal spirit creatures as a woman, his wife, the mother of his sons. (Rev. 12:1; Gal. 4:26) Also, the spirit-anointed congregation of Jesus Christ is spoken of as his bride. (Rev. 19:7; 21:2, 9) And from a spiritual standpoint there is no distinction between male and female among those called to share in the heavenly Kingdom with Christ. —Gal. 3:26-28.

Should women be ministers?

Those charged with oversight of a congregation are described in the Bible as being males. The 12 apostles of Jesus

Christ were all males, and those later appointed to be overseers and ministerial servants in Christian congregations were males. (Matt. 10:1-4; 1 Tim. 3:2, 12) Women are counseled to "learn in silence with full submissiveness" at congregation meetings, in that they do not raise questions challenging the men in the congregation. The women are 'not to speak' at such meetings if what they might say would demonstrate lack of subjection. (1 Tim. 2:11, 12; 1 Cor. 14: 33, 34) Thus, although women make valuable contributions to the activity of the congregation, there is no provision for them to preside, or to take the lead by instructing the congregation, when qualified men are present.

But may women be preachers, proclaimers, ministers of the good news, outside the congregation meetings? At Pentecost of 33 C.E. holy spirit was poured out on both men and women. In explanation, the apostle Peter quoted Joel 2: 28, 29, saying: "'In the last days,' God says, 'I shall pour out some of my spirit upon every sort of flesh, and your sons *and your daughters* will prophesy and your young men will see visions and your old men will dream dreams; and even upon my men slaves *and upon my women slaves* I will pour out some of my spirit in those days, and they will prophesy.'" (Acts 2:17, 18) In like manner today, women properly share in the Christian ministry, preaching from house to house and conducting home Bible studies.—See also Psalm 68:11; Philippians 4:2, 3.

Why do Christian women wear head coverings on certain occasions?

1 Cor. 11:3-10: "The head of every man is the Christ; in turn the head of a woman is the man; in turn the head of the Christ is God. . . . Every woman that prays or prophesies with her head uncovered shames her head . . . For a man ought not to have his head covered, as he is God's image and glory; but the woman is man's glory. For man is not out of woman, but woman out of man; and, what is more, man was not created for the sake of the woman, but woman for the sake of the man. That is why the woman ought to have a sign of authority upon her head because of the angels." (When a

Christian woman wears a head covering on appropriate occasions, this is an evidence of her respect for the headship arrangement that was instituted by God. Christ respects theocratic headship; man and woman are also obligated to do so. The first man, Adam, was not produced by birth from a woman but was created by God. When creating Eve, God used a rib from Adam as a foundation, and God stated that she was to be a helper for Adam. Thus to man, who was produced first, was assigned the position of head. The man does not wear a head covering when 'praying or prophesying' because, *in regard to headship,* man is "God's image," having no earthly head in matters relating to his family. However, for a woman to 'pray or prophesy' without a head covering would show disrespect for man's God-assigned position and would shame him. Even the angels, who are members of Jehovah's wifelike heavenly organization, observe the "sign of authority" worn by faithful Christian women and are reminded of their own subjection to Jehovah.)

When is it necessary for a woman to wear a head covering?

When she "prays or prophesies," as stated at 1 Corinthians 11:5. This does not mean that a head covering is needed when she prays privately or when she converses with others about Bible prophecy. However, she should wear such a head covering as an outward sign of her respect for man's headship when she cares for *matters pertaining to worship that would ordinarily be cared for by her husband or by another man.* If she prays aloud on behalf of herself and others or conducts a formal Bible study, thus doing the teaching, *in the presence of her husband,* she should wear a head covering, even if he does not share her faith. But since she is divinely authorized to teach her children, no head covering is needed when praying or studying with her undedicated young ones at times when her husband is not present. If, in an exceptional circumstance, *a dedicated male member of the congregation is present* or when she is accompanied by a visiting traveling overseer, then, when she conducts a prearranged Bible study, she should cover her head, but he should offer the prayer.

Is it proper for women to wear cosmetics or jewelry?

1 Pet. 3:3, 4: "Do not let your adornment be that of the external braiding of the hair and of the putting on of gold ornaments or the wearing of outer garments, but let it be the secret person of the heart in the incorruptible apparel of the quiet and mild spirit, which is of great value in the eyes of God." (Does this mean that women should wear no ornaments? Certainly not; just as it obviously does not mean that they should not wear outer garments. But they are here encouraged to be balanced in their attitude regarding grooming and dress, putting the primary emphasis on spiritual adornment.)

1 Tim. 2:9, 10: "I desire the women to adorn themselves in well-arranged dress, with modesty and soundness of mind, not with styles of hair braiding and gold or pearls or very expensive garb, but in the way that befits women professing to reverence God, namely, through good works." (What really counts with God—one's outward appearance or one's heart condition? Would God be pleased if a woman wore no cosmetics or jewelry but lived immorally? Or would he approve women who are modest and sound in mind in their use of cosmetics and jewelry and who primarily adorn themselves with godly qualities and Christian conduct? Jehovah says: "Not the way man sees is the way God sees, because mere man sees what appears to the eyes; but as for Jehovah, he sees what the heart is."—1 Sam. 16:7.)

Prov. 31:30: "Charm may be false, and prettiness may be vain; but the woman that fears Jehovah is the one that procures praise for herself."

World

Definition: When translated from the Greek word *ko'smos,* "world" can mean (1) humankind as a whole, apart from their moral condition or course of life, (2) the framework of human circumstances into which a person is born and in which he lives, or (3) the mass of mankind apart from Jehovah's approved servants. Some Bible translators have conveyed inaccurate impressions by also using "world" as the equivalent of Greek terms that mean "earth," "inhabited earth," and "system of things." The following discussion focuses its principal attention on the third of the numbered meanings of "world" as given above.

Will the world be destroyed by fire?

2 Pet. 3:7: "By the same word [of God] the heavens and the earth that are now are stored up for fire and are being reserved to the day of judgment and of destruction of the ungodly men." (Notice that it is "the ungodly men," not humankind as a whole, who are to be destroyed. Similarly, verse 6 refers to destruction of "the world" in Noah's day. Wicked people were destroyed, but the earth as well as God-fearing Noah and his household remained. Is the "fire" in the coming day of judgment going to be literal, or is it symbolic of complete destruction? What effect would literal fire have on such literal heavenly bodies as the already intensely hot sun and stars? For further consideration of this text, see pages 113-115, under "Earth.")

Prov. 2:21, 22: "The upright are the ones that will reside in the earth, and the blameless are the ones that will be left over in it. As regards the wicked, they will be cut off from the very earth; and as for the treacherous, they will be torn away from it."

Who rules this world—God or Satan?

Dan. 4:35: "[The Most High God, Jehovah,] is doing according to his own will among the army of the heavens and the inhabitants of the earth. And there exists no one that can check his hand or that can say to him, 'What have you been doing?'" (In a similar vein, Jeremiah 10:6, 7 refers to Jehovah as "King of the nations" because he is the Superlative King, the one who can and will call to account human kings and the nations over which they rule. As the earth's Creator, Jehovah is its rightful Ruler; he has never abdicated that position.)

John 14:30: "[Jesus said:] The ruler of the world is coming. And he has no hold on me." (This ruler obviously is not Jehovah God, whose will Jesus always performs loyally. This "ruler of the world" must be "the wicked one," Satan the Devil, in whose power "the whole world is lying," as stated at 1 John 5:19. Although mankind lives on a planet that belongs to God, the world that is made up of those who are not Jehovah's obedient servants is under Satan's control because such people obey him. Those who wholeheartedly submit to Jehovah's rulership are not part of that world. Compare 2 Corinthians 4:4.)

Rev. 13:2: "The dragon [Satan the Devil] gave to the beast its power and its throne and great authority." (Comparison of the description of this "beast" with Daniel 7 indicates that it represents human government, not just one such but the global system of political rulership. That Satan is its ruler agrees with Luke 4:5-7, also with Revelation 16: 14, 16, which depicts demonic utterances as leading the rulers of all the earth to war against God at Armageddon. Satan's rulership of the world is one that is merely tolerated by God until His appointed time arrives for settling the issue of universal sovereignty.)

Rev. 11:15: "Loud voices occurred in heaven, saying: 'The kingdom of the world did become the kingdom of our Lord [Jehovah] and of his Christ.'" (When this occurred in 1914, "the last days" for the present wicked system began. A new manifestation of Jehovah's sovereignty appeared, this time through his own Son as Messianic Ruler. Soon the wicked world will be destroyed, and Satan, its wicked spirit ruler, will be abyssed, unable to influence mankind.)

What is the attitude of true Christians toward the world and toward people who are part of the world?

John 15:19: "You [Jesus' followers] are no part of the world, but I have chosen you out of the world." (Thus true Christians are no part of the mass of human society that is alienated from God. They care for normal human activities, but they shun attitudes, speech, and conduct that are characteristic of the world and that conflict with Jehovah's righteous ways.) (See pages 269-276, also 389-393.)

Jas. 4:4: "Adulteresses, do you not know that the friendship with the world is enmity with God? Whoever, therefore, wants to be a friend of the world is constituting himself an enemy of God." (Because Christians are imperfect, they may at times get soiled through contacts with the world. But when counseled from God's Word, they repent and correct their ways. However, if some, by deliberate choice, ally themselves with the world or imitate its spirit, they show that they no longer are true Christians but have become part of the world that is at enmity with God.)

Rom. 13:1: "Let every soul be in subjection to the superior authorities, for there is no authority except by God; the existing authorities stand placed in their relative positions by God." (Those who heed this counsel are not rebels, trying to overthrow governments of the world. They subject themselves to the authority of political rulers, obeying them as long as the demands of such rulers do not conflict with God's requirements. Such governments were foreseen and foretold by God. They exercise authority, not because he empowered them, but by his permission. In his due time he will also remove them.)

Gal. 6:10: "As long as we have time favorable for it, let us work what is good toward all, but especially toward those related to us in the faith." (So, true Christians do not hold back from doing good to their fellowmen. They imitate God, who makes the sun shine upon both wicked people and good. —Matt. 5:43-48.)

Matt. 5:14-16: "You are the light of the world. . . . Let your light shine before men, that they may see your fine works and give glory to your Father who is in the heavens." (For others to give glory to God because of what Christians do, it is obvious that those who are Christians must be active witnesses to the world concerning God's name and purpose. It is to this activity that true Christians give primary emphasis.)

What is the meaning of present world conditions?

See the main heading "Last Days."

Index

This Index does not list every aspect of each principal subject. To locate other details, turn to appropriate main heading(s) on the preceding pages and read the subheadings.

Scriptures Often Misapplied

Would you welcome more information or a free home Bible study?

Write Watch Tower at appropriate address below.

ALASKA 99507: 2552 East 48th Ave., Anchorage. **ARGENTINA:** Casilla de Correo 83, 1427 Buenos Aires. **AUSTRALIA:** Box 280, Ingleburn, N.S.W. 2565. **AUSTRIA:** Postfach 67, A-1134 Vienna [13 Gallgasse 42-44, Vienna]. **BAHAMAS:** Box N-1247, Nassau, N.P. **BARBADOS:** Fontabelle Rd., Bridgetown. **BELGIUM:** rue d'Argile 60, B-1950 Kraainem. **BELIZE:** Box 257, Belize City. **BOLIVIA:** Casilla No. 1440, La Paz. **BRAZIL:** Caixa Postal 92, 18270 Tatuí, SP. **CANADA L7G 4Y4:** Box 4100, Halton Hills (Georgetown), Ontario. **CHILE:** Casilla 267, Puente Alto [Av. Concha y Toro 3456, Puente Alto]. **COLOMBIA:** Apartado Aéreo 85058, Bogotá 8, D.E. **COSTA RICA:** Apartado 10043, San José. **CÔTE D'IVOIRE (IVORY COAST):** 06 B.P. 393, Abidjan 06. **CYPRUS:** P. O. Box 33, Dhali, Nicosia. **CZECHOSLOVAKIA:** Saveljevova 18, CZ-14000 Prague. **DENMARK:** Stenhusvej 28, DK-4300 Holbæk. **DOMINICAN REPUBLIC:** Apartado 1742, Santo Domingo. **ECUADOR:** Casilla 4512, Guayaquil. **EL SALVADOR:** Apartado Postal 401, San Salvador. **ENGLAND NW7 1RN:** The Ridgeway, London. **FIJI:** Box 23, Suva. **FINLAND:** Postbox 68, SF-01301 Vantaa 30. **FRANCE:** B.P. 63, F-92105 Boulogne-Billancourt Cedex. **FRENCH GUIANA:** 41, Résidence Les Grenadilles, 97354 Montjoly. **GERMANY:** Postfach 20, W-6251 Selters/Taunus 1. **GHANA:** Box 760, Accra. **GREECE:** 77 Leoforos Kifisias, GR-151 24 Marousi. **GUADELOUPE:** B.P. 239, 97156 Pointe-à-Pitre Cedex. **GUAM 96913:** 143 Jehovah St., Barrigada. **GUATEMALA:** 17 Calle 13-63, Zona 11, 01011 Guatemala. **GUYANA:** 50 Brickdam, Georgetown 16. **HAITI:** Post Box 185, Port-au-Prince. **HAWAII 96819:** 2055 Kam IV Rd., Honolulu. **HONDURAS:** Apartado 147, Tegucigalpa. **HONG KONG:** 4 Kent Road, Kowloon Tong. **HUNGARY:** Pf. 223, H-1425 Budapest. **ICELAND:** P. O. Box 8496, IS-128 Reykjavík. **INDIA:** Post Bag 10, Lonavla, Pune Dis., Mah. 410 401. **IRELAND:** 29A Jamestown Road, Finglas, Dublin 11. **ISRAEL:** P. O. Box 961, 61-009 Tel Aviv. **ITALY:** Via della Bufalotta 1281, I-00138 Rome RM. **JAMAICA:** Box 180, Kingston 10. **JAPAN:** 1271 Nakashinden, Ebina City, Kanagawa Pref., 243-04. **KENYA:** Box 47788, Nairobi. **KOREA, REPUBLIC OF:** Box 33 Pyungtaek P. O., Kyunggido, 450-600. **LEEWARD ISLANDS:** Box 119, St. Johns, Antigua. **LIBERIA:** P.O. Box 10-0380, 1000 Monrovia 10. **LUXEMBOURG:** B.P. 2186, L-1021 Luxembourg, G. D. **MADAGASCAR:** B. P. 511, Antananarivo 101. **MALAYSIA:** 28 Jalan Kampar, Off Jalan Landasan, 41300 Klang, Sel. **MARTINIQUE:** Cours Campeche, Morne Tartenson, 97200 Fort de France. **MAURITIUS:** P.O. Box 54, 5 Osman Ave., Vacoas. **MEXICO:** Apartado Postal 896, 06002 Mexico, D. F. **MYANMAR:** P.O. Box 62, Yangon. **NETHERLANDS:** Noordbargerstraat 77, NL-7812 AA Emmen. **NETHERLANDS ANTILLES:** Oosterbeekstraat 11, Willemstad, Curaçao. **NEW CALEDONIA:** B.P. 787, Nouméa. **NEW ZEALAND:** P.O. Box 142, Manurewa. **NIGERIA:** P.M.B. 1090, Benin City, Bendel State. **NORWAY:** Gaupeveien 24, N-1914 Ytre Enebakk. **PAKISTAN:** 197-A Ahmad Block, New Garden Town, Lahore 54600. **PANAMA:** Apartado 6-2671, Zona 6A, El Dorado. **PAPUA NEW GUINEA:** Box 636, Boroko, N.C.D. **PARAGUAY:** Diaz de Solís 1485 esq. C.A. López, Sajonia, Casilla de Correo 482, Asunción. **PERU:** Casilla 18-1055, Lima [Av. El Cortijo 329, Monterrico 33]. **PHILIPPINES, REPUBLIC OF:** P. O. Box 2044, 1099 Manila [186 Roosevelt Ave., San Francisco del Monte, 1105 Quezon City]. **POLAND:** prz. poczt. 23, 00-991 Warszawa 44. **PORTUGAL:** Apartado 91, P-2766 Estoril Codex [Rua Conde Barão, 511, Alcabideche, P-2765 Estoril]. **PUERTO RICO 00927:** Calle Ónix 23, Urb. Bucaré, Río Piedras. **SENEGAL:** B.P. 3107, Dakar. **SIERRA LEONE:** P. O. Box 136, Freetown. **SOLOMON ISLANDS:** P.O. Box 166, Honiara. **SOUTH AFRICA:** Private Bag 2067, Krugersdorp, 1740. **SPAIN:** Apartado postal 132, E-28850 Torrejón de Ardoz (Madrid). **SRI LANKA, REP. OF:** 62 Layard's Road, Colombo 5. **SURINAME:** P. O. Box 49, Paramaribo. **SWEDEN:** Box 5, S-732 21 Arboga. **SWITZERLAND:** Ulmenweg 45, P.O. Box 225, CH-3602 Thun. **TAHITI:** B.P. 518, Papeete. **TAIWAN:** 107 Yun Ho Street, Taipei 10613. **THAILAND:** 69/1 Soi Phasuk, Sukhumwit Rd., Soi 2, Bangkok 10 110. **TRINIDAD AND TOBAGO, REP. OF:** Lower Rapsey Street & Laxmi Lane, Curepe. **UNITED STATES OF AMERICA:** 25 Columbia Heights, Brooklyn, N.Y. 11201. **URUGUAY:** Francisco Bauzá 3372, 11.600 Montevideo. **VENEZUELA:** Apartado 20.364, Caracas, DF 1020A. **WESTERN SAMOA:** P. O. Box 673, Apia. **YUGOSLAVIA:** Pp. 417, YU-41001 Zagreb. **ZAMBIA, REP. OF:** Box 21598, Kitwe. **ZIMBABWE:** 35 Fife Avenue, Harare.